HTML

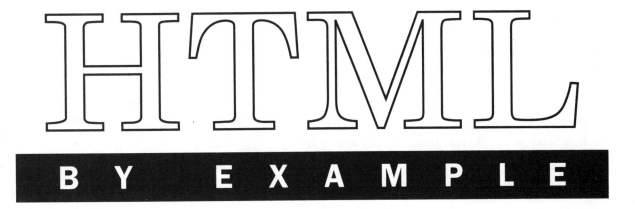

BY EXAMPLE

201 West 103rd Street
Indianapolis, Indiana 46290

Ann Navarro

Todd Stauffer

HTML by Example

International Standard Book Number: 0-7897-2228-3

Library of Congress Catalog Card Number: 99-68217

Printed in the United States of America

First Printing: December 1999

01   00   4   3   2

Trademarks

Warning and Disclaimer

Publisher
Dean Miller

Acquisitions Editor
Randy Haubner

Development Editor
Sean Dixon

Managing Editor
Matt Purcell

Project Editor
Natalie Harris

Copy Editor
Gayle Johnson

Indexer
Aamir Burki

Proofreaders
Andrew Beaster

Benjamin Berg

Kelly Talbot

Technical Editors
Bill Bruns

Bob Correll

Team Coordinator
Cindy Teeters

Interior Design
Karen Ruggles

Cover Design
Rader Design

Layout Technician
Stacey DeRome

Ayanna Lacey

Heather Hiatt Miller

Contents at a Glance

Table of Contents

Dedication

For Dave: Just for being you.

About the Author

Ann Navarro founded WebGeek Communications in January of 1996 as the result of having become instantly enamored of the Web the first time she saw it back in 1994. She serves on the Governing Board of the HTML Writers Guild, the world's largest association of Web developers, and she also holds the position of director, Online Education. Navarro currently participates in the W3C HTML Working Group, helping to craft the documents that will become the XHTML Recommendations. She is married to Dave, who's an even bigger geek than she is, and they live happily in Port Charlotte, Florida, in a house with more computing power than most small countries. The power and telephone companies send them gifts each year at Christmas.

Todd Stauffer is the author of more than a dozen computer books, including *Using Your Mac* and *Using the Internet with Your Mac* for MCP. He's also the author of *Macworld Mac Upgrade and Repair Bible* for IDG Books and is the co-author of *PC Upgrade and Repair Answers!* for Osborne/McGraw Hill.

Aside from writing computer books, Todd is co-host of *Disk Doctors*, an Emmy-nominated, nationally televised show on JEC Knowledge TV (http://www.knowledgetv.com). He's also an online editor for *NetProfessional Magazine* and a writer for a number of Web sites and publications, including CMP's Techweb, The Mac Report, Inside Line, Inside Mac Games, and Webintosh.

Todd is the Mac Chat columnist for *Peak Computing Magazine* and has hosted regional computing radio shows in Denver and Colorado Springs. He publishes a number of Web sites and acts as a Web consultant for print newspapers and publications. Since graduating from Texas A&M University with a degree in English literature, Todd has worked as a magazine editor, advertising writer, and technical writer, all in computing fields.

You can reach Todd at tstauffer@aol.com or through his site at http://www.shutup101.com/todd/ on the World Wide Web.

Acknowledgments

A good book is never a solo effort. For those who have never peeked behind the scenes at the publishing industry, discovering just how many people are involved in a single book project is a real eye-opener. This is where I take the opportunity to thank each of them, including Randy Haubner, Executive Editor; Sean Dixon, Development Editor; Natalie Harris, Project Editor; Gayle Johnson, Copy Editor; and Bill Bruns and Bob Correll, Technical Editors.

Thanks to Sebastian Schnitzenbaumer of Stack Overflow, and the rest of the HTML Working Group, for the camaraderie and entertainment in Munich. It was a much-needed mental vacation, even as I approached final deadlines.

And, as always, thanks to my agent, David Rogelberg, and Neil Salkind of Studio B Productions. Your uncanny knack for finding just the right project at just the right time is a very welcome part of my life.

Introduction

If you're ready to jump into the world of creating Web pages using HTML, you've found the right book—regardless of your previous experience with programming or the World Wide Web. That's because *HTML by Example* uses a "hands-on" approach to creating Web pages that will make learning HTML both easy and fun! Forget about tired reference manuals or overly technical tomes that make HTML seem like rocket science. It's not! If you've got a simple text editor on nearly any computer platform (Windows, Macintosh, UNIX, Linux, and so on), the only other tool you need is this book. Now you're ready to create your own presence on the Web.

What's the *By Example* Advantage?

There are two major reasons why learning HTML is easier when it's *By Example*. First, HTML isn't a typical programming language. In fact, it isn't a programming language at all. It's a *mark-up* language that builds on very basic concepts that are all somewhat interrelated. Learning by example allows you to start with the initial concepts and learn to make complex Web pages come to life easily.

Second, with the HTML examples that will be available for download from the Web, *HTML by Example* gives you a major head start in Web site creation. Why? Because if you see an example that's similar to what you want to create, you can modify the example to suit your needs. It's possible to have a Web page created within minutes when using this material! Just copy and paste.

Who Should Use This Book?

Before you get to the point of actually creating HTML documents (Web pages), you'll go through a little refresher course on the Internet and the World Wide Web. So, even if you're not terribly familiar with the Web, I'll try to get you there before throwing any strange-looking code or addresses at you.

Essentially, all you need to use this book is a rudimentary grasp of the Internet and the Web, and a desire to create your own place there. If you've just heard of the Web, or even if you've been surfing for a while and want to know more about Web page creation, you've found the right book.

Programmers and graphic artists will also find this book useful for making the transition to the Web—though again, Web design isn't nearly as tough as some programming tasks, so traditional graphic artists should be comfortable very quickly when working in the digital space. Later in this book, you'll learn how to make your pages cutting-edge by incorporating scripting, multimedia objects, and more. But even there, programming is not a prerequisite.

Why Should You Learn HTML?

The World Wide Web is by far the fastest growing part of the Internet, and thousands of new sites are added daily. Business and commerce have now embraced the Web to the point that not having a Web site can seriously limit a company's potential. This makes job candidates with HTML experience on their resumes very attractive.

Creative people, such as writers, designers, and artists, should also learn more about the Web. The worlds of commercial art and advertising are now focusing on Web space along with traditional print and broadcast media. A solid understanding of HTML will take you a long way into the future of your craft.

By the same token, nearly any computer professional should have some notion of how HTML works and why the Web is based on it. But that doesn't mean it takes a rocket scientist to create Web pages. Office workers, editors, public relations specialists, salespeople, real estate agents, financial advisors, and consultants of all flavors should all have a Web presence, and they can benefit from doing it themselves.

The Web is so diverse that it's impossible to categorize all the reasons to learn about HTML page creation. Home office pages, small businesses online, family photo albums, and even hobbyists all benefit from establishing their small corner in cyberspace—and are finding new contacts, friends, and even lost family members in the process.

What Tools Do You Need?

For the approach you're taking to Web creation, all you need is a text-editing program such as Windows's Notepad, SimpleText on the Mac, or VI and Emacs on UNIX platforms. Any basic ASCII text editor will work fine.

A number of HTML editing programs are available, in both shareware and commercial versions, but you won't be starting with them (although a few of the more popular ones that are freely available are discussed in the final chapters of this book). The reasoning behind this is simple: Even the most advanced HTML editors require an understanding of HTML if you're going to create anything more than the most rudimentary of pages, and no one likes to stick with the basics for long after they discover how much fun HTML can be!

Once you're through with this book (which shouldn't take long!) and you've got a solid grasp of HTML, go ahead and try out some of the HTML authoring tools mentioned here, or that you find elsewhere on the Web. They can make some basic tasks go much quicker for many people, though you'll still want to fire up your trusty text editor to make sure that the end result is exactly as you intended it to be.

You'll also need a stand-alone Web browser program or two for viewing and critiquing your documents. If you don't have a Web browser program (such as Netscape Navigator or Microsoft Internet Explorer), several popular versions are available on the Web for free download. You don't necessarily need an Internet connection for most of this book, but having one will allow you to visit sites that I mention as being particularly informative or illustrative, and will also allow you to download the HTML examples in the book from the Web by browsing to `http://www.mcp.com/product_info` and typing in this book's ISBN, 0789722283.

How This Book Works

Each chapter starts by explaining a particular concept, giving examples in snippets of HTML markup as you go along. Once you've got that concept under your belt, you'll be ready to work with a full-fledged example. You can either type in the example or download it from the Web. Some of the examples will also suggest that you modify the text to make it more suitable for you personally. When you're done, you can simply view the document in your Web browser.

The key to the organization of this book is simple: It's progressive. You'll start out very simply, by going over Web concepts and creating basic pages. From there, you'll learn about the formal standards of HTML (known officially as "Recommendations") and how to decide which one is right for you. Then you'll add graphics, multimedia, and scripting, until your pages rival some of the most exciting sites available on the Web.

You'll also notice that nearly every chapter includes review questions and exercises to help you reinforce what you've learned. If you gave up review questions in grammar school, that's fine. Just skip to the next chapter. If you'd like to make sure you've covered all the material, though, the "Summary" section will help you know for sure that you're ready to move on.

Overview of Chapters

This book is divided into logical parts and chapters to help you find the lessons that are most appropriate for your knowledge level. What follows is a description of each part of this book, including a look at each chapter.

Part I: Internet, Web, and HTML Fundamentals

Chapter 1, "What Is HTML?," introduces you to the fundamentals of creating documents for the Web. Chapter 2, "The World Wide Web and Web Servers," discusses the different conventions used to address computers, servers, and services on the Internet. Chapter 3, "How Web Browsers Work," takes a look at how the typical Web browser program reads the HTML documents you create and shows you what you need to consider to create better pages.

Chapter 4, "HTML's Role on the Web," is concerned with the standards that have been developed for HTML, helping you decide how to best use them on your pages. Chapter 5, "What You Need for a Web Site," rounds out Part I with a discussion of the arrangements you need to make your Web pages visible to the online world.

Part II: Creating Basic Pages with HTML 4

This part of the book discusses creating a basic Web page using techniques found in HTML 4. Chapter 6, "Creating a Web Page and Entering Text," and Chapter 7, "Changing and Customizing HTML Text," show you how to get started with your Web document and emphasize regular text. In Chapter 8, "Displaying Text in Lists," you learn about the various types of HTML lists that can be used to organize text in a more readable way.

Chapter 9, "Adding Graphics to Your Web Pages," is your first look at adding basic images to enhance your Web page presentation. Chapter 10, "Hypertext and Creating Links," and Chapter 11, "Using Links with Other HTML Tags," show you how to put hypertext into your HTML pages by adding clickable links to other pages or Web sites.

Part III: Interactive HTML

Here's where things really start to get fun. Still using only HTML 4 elements (although these are not all supported by every Web browser anymore), the three chapters in Part III discuss making your Web site truly interactive. In Chapter 12, "Adding Tables to Your Documents," we discuss arranging tabular data within your page in a way that will make sense. Chapter 13, "HTML Forms," and Chapter 14, "Form Design and Data Gathering with CGI Scripts," show you how to gather information from your users, whether it's for statistical data, online ordering, or just for fun.

Part IV: Page Layout and Formatting

These chapters move you beyond the basics and into some of the more inventive aspects of HTML 4.

You'll start with Chapter 15, "Frames," which provides a whole new design paradigm for displaying different segments of content in one visual space. Chapter 16, "Images, Multimedia Objects, and Background Graphics," and Chapter 17, "Client-Side Image Maps," bring your pages to life.

Chapter 18, "Enhancing Your Pages with Style Sheets," introduces you to the new standard that lets you modify colors, margins, fonts, and a myriad of other typographical and layout conventions.

Next up are the skills you need to check your work. In Chapter 19, "Validating Your HTML," you learn that adhering to the standards set forth in HTML 4 not only is the "right thing to do" but also helps everyone see your pages just as you intended, no matter how they're accessing the Web.

Part V: Internet Programming and Advanced Web Technologies

In this section of the book, you delve into some of the most cutting-edge and exciting technologies to be introduced to the World Wide Web. Chapter 20, "Using Java and JavaScript," and Chapter 21, "JavaScript Objects and Functions," are an easy-to-follow look at the world of JavaScript, showing you how to do your own programming in one of the most advanced scripting languages available for Web developers.

Chapter 22, "Adding Portable Documents to Web Sites," introduces you to the concept of portable documents and offers advice for creating your own "nearly-free" portable documents for distribution on the Web.

Part VI: HTML Editors and Tools

In this section, we discuss some of the more popular applications for creating Web pages quickly and easily. As Web development becomes more popular, the tools become more advanced. Chapter 23, "Creating HTML Documents with Netscape Composer," introduces you to the all-in-one solution to Web browsing and editing from Netscape Corporation. Chapter 24, "Using Microsoft FrontPage Express," discusses Microsoft's powerful editing tool that ships with Windows 98.

Part VII: HTML Examples

This last part of the book has only one chapter, Chapter 25, "HTML Examples," but there's a lot to it. Here, you'll take a look at two completely different reasons to create a Web site: personal and business. In each, you'll review some of the basic and advanced Web concepts you've encountered throughout the book. The best part is that all of these pages are on the included CD-ROM. If you find a page that does something you want to add to your Web site, just copy it from the CD and alter it to suit your needs!

Conventions Used in This Book

This books uses the following typeface conventions:

Typeface	Meaning
Italic	Terms used the first time
`Computer type`	Text that you type, code listings, commands, HTML tags, Internet addresses, attributes
`Italic computer type`	Placeholders in code—words that stand for what you actually type

NOTE

Notes provide additional information related to a particular topic.

TIP

Tips provide quick and helpful information to assist you along the way.

EXAMPLE

The Other Advantage

In writing computer-oriented books, I've invested not only a significant amount of time and effort, but also a sincere hope that you, the reader, find the information here to be accurate, valuable, and helpful. But if I don't hear from you, it's difficult for me to know whether these goals were met. Therefore, I want you to let me know how I did by sending me email. I will take any question, concern, praise, or complaint you have about this book and its examples, errors, or anything else that comes up. I'll do my best to provide the right answer or refer you to a place where you can find the information you need, or someone to ask who may have more experience in the given topic than I do. Write me at byexample@webgeek.com.

It is very important to me that you are satisfied with everything you come across in this book. If you get through a chapter and its review questions and still have trouble with a concept, take a peek at the Web site I'll be maintaining for this book to see if someone else has encountered the same problem. Updates, bits of errata, and anything else related to questions and problems readers have had will be posted there. You can find it at http://www.webgeek.com/books/example/. The most important thing to remember is that I don't want you wasting time on an error or on a concept I explained poorly. So do look there or email me before you spend too much time hitting yourself over the head.

If you've created something you're particularly proud of, drop me a line about that too! I love to hear my readers' success stories.

Part I

Internet, Web, and HTML Fundamentals

What Is HTML?

The World Wide Web and Web Servers

How Web Browsers Work

HTML's Role on the Web

What You Need for a Web Site

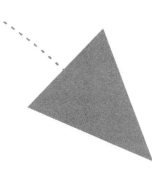

What Is HTML?

The World Wide Web has enjoyed unprecedented growth since it jumped from the world of academia into the public consciousness in the early 1990s. What began as a means to share research data has become an integral part of how we work, play, and shop today.

Think about how ingrained the Net has become to us. You'll just as often hear "What's your e-mail address?" as you will "Can I get your phone number?" Nearly every major company (and many smaller ones) advertising on television these days include a "dot.com" address for viewers to visit to receive more information. Even respected news programs such as NBC's Dateline have gone "interactive" with viewers answering online opinion polls in response to stories as they air.

Beyond the modern conveniences of Christmas shopping or checking your bank balance online, one aspect of the Web has now touched millions of individuals in a way we never could have imagined as recently as ten years ago: communication.

Even before corporate America discovered e-commerce, the Web has been a place where individuals can carve out their own corner of cyberspace for themselves. People publish Web pages that are purely personal: their thoughts, favorite pictures, resumes, tributes to their favorite authors and singers, and even online journals for those who are more exhibitionistic. The key to this freedom of expression is the language in which Web pages are created: the Hypertext Markup Language, or HTML.

This chapter teaches you the following:

- What HTML is
- The history of HTML
- How HTML marks up text for display as a Web page
- Who decides what goes in the HTML standard

HTML as a Publishing Tool

As soon as the first text-editing program was created for the computer, people began to shift from pen-and-paper or the typewriter to the computer for their publishing needs. Certainly, most of us with any experience at it are quicker typists than we are at handwriting. In the early days of desktop publishing, we used special formatting codes to indicate line breaks, new fonts, margins, and all the other instructions needed to display our work as we intended. The codes could be fairly cryptic, but they were easy enough to remember after you'd been at it for a while.

As the personal computer became more common in the workplace and in our homes, word processors advanced to the stage where the average user could perform fairly sophisticated layout and design tasks for the printed page using a *graphical user interface (GUI)* instead of the codes required in previous software versions. Anyone who's used Microsoft Word today knows how easy it is to highlight a section of text and click the Bold button and have the words transformed right on the screen.

Although programs are quickly being developed to offer similar features for HTML development, these tend to be less-than-ideal solutions. Currently, anyone who decides to learn HTML must know some codes, memorize some syntax, and develop pages for the World Wide Web without the benefit of seeing all the fonts, emphasis, and paragraph breaks beforehand.

But anyone who has had any success with the word processing programs of 10 or 15 years ago (or desktop publishing programs as recently as five years ago) will have little or no trouble learning HTML. Ultimately, you'll see that HTML's basic structure makes a lot of sense for this emerging medium—the World Wide Web. And, as with most things computer-oriented, you'll find that once you've spent a few moments with it, HTML isn't nearly as difficult as you might have originally imagined.

HTML Is Not a Programming Language

As its name indicates, HTML isn't a programming language, but a markup language. Some Web developers would like nothing better than to say, "HTML is a very difficult programming language that has taken me years to master. So I'll have to charge you $100 an hour to develop your Web pages." However, this simply isn't the case. As I've already hinted, creating an HTML document is not much more difficult than using a copy of WordPerfect 2000 with the Reveal Codes setting enabled. The catch, as with desktop publishing or any other form of document creation, is in doing it well.

After you finish this book, you'll be well down the path toward creating finely crafted HTML pages.

TIP

Remember the definition of HTML: *Hypertext Markup Language*. In HTML itself, there is no programming—just the "marking up" of regular text for emphasis and organization.

I prefer to call people who work with HTML "designers" or "developers," not "programmers." Some designers might bemoan what they see as the limited design work that can be accomplished with HTML, and anyone used to working with FrameMaker, Quark XPress, or Adobe PageMaker might be more than a little frustrated. But the best pages are still those created by professional artists, writers, and others with a strong sense of design.

As Web page development matures, we are starting to see more concessions to the professional designers, as well as an expansion into realms that do require a certain level of computer programming expertise. Creating scripts or applets (small programs) in the Java language, for instance, is an area where Web page development meets computer programming. It's also a relatively distinct arena from HTML, and you can easily be an expert in HTML without ever programming much of anything.

The basics of HTML are not programming, and for the uninitiated in both realms, HTML is much more easily grasped than most programming languages. If you're familiar with the World Wide Web, you've used a Web browser such as Netscape, Internet Explorer, Mosaic, or Lynx, and if you have any experience with a word processor or text editor such as Notepad, SimpleText, or Emacs, you're familiar with the basic tools required for learning HTML.

A Short History of HTML

HTML was first proposed in 1989. It took shape as a subset of SGML (Standard Generalized Markup Language), which is a higher-level markup language that has long been a favorite of the Department of Defense and many other organizations with a truly astounding volume of documents to manage. Like HTML, it describes formatting and hypertext links, and it defines different components of a document. HTML is definitely the simpler of the two, and although they are related, few browsers support both.

Because HTML was conceived for transmission over the Internet (in the form of Web pages), it is much simpler than SGML, which is more of an application-oriented document format. While it's true that many programs can load, edit, create, and save files in the SGML format (just as many programs can create and save files in the Microsoft Word format), SGML is not exactly ideal for transmission across the Internet to many different types of computers, users, and browser applications.

HTML is more suited to this task. Designed with these considerations in mind, HTML lets you, the designer, create pages that can be read on any type of computer, using any Web browser software, that can be connected to the Web. Even users who are unable to view your graphics, for instance, can experience the bulk of what you're communicating if you design your HTML pages properly.

At the same time, HTML is simple enough that typical computer users can generate HTML documents without the benefit of a special application. Creating a Microsoft Word–format document by hand would be rather difficult (including all the required text sizes, fonts, page breaks, columns, margins, and other information) even if it weren't a *proprietary*—that is, non-public—document format.

HTML is a public standard, and it's simple enough that you can get through a book such as this one and have a very strong ability to create HTML documents from scratch. This simplicity is part of a trade-off because HTML-format documents don't offer nearly the precision of control or depth of formatting options that a WordPerfect- or Adobe PageMaker–formatted document would. But that's really okay!

EXAMPLE

Marking Up Text

The most basic element of any HTML page (and, therefore, any page on the Web) is ASCII text. Web browsers are smart enough that you could simply write a single paragraph of regular text—generated in a text editor and saved as a text file—and have it be displayed in the browser (see Figure 1.1). Here's an example:

> Welcome to my home on the World Wide Web. As you can see, my page isn't completely developed yet, but there were some things I simply had to say before I could get anything else done. My name is Stephanie Bradley, and I'm a real estate developer located in Miami. If you'd like, you can reach my office at 555-4675.

NOTE

Although it's possible, you would never want to display plain text on the Web without conforming to certain HTML conventions. These are explained in Chapter 6, "Creating a Web Page and Entering Text."

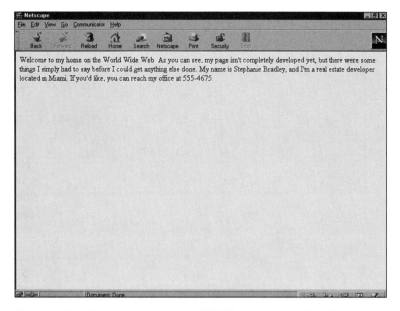

Figure 1.1: *Text is so basic to HTML that it can be displayed in a Web browser with no additional commands or codes.*

Remember that HTML-formatted documents aren't that far removed from documents created by a word processing program, which are also basically text. Marking up text, then, simply means that you add certain commands, or tags, to your document in order to tell a Web browser how you want the document displayed.

One of the most basic uses for HTML tags is to tell a browser that you want certain text to be emphasized on the page. The HTML document standard allows for a couple of different types of emphasis. With explicit formatting, you choose to make something italic as opposed to bold. With implicit formatting, the browser decides how to format the emphasized text.

EXAMPLE

Using part of the preceding example, an HTML tag used for emphasis might look something like this:

```
Welcome to <EM>my home</EM> on the World Wide Web.
```

In this example, <EM> and </EM> are HTML tags that tell the Web browser which text (in this example, my home) is to be emphasized when displayed (see Figure 1.2).

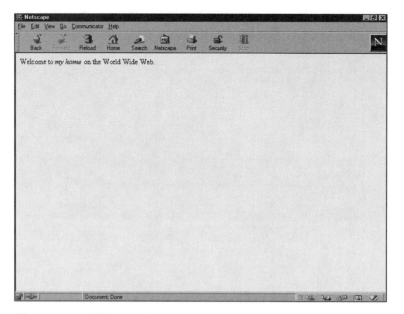

Figure 1.2: HTML tags can be used to mark certain text for emphasis.

The browser isn't just displaying regular text; it has also taken into account the way you want the text to be displayed according to the HTML tags you've added. Tags are a lot like margin notes you might make with a red pen when editing or correcting term papers or corporate reports. After you've entered the basic text in a Web document, you add HTML markup elements to tell the browser how you want things organized and displayed on the page.

You'll learn more about the specific types of tags in Chapter 6, but for now, the most important distinction is between text and HTML tags. All HTML documents will be basically text, as are all word processing documents and most desktop publishing documents. The only difference, then, is how the text is described for display on the screen.

In most word processing documents, the "markup" that describes the emphasis and organization of text is hidden from the user. HTML, however, is a little more primitive than that, because it allows you to manually enter your text markup tags to determine how the text will appear. You can't do this with a Microsoft Word document, but, then again, Microsoft Word documents aren't the standard for all Web pages and browsers on the Internet!

Who Decides What HTML Is?

HTML has had several "keepers" since its inception. The first large group to control it was the Internet Engineering Task Force (IETF), who created an HTML Working Group in 1994. This group established the HTML 2.0 specification, as well as the proposed HTML 3.0 version, completing their work in 1996.

In the same 1994 time frame, an international industry consortium was formed, calling itself the World Wide Web Consortium (W3C). The organization is now cohosted by three academic institutions: In the United States, the host is the Massachusetts Institute of Technology Laboratory for Computer Science (MIT/LCS), the Institut Nationalde Recherche en Informatique et en Automatique (INRIA) is the host in Europe (France), and in Asia, the host is the Keio University Shonan Fujisawa campus in Japan.

Over 350 companies are now members of the W3C, representing academic interests such as the University of Bristol in the UK; software vendors both large and small such as Microsoft, Netscape, and Opera Software; other industry groups such as the HTML Writers Guild, The Open Group, and the Web3D Consortium; and many more.

In 1996, when the IETF HTML Working Group finished its task, the W3C instituted a new HTML Working Group, which produced HTML 3.2 in 1996 and HTML 4.0 in 1998. Work continues to this day, with recent specifications for HTML 4.01 and XHTML, the Extensible Hypertext Markup Language, which is the next version of HTML written in XML syntax.

The World Wide Web Consortium

Tim Berners-Lee is credited with first creating HTML when he was working as a scientist at CERN, the European Laboratory for Particle Physics. Up until the time when the IETF HTML Working Group took over responsibility for the standard, it was largely an informal effort.

Still very much involved in the evolution of the standard, Berners-Lee serves as director of the World Wide Web Consortium. In addition to work on HTML, the W3C oversees specification efforts in the fields of XML (the Extensible Markup Language), Cascading Style Sheets for advanced presentational aspects of Web pages, multimedia development with SMIL, privacy and meta data in e-commerce, the Web Accessibility Initiative, and much more.

The Working Groups of the W3C, who produce the recommendations for all these technologies, are formed from participating employees of the Consortium member companies and, in some cases, individual invited experts. Some in the Internet community have complained that this process isn't sufficiently open to the public, but what is clear is that an enormous amount of highly technical work has been developed over the past five years through the efforts of these hard-working individuals, and the Web as a whole has enjoyed significant gains.

Additional Information on HTML Standards and Organizations

For more information on the World Wide Web Consortium, consult the W3C Web site at http://www.w3.org/. This site will probably be the most useful as you continue to learn more about HTML and emerging new standards.

The HTML activity has detailed information available at http://www.w3.org/MarkUp/. You can view some of the original proposals from Berners-Lee, as well as see the path that HTML has taken over the years to where we are today—working on HTML 4.01 and XHTML.

What's Next?

HTML is a document format, somewhat like word processing or desktop publishing formats, but considerably less complicated and based on more open standards. Creating HTML programs isn't really programming, although some programming can be necessary in other aspects of Web page creation. The World Wide Web Consortium (W3C) is now the keeper of the HTML standard.

In Chapter 2, we will take a look at the World Wide Web and the various services available on the Internet.

Review Questions

1. Is HTML a programming language?

2. True or false: HTML documents can be created with nothing more than a text-editing program.

3. What other markup language is HTML based on?

4. True or false: You can directly edit a WordPerfect-format document.

5. Is the HTML Working Group a subsidiary of the World Wide Web Consortium?

6. Is HTML the only specification that the W3C works on?

The World Wide Web and Web Servers

Probably the most important thing to remember about the World Wide Web and the Internet in general is that they are global in scale and often a very cooperative venture. Information on the Web tends to be distributed around the world. Therefore, it's just as easy for you to access a site in New Zealand or Japan as it is to access Web information in your own area.

The basic reason for learning HTML is to create pages for the World Wide Web. Before you start, though, you'll want to know a little about how this whole process works. This chapter teaches you the following:

- What the major Web browsing programs are and what features they offer

- How the Web works

- Some of the terms associated with surfing the Web

- The different services available on the Internet and how they interact with the Web

What's the World Wide Web?

The World Wide Web is a part of the Internet. It relies on a common set of protocols that allow a server computer configured a certain way to distribute documents across the Internet in a standard way. This Web standard allows programs on many different computer platforms (such as Windows 95/98/NT, MacOS, Linux, UNIX, and so on) to properly format and display the information served. These programs are called *Web browsers*.

NOTE

Note that the Web is composed of different sites around the world. A *site* is basically just a collection of HTML documents that you can access with your Web browser. HTML documents offered for viewing by Que Corporation, the publisher of this book, are organized into a site that can be found at `http://www.mcp.com/que`. There are also many personal Web sites. For instance, my company, WebGeek Communications, has a site at `http://www.webgeek.com`.

The Web is fairly unique among Internet services (which also include email, FTP, Gopher, and more) in that its protocols allow the Web server to send information of many different types (text, sound, graphics) as well as offer access to those other Internet services. Most Web browsers are just as capable of displaying email or Usenet newsgroup messages as of displaying Web pages written in HTML (see Figure 2.1).

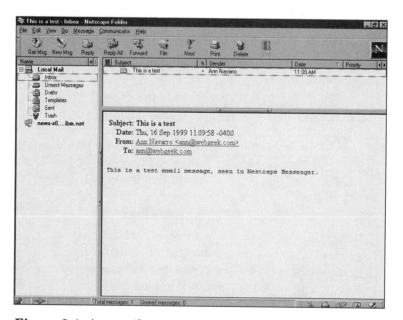

Figure 2.1: *An email message as displayed through Netscape Communicator's email module.*

This flexibility is part of what has fueled the success and popularity of the Web. Not only do the Web protocols allow more interactive multimedia presentations of information, but the typical Web browser can also offer its user access to other Internet resources, making a Web browser perhaps a user's most valuable Internet application.

Servers and Hosts

The Internet community uses the words *host* and *server* when talking about the types of computers you'll encounter. But what do these names mean?

I like to use the analogy of a party. At a party, a host or hostess will welcome you into his or her home and point you to the various things you can do at the party. He or she will show you where to put your coat, point you to the refreshments, and tell you about his or her home.

Now, depending on how large or lavish the party is, you might also have servers. Servers perform specific tasks such as bringing you beverages or food, opening the door, taking your coat, or moving furniture around. At a small party, the host might act as a server. At larger parties, the host coordinates the servers.

That's how hosts and servers work on the Internet. A host computer is generally a computer that allows its local users to gain access to Internet services. It might also allow other users to gain access to information in its organization. One computer in my office acts as our local host. It directs traffic not only between our computers and the Internet, but between our computers locally. If I need to print portions of a current manuscript, my request is funneled through to the specific machine that is the print server.

However, depending on the size of the organization's Internet site, the host often doesn't serve that information itself. Instead, it relies on server computers that have more specific functions, such as serving HTML documents, shareware programs, or Usenet news. The servers will be accessed through the host, though, so it's really only important to know the host address on the Internet—just like in the real world.

The Hypertext Concept: Web Links

Unlike any other Internet service or protocol, the World Wide Web is based on a concept of information retrieval called *hypertext*. In a hypertext document, certain words within the text are marked as *links* to other areas of the current document or to other documents (see Figure 2.2). The basic Windows help engine (like many other online help programs) uses this same hypertext concept to distribute information.

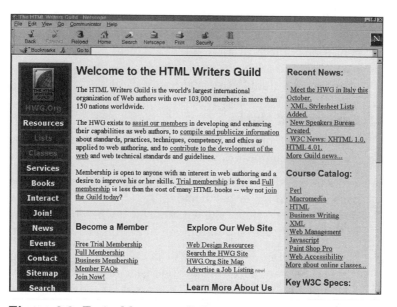

Figure 2.2: *Typical hypertext links in a Web document.*

As you can see in the figure, links can be text or graphics. The user moves to a related area by moving the mouse pointer to the link and clicking once. This generally causes the current Web document to be erased from the browser's window, and a new document is loaded in its place.

NOTE

Links can point to another part of the same document, in which case clicking the link will cause the browser to move to a new part of the currently displayed document.

Consider, then, that this hypertext concept will affect the way information is presented and read on the Web. A normal printed book (like this one) presents its information in a very linear way. Hypertext, on the other hand, is a little more synergistic.

On the World Wide Web, this synergy can be taken to an extreme. For instance, you might use hypertext to define a word within a sentence. Suppose that I see the following example on a Web page:

> The majority of dinosaurs found in this region were <u>herbivores</u>, and surprisingly docile.

I can assume that the word *herbivores* is a hypertext link. That link might take me to a definition of the word *herbivore* that this particular author has provided for his readers. This link might also take me to a completely different Web site, written by another person or group altogether. It might take me to a recent university study about herbivores in general, for instance, or a drawing of a plant-eating dinosaur done by a 10-year-old student in Australia.

Thinking in Hypertext

EXAMPLE

For just a moment, imagine that you're reading a hypertext document instead of a printed page.

If, for instance, you were reading a Web page about our hobbies, you'd find that one of the things that interests Todd most is <u>private airplanes</u>. Clicking that link might take you to a new Web site dedicated to the discussion of personal aircraft, including a link to <u>Cessna Aircraft</u>'s Web site. Once there, you could read about Cessna's particular offerings, prices, and perhaps a <u>testimonial</u> offered by a recent satisfied customer. Clicking this link whisks you away to that customer's personal Web site, where you read his accolades for Cessna. Then you notice that he's a professor at <u>Yale</u> and has provided a link for more information. Clicking the Yale link takes you to the university's Web site, where you can see different sorts of information about registration, classes, research projects, alumni, faculty, and other interesting tidbits.

This offers important implications for HTML writers. For one, you've got to take into consideration this particular style of presenting information. Also, building a good Web site often means being aware of other offerings on the Web and creating links to other people's pages that coincide with or expand upon the information you're presenting.

The Web Page

The World Wide Web is composed of millions of Web pages, each of which is served to a browser (when requested) one page at a time. A Web *page* is generally a single HTML document, which might include text, graphics, sound files, and hypertext links. Each HTML document you create is a single Web page, regardless of the length of the document or the amount of information included (see Figure 2.3).

The Web page shown in Figure 2.3 contains more information than can be shown on the screen at one time, but *scrolling down* the page (by clicking the scrollbar to the right of the browser window) reveals the rest of that particular document. Note, though, that scrolling doesn't present you with a new Web page; it simply puts more of the same page into view.

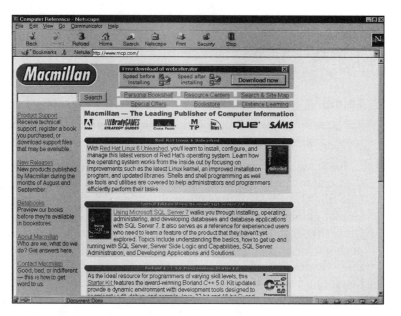

Figure 2.3: *A typical Web page as viewed through Netscape Navigator.*

TIP

Most browser programs have a text box at the top of the screen called the *location* or *address* box that tells you the name of the HTML document being displayed. HTML document names most often end with the extension .html or .htm. You might also see .cfm, .asp, .shtml, or several others.

The Web Site

A Web site is a collection of Web pages under the control of a particular person or group. Generally, a Web site offers a certain amount of organization of its internal information. You might start with an *index* or *default* page for a Web site and then use hypertext links to access more detailed information. Another page within the Web site might offer links to other interesting sites on the Web, information about the organization, or just about anything else.

Web site organization is an important consideration for any HTML designer, including those designing and building corporate Web sites. The typical corporate Web site needs to offer a number of different types of information, each of which might merit its own Web page or pages.

A Corporate Web Site

The typical corporate Web site starts with an index page that quickly introduces users to the information the site has to offer. Perhaps *index* is a misnomer because this page usually acts as a sort of table of contents for the Web site (see Figure 2.4).

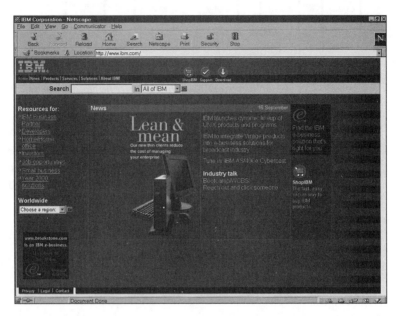

Figure 2.4: *This corporate index page offers links to different parts of the Web site.*

The rest of the pages within the hypothetical corporate Web site from Figure 2.4 are accessed from a similar index page, typically referred to as the *home* page, allowing users to move directly to the information they want. If users are interested in getting phone numbers and addresses for a company, for instance, they might click a link that takes them to an *About the Company* page. If they're interested in the company's products, they'd click another link that would take them to a product demo page.

By organizing the site in this way, the designer makes sure that users can get to every Web page that's part of the site while allowing them to go directly to the pages that interest them most.

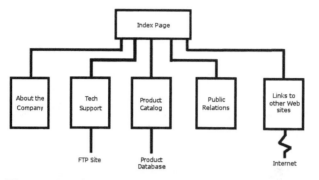

Figure 2.5: *An organizational chart for a basic corporate Web site.*

Intranets Versus the Internet

Another use of HTML and Web technology worth talking about is the growing popularity of *intranets,* or Internet-like networks within companies. In the Web organizational chart shown in Figure 2.5, notice that most of the information presented is geared toward external users.

This same technology can be applied to Web sites for internal uses, allowing employees to access often-used forms, company news, announcements, and clarifications. For instance, the Human Resources department might make job listings and the company's address available on the Internet but would discuss changes to the company's health insurance policies on their intranet.

In fact, many companies are even using HTML to create *front ends* to corporate databases and other shared resources. Using a Web browser application, employees can access data stored on the company's internal network. This takes some programming expertise (usually using CGI-BIN scripts, discussed briefly in Chapter 14, "Form Design and Data Gathering with CGI Scripts"), but the majority of the work is done in HTML.

Fortunately, designing intranet sites isn't that different from designing Internet sites. The skills you'll gain in this book will be equally applicable to both. The only real difference is a question of organization and the type of information you'll want to offer on your intranet. Generally, this information will include the sort of things that are not for public consumption.

Hypermedia: Text and Graphics on the Web

With graphical browsers such as Internet Explorer and Netscape Navigator, the hypertext concept of the Web was introduced to the world of multimedia, resulting in the hypermedia links that are possible in HTML.

This really isn't much different from the hypertext links you learned about in the previous section; the only difference is that hypermedia links point to files other than HTML documents. For instance, a hypermedia link might point to an audio file, a QuickTime movie file, or a graphics file such as a GIF- or JPEG-format graphic (see Figure 2.6).

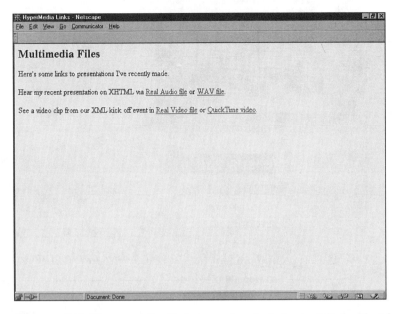

Figure 2.6: *Hypermedia links are simply hypertext links that lead to non-HTML documents.*

Because of the flexibility of the Web protocol, these files can be sent by a Web server just as easily as can an HTML document. All you need to do is create the link to a multimedia file. When users click that link, the multimedia file will be sent over the Web to their browser programs.

Plug-Ins: The Helper Applications

Once the multimedia file is received by the user's Web browser, it's up to the browser to decide how to display or use that multimedia file. Some browsers have certain abilities built in—especially the basics, such as displaying graphics files or plain ASCII text files. At other times, browsers will employ the services of a helper application, also often referred to as a *plug-in* (see Figure 2.7).

Most of these helper applications are plug-in programs that are available as commercial or shareware applications. The browser will generally need to be configured to recognize particular types of multimedia files that, in turn, will cause the browser to load the appropriate plug-in. Once loaded, the downloaded multimedia file will be fed to the helper applications, which can play or display the multimedia file.

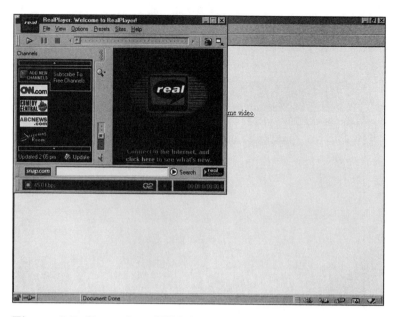

Figure 2.7: *Examples of Web browser helper applications.*

TIP

Don't worry too much about configuring your browser. The installation process for most helper applications sets the file recognition information automatically.

The two terms, *helper application* and *plug-in*, tend to be used interchangeably today. Historically, a helper is an application that is launched to handle a file and runs outside of the browser. The RealPlayer application shown in Figure 2.7 is most accurately labeled as a helper application.

Plug-ins, on the other hand, are additional program code that is actually incorporated into your browser when you install it. The end result is that the browser itself is now capable of handling the files in question. You'll notice this most frequently with plug-ins such as Shockwave and Flash.

Common Multimedia Formats

It seems that multimedia formats are constantly being added and improved for the Web. Some of the more common types of multimedia files are listed in Table 2.1 with their associated file extensions. This list isn't exhaustive, but it should give you an idea of the types of files that can be distributed on the Web.

Table 2.1: Common Multimedia File Types

File Format	Type of File	Extension
Sun Systems sound	Audio	.au
Windows sound	Audio	.wav
Audio Interchange	Audio	.aiff, .aifc
MPEG audio	Audio	.mpg, .mpeg
MP3	Audio	.mp3
SoundBlaster voice	Audio	.voc
RealAudio	Audio	.ra, .ram
CompuServe GIF	Graphics	.gif
JPEG (compressed)	Graphics	.jpg, .jpeg
TIFF	Graphics	.tif, .tiff
Windows bitmap	Graphics	.bmp
Apple picture	Graphics	.pict
Fractal animations	Animation	.fli, .flc
VRML	3D world animation	.wrl
MPEG video	Video	.mpg, mpeg
QuickTime	Video	.mov, .moov, .qt
Video for Windows	Video	.avi
Macromedia Shockwave	Multimedia presentation	.dcr
ASCII text	Plain text	.txt, .text
Postscript	Formatted text	.ps
Adobe Acrobat	Formatted text	.pdf

Not all of these different file formats necessarily require special helper applications. Many sound helpers play the majority of different sound files, for instance, and some graphics programs can handle multiple file types. For the most part, you will need different helper applications for the various video, animation, and formatted text types.

Internet Services and Addresses

Aside from being hypertext-based and capable of transferring a number of multimedia file formats, the Web is unique in its ability to access other Internet services. Being the youngest of the Internet services, the Web can access all of its older siblings, including Internet email, Usenet newsgroups,

Gopher servers, and FTP servers. Before you can access these services, though, you need to know what they do and how their addressing schemes work.

Internet Email

Internet email is designed for the transmission of ASCII text messages from one Internet user to another, specified user. Like mail delivered by the U.S. Post Office, Internet email allows you to address your messages to a particular person. After it's sent, it eventually arrives in that person's email box (generally an Internet-connected computer where he or she has an account), and your recipient can read, forward, or reply to the message.

Internet email addresses follow certain conventions:

`username@sub-domain.domain.first-level domain`

username is the name of the account with the computer, *sub-domain* is an optional internal designation, *domain* is the name assigned to the host organization's Internet presence, and *first-level domain* is a two- or three-letter code that identifies the type of organization that controls the host computer.

An example of a simple email address (mine) is ann@webgeek.com, where ann is the username, webgeek is the domain, and com is the first-level domain. .com is a three-letter code representing a *commercial* entity. Table 2.2 lists the most common first-level domain names.

Table 2.2: Common First-level Domain Names

First-Level Domain	Organization Type
.com	Commercial
.edu	Educational
.org	Organization/association
.net	Computer network
.gov	Government
.mil	Military installation
.ca	Canadian domain
.fr	French domain
.au	Australian domain
.uk	United Kingdom domain
.jp	Japanese domain

You might have noticed that my address doesn't include a hostname or a subdomain. For this particular address, it is unnecessary because WebGeek handles all incoming Internet email through the gateway. Put simply, that means that the server that answers for the `webgeek.com` domain routes all the mail to the appropriate mailboxes; it doesn't need to be directly addressed to an individual mail server.

Consider `Todd@lechery.isc.tamu.edu`. This is an address that Todd had a few years ago when he worked at Texas A&M University. (He no longer receives email at that address.) Notice how it uses all of the possible parts of an Internet address. `Todd` is the username, `lechery` is a host computer (in this case, an actual computer named "lechery"), `isc` is a subdomain name that represents the computers in the Institute for Scientific Computation, `tamu` is the domain name for all Internet-connected computers at Texas A&M University, and `edu` is the three-letter code for *educational,* which is the type of organization that Texas A&M is considered to be on the Internet.

Usenet Newsgroups

The next Internet service we'll talk about is Usenet newsgroups. These are discussion groups on the Internet where people gather to post messages and replies on thousands of topics, including computing, popular entertainers, sports, dating, politics, and classified advertising. Usenet is a very popular Internet service, and most Web browsers have some built-in ability to read Usenet discussion groups.

NOTE

Although you'll hear the word "news" a lot when you talk about Usenet, not too many newsgroups offer the kind of news you expect from a newspaper or CNN. In general, Usenet is comprised of discussion groups such as the forums on CompuServe or the message areas on America Online.

Like Internet email, Usenet discussion groups have their own system of organization to help you find things. This system uses ideas and syntax that are similar to email addresses, but you'll notice that Usenet doesn't require that you find specific hosts and servers on the Internet—just a particular group. Usenet newsgroup names use the following format:

`first-level name.second-level.third.fourth...`

The first-level name indicates what type of Usenet group this is, the second narrows the subject a bit, and the address continues until it more or less completely describes the group. For instance, the following are both examples of Usenet newsgroup addresses:

`co.general`

`comp.sys.ibm.pc.misc`

In the first example, the first-level name co means that this is a local Usenet group for the Colorado area, and general shows that it's for discussion of general topics. In the second example, comp is a common first-level name that suggests that this is an internationally available newsgroup about some sort of computing issue (see Table 2.3). The other levels of the name provide more detailed information about the group.

Table 2.3: Common Usenet First-level Newsgroup Names

First-Level Name	Description
alt	Alternative groups
biz	Business issues
clari	Clarinet news stories
comp	Computing topics
misc	Other general discussions
news	General news about and help with Usenet
rec	Recreational topics
sci	Scientific discussions
soc	Social issues
talk	Debate-oriented groups

FTP

The File Transfer Protocol (FTP) is the Internet service that allows computers to transfer binary files (programs and documents) across the Internet. This is the uploading/downloading protocol that you might use to obtain copies of shareware or freeware programs, or that might be useful for downloading new software drivers from a particular computer hardware company.

FTP addresses use the following format:

`host.sub-domain.domain.first-level domain`

An FTP address is simply the Internet address of a particular host computer. The following example is the FTP address for downloading driver updates and other software from the Iomega site (makers of Zip drives):

`ftp.iomega.com`

In most cases, FTP connections also require some sort of login procedure, which means that you'll need a username and password from the system administrator to gain access. The majority of public FTP sites, however, are anonymous sites that allow anyone to access their files. For these sites, the username is generally anonymous, and you're asked to enter your email address for the system's password.

NOTE

Many Web browsers can access only anonymous FTP sites. You might still need a dedicated FTP program to access FTP sites that require an account username and password.

Web Servers

Most of us won't have an occasion to truly run our own Web servers. However, there are still details about them that you should be familiar with because you'll still be interacting with them if you choose to create a Web site that's housed at your ISP.

A server, as we've discussed previously, refers to a machine that performs a specific task. In this case, it's a machine that stores and sends out the individual files that make up a Web site. The actual process of receiving and responding to requests for files is handled by Web server software.

TIP

In most instances, you'll be able to tell whether someone is talking about the Web server as a piece of hardware or as a software program by the context in which it's mentioned.

Web server software is available for just about any operating system platform, but the most popular ones are run on Windows NT or a UNIX variant. Three of them, Microsoft's Internet Information Server (IIS), Microsoft Personal Web Server (PWS), and Apache, are discussed in this section.

Microsoft Internet Information Server (IIS)

Considered the front-runner in the Windows NT Web server market, Internet Information Server is incorporated into the Windows NT Server operating system. Because it's freely available and already installed on NT Server machines, it's no wonder it tends to be popular. But beyond its cost-effectiveness, IIS is also a competitive entry in this market for its ease of administration, integrated support for NT-style security authentication, and the large number of database formats it supports.

IIS is increasingly popular in the ISP market, due in large part to its integrated support for Microsoft's HTML authoring tool, FrontPage. Microsoft has created extensions to IIS that provides both added functionality to the authoring environment and an easy wizard-based approach to Web site tasks such as search engines, guest books, and date/time stamps.

When working with IIS, keep in mind that like most other Windows applications, filenames are handled without regard to case. That is, Index.html, INDEX.HTML, and index.html are all considered to be the same file.

Microsoft Personal Web Server (PWS)

Microsoft's Personal Web Server is fun, in that you can install and run it on any desktop or laptop machine that's running Windows 95 or 98; it doesn't have to be a computer designated as a server.

PWS can be obtained by downloading the Windows NT Option Pack. Don't let that name confuse you even if you're not running Windows NT Workstation, but instead are running Windows 95 or 98, you still want to download the NT Option Pack to obtain Personal Web Server. (You can start from http://www.microsoft.com/windows/ie/pws/default.htm?RLD=23).

Many HTML authors find PWS convenient for testing the development of an entire Web site locally, before transferring the files to a Web server that's actually connected to the Internet. PWS is fully capable of handling ASP, ISAPI, and CGI interactions, you can be sure of your site's functionality before exposing it to the public.

As with IIS, Personal Web Server treats filenames without regard to case. INDEX.HTML is the same as index.html or any other variant.

Apache

The Apache Web Server is truly the workhorse of the Web. Unique among the myriad of commercial Web server offerings, Apache, like many UNIX/Linux projects, was written by a group of enthusiastic programmers on a purely volunteer basis. Anyone is free to offer suggestions, program code that improves its functionality, and help in maintaining and supporting the project. The Apache Software Foundation (http://www.apache.org) was established to ensure the organized promotion and growth of all that is involved in a project of this scope.

You can download and install Apache in one of two ways: by downloading the source code and compiling it yourself with a C compiler (not for the inexperienced or the faint of heart!) or by downloading one of the precompiled binary versions available for over 20 operating system platforms.

If your ISP or company system runs Apache on a UNIX or Linux system, keep in mind that those operating systems do pay attention to case in filenames, unlike the two Windows products in the previous section. In that case, Index.html can exist independently of INDEX.HTML and any other variation. You need to be careful to keep a consistent scheme for filename case both when saving, and referring to them in your HTML documents (as you'll learn to do later).

What's Next?

The World Wide Web is the youngest and most unique of the Internet services. Its protocols allow it to transmit both text and multimedia file formats to users while also allowing Web browsers to access other Internet services. The Web is based on a concept called hypertext, which means that text within the paragraphs on a Web page is designed to act as links to other Web pages. There is no hierarchy on the Web, which is only loosely organized by the system of links.

Other services that can be accessed via the Web include Usenet, email, and FTP. Each of these older Internet services has its own scheme for formulating addresses. Most of the services require a server computer of some sort to allow Internet applications to access their information. The server computers have specific addresses on the Web that you need to know in order to contact the servers.

In Chapter 3, we will look at several Web browser programs and how they display HTML documents.

Review Questions

1. Why are Web protocols considered flexible by Internet standards?

2. What does hypertext mean? Where else might the typical computer user encounter hypertext?

3. True or false: Hypermedia links are hypertext links to newswire stories.

4. What makes a Web site different from a Web page?

5. What is the purpose of having helper applications?

6. Why are file extensions important to Web browsers?

7. Among Usenet, Internet email, and FTP, what two Internet services use similar addressing schemes?

8. What should you enter as the password to an anonymous FTP site?

9. What Web server can be installed on a Windows 98 desktop computer?

10. True or false: All Web servers treat filenames in a case-sensitive manner.

Review Exercises

1. If you have an Internet account or an account with an online service, use your email address to determine your service's domain name and first-level domain.

2. If you have an FTP application, see if your ISP offers an FTP site. Try an address in the format `ftp.ispdomain.first-level domain.` An example might be `ftp.service.net`.

3. Using your Web browser, attempt to connect to an FTP address such as `ftp.download.com`. What happens?

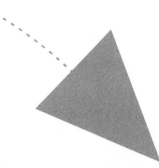

How Web Browsers Work

The HTML we write is displayed primarily in applications called Web browsers. Although we're beginning to see HTML appear in other arenas, such as online help modules, its primary use is still the creation of Web pages that will be displayed in Web browsers. Therefore, it's important to get to know these browsers.

This chapter teaches you the following:

- About some popular Web browser applications
- How Web browsers interact with Web servers
- How browsers interact with the other Internet services that are available to them, including the following:
  - How Uniform Resource Locators (URLs) work
  - The fundamentals of Web protocols
  - How a Web browser reads a Web page

Web Browser Applications

All Web browsers are capable of certain basic tasks, such as finding and loading new Web pages and displaying them following HTML standards and conventions. Each browser tends to have its own quirks, however, based in part on the vagueness in (or lack of) display directives found in the HTML specifications. The more documents you create, the quicker you'll get used to them.

NOTE

This book cannot provide an exhaustive survey of the Web browsers available. It is fair to say, though, that it covers the most popular ones.

NCSA Mosaic

Worth mentioning for its historic value, though not its current popularity, the Mosaic browser, shown in Figure 3.1, was first developed by the National Center for Supercomputing Applications (NCSA) in 1993. It was the first widely available graphical browser for Web users. Versions have been written for Windows, Macintosh, and various UNIX platforms. It was also the basis of a number of other browsers on the market—most notably those created and licensed by SpyGlass Corp.

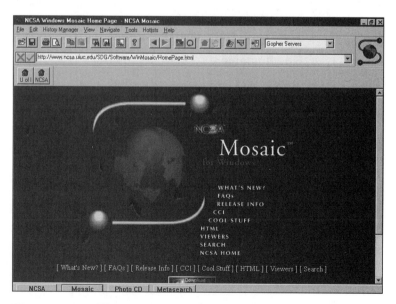

Figure 3.1: *NCSA Mosaic for Windows 95.*

As of January 1997, the Mosaic development team announced that it would not produce any new versions of the Mosaic browser. In part, at least, this is likely because of the explosive growth in popularity of two newer browsers, discussed next, and a desire to shift the efforts of the team to new projects.

Netscape Navigator

Sharing the title of "most popular" Web browser currently available, Netscape Navigator (often simply referred to as Netscape) made a splash on the Internet in 1995 with its totally free first version. Created in part by programmers who had worked on the original NCSA project, Netscape quickly became known as the finest second-generation Web browser. It was noted for both its flexibility and its speed gains over Mosaic—especially for modem connections.

Netscape's popularity continued to rise as innovations in later versions introduced its cability to accept plug-ins, or helper applications, that actually extended the cabilities of the browser program. Users who have the Macromedia Shockwave plug-in, for instance, can view Macromedia presentation files that are embedded within HTML documents in Navigator's window (instead of loading a separate helper application).

Netscape, shown in Figure 3.2, is available free of charge for Windows, Mac, and UNIX users. It can be downloaded from the Web from a variety of sources, including Netscape's download center at `http://www.netscape.com/computing/download/index.html` or by FTP at `ftp.netscape.com`.

When it was introduced, Netscape's main advantages were speed and the ability to display more graphics formats than Mosaic. Since that time, however, Netscape has introduced security features and other technologies (such as a built-in email program and built-in Usenet newsreader) that have continued to lead the way in browser innovation.

Another advantage came with the support of Java applets and JavaScript authoring within Netscape itself. Again, Java applets can be embedded in the Netscape browser window, allowing the user access to truly dynamic pages that can be an interface for anything from simple games to stock quotes to bank-by-computer information. JavaScript gives Web designers programmatic control over their pages, allowing them to check HTML form entries, to load different pages based on user input, and to do much more.

Today, Netscape offers support for most current Web-related languages and specifications, including HTML 4, Cascading Style Sheets (which you'll learn about later in Chapter 18, "Cascading Style Sheets"), and a vast array of plug-ins, helpers, and other multimedia enhancements.

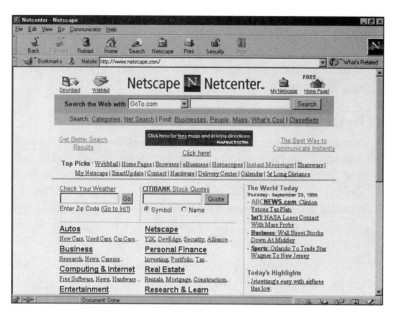

Figure 3.2: *Netscape Navigator for Windows.*

Netscape Navigator is available either as a standalone Web browser or as a component of the larger package known as Netscape Communicator. The current Communicator (version 4.7 as we went to press) bundles these programs together (some items are available only on the Windows platform):

- **Navigator** The browser itself.

- **Messenger** An integrated email and usenet newsreader client.

- **Composer** Netscape's HTML authoring tool.

- **AOL Instant Messenger 3.0** A real-time chat utility.

- **Three audio/video tools** Netscape Radio, RealPlayer G2, and Winamp.

- **PalmPilot Synch Tools** Synchronize your PDA browser with your desktop.

When using the Communicator package, you can choose which items you wish to install and leave out those you don't think you'll use. Netscape's SmartUpdate feature in Communicator allows for easy upgrades as new features or bug fixes become available. No more downloading 10–15 megabyte files each time!

Microsoft Internet Explorer

Another entry in the free Web browser market is Internet Explorer, a Web browser created by Microsoft (see Figure 3.3). Originally based on the Mosaic technology, and in fact still licensed (in part) for distribution by SpyGlass, Internet Explorer is a contender along with Netscape Navigator for the "most popular" title. Microsoft's browser is available for Windows 95/98, Windows NT, and Macintosh platforms. It can be found on the Web at `http://www.microsoft.com/IE/` or by FTP at `ftp.microsoft.com`.

TIP

Current installations of Windows 95/98 and Windows NT come with a version of Internet Explorer already installed. Depending on which version of Windows you have, it might not be the most recent version of IE. Check the version number by using Internet Explorer's Help menu, then choose About Internet Explorer. The current version (as of press time) was Internet Explorer 5.

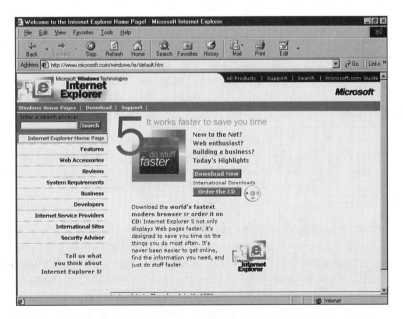

Figure 3.3: *Microsoft Internet Explorer 5.0 for Windows 98.*

Internet Explorer, like Netscape Navigator, supports most of the HTML 4 recommendation, along with Cascading Style Sheets, and even XML (though in a rather awkward proprietary manner). Most designers prefer IE's support for CSS, though even it isn't complete. Both Navigator and Internet Explorer could use improvements on that front.

Microsoft has packaged a number of tools to go with Internet Explorer, which can be downloaded individually or as an entire suite. Added features include the following:

- **Outlook Express** Integrated mail and news reader
- **Windows Media Player** Handles audio and video files
- **Net Meeting** Real-time audio/video chat
- **FrontPage Express** Microsoft's miniature Web authoring tool

Lynx

Lynx and similar browsers (such as Cello and specialized systems such as screen readers and Braille browsers) are a little different from the others discussed so far because they lack the ability to display graphics. It might be surprising that people still rely on text-based browsers to access the Web, but it remains true that not everyone has a high-speed connection to the Internet. In fact, some users don't even have a graphical operating system (such as Windows and MacOS) for their computer.

Most often you'll find such basic terminal access to the Internet in school and university computer labs, or other "dumb terminal" environments, where each machine isn't a fully equipped desktop workstation. So, these users aren't necessarily living the "Dark Ages" of computing by choice.

Lynx was originally written for the UNIX platform. In fact, it is the browser used by most service providers for text-based accounts. There is also an MS-DOS version that offers users browsing capabilities in a text-only format (see Figure 3.4). The DOS version can be used on any Windows platform simply by running it from the MS-DOS command prompt.

Special considerations must go into your HTML documents if they will support text-based browsers such as Lynx. Fortunately, as you'll see in upcoming chapters, HTML by its very nature favors a text-based display, and HTML 4.0 in particular incorporates "accessibility" features that help all nontraditional displays, such as the screen readers and braille devices mentioned previously, manage all the information being presented to them.

Uniform Resource Locators

Now that you've looked at the various Web browsers that might be accessing your Web site, let's talk about something they all have in common: the use of *Uniform Resource Locators* (URLs). What's a URL? If you remember our discussion from the preceding chapter, you might recall that I mentioned that most Internet services have "addresses" for accessing information within that service.

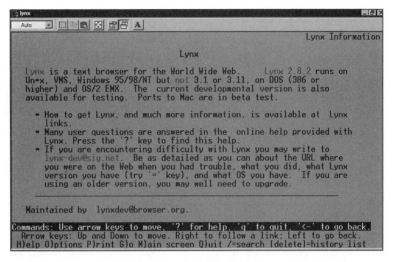

Figure 3.4: *The DOS version of the Lynx browser.*

Each of these addresses is a bit different. For instance, you would send an email message to my mailbox used for book-related topics by using `books@webgeek.com` in an email application.

On the other hand, to access the Netscape FTP site mentioned previously, you would enter `ftp.netscape.com` in the FTP application you are using.

The World Wide Web also has its own addressing scheme, but it's slightly more advanced than the schemes of its predecessors. Not only is the Web newer, but its addresses have to be more sophisticated because of the Web's unique ability to access all the different Internet services.

URLs are these special addresses. Web page authors should be familiar with the addressing schemes found on the Internet because you will be incorporating those addresses in your pages when you create links to other documents. Linking is discussed in detail in Chapter 10, "Hypertext and Creating Links."

A URL follows a format like this:

`protocol://host.domain.first-level domain/path/filename.ext`

or

`protocol:host.domain.first-level domain`

An example of a URL to access a Web document would be `http://www.microsoft.com/windows/default.asp`.

Let's look at that address carefully. According to the format for a URL, `http://` is the protocol, www is the host computer you're accessing, microsoft is the domain, and com is the first-level domain type for this system. That's followed by / to suggest that a path statement is coming next.

The path statement tells you that you're looking at the document default.asp, located in the directory windows.

NOTE

An .asp file is a special type of HTML file known as an Active Server Page that incorporates some server-side processing techniques. For our current illustrative purposes, consider it an HTML file.

NOTE

If you're familiar with DOS, Windows, or UNIX, you will probably recognize path statements right away. MacOS users and others simply need to realize that a path statement offers a "path" to a specific file on the server computer's hard drive. A Web browser needs to know in exactly which directories and subdirectories (folders and subfolders) a file can be found, so a path statement is a standard part of any URL.

The URL has two basic advantages. First, it allows you to explicitly indicate the type of Internet service involved. HTTP, for instance, indicates the *Hypertext Transfer Protocol*—the basic protocol for transferring Web documents. You'll look at this part of the URL in a moment.

Second, the URL system of addressing makes every single document, program, and file on the Internet a separately addressable entity. Why is this useful?

EXAMPLE

The URL Advantage

For this example, all you need to do is load your Web browser (whichever one you happen to use) and find the text box or similar interface element that allows you to enter a URL manually to access Web pages (see Figure 3.5). The point of this example is to show you the benefits of using URLs for the Web. With FTP, you really only need to know a host address. But on the Web, knowing just the host address often isn't enough.

Figure 3.5: The Go To/Location text box in Netscape for Windows allows you to enter a URL manually.

Once you've located the appropriate entry box, enter www.mcp.com. Depending on the browser you're using, you'll more than likely need to press Enter or Return after typing this address.

What happens then depends on your Web browser. Some browsers will give you an error, which isn't exactly perfect for this example, but it does prove that you need more than just a server address to get around on the Web. Others will take you directly to the Macmillan Computer Publishing Web site.

TIP

If your browser gives you an error, enter http://www.mcp.com. Some browsers require at least a partial URL. Others guess the protocol from the type of server address entered.

Notice that www.mcp.com follows the addressing conventions established for Internet services such as FTP and Gopher. The problem is that if the Web used this method for addresses, you'd have to begin at the first page of the Web site every time you wanted to access one of the hundreds of pages available from Macmillan.

To get around that, a URL provides your Web browser with more information. Try typing http://www.mcp.com/que/index.html in your Web browser, and then press Enter or Return (as appropriate).

All Web browsers should easily handle this address. With a URL, you can be much more specific about the document you want to see because every document on the Internet has an individual address. In this case, you've instructed your Web browser to go directly to the Que directory on Macmillan's Web site and load the HTML document called index.html.

The Different Protocols for URLs

You've already looked at Internet addresses such as www.mcp.com in depth, and you should be familiar with the concept of a path statement. That leaves just one part of a URL that's new to you: the protocol.

I've already mentioned that HTTP is the protocol most often used by Web browsers to access HTML pages. Table 3.1 shows some of the other protocols that can be part of a URL.

Table 3.1: Possible Protocols for a URL

Protocol	What It Accesses
http://	HTML documents
https://	Some "secure" HTML documents
file://	HTML documents on your hard drive
ftp://	FTP sites and files
news://	Usenet newsgroups on a particular news server
mailto:	Email messages
telnet:	Direct connection from your computer to the server using a "shell" account.

By entering one of these protocols, followed by an Internet server address and a path statement, you can access nearly any document, directory, file, or program available on the Internet or on your own hard drive.

NOTE

The mailto: and telnet: protocols have slightly different requirements to create a URL. mailto: is followed by a simple email address, and telnet: is followed by just a server address. Also notice that file:// is often slightly different for different browsers. The colon acts as a separator between the protocol and the address. The double slash //, when used, indicates conformance to the common Internet scheme syntax developed by the Internet Engineering Task Force.

EXAMPLE

Accessing Other Internet Services with URLs

Fortunately, by simply changing the protocol of a particular URL, you can access most Internet services directly from your browser. For this example, you'll need to load your Web browser once more and enter ftp://ftp.cdrom.com/pub/win95/.

This should result in a listing of the subdirectory demos located on the FTP server ftp.cdrom.com. Notice that you didn't enter a document name because, if you're using the FTP protocol, the document or file will be automatically downloaded.

TIP

If your browser tells you that there are too many users presently connected for you to connect to this FTP site, wait a moment or two, and then click the Reload button or otherwise reload this URL with your browser.

Not all browsers support the mailto: command—let's see if yours does. In your browser's URL window, type mailto:books@webgeek.com and press Enter or Return if necessary.

If your browser supports the `mailto:` protocol command, you should see a new window, complete with my email address in the Mail To field. If your browser doesn't have an integrated email client, your default mail client might launch and create a new email message, as happens on my system with Eudora Pro (see Figure 3.6).

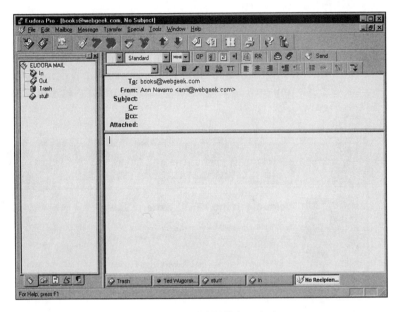

Figure 3.6: *A* `mailto:` *protocol URL in action.*

Some browsers, or browser/email client combinations, don't handle `mailto:` protocols. Don't worry if you find yourself in this situation; you're not alone by any means.

How Web Browsers Access HTML Documents

When you enter a URL in the URL field on your browser, the browser goes through the following three basic steps:

1. It determines what protocol to use.

2. It looks up and contacts the server at the address specified.

3. It requests the specific document (including its path statement) from the server computer.

Using all this information, your browser was able to access the variety of Internet services discussed in Table 3.1 and in the subsequent example. But what does this have to do with HTML design? Just about everything.

In HTML, a hypertext link is simply a clickable URL. Every time you create a link in a Web document, you assign a URL to that link. When that link is clicked by a user, the URL is fed to the browser, which then goes through the procedure just outlined to try and retrieve it.

Watching the Link

EXAMPLE

If you've used your Web browser much, you've watched this happen countless times, even if you didn't realize it. If you're using Netscape or a similar browser, start by pointing your mouse pointer at just about any link you can find. You might notice that when your mouse pointer is touching the link, a URL appears in the status bar—probably at the bottom of the page (see Figure 3.7).

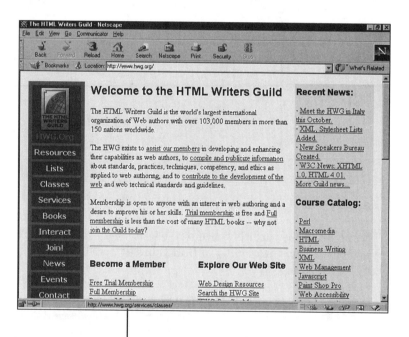

A URL associated with a link on this page

Figure 3.7: A URL in the status bar of Netscape Navigator.

That's the URL associated with the link to which you're pointing. Clicking that link will cause the browser to accept that URL as its next command, in much the same way that you manually entered URLs in the earlier example. To see this happen, click the link once. Now check the URL field that you used before to enter URLs (see Figure 3.8). You should see the same URL that was associated with the link to which your mouse pointer was pointing. Then, after a few seconds, you should be at the new page.

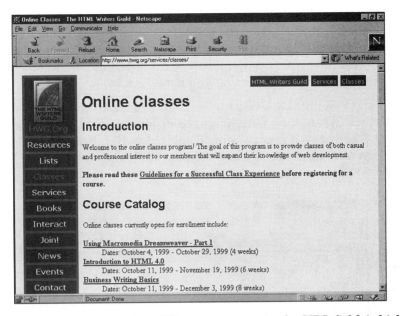

Figure 3.8: *The link's URL now appears in the URL field (which is Location in Netscape).*

What Can Be Sent on the Web?

Part of the magic of the HTTP protocol is that it is fairly unlimited (by Internet standards) in the sort of files that it can send and receive. For instance, like Internet email, much of what is sent on the Web (via the HTTP protocol) is ASCII text. But HTTP isn't limited to ASCII text.

NOTE

Two different types of files can be sent over various Internet services: ASCII text files (plain text) and binary files. Binary files are any documents created by applications (such as word processing or graphics applications), or even the applications themselves. It's easiest to think of binary files as anything that isn't an ASCII file.

In fact, HTTP can send both of the major types of files—ASCII and binary—using the same protocol. This means that both plain text files (such as Usenet messages and HTML documents) and binaries (such as downloadable programs or graphics files) can be sent via the Web without any major effort on the part of the user. In certain cases, the HTML author will have to make a distinction (for instance, as to whether a graphics file should be displayed or downloaded to the user's machine), but for the most part, the browser figures this stuff out by itself.

How exactly does it figure these things out? Usually by a combination of the protocol selected and the extension to the filename in question. For instance, a file called index.html that's accessed using a URL that starts with the `http://` protocol will be displayed in a browser as an HTML file, complete with formatting and hypertext links.

EXAMPLE

However, if that same file is renamed index.txt, even if it's loaded with an `http://` protocol URL, it will be displayed in the browser as a simple ASCII file, just as if it were being displayed in NotePad, SimpleText, or Emacs. Why is this? Because the extension tells the Web browser how to display the file (see Figures 3.9 and 3.10).

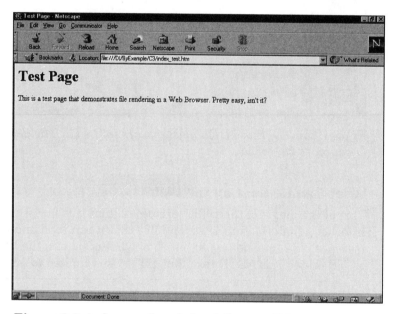

Figure 3.9: *index_test.htm is loaded as an HTML document by the browser.*

You might recall from Chapter 1, "What Is HTML?," that much of an HTML document is "text" (the rest being HTML codes). In fact, all of an HTML document is ASCII text, as is demonstrated in Figure 3.9. It is only the extension .html (or .htm on DOS-based Web servers) that tells a Web browser that it needs to interpret some of the text as HTML commands within a particular ASCII text document.

TIP

Because HTML documents are ASCII text, it's possible to create them in simple text editor programs. A Microsoft Word document, on the other hand, is not ASCII text—it's saved in a binary format. Therefore, you can't always use the concept of "it contains text" to judge ASCII versus binary.

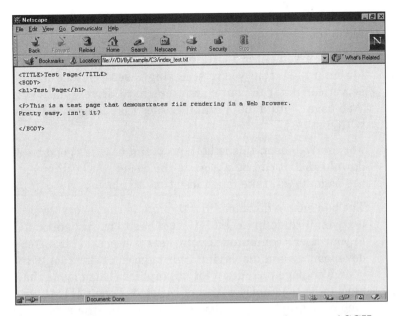

Figure 3.10: *index_test.txt is displayed simply as an ASCII text file.*

Binaries on the Web

When a binary document such as a graphics file is sent over the Web, it's important that it have the appropriate extension. That's how Web browsers know whether a document should be viewed in the browser window (like a JPG- or GIF-format graphic) or it should be saved to the hard drive (like a ZIP or StuffIt archive file).

To the HTML designer, this means two things. First, you should recognize that your HTML pages can offer just about any other type of file for transport across the Web. If you want to send graphics, games, WordPerfect documents, or just about anything else, just put a hypertext link to that file on your Web page.

Second, you need to remember that the most important part of a filename, at least for HTML purposes, is its extension. If you fail to put the correct extension on a filename, your user's browser won't know what to do with it. If you're trying to display a graphic on your Web page, for instance, but you put a .txt extension on it, it isn't likely to display.

Everything Is Downloaded

There's one other thing you should realize about the Web and Web browsers before you begin developing Web pages. Very simply, everything you view in a Web browser has to be downloaded from the Web site first. What do I mean by this?

Whenever you enter a URL or click a hypertext link, the HTML document (or binary file) that you're accessing is sent, in its entirety, from the Web server computer to your computer's hard drive. That's why, for instance, Web pages with a lot of graphics files take longer to display than Web pages with just text.

For the Web user, this is both good and bad. It's good because once a page is downloaded, it can be placed in the cache so that the next time you access the page, it will take much less time to display.

The bad side of downloading, though, is that every graphic and all of the text you include in an HTML page has to be transmitted over the Internet to your user's computer. If your user is accessing the Web over a modem, downloading and displaying your page can take a long time—especially if your Web page includes a lot of graphics. This means that HTML designers have to be constantly aware of the size of their HTML documents and their Web page graphics in order to avoid causing their users unnecessary irritation and wasted time.

NOTE

It can take up to 15 seconds (on average) for a 25KB graphic to be transmitted over a 56Kbps modem connection. So a 100KB Web page could take a full minute to transfer—the length of up to four television commercials.

What's Next?

There are a number of popular Web browser applications that Web designers should take into consideration when designing their Web pages. Each has its own strengths, yet all render HTML files in about the same way, albeit with a few quirks you'll discover.

The Web uses a particular style of Internet address called a URL, which allows it to address individually any document on the Internet. This offers an advantage over other Internet address schemes because it specifies the Internet service protocols desired and points directly at documents.

It's important for the Web designer to remember that everything on a Web page is downloaded, including text and graphics. The larger the graphics on a Web page, the longer it will take to display. This is also an advantage, though, because pages can be cached for future use.

Next up in Chapter 4, "HTML's Role on the Web," you'll learn about HTML's role on the Web. We'll discuss how companies can benefit from being online, how sites can incorporate "Web applications" to address customer needs, and how HTML keeps pace with the ever-changing nature of the World Wide Web.

Review Questions

1. Which browser was the first graphical browser on the market? Which is currently the most popular?

2. What makes the Lynx browser different from the others discussed?

3. Is the following a URL, a server address, or a path statement?

   www.mcp.com

4. What makes the `mailto:` command different from a standard URL?

5. What ASCII character comes between each folder or directory in a path statement?

6. If I entered the following in my browser's URL field (and pressed Enter or Return, if necessary), would it download a file?

   http://ftp.cdrom.com/pub/win95/games/four.zip

7. True or false: Graphics displayed on a Web page are downloaded to the user's computer, which is why they often take extra time to display.

8. Are the following files ASCII files or binary files?

   An Adobe Photoshop picture

   An HTML page

   A Microsoft Word document

   An Excel spreadsheet

Review Exercises

1. Use your current Web browser to access one of the FTP sites mentioned in the "Web Browser Applications" section of this chapter. Notice how browsers handle FTP connections.

2. Use an `ftp://` URL to download one of those other Web browsers (or another file) directly. Hint: You'll need to figure out the path to the file first.

3. If your ISP allows it, use a modem communications program to dial up your shell account, and then use Lynx or a similar text browser based on their server through your ISP's connection. Notice how different the Web is without graphics and a mouse!

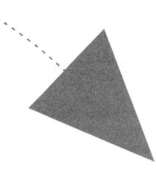

HTML's Role on the Web

You've already seen how HTML is used to emphasize text in Web documents. And you've seen how hypertext and hypermedia links can be used to maneuver on the Web, access information, and download different file formats.

This chapter teaches you the following:

- Where HTML is today and where it's going in the future
- The advantages of Web pages compared to other Internet services
- How HTML has changed with the Web
- How to recognize and understand the different flavors of HTML
- How to decide what types of HTML you will use

Why Create Web Pages?

Having learned exactly how the Web works, you can move on to why you might want to create Web pages. There are a number of reasons you might want to do this; more than likely, you've already got some ideas. Consider the following possible examples:

- **Small businesses**   The Web is an ideal way for small businesses to communicate with both existing customers and potential customers. In terms of advertising dollars, it can be one of the most inexpensive buys in town! If you haven't already, it's a good idea to put up some Web pages that explain the services you provide from your small business or home office. Then put your URL on your business cards or brochures and other advertising so that customers know where to go for detailed information about you.

- **Large businesses**   Large businesses should be on the Web too, especially technical and customer-service–oriented businesses. The Web is a wonderfully unique way to provide customer service, technical support, and informational services at a relatively low cost to the business. A good Web designer and a creative Information Systems (IS) staff can put together some very unique services that might save a business tons of customer support dollars (see Figure 4.1).

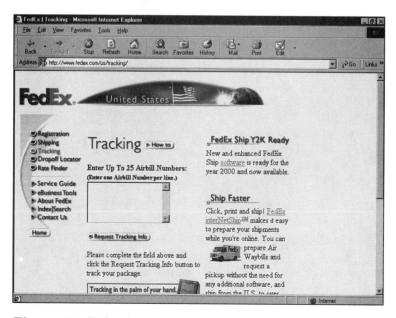

Figure 4.1: *Federal Express has come up with a great reason to use the Web—customers can track packages without calling an 800 number.*

- **Community groups**   Do you participate in a group in your community, such as a neighborhood, church, or school organization? If you do, a Web page is a great way to offer information about the group, present a meeting schedule, post announcements, and recruit new members. The Web page can even be a great way to inform members of changes to the club or the schedule, or to praise members for accomplishments.

- **Hobbies**   Even if your major hobbies aren't computer-related, you can create a Web page and put it on the World Wide Web. Eventually, people with the same interests as you will be visiting your page, sending you email, and helping you find more information about your hobby. You might even find others who've put up similar Web pages, and you'll be able to add links to their information on your page.

- **Personal or family pages**   What else can you put on a Web page? Your resume; samples of your work; samples of your kids' work; pictures of the house, car, or kittens you're selling; and even clips from home movies. It's a good way to make up-to-the-minute photos available to your family. It's also a great place to post writing samples and old articles about yourself or your family from the local paper.

Web Applications

Another emerging use for HTML on the Web is as a basis for something called a *Web application*. In essence, a Web application is a Web site designed to do more than simply present pages and hypermedia links to its users; it actually acts as a front end for data-processing.

For instance, consider the notion of a Web site designed to give the company's salespeople the ability to access product information and confirm orders while on the road. Using HTML, the basic interface for the sales database can be made available on the Web. With the appropriate browser software and an Internet connection (perhaps even over a cellular modem), the salesperson for your company has nearly instant access to the information she needs.

Once the data is centered on the page, it is passed by the Web server to programs (often referred to as CGI-BIN scripts for applications, as discussed in Chapter 14, "Form Design and Data Gathering with CGI Scripts") that process information—looking up the product in the database or taking the order. The results of these programs can be generated completely with HTML markup so that the answers can be viewed by the salesperson in her Web browser.

Searching on the Web

Not all Web applications are necessarily business-related—and even the applications that are don't necessarily have to be limited to employee use. Consider one of the most popular Web applications available: the Web-based search engine.

These Web applications use HTML pages to offer an interface to a database of Web sites around the world. You begin by accessing the page and entering keywords, which the Web application passes to a processing program. The program uses your keywords to check the database of Web pages, and then it generates an HTML page with the results.

The URL for that results page is returned to the Web server, which treats it as a standard link. The browser loads the newly created page, complete with hypertext links to the possible database matches.

Let's take a look at the popular Yahoo! Web directory application. Start out by entering `http://www.yahoo.com/` in your browser and pressing Enter or Return.

Once the page is loaded, it should look something like Figure 4.2. In the field on the Web page that allows you to enter text, enter a few keywords that might suggest a hobby that interests you. One of my hobbies is cooking, so I might try entering `cooking`, `food`, `gourmet`, or something similar.

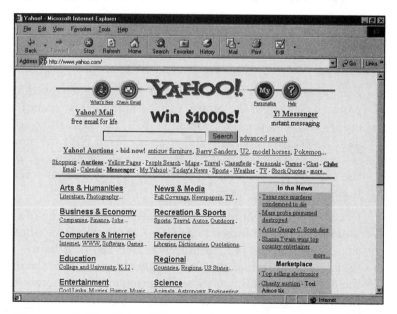

Figure 4.2: *The Yahoo! Web directory application.*

Click the Search button on the Web page, and the Yahoo! engine will begin searching for related Web pages. When it's finished, you are presented with a list of hypertext links. Click any link to view the related pages and see whether they offer the information you are seeking.

Advantages and Disadvantages of the Web

Most small or large businesses have a compelling reason to create a presence on the World Wide Web. It's an important new medium for communications that is relatively inexpensive to implement, it's a boon for dealing with customer service issues, and it's gaining popularity in leaps and bounds. But any good HTML designer should realize that there are also certain disadvantages to the Web.

Advantages

There are many good reasons to commit to creating a presence on the World Wide Web. I've already hinted at some of these in this chapter, but let's look at them in detail. Most of these are geared toward businesses, but you'll notice that these advantages are available to any Web site:

- **Multimedia presentations** A Web site allows you to do things that are simply not possible in any other medium. Because it combines the visual impact of television, the informational utility of print, and the personal appeal of radio, the Web is an effective tool for taking marketing information to another level. Products can be explained and offered in depth, along with pictures, video, sound, and even animation.

- **Interactivity** There are a number of different areas where the fact that your user can interactively determine what to view or hear can really make the difference for a business. Especially important is the added value that the Web gives you for customer service, technical or product support, and immediate feedback. While most of any Web site is automated, it gives you an opportunity to answer frequently asked questions and point customers to resources that might help them solve problems on their own. While this might seem like an advantage reserved for computer companies, consider the implications for service-oriented industries such as travel, consulting, catalog sales, and business-to-business sales. If the Web site can answer a basic question 20 times in a day instead of one of your telephone customer service agents, the company can quickly realize significant cost savings while still providing their customers with the information they need.

- **Flexibility**   If your business relies on printing or publishing and the media, you can immediately see the advantage of the Web. Changes on the Web are relatively instantaneous, and the speed with which an update can be made is measured in minutes, not weeks. Consider a financial planner's or real estate agent's sales newsletter. Instant changes on World Wide Web give their net-savvy clients a time-based edge. Incorporating the Web into the services you offer a client gives you an added value in their eyes, especially in time-sensitive industries. The travel planner's site can immediately feature specials and discounts provided by the major airlines, just minutes after the information has been released. The "wired" traveler, then, is more likely to find out about the sale early, and secure seats that are prone to sell out fast. If she waited to see the fare sale notice in her local paper's weekly travel section, she could be several days too late to secure the trip she was shopping for.

EXAMPLE

Travel Agent Web Site

Let's roll all these advantages into a hypothetical Web site for a travel agency to show exactly what we mean. All-Rite Travel has decided that it needs a Web site and is trying to determine the ways in which the site will help win and keep customers. The agency relies on professionally designed and printed brochures that are updated annually to distribute general information about the agency and its services. It has a quarterly newsletter for repeat customers, and it generates laser-printer fliers and mailers for special deals. Figure 4.3 shows the index page for All-Rite Travel's site.

MULTIMEDIA AND INTERACTIVITY

First of all, the agency's presentations can be multimedia-oriented. Taking advantage of the Web allows you to provide sound, graphics, and even video of travel destinations across the Web. If the agency has pictures of accommodations in a vacation resort, for instance, it can put those on its site. Sounds, video, or text generated by travel writers or photographers can also be added. A map to its offices, links for customers to send email, and information about its affiliations can all be online.

And using hypertext, All-Rite can pick from relatively unlimited resources for more information. It would take only a few hours to build links to all the Chambers of Commerce in major U.S. metropolitan areas. Links to airlines, major hotel chains, limousine services, car rentals, and credit card companies can all be added.

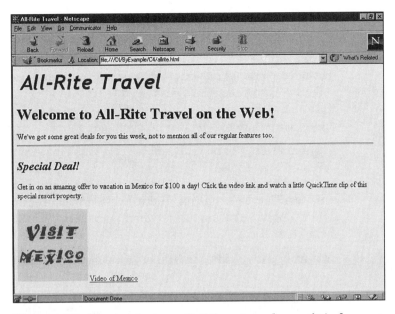

Figure 4.3: *Here's what our fictitious travel agent's index page might look like.*

FLEXIBILITY

Although All-Rite would probably want to continue with its print advertising and brochures, the possibilities for offering information over the Web are enticing. Because customers can take as little or as much information as they want, the Web can house all sorts of extras. Special employee pages can tell customers which agent is most specialized in their area of interest. Articles written by agents and other specialists can give tips on restaurants, travel safety, saving money, and tracking expenses on corporate trips.

The Web page could be instantly updated with new packages or the best deals the agency comes across—as they happen. The moment you are ready to make a sales notice or offer a special price, you can do so on the Web. Once All-Rite's customers are used to its Web presence, those with a special interest in traveling can easily check the Web site every few days for the latest offerings.

Disadvantages

You might not think that there would be disadvantages in having a Web site because most people and companies would use a Web site to enhance their marketing and customer service efforts, not supplant them. That said, there are a few hurdles to leap, and they should definitely be considered before your Web project takes off:

- **Learning curve**   It will take a while for folks to learn HTML, figure out how to upload pages, create appropriate graphics, and design effective Web sites. You'll also need to find an effective and helpful Internet service provider (or a similar in-house IS employee of the larger corporation) who can help you get online.

- **Appearance**   To be truly effective, a Web site also needs to be attractive and easy to use. For many companies, especially larger ones, that will mean using professional artists, writers, and designers. Beginning this task can be daunting, and it will require a reasonable budget, which might be intimidating when management isn't sure what the benefits will be.

- **Maintenance and timeliness**   One of the worst things that can happen to a Web site is for it to sit dormant for weeks or months because it was the pet project of an employee who has less time for it than she anticipated or because every change to the Web site must first be approved by a committee. It's important that a Web developer be relatively free to spend time on the project and that someone be available to make timely decisions. Without this, the Web site loses some of its inherent advantages.

- **Security**   Transmitting data via Internet technology, including the Web, can potentially be an unsecured process. For data to be transmitted over the Web, it must pass through a number of different servers and hosts, and any of the information you offer could potentially be read or held by any of these system operators. Luckily, advances in secure server technologies and other privacy measures have allowed the broad acceptance of e-commerce that we're now seeing. Despite that, companies should still protect sensitive internal data behind an appropriate firewall or server security systems.

- **Copyright issues**   The lack of security is also applicable for the Web designer. Nearly anything you create on the Web can easily be read or copied by anyone with Web access. This can be intimidating to both artists and publishers who want to make sure that Internet access doesn't devalue their published (and profitable) efforts. We expect that case law will soon catch up with the Internet in this regard.

- **Cost**   Depending on the size of your organization and the expertise of its people, a Web site can quickly become expensive. Learning HTML and creating a reasonable site isn't that difficult (as you'll see in this book), but maintaining the appropriate equipment; paying dedicated staffers; and bringing in consultants, designers, programmers, and IS technicians as a site grows can quickly expand the budget. The advantages will often outweigh these costs, but any Web developer should be aware that Web sites tend to get bigger and more time-consuming as time goes on.

SECURE CONNECTIONS ON THE INTERNET

Some Web server software packages offer an implementation of the *secure sockets layer* (SSL), a protocol that sits "on top" of TCP/IP (the Internet networking protocol) and "below" HTTP. Its purpose is to secure the transmission of HTTP data over the Web.

With an SSL server (usually designated by its `https://`-protocol URL) and an SSL-capable browser program, transmissions over the Web are encrypted in such a way that users trying to read the data as it passes over the Internet are treated to nothing but garbled text.

SSL is a feature of most current Web servers today and is designed to allow users to access a Web site in a secure fashion so that credit cards and other personal information can be passed with relative assurance.

Although this is not directly relevant to HTML designers, if you have the opportunity to create a commercial Web site (or otherwise ask for personal information from users), you might look into the possibility of using an SSL-based secure Web server to offer your users peace of mind. And, although SSL isn't the only security scheme, it's the most widely supported.

HTML and the Changing World Wide Web

You already know that the Web is really only a few years old and that graphical browsers have been around since only late 1993. So how could the Web have had enough time to change dramatically? In the computer world, it doesn't take long.

The Web and HTML were initially designed for use by academics in a fairly limited way: They planned to collaborate on physics projects and share information in a hypertext format. Publishing on the Web meant that they could put experimental data and their conclusions on the Internet, with links to other data and other researchers' notes, or even links that would download graphs and charts.

A few years later, people are talking about the Web as if it were the greatest thing since sliced bread. The World Wide Web is touted as the next logical medium for publication. It's the printing press of the future, where everyone who puts together a newsletter, magazine, sales brochure, or (in some cases) television show will have to have a presence.

Sounds pretty demanding, doesn't it?

The Forced Evolution of HTML

Along with these changing demands for the Web have come changing demands for HTML. It's only in the last two to three years or so that professional designers, writers, layout artists, and their ilk have begun to take an interest in the Web. And what did they find when they got there? They found that the feature-rich environment they were used to working in didn't directly translate to HTML.

HTML has certainly made advances since the first days of its Henry Ford-type pages. You could have any background color as long as it was gunship grey, and you couldn't justify and align text with images. But designers are still pressing forward with desires for the pixel-perfect control they're used to in print formats. Luckily, more and more of their wishes are coming true.

The Current State of HTML

With these commercial demands have come different solutions. Stylistic issues are now primarily addressed with a technology called Cascading Style Sheets (CSS), which will be introduced in Chapter 18, "Cascading Style Sheets." Database connectivity is possible using Active Server Pages, scripting language, and even XML.

The W3C's most recent effort in HTML is the HTML 4.01 Recommendation. HTML 4.01 is an update to HTML 4.0, which gained official standing in early 1998. HTML 4.01 is undergoing Proposed Recommendation review as this book goes to press, and we expect it to be formally adopted by the time you read this.

New work in the HTML arena is focusing on blending HTML with XML, the Extensible Markup Language. XML could be described as "pure structure" because its elements simply bound content and don't imply presentation as some HTML elements do (which you'll discover in the next few chapters). This new hybrid, referred to as the Extensible Hypertext Markup Language, or XHTML, is actively being developed as we go to press. Watch for more news on this from the W3C in the coming months.

What Can HTML Do?

Publishing on the Web with HTML is nearly limitless. Designers have been able to break the boundaries placed on print media to develop interactive and nonlinear experiences. The most successful of these artists understand one of the most basic concepts about Web publishing: The Web is not paper.

If you have your heart set on your Web site looking exactly like the layout you can produce using Microsoft's Publisher, or QuarkXPress, you'll be disappointed. When working with paper, you know exactly what your target media is, that is, 8 1/2 by 11-inch paper, a tri-fold brochure, and so on. On the Web, you won't know whether your site is being viewed on a 21-inch desktop monitor set to a resolution of 1600×1200 pixels with Internet Explorer opened to full screen, or on a Web-enabled PDA with a gray-scale viewscreen just 400×300 pixels in size.

No matter how you design your Web pages, they're going to look different in those two environmental extremes, just as they'll look slightly different in more traditional settings. Keeping that in mind, the HTML skills you'll learn in this book give you the freedom to create lushly illustrated and aesthetically pleasing designs. Let your imagination take over!

What's Next?

There are certain advantages to the Web, such as multimedia, interactivity, timeliness, and a certain air of "tech awareness" that make creating HTML pages something of a necessity for businesses and a good idea for families, too. There are disadvantages as well, including the cost in time and money, the learning curve for Web design, and the constant need to update.

HTML has been evolving over the years in part due to the input of millions of people, larger businesses, and commercial artists. The current state of HTML is the HTML 4.0 Recommendation. An updated version HTML 4.01 is about to be passed on to Recommendation (specification) status.

HTML and it's related Web specifications provide the Web designer with nearly unlimited freedom of expression. The one key caveat to remember is that you'll never know in just what type of visual environment your site is being viewed. It could be a large desktop monitor, a small PDA, or any of a host of other devices. Each system will display your work in a slightly different manner based on the size of the screen, the browser, and the capabilities of the device.

Next up in Chapter 5 you'll learn what you need to be ready to create a Web site. We'll cover finding a Web server, selecting an ISP, and Web site organization techniques.

Review Questions

1. Is it possible for a Web site to actually save businesses money? What business services are often enhanced by Web sites?

2. Why is the Web's multimedia capability an advantage in using the Web for your business?

3. Explain why the Web's flexibility was an advantage for our fictional travel agent in the Travel Agent Web Site example.

4. What's one of the worst things that can happen to a Web site?

5. What is a Web application?

6. The Web was originally conceived as a research tool. What has it been touted as recently?

Review Exercises

1. Using two different browsers, perhaps Netscape and Internet Explorer, load the home pages of both companies (http://www.netscape.com and http://www.microsoft.com). Do you see any small differences in how the pages display? Those are the quirks between them that were mentioned.

2. With your browser, access several large corporate sites, such as http://www.ibm.com/, http://www.nabisco.com, or http://www.twa.com. Notice the types of information they offer and how the information is presented.

3. If your ISP offers a page of local business links (or if you can find some via a Web search engine), take a look at them and consider how (and if) you would improve them. What do they do better or worse than the large corporate sites?

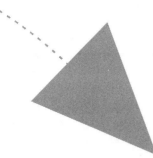

What You Need for a Web Site

Although creating HTML pages is easily the most time-consuming part of building your Web site, another equally important part is figuring out how you will get those pages on the Web. You'll need Web server software, an Internet connection, a Web URL for your pages, and a system for organizing your pages and graphics. Depending on how you gain access and how complicated your site is, just getting your first page up on the Web can take a certain amount of planning.

This chapter teaches you

- How to choose Web server software
- What kind of Internet connections are available
- When to look for Web hosting services
- Web Site organization techniques

Finding a Web Server

Before you can display your HTML pages on the Web, you'll need access to a Web server. This may already be taken care of for you, especially if you work with an Information Systems (IS) department in a larger corporation. If this is the case, you'll just need to know how and where to send your HTML files when you want to update the site. Otherwise, you'll need to make some arrangements on your own.

It isn't terribly difficult to set up your own Web server—especially if you already have a high-speed connection to the Internet. If you access the Internet through an Internet Service Provider (ISP), you'll want to discuss this with them. More than likely, they will be willing to provide you with space on their Web server computers. If your Web site is a fairly small venture, or if you're not ready for a heavy investment in equipment, using your ISP's Web server is a great (and very common) alternative.

What Is a Web Server?

In its essence, it's the job of a Web server to accept connections from Web browsers all over the Internet and, when requested, send them the HTML documents that are available from your site. This is done using the HTTP protocol, discussed in Chapter 2, "The World Wide Web and Web Servers."

A Web server is simply a computer with an Internet connection that runs software designed to send out HTML pages and other file formats (such as multimedia files). The server computer should have a relatively high-speed connection to the Internet (faster than any available modem connections, for instance) and should be powerful enough to deal with a number of simultaneous connections from the Internet.

Web server software generally requires a fairly robust operating system (like UNIX, Windows NT, Linux, or Solaris), although software is available for other platforms. Which software you use depends on your level of experience with Internet connections and various operating systems.

Speed of the Server Connection

The other major consideration is how popular your Web site will be. The more hits, or connections, your Web server receives at one time, the more powerful the computer should be, and the faster your connection to the Internet. What do we mean by a fast connection?

Most Internet connections are measured in terms of bits per second (bps), which translates loosely as "how many bits of data can be transmitted across the Internet in a second." In computerese, it takes eight bits to make up one byte of computer information—and a byte is what is required to create one character of text.

The typical modem connection today is up to 56,700 bps, which translates to roughly 7,372 characters (bytes) transferred every second. Therefore, if a typical page of text contains 1,200 words, and each word has an average of six characters, this connection would yield roughly a one-page-per-second transmission rate. This is achieved through hardware compression. Each page of text is compressed by the modem to make it smaller, and then it is transmitted. The receiving modem decompresses the text to its original state.

Files that have been precompressed, such as GIF and ZIP files, do not travel so quickly, because the modem can't make them any smaller. With compressed files, transmission slows to roughly 4,812 bytes per second. A 100 KB ZIP file would take approximately 24 seconds to download.

In the United States, FCC regulations do not permit 56 Kbps modems to actually run at the full 56 Kbps speed. With perfectly clean (no static) phone lines, typical connection speeds are between 42 and 48 Kbps. If your telephone line experiences a lot of "noise," that speed could be further reduced to 34 to 40 Kbps.

An often-overlooked fact regarding 56 Kbps modems is that the faster transfer rates are only for data being sent *to* your computer by your Internet Service Provider. Any data sent *from* your computer out onto the Internet (such as email, or a file uploaded to your Web server) is done at a 33.6 Kbps connection rate. This is because the available "communications channels" on your phone line are divided unevenly in order to achieve the faster download speed. Roughly two-thirds of your phone connection is devoted to downloading data from the Internet. Only one-third is for sending data back out onto the Internet.

Types of Internet Connections

So your server will need a faster connection. But how do you get one? If Internet access is available to you through your company's Local Area Network (LAN), you probably already have a high-speed connection. Ask around your IT department. If you're running a small business or home office, you won't have to worry about high speed if you make your Web pages available on your ISP's Web server.

If you're going to use your own Web server computer, however, you'll need a high-speed Internet connection that you can connect to that computer. Table 5.1 details some of the possible connections.

Table 5.1: Internet Connection Speeds and Technologies

Connection Speed	Connection Technology
28.8/56.7 Kbps	High-speed modem
56 Kbps	56 Kbps leased line
64 Kbps	Single-B-Channel ISDN
128 Kbps	Basic-rate ISDN
Up to 1.5 Mbps	Primary-rate ISDN (U.S.)
1.5 Mbps	T-1 dedicated line
Up to 9 Mbps	DSL line (downstream; up to 640 Kbps upstream)
45 Mbps	T-3 dedicated line

The minimum for an acceptable Web server connection is probably a basic-rate ISDN (Integrated Services Digital Network) connection, which offers 128,000 bps connections to the Internet. ISDN technology uses your existing phone wiring to provide an enhanced digital telephone connection. Using a special network adapter card for your computer, you can use the ISDN line to dial an appropriately equipped ISP. You can also use the ISDN connection for regular telephone calls.

NOTE

ISDN is a service of your local telephone company, so you should contact them for more information. Also be aware that emerging technologies such as cable modems (offered by your cable TV company) may be another high-speed alternative.

The basic-rate ISDN connection is still somewhat slow, depending on your Web site's traffic (that is, the number of visitors to your site). But it's also the most reasonably priced, generally falling between $50 and $150 a month for the ISDN line (from your local phone company), with $50 to $300 for the ISDN account (from your ISP) and $300 to $1,000 to purchase the ISDN equipment.

TIP

Relatively low-cost ISDN "modems" in the $100 to $300 range are becoming more common for both PCs and Macs.

A T-1 line is the typical minimum connection for an ISP or a large business. These lines generally cost thousands of dollars per month for Internet access, as do primary-rate ISDN connections. T-3 lines currently serve as the backbone of the Internet and are generally found only at connecting university, government, and supercomputing organizations.

Dealing with an ISP

For any sort of connection to the Internet, you'll probably need to deal with an Internet Service Provider. These companies offer dial-up and special high-speed connections to the Internet, as well as generally offering Web and other types of Internet servers for your use.

> **NOTE**
>
> Looking for a provider for your Web page? With your Web browser, you can access some lists of ISPs around the country (and world) at http://thelist.internet.com or http://www.yahoo.com/Business_and_Economy/Companies/Internet_Services/Web_Presence_Providers/. The latter includes a listing of free Web page providers. You might also check with your current ISP for Web deals. Many popular online services offer free or cheap Web space.

For a typical smaller Web site, you'll want to buy space on your ISP's Web site. Generally this will give you a URL that begins with the name of the ISP's host computer but points to a special directory for your HTML pages, such as http://www.*isp*.com/*username*/index.html.

With many Web server programs, the default page that is first loaded is named index.html, so that's the name you'll use for the first page you'd like presented to users when they access your Web site.

Determining Costs

If you're looking for an ISP for your Web site (as opposed to using your company's computers or your current ISP), it's important to consider two factors. Most ISPs will charge you based on how much disk space your Web site consumes, but some also charge based on how much throughput is registered for your pages.

Throughput can be thought of as the average amount of information transferred from your site to a user multiplied by the number of users who access your Web site:

average amount of information × number of users = throughput

For instance, if each user who accesses your site transfers an average of 50 KB, and 1,000 users access your site in a month, your throughput for that month would be 5 MB of data. If your ISP charges $1 per megabyte of throughput, you'll be charged $5 (not including the disk space charges and any monthly fees that the ISP may charge).

So why charge for throughput? If hundreds of people access your site at any given time, this means that many fewer people can access other services provided by the ISP, so they charge you more. Consider a scenario in which people download a 250 KB shareware program from your Web site, and over 10,000 people access your Web site in a month. This translates to approximately 2.5 gigabytes of data transferred, for which you might be charged $2,500 (at $1 per megabyte).

TIP

Look for Web sites that offer monthly maximums and special deals to avoid surprise bills for hundreds or thousands of dollars.

A sum of $2,500 is a little high for that sort of traffic, but it does bring up a good point: Many ISPs will limit your site to a certain amount of data transferred or a certain number of visitors per month (for a particular price plan). To get past these limitations, you may have to opt for the next-higher plan available from the ISP or accept additional charges for extra throughput.

Whichever pricing plan your ISP has, do check with them about any maximum usage caps. If your site gets "discovered" and has multi-megabytes of daily throughput, some providers may not be willing to continue carrying your site for the previously stated costs.

What You Need to Know

Once you've decided on an ISP that you feel is reasonably priced, you're ready to create your HTML pages and upload them to the server. To do all this correctly, you'll probably need to ask a few questions:

- **What is my site's default URL?**   This should be something like the ISP's host address along with a directory for your username. For instance, if my username is anavarro and my ISP's Web server is www.webco.net, the default URL for my site might be http://www.webco.net/anavarro/. Different ISPs will organize this in different ways, so you'll need to make sure you get this right.

NOTE

Many ISPs will give you the option, sometimes at an increased price, of creating your own domain name for your site. Then users could access your site at http://www.yourname.com/.

- **How do I upload files to my site's directory?**   You should get instructions for accessing your Web site's directory on the Web server computer using either FTP or a UNIX shell account. We'll discuss this more in the section "Updating Your Web Site," later in this chapter.

- **Are there any limitations to the names I can give my files?** The operating system in use by the Web server may not be instantly obvious to you. If this is the case, you'll want to ask if there is a certain filename length or a certain file-naming formats and conventions (such as case sensitivity) that you need to follow.

- **Can I create subdirectories within my main Web site directory?** Most Web servers will give you this capability, but some will not allow you to create new subdirectories.

- **What support is offered for CGI programming?** Some servers won't allow you to add CGI scripts to your Web site for processing forms or adding other interactive features. Others will, but they require you to pay extra, pay to have the provider write those scripts (regardless of your ability), or only use pre-written generic scripts that they make available to clients. Some ISPs take this stance due to the possibility of poorly written scripts causing extra loads on the server's processors, and unnecessarily tying up computing cycles. In a worst-case scenario, a broken script can take a system down. therefore, if you plan a highly interactive site, you should ask about CGI support and their policies for its use.

Organizing a Web Site

The most important thing to remember when organizing a Web site is how the server computer you're using will differ from the computer you use to create Web pages. This is because you'll need to know the exact path to the HTML pages and multimedia files you use in creating your Web page. As we've seen before, a URL requires both a server name and a path statement to the file. This includes files that you've placed on your own Web server—so while you're creating your Web pages, you'll need to know where your files will eventually be.

Although there are a number of different ways to arrange a Web site, there are some rules of thumb to keep in mind. For the most part, any organization you create for your Web site files should be designed to make updating your pages easy in the future. If you have to move all your files around every time you change something on a Web page, you'll also be forced to change all the hypertext links on many other pages—and that can be incredibly time-consuming.

Let's look at a couple of different types of organization for Web sites:

- **Single-directory sites** Smaller sites (those with just a few HTML pages and graphics) can often get by with a single directory on the Web server. All your graphics and HTML pages are in this one directory. One of the biggest advantages of this system is that links to local files and graphics require no special path statements.

- **Directory by function**   One way to organize more complicated sites is to put each section of related Web pages in the same directory. For instance, in your main directory you might offer only your first (index) page and its associated graphics. For a business site, you'd have subdirectories for About the Business, Product Information, Technical Support, and so on. In each of these subdirectories, you'd include all the related HTML files and the graphics for those pages.

- **Directory by file type**   Some people prefer to create subdirectories according to the type of file as opposed to the content of the page. Your main directory may have only the index page of your site. Other subdirectories might be Graphics, Web Pages, Downloadable Files, and so on. The main advantage in organizing this way is that files generally have to be replaced only once. If you use a graphic on a number of different pages, for instance, you replace it once in the Graphics subdirectory, and all the HTML pages that access this graphic will use the new one.

- **Hybrid**   The best way to organize a large site might be a hybrid of the last two methods just discussed. Creating separate subdirectories for nonrecurring items (such as individual Web pages in each category) while creating other subdirectories for items used multiple times (such as graphics) lets you get to all the files in an efficient way.

Naming Your Files

We've already mentioned that file extensions are an important part of all the filenames you use for your Web site. Because other Web browsers may rely on the file extension to know what sort of document or file it is, you'll need to include the appropriate extensions with all your Web site files.

Your Web site will almost always begin with a file called index.html. Most Web server software programs will automatically load this page if the URL of your site is accessed without a specific path and file reference. For example, entering `http://www.hwg.org/` in your browser actually results in the URL `http://www.hwg.org/index.html` being loaded into your browser. Your Web site's first page (whether it's a "front door" page or the first page of your site) should be designed with this in mind.

The other consideration for naming your files is the organization you plan to use for your site. If you're using a single-directory organization, your filenames should be as unique as possible, and graphics and other files should probably have names that relate to associated Web pages. For instance:

```
about-company.html
about-header.jpg
about-ceo-photo.jpg
```

When possible, these names will help you determine which files are associated with which HTML pages when you go to update those files.

For graphics and other files that show up on multiple pages, you might want to come up with a memorable prefix, like gen or site, so that you can easily replace these universal files when necessary.

TIP

Not everyone finds the naming system just described very intuitive. The idea is to find something meaningful for both you and anyone else who may need to update or take over maintenance of your site.

EXAMPLE

Organizing a Site

To create a reasonably sized site for my home-business Web site, I'm going to use the hybrid style of organization. My site has three different sections: About My Business, Services, and Samples. Each of these sections will have its own directory structure. Graphics will be in their own subdirectory, as will downloadable files that I'm including (see Figure 5.1).

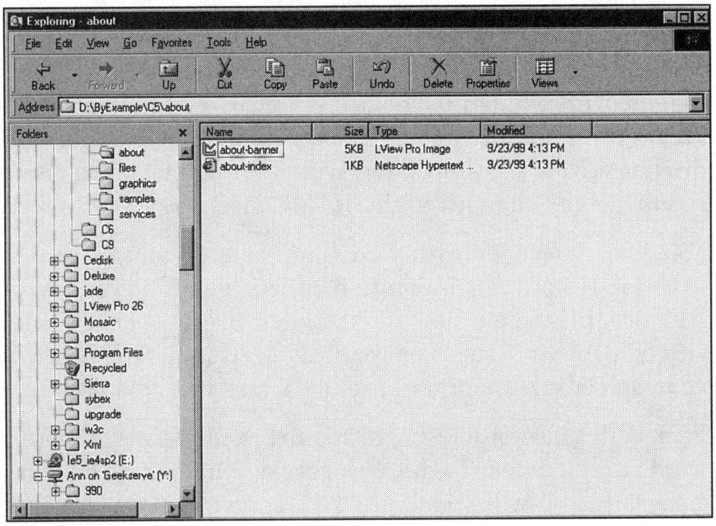

Figure 5.1: *The directory organization for my site.*

The directory names, then, will be as follows:

about

services

samples

graphics

files

Files and graphics are named for where they appear, unless they show up in multiple Web pages. For this site, the prefixes I'm using are as follows:

about_

serv_

samp_

gen_

index_

By naming files in this way, I'll be able to replace any graphics or update my sample files easily—without being forced to load each file or graphic to figure out what it is. Making the names as descriptive as possible (aside from the prefix) will help too, as in the following:

about-photo-me.jpg

samp-resume1.doc

sampl-catalog-copy.txt

Updating Your Web Site

If you organize your site well, updating the site is simply a matter of replacing an outdated file with a new file using the same filename. For instance, if I wanted to replace the picture of me in the previous example, I'd simply name the new file, about-photo-me.jpg, and save it in the same directory. Now the associated Web page will load the new graphic without requiring any changes to the HTML markup.

You'll need to check with your company's IT contact or your ISP to figure out exactly how you'll update files. With an ISP, you can generally use an FTP program to put new files in your directory organization on the Web site. You might instead be required to use a UNIX-based shell account for your uploading. In either case, it's a fairly simple process.

Your Web space provider will require you to enter a username and password to gain access to the Web server, whether by FTP or shell account. Generally, you will point your FTP server to the Web server itself (for instance, www.isp.com), unless the provider has created a mirror site to avoid direct access to the Web server.

NOTE

A *mirror site* is generally an exact replica of a Web server's hard disk, but it is kept separate for security reasons. For instance, you might not be able to directly access your company's Web site files—but you can change a mirror of that Web server, and your changes will be handled by knowledgeable Internet specialists. Many companies prefer to isolate their Web servers from their corporate network so that important data is impossible to access from outside the company.

The term *mirror* is more generally used to represent any more-or-less exact copies of an Internet server. The FTP site `mirrors.aol.com`, for instance, offers copies of nearly every shareware file available on other popular FTP servers around the world. This gives more users access to the same files at the same time.

After clearing the security procedure, you'll most likely be in your personal Web site's main directory. (If not, you'll need to use the `cd` command in UNIX or otherwise change directories in your FTP program.) From that point, you can update files using the `Put` command. Simply upload the updated files with the same names as the outdated files—in nearly every case, the old files will simply be overwritten. If you're using new files, upload them using the names and paths that your Web page links use to refer to them.

TIP

It's a good idea to maintain a folder or directory on your own hard drive that is as identical as possible to the Web site you make available on a server so that you can test your organization and filenames.

What's Next?

Before you can start showing the world your HTML pages, you need to find a Web server where you can store them. This server can be a corporate server, an Internet Service Provider, or a computer you maintain yourself. In any case, it needs to run Web server software and have a high-speed Internet connection.

Once you've established where you'll put your HTML files, you need to decide how you'll organize them. There are four basic ways to do this: in one directory, in directories organized by function, in directories organized by file type, or a hybrid of the latter two. For larger sites, a hybrid is most effective.

An important part of your Web site organization is the way you name files. The best way to do this is to be as descriptive as possible, while using name prefixes that best describe which Web pages are used to access these files. This will also help immensely when it's time to troubleshoot your Web site or update some of the files.

Next up in Chapter 6, you'll create your first Web page using HTML. We'll start by reviewing several pieces of HTML markup that are required to be in every HTML document, then add some text to complete the page.

Review Questions

1. True or false: You'll need an extra, very powerful computer if you expect to have a Web site on the Internet.

2. Aside from the computer itself, what two basic things does a Web server require to operate?

3. If bps stands for bits per second, what does Kbps stand for? How is this different from Mbps?

4. How can you find out if ISDN phone service is available in your area?

5. What is throughput? Why do some Internet service providers charge based on throughput?

6. If your Web server runs the MS-DOS operating system, what are your filename limitations?

7. Explain the hybrid style of Web site organization.

8. The file, about-ceo-photo.jpg, is most likely what sort of file? What might the HTML page that it is linked to be about?

9. What is the FTP command for uploading files over the Internet? Does "uploading" mean you're currently sending the file or receiving the file?

Review Exercises

1. After you have a Web site available to you, test it by creating a text file called text.txt. (Just use NotePad, SimpleText, VI, or a similar text editor and type something in this file.) Then, upload the file to your Web server. After it's there, use your Web browser to access it, using the appropriate URL. An example might be `http://www.webgeek.com/anavarro/text.txt`. After you get it to appear in your browser, you'll know you're on the right track!

2. Create a special hierarchy of directories on your own hard drive that mirror the type of organization you're going to use for the Web site. When possible, your lowest-level directory should be named the same as your directory on the Web server.

3. Access your ISP's other Web pages and, from the URLs, attempt to determine what OS the ISP is using for its Web server. (Is it UNIX? Linux? Windows NT? It may be difficult, but not impossible, to tell.) Once you've guessed, contact your ISP to figure out if you're right. Don't forget that you'll need to use that OS's naming conventions when you create your site.

Part II

Creating Basic Pages with HTML 4

Creating a Web Page and Entering Text

Changing and Customizing HTML Text

Displaying Text in Lists

Adding Graphics to Your Web Pages

Hypertext and Creating Links

Using Links with Other HTML Tags

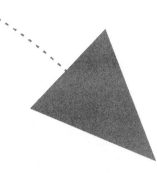

6

Creating a Web Page and Entering Text

With the basics behind you, it's time to start creating your first HTML pages. As has already been mentioned, the basic building block of an HTML page is text. To create these pages, all you really need is a text editor and a Web browser for testing your creation (you'll eventually need a graphics program to create and edit your graphics, too). So let's look at the basic tools for Web publishing and then create your own HTML template.

This chapter teaches you

- What type of program to use when creating Web pages
- Which HTML "tags" are required in every HTML document
- How to enter text in a Web page
- How to preview your work in a Web browser

The Tools for Web Publishing

I've already mentioned that all you need is a text editor. In Windows, that's Notepad. For Mac users, SimpleText is the perfect HTML editor. UNIX users can opt for vi or Emacs. Basically, all you need to remember is that even though HTML pages have .htm or .html file extensions, they are simply ASCII text files. Any program that generates ASCII text files will work fine as an HTML editor.

You'll also need a Web browser to check the appearance of your Web page as you create it. All Web browsers should have the ability to load local pages from your hard drive, just as they can load HTML pages across the Web (see Figure 6.1).

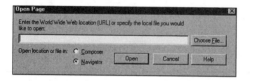

Figure 6.1: *In Netscape Navigator 4.51 for Windows 98, the File, Open Page command opens the Open Page dialog box. It contains the Choose File button that allows you to search for the file on your hard drive.*

You may have heard of some dedicated HTML editing programs that are designed to make your work in HTML easier. They do indeed exist, and they can be very useful. Unfortunately, many of them also hide the HTML codes from the designer, so they would be difficult for you to use as you learn how HTML works. However, once you understand HTML, it can be a great benefit to use one of these editors.

Required Tags

The first HTML tags you will look at are the tags that are required for every HTML page you create. They define the different parts of the document, as well as information about the document itself.

To begin each HTML page, you must have what's known as a *document type definition* (often shortened to *doctype*). This is a tag that declares that you're writing your page in HTML and says what version you're working with. This will be important later when you go to validate your pages. Validation is kind of like a spell checker and grammar checker for HTML files. It can help you catch errors that might otherwise make your pages look funny.

Throughout most of this book, we'll be using what's known as the HTML 4.0 Transitional doctype. The meaning of this tag, and other possible doctype versions, are discussed later, in Chapter 19. For now, what you need to know is that it looks like this:

```
<!DOCTYPE HTML PUBLIC "-//W3C//DTD HTML 4.0 Transitional//EN">
```

The doctype tag is one of the few exceptions to the "case isn't sensitive" rule. The doctype must be written exactly as it's shown here—spacing, capitalization, punctuation, and all.

The Document <HEAD>

Just like a magazine article, an HTML document has two distinct parts: a head and a body. The head of the HTML document is where you enter the title of the page. It's also used for some more-advanced commands that you'll study later in Chapters 10, and 19 through 21.

Both the head and the body are bound within another piece of markup, the <HTML> tag. So to begin your first document and create the head portion, type the following into your text editor:

```
<!DOCTYPE HTML PUBLIC "-//W3C//DTD HTML 4.0 Transitional//EN">

<HTML>
<HEAD>

<TITLE>My First Page</TITLE>

</HEAD>
```

This tells a Web browser what information should be considered to be in the head portion of the document, and what it should call the document in the title bar of the browser window.

If you've got a head, you need a body. The body is where you'll do most of your work—you'll enter text, headlines, graphics, and all your other Web goodies. To add the body section, start after the </HEAD> tag and enter the following:

```
<BODY>

</BODY>
```

Between these two tags, you'll eventually enter the rest of the text and graphics for your Web page.

Now, at least as far as your Web browser is concerned, you have a complete Web document!

EXAMPLE

Creating an HTML Template

Let's take what you know and create a template. By saving this template as a generic text file, you'll have a quick way to create new HTML files without retyping tags that are common across all files each time. Simply load the template and use the File, Save As command to save it as your new Web page.

Start by entering the following in a blank text file:

```
<!DOCTYPE HTML PUBLIC "-//W3C//DTD HTML 4.0 Transitional//EN">
<HTML>
<HEAD>
<TITLE>Enter Title Here</TITLE>
</HEAD>
<BODY>
</BODY>
</HTML>
```

And that's it. Now save this as an ASCII text file called template.html. Now, whenever you're ready to create a new HTML document, simply load template.html into your text editor and use the Save As command to rename it.

EXAMPLE

Hello World

When you're learning a new programming language, it's traditional that the first program you create be designed to say "Hello World." Well, HTML isn't a programming language, but I can use the Hello World example to prove that your template is a complete Web document.

Load the template.html file into your text editor, and use the Save As command to rename it hello.html or something similar. Now, edit the document so that it looks like this:

```
<!DOCTYPE HTML PUBLIC "-//W3C//DTD HTML 4.0 Transitional//EN">
<HTML>
<HEAD>
<TITLE>Hello World Page</TITLE>
</HEAD>
<BODY>
Hello World!
</BODY>
</HTML>
```

Select the File, Save command from your text editor. Now start your Web browser and select the Open (or similar) command from the File menu. In the dialog box, find the document hello.html and click OK to load it into your Web browser. If everything goes as planned, your browser should display something similar to Figure 6.2.

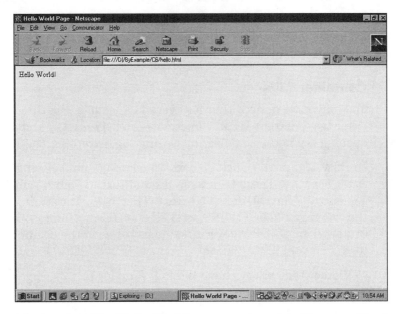

Figure 6.2: *The Hello World page as viewed in Netscape Navigator.*

And that's a Web page!

Understanding Tags: Container and Empty Tags

In creating your HTML template, you've already dealt with some of the most basic tags in HTML. The first thing you should notice about these HTML tags is that all tags include < and > on either side of the tag's command. This is how HTML recognizes tags. If you don't use the brackets, a Web browser will assume your commands are text that you want displayed—even if that text is the same as an HTML command.

While a Web browser would consider the following to be a tag:

`<HTML>`

that same Web browser would interpret the following as text to be displayed onscreen:

`HTML`

TIP

Tags are not case sensitive, so they don't have to be all-uppercase—even though that's how they appear in this book. Some people feel that uppercase makes the tags really stand out when you're reviewing the source of your pages later. Others prefer the look of lowercase. In HTML, with very few exceptions, the choice is yours.

Because tags aren't considered text by the document, they also don't show up in the document. If the browser interprets something as a tag, it won't appear in the browser window.

Container Tags

You may have noticed that for every tag, such as the title tag, you actually enter two different HTML functions—an *opening* tag and a *closing* tag. The opening tag is the same as the closing tag, except for the / after the <.

In HTML, tags that include both an opening and a closing tag are called *container* tags. These tags wrap around text in your document and perform some sort of formatting on the text. They hold, or contain, the text between the two tags. The <TITLE>, <HTML>, <HEAD>, and <BODY> tags are all container tags—the relevant text goes between the opening and closing tags.

Container tags always have the following form:

```
<TAG>text and markup being formatted or defined</TAG>
```

In fact, you were introduced to a fairly common container tag in the first chapter of this book—the <EM> (emphasis) tag. Here's an example of the emphasis tag:

```
Here's some <EM>really important</EM> text.
```

Because <EM> is an implicit formatting tag, it's up to the browser to decide what to do to the text between the opening and closing tags. But only the words "really important" will be affected in this example, since they're the only text that is being "contained" by the tags.

By *implicit*, I mean that the rules for HTML don't tell the browser programmers exactly what the emphasized text should look like. That is, HTML doesn't say, "Make this text two sizes bigger than the rest of the text, and change its color," though that would be a perfectly technically acceptable choice. So the programming team who created each browser must decide how it will visually emphasize the text contained in the tag. The earliest Web browsers that offered support for the <EM> tag chose to use an italicized font for the visual emphasis. This treatment caught on, and became the traditional rendering of <EM>. Though most browsers today do this, it's important to remember that HTML doesn't require them to, so it shouldn't be relied upon to always produce italics. We'll talk more about implicit tags in Chapter 7.

Empty Tags

All other tags in HTML fall into one other category—*empty* tags. These tags have only an opening tag—there is no closing tag. The reason for this is that empty tags don't act on blocks of text. Instead, they do something all on their own. An example of this would be the <HR> (horizontal rule) tag. This tag draws a line across the width of your document. For example:

```
The following is a horizontal line:

<HR>

The rest of this is just more text.
```

When viewed in a Web browser, the two sentences will be separated by a horizontal line, as shown in Figure 6.3.

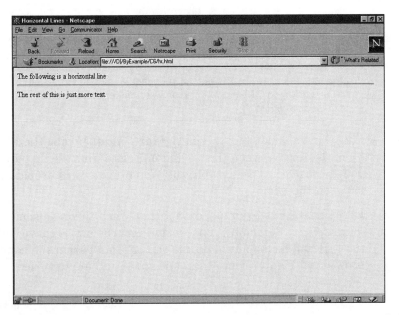

Figure 6.3: *Empty tags like* <HR> *for horizontal lines perform functions on their own.*

Entering Paragraph Text on Your Web Page

With your template prepared, and with an understanding of the two types of tags in HTML, you're ready to enter text on a Web page. As mentioned earlier, all the text that you enter on a page should come between the <BODY> and </BODY> tags. Like <EM>, the body tags are container tags that tell a Web browser what parts of the HTML document should be displayed in the browser window.

While you could just type text into an HTML document and it will be displayed in the browser, it should be in another container tag, such as the <P> (paragraph) tag. This tag is used to show a Web browser what text in your document constitutes a paragraph.

The paragraph tag uses the following format:

```
<P>Here is the text for my paragraph. It doesn't matter how long it is, how many
spaces are between the words, or when I decide to press the Enter key. It will
create a new paragraph only when I end the tag and begin with another one.
</P>
<P> Here's the next paragraph. </P>
```

NOTE

Although it is technically a container tag, the closing </P> tag is considered optional by HTML 4.0. This tends to cause a little confusion. Many people end up using <P> as an empty tag, assuming that it's designed to insert a line break at the end of paragraphs (or even to create multiple blank lines). That's not its purpose. Using <P> as a container, as I've shown previously, gets the most reliable results in all different types of browsers. In well-written HTML, the container is used to isolate all the text you want to call a "paragraph." Then it lets the browser render that in the way its programmers feel is most appropriate.

Like the emphasis tag, the paragraph container tells the Web browser that all of the text between the on and off tags is in a single paragraph. When you start another paragraph, the Web browser will drop down a line between the two.

Here's that same example, except that you'll throw in some returns and extra spaces. Remember, spaces and returns almost never affect the way the text will be displayed on the screen. In a paragraph container, the browser will ignore more than one space and any returns.

```
<P>Here is the text for my    paragraph.
It doesn't matter how long it is, how many spaces    are      between the words,
or when I decide to press the Enter key. It will create a new paragraph
only when I end the tag and begin with another one. </P>
<P> Here's the next paragraph. </P>
```

Both this example and the previous example will be displayed in the Web browser in exactly the same way.

The
 Tag for Line Breaks

But what if you want to decide where a line will end? Consider the example of entering an address in a Web document:

```
<P>

Richard Smith

14234 Main Street

Anycity, NY 00001

</P>
```

It looks about right when you type it into your text editor. However, when it is displayed in a Web browser, it looks like Figure 6.4.

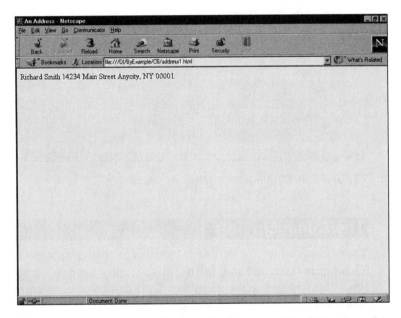

Figure 6.4: *The Post Office might have trouble delivering this.*

We already know what the problem is: Web browsers ignore extra spaces and returns! But if you put each of those lines in a paragraph container, you'd end up with a space between each line, and that would look wrong, too.

The answer is the empty tag <BR>, which forces a line return in your Web document. Properly formatted, your address would look like this:

```
<P>

Richard Smith<BR>

14234 Main Street<BR>
```

```
Anycity, NY 00001<BR>
</P>
```

And it would look just right in your Web browser, as shown in Figure 6.5.

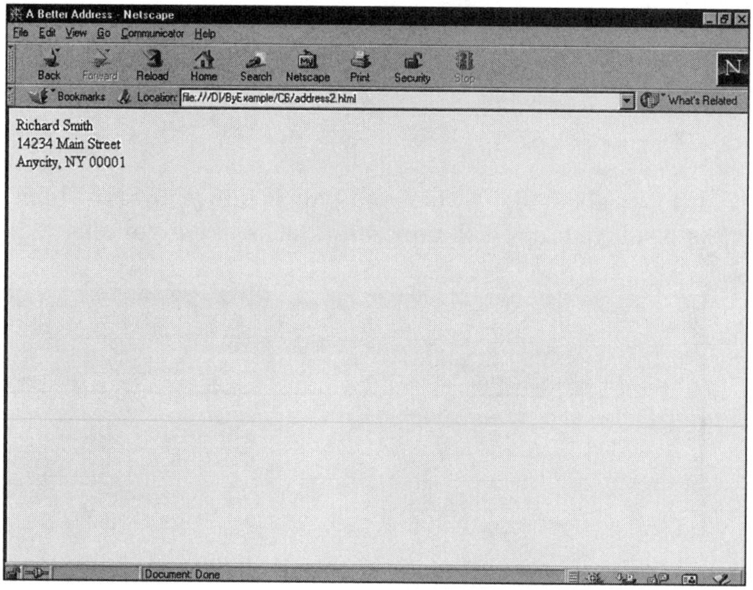

Figure 6.5: *This address looks much better.*

The Comment Tag

There's one other tag I'd like to discuss in this chapter—the comment tag. This tag is fairly unique, in that it's actually used to make the Web browser ignore anything the tag contains. That can be text, hypertext links, image links—even small scripts and programs.

For now, you'll use the comment tag to hide text. The point in hiding text is that it allows you to create a private message that is intended to remind you of something or to help those who view the raw HTML document understand what you're doing. That's why it's called the comment tag. For instance:

```
<!-- This is a comment that won't display in a browser -->
```

The comment tag isn't the most elegant in HTML, but it usually works. Anything you type between `<!--` and `-->` should be ignored by the browser. Even multiple lines are ignored: As with most tags, the comment tag ignores returns.

NOTE

Notice that the comment example shown here has exactly two hyphens and a space after the <! and before any text. This syntax is required to produce a valid comment tag. The same situation goes for the closing comment: A space and two hyphens occur before the >.

Generally, you'll use the comment tag for your own benefit. Perhaps you'll want to mark a point in a particular HTML document where you need to remember to update some text, or maybe you'll want to explain a particularly confusing part of your page. Since it's fairly easy for anyone to view your raw HTML document, you might also use the comment tag to create a copyright message or give information about yourself (see the next section for more about protecting your source).

Viewing the Source of a Web Page

Have you ever been out on the Web looking at a particularly well-designed HTML document and wondered how they did it?

Most browsers will let you view the document source for any Web page they can load. This allows you to download the raw HTML codes and ASCII text, just as if you'd created the page yourself.

To do this, select the View Source command from your Web browser's View menu (this command may differ slightly, so look for a similar name if you can't find View Source). What results is the plain ASCII text file that was used to create that Web page.

Depending on your browser, this source file will either be displayed in the browser window or saved to your hard drive and displayed in the default text editor. If the source is displayed in the browser window, select File, Save As from the original browser display to save the source to your hard drive.

Just because you can view and save HTML source doesn't mean you can do whatever you want with it. Documents published to the Web are still owned by the people who produced them under the terms of copyright law. Indeed, you might find comments used to declare this, such as the following:

```
<!--Contents of this document Copyright 1999, Ann Navarro. Please do not copy
or otherwise reproduce the source HTML code of this document without
permission.-->
```

This isn't to say that you shouldn't also offer a visible copyright notice or other legal disclaimers. But comments within the code tend to talk directly to folks a little more informally. Using a comment tag like this is a great way to encourage other Web designers to ask you before using your HTML pages for their own private use. (But if they don't ask, any legal problems are your own, I'm afraid.)

NOTE

Don't let this confuse you, but the comment tag is an unusual one. It's not really a container tag, since it doesn't have two similar tags that are differentiated only by / in the second tag. At the same time, it's difficult to describe as an empty tag, since it does do something to text in the document.

EXAMPLE

Creating a Complete Web Page

Let's take everything you've learned and build a complete Web page. Start by loading the template and using Save As to create a new document for this example. (Call it test1.html or something similar.)

Now, create a document that looks something like the following. You should have to change only the title text; enter the other text between the body tags.

```
<!DOCTYPE HTML PUBLIC "-//W3C//DTD HTML 4.0 Transitional//EN">

<HTML>

<HEAD>

<TITLE>The Testing Tags Page</TITLE>

<!-- This page is Copyright 1999, Ann Navarro -->

</HEAD>

<BODY>

<P>On this page we're reviewing the different types of tags that we've learned
in this chapter. For instance, this is the first paragraph.</P>

<P>In the second paragraph, I'm going to include the name and address of one of
my favorite people. Hopefully it's formatted correctly.<BR>

Tom Smith<BR>

1010 Elm Street<BR>

Anywhere, US 10001<BR>

</P>

<HR>

<P>Now I'll start a <EM>completely new</EM> idea, since it's coming after a
horizontal line.</P>

<!-- Don't forget to update this page with the completely new idea here. -->

</BODY>

</HTML>
```

When you've finished entering the text and tags (you can use your own text if you like; just try to use all of the tags we've reviewed in the chapter), use the Save command in your text editor. Now switch to your Web browser and load your new page using the Open File (or similar) command.

If everything went well, the text should look something like Figure 6.6.

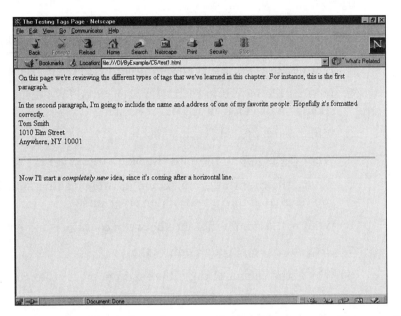

Figure 6.6: *Here's how the example should appear in Netscape Navigator. Notice that the comments do not appear.*

What's Next?

A good text editor and a Web browser program are all you need to start creating Web pages. Using these tools, you can create a template for your Web pages that includes all of the appropriate document tags. Since these are almost always the same for every HTML document, you can reuse the template without retyping.

There are two basic types of HTML tags: container tags and empty tags. The major difference between the two is that container tags feature both an on and an off component (usually the same tag, with a slash (/) before the name of the off tag). This is because container tags act on specific blocks of text, while empty tags generally perform some function on their own.

The most basic tags for entering text are the paragraph, line break, comment, and horizontal line tags. The comment tag is a special case: It's designed to keep text from being displayed by a Web browser. Entering text on a Web page is a simple matter of typing between the body tags, with an eye toward using the basic tags correctly.

Now that you've gotten the basics down, we'll move on to additional text formatting techniques in Chapter 7. You'll learn about changing the text style, making citations and quoting passages of other text, and preformatting text.

Review Questions

1. Is it necessary to use a special program to create HTML pages?

2. In what file format are HTML pages saved? What file extension should be used for an HTML document?

3. What are the four basic document tags?

4. What tag is appropriate for the head area of an HTML document?

5. What's the first thing you should do after loading an HTML template you've created into a text editor program?

6. What is the main difference between container and empty tags?

7. Give one example of an empty tag.

8. Why is the comment tag different from most other container tags?

9. True or false: All text for your Web page should be typed between the body container tags.

10. Aside from line spacing, what is the main difference between the <BR> and <P> tags?

Review Exercises

1. Create a document that uses nothing but <P> container tags to break up text. Then create a document that uses nothing but <BR> tags. What's the difference in your browser?

2. Create a new document that takes the format of a business letter. Combine <P> and <BR> tags to properly separate the different parts of the document, such as the address, greeting, content, and signature. What works best for each?

3. Add a standard "header comment" to your template using the comment tag. This is a great idea, especially if you develop HTML pages for your company. After all, documenting your efforts is what the comment tag is all about. Here's an example for a template that can be altered every time you create a new document:

```
<!---
Page Designer: Ann Navarro
Creation Date: 01 February 00
Revision Date: 15 February 00
File type: HTML 4.0 --->
```

4. Use your Web browser to view and save the main source code for the following Web document: `http://www.mcp.com`.

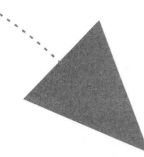

Changing and Customizing HTML Text

Now that you've gotten the hang of putting text into your HTML pages, it's time to organize them in a way that makes your documents more readable. HTML provides several neat ways of making important text stand out and creating other emphasis as needed.

This chapter teachers you

- How to manage structural headings
- The difference between implicit and explicit text emphasis
- How to emphasize your text with specific semantics

Creating Headings

One of the first things you might have wondered when you were entering text in Chapter 6 is, "How can I change the size of the text?" HTML 4 provides several ways of doing this: headings, inline container tags, font tags, and style sheets. We'll take a look at many of these techniques here in this chapter, and you'll be introduced to style sheets later, in Chapter 18.

Heading tags are containers, intended to be used as, well, headings! The text you see in the larger bold font "Creating Headings" is, indeed, a heading. If you'll think back to your English Composition classes, you may have written papers that used headings. A top-level or level one heading is often the title of a work, or, say, the headline for a newspaper. Second-level headings cover major subtopics and are generally presented in smaller or less "stand out" ways.

EXAMPLE

In HTML, headings range from level 1 to level 6, in which level 1 is the primary, or "largest." The following is an example of using headings in a document (see Figure 7.1 for the results):

```
<H1>Header Level One is the largest for headlines or page titles</H1>

<H2>Level Two is a little smaller for major subheads</H2>

<H3>Level Three is again smaller, for minor subheads</H3>

<P>This is regular text.</P>

<H4>Level Four</H4>

<H5>Level Five</H5>

<H6>Level Six</H6>
```

Although some browsers display these in descending sizes, HTML doesn't actually require them to do so. A browser programmer could choose to use different colors or fonts to differentiate between the levels. However, they'd do so with the risks associated with violating "tradition." Most people expect headings to decrease in size as they go down a level, so that's what most browsers do with them.

Another interesting thing to note is that headings always reside on their own line when displayed in most Web browsers, even if you just keep typing after you close it. The following:

```
<H1>This is a header</H1> And this is plain text.
```

offers the same results as this:

```
<H2>This is also a header</H2>

<P>And this is also plain text</P>
```

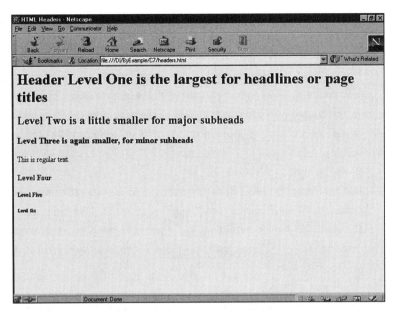

Figure 7.1: *HTML header tags at work. Notice that the fourth entry is regular text in a paragraph container.*

In both cases, the Web browser will place the heading text and plain text on different lines, with the heading text generally appearing larger and the plain text appearing "normal" in size.

NOTE

The HTML standard does state that using a particular header level requires that the larger header tag must have been used previously. (For example, <H3> couldn't be used unless <H2> had already been used.) These really shouldn't be used just for the size they render on a particular browser. If you want to change the look of a heading, you can do so with CSS.

EXAMPLE

A Topical Discussion

Now, with the addition of header tags, you're suddenly able to add a level of organization to your pages that was lacking previously. Using the horizontal line and emphasis tags you saw in Chapter 6, it's possible to create a very useful text-oriented HTML document with what you now know.

Let's start with just headers and regular text. Load your HTML template into a text editor and save it as a new HTML document (headers.html or something similar). Then fill in the template's body section using both header containers and paragraph containers, as shown in Listing 7.1.

Listing 7.1: headers.html: The Template's HTML Body Section

```
<BODY>
<H1>Welcome to my home on the Web</H1>
<P>Hi there! My name is Mark Williamson, and I'm an active participant in the
Web. Aside from my Internet journeys I'm also a big fan of the science-fiction
writer Wilhelm Norris, and I love collecting models of television spacecraft.
As far as the boring stuff goes, I work as a Macintosh programmer in Carmel,
California.</P>
<H2>My Work</H2>
<P>I've recently moved from programming in a Microsoft Windows environment to
a Macintosh environment, and I must admit that I've been more than a little
overwhelmed. Fortunately I've had good help from local user groups and my
co-workers...plus, they've introduced me to some exceptional tools for Mac
programming.</P>
<H3>ProGraph</H3>
<P>If you've never worked in a visual programming environment, you're in for a
treat. With my background in Windows and UNIX C programming, I was surprised
how quickly I picked up this object-oriented concept. I definitely recommend
it!</P>
<H3>MetroWerks</H3>
<P>I can't imagine I even need to say anything about this. It's hands-down the
best C and C++ development environment ever created for Macintosh. In my
opinion, it's the best created for any platform!</P>
<P>This document contains opinions that are my own and do not necessarily
reflect those of my employer.</P>
</BODY>
```

Entering text and using header tags in this way allows you to create a document that has more of the feel of a well-outlined magazine article, or even a chapter in a book. You may have noticed that this book uses different-sized headlines to suggest that you're digging deeper into a subject (smaller headlines) or beginning a new subject (bigger headlines). HTML allows you to do the same thing with heading tags (see Figure 7.2).

Larger headings indicate broader subjects ———

Smaller headers dig deeper ———

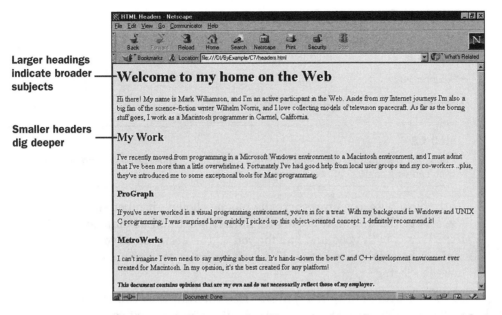

Figure 7.2: *Inserting heading containers between paragraphs makes for a more readable page.*

Implicit and Explicit Text Emphasis

Implicit tags are those that allow the browser to choose, within limitations, how the marked-up text will be displayed. Heading tags are actually an example of an implicit tag, since the HTML designer has no control over how much bigger or smaller a header tag will be. Although most browsers render heading tags in somewhat similar ways, others (for instance, non-graphical browsers) have to come up with another system for emphasis, such as underlining or highlighting the text.

Because HTML was originally created with the overriding mission of being displayed on nearly any computer system, implicit tags for emphasis were a necessity. HTML allows the designer to decide what text will be emphasized. But only explicit tags tell the Web browser how to render that text.

Explicit Styles

Explicit tags are also often called *physical tags,* since they very specifically tell the Web browser how you want the text to physically appear. The browser is given no choice in the matter.

The basic explicit tags are containers that let you mark text as bold, italic, or underlined (see Table 7.1).

Table 7.1: HTML Physical Container Tags

Tags	Meaning
<B>*content*</B>	Bold text
<I>*content*</I>	Italic text
<U>*content*</U>	Underlined text

NOTE

Underlining should be used with extreme caution. Since most browsers underline links, you can very easily confuse your readers by using it.

With these tags, the browser really has no choice—it must either display the text as defined or, if it can't do that, it must add no emphasis to the text. This is both good and bad for you as the designer. If you prefer that text not be emphasized at all if it can't be italic, for example, you should use the <I> tag.

EXAMPLE

Another feature of explicit (physical) tags is that they can generally be used in combination with other tags. As you'll see in the next section, it isn't always a good idea to use them with implicit tags. For instance, most graphic browsers will render the following example by applying both tags to the text (see Figure 7.3):

```
<H1><I>Welcome Home!</I></H1>
<B><I>This is bold and italic</I></B>
```

Implicit HTML Tags

Implicit styles are often called *logical* styles since they allow the browser some freedom in how it will display the text. These tags, like the heading tags, are generally relative to one another, depending on the browser being used to view them. Table 7.2 lists some of the common implicit (logical) tags.

Table 7.2: Some Basic Logical HTML Tags

Tags	Meaning	Generally Rendered As
<EM>*content*</EM>	Emphasis	Italic text
<STRONG>*content*</STRONG>	Strong emphasis	Bold text
<TT>*content*</TT>	Teletype	Monospaced text

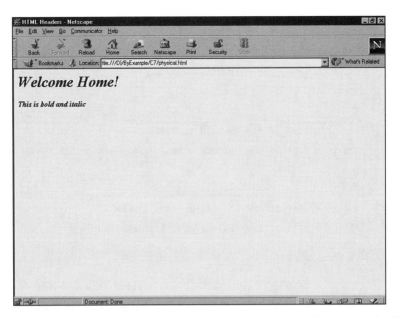

Figure 7.3: *Most browsers can render two physical tags applied to the same selection of text.*

Table 7.2 tells you how these tags are often rendered in graphical Web browsers. There's no rule for this, though, and the tags don't necessarily have to be rendered in that way.

There are two other distinctions between these tags and the physical tags (such as bold and italic) that we've already discussed. First, these logical tags will always be rendered by any Web browser that views them. Even text browsers (which are unable to show italic text) will display the <EM> or <STRONG> tags by underlining, boldfacing, or highlighting the text.

Second, these tags are generally ineffective when used together. Whereas <B><I>text</I></B> will sometimes offer useful results, <EM><STRONG>text</STRONG></EM> may not do what you've intended. Combining these tags with other tags (such as heading tags or physical tags) can be either ineffective or redundant.

EXAMPLE

Physical Tags Versus Logical Tags

Here's a great way to kill two birds with one stone. With this example you can get a feel for using both the physical and the logical tags just discussed. At the same time, you can also test these tags in your browser to see how they're displayed. (If you have more than one browser, test this example in all of them. That way you can see how different browsers interpret logical tags.)

To begin, load your template file in a text editor, and rename it something intuitive, like tagtest1.html. Then, enter the text between the body tags as it appears in Listing 7.2.

Listing 7.2: tagtest1.html: HTML Body Tags Text

```
<BODY>
<P>
This is a test of the <B>bold tag</B><BR>
This is a test of the <STRONG>strong emphasis tag</STRONG><BR>
</P>
<P>
This is a test of the <I>italics tag</I><BR>
This is a test of the <EM>emphasis tag</EM><BR>
</P>
<P>
This is a test of the <B><I>bold and italics tags together</I></B><BR>
This is a test of the <STRONG><EM>strong and emphasis tags together</EM>
</STRONG><BR>
</P>
<P>
While we're at it, does <U>underlined text</U> appear in this browser?<BR>
And what does <TT>teletype text</TT> look like?<BR>
</P>
</BODY>
```

When you've finished entering this text, save the file again in your text editor, and then choose the Load File command in your Web browser to display the HTML document. If you have other Web browsers, see how those respond to the tags, too (see Figure 7.4).

Other Implicits: Programming, Quoting, and Citing

Many of the features currently found in HTML were developed in the "wild, early days" of HTML, when unique "extensions" to HTML were commonplace as browsers competed for market share. Many of them were adopted into HTML under version 3.2, and were carried over into HTML 4. For the most part, these tags are implicit (logical) and aimed directly at certain areas of expertise. At the same time, however, the bulk of these tags will look very similar in a Web browser.

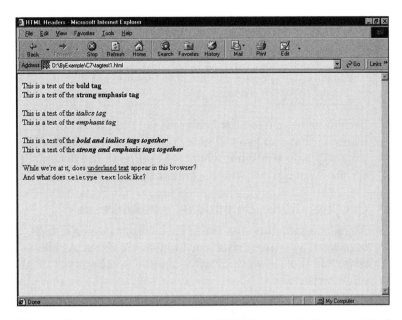

Figure 7.4: *Implicit and explicit HTML codes in Internet Explorer 5.0 for Windows NT.*

Programmer's HTML Tags

One of the early, more common uses for HTML was for documenting computer programs and offering tips or advice to computer programmers. Part of the HTML 4 standard, then, offers some implicit (logical) HTML tags that allow HTML designers to mark text in a way that makes it easier to present computer programming codes. Those tags are listed in Table 7.3.

Table 7.3: HTML Tags for Computer Programming

Tags	Meaning	Generally Rendered As
<CODE>*content*</CODE>	Programming lines	Monospaced (like <TT>)
<KBD>*content*</KBD>	Keyboard text	Monospaced
<SAMP>*content*</SAMP>	Sample output	Monospaced
<VAR>*content*</VAR>	Variable	Italic

Notice that most of these tags are often displayed in exactly the same way—in the default monospaced font for the browser. Then why use them?

First, not all browsers will necessarily follow the "general" way. Some browsers will actually render these tags in slightly different ways from one another, so that <SAMP>, for instance, might appear in a slightly larger font than <CODE>.

NOTE

These tags had more meaning with earlier browsers like Mosaic, which used to allow users to define their own presentation for specific tags. In an era in which browsers give the designer control over actual font families and sizes (see Chapter 18), these tags are used less and less.

Second, using these tags is a great way to internally document your HTML pages so that you can tell at a glance what certain text is supposed to be. This will help you later, when you return to the document to update it or fix errors—especially as the document becomes more complex.

Quoting, Citing, Definitions, and Addresses

Along the same lines as the HTML "programmer's" tags, certain implicit tags work as typographer's or publisher's codes. As shown in Table 7.4, these codes often work in ways similar to others you've already seen—with a few twists.

Table 7.4: HTML Publisher-Style Tags

Tags	Meaning	Generally Rendered As
`<CITE>`*content*`</CITE>`	Bibliographical citation	Italic text
`<BLOCKQUOTE>`*content*`</BLOCKQUOTE>`	Block of quoted text	Indented text
`<DFN>`*content*`</DFN>`	Term definition	Regular text
`<ADDRESS>`*content*`</ADDRESS>`	Street or e-mail address	Italic text

Note that the `<CITE>` tag generally won't be rendered any differently from the italic, emphasis, or variable tags you've seen previously. The `<DFN>` tag is often not rendered as any special sort of text at all, whereas the `<ADDRESS>` tag is identical in function to the italics tag.

So the best use for these tags (with the exception of the `<BLOCKQUOTE>` tag) is as internal documentation of your HTML documents. Remember, of course, that some browsers may render them slightly differently from what is suggested in Table 7.4.

EXAMPLE

Using the `<BLOCKQUOTE>` and `<ADDRESS>` Tags

The only really new tag in Table 7.4 is the `<BLOCKQUOTE>` tag. This tag usually indents the left margin of regular text in the browser window, just as you might find a blocked quotation formatted in a printed document.

Although the `<ADDRESS>` tag is similar to italics or emphasis, I've thrown in an example of using it correctly. Remember to include a line break after each line of the address.

To begin this example, create and save a new HTML document from the template you created in Chapter 6. Enter Listing 7.3 between the body tags.

Listing 7.3: emphasis.html: The <BLOCKQUOTE> and <ADDRESS> Tags

```
<BODY>
<P>I believe it was Abraham Lincoln who once said (emphasis is mine):
<BLOCKQUOTE>Four score and seven years ago our <B>forefathers</B> brought
forth on this continent a new nation, conceived in <I>liberty</I> and
dedicated to the proposition that all men are created <EM>equal</EM>.
</BLOCKQUOTE>
It was something like that, wasn't it?
</P>
<P>If you liked this quote, feel free to write me at:<BR>
<ADDRESS>
Rich Memory<BR>
4242 Sumtin Street<BR>
Big City, ST 12435<BR>
</ADDRESS>
</P>
</BODY>
```

What does all of this look like? Take a look at Figure 7.5. <BLOCKQUOTE>, unlike some of the tags you've looked at, really does offer unique abilities that make it worth using in your documents.

Preformatted Text

You might recall that earlier I said that spaces and returns between tags (like the paragraph tag) don't matter. Well, there is at least one exception to this rule: the <PRE> tag.

The <PRE> (preformatted text) tag is designed to allow you to keep the exact spacing and returns that you've put between the on and off tags. The basic reasoning behind this tag is the notion that every once in a while you'd like your text to stay exactly where you put it. You've probably noticed by now that Web browsers omit extra spaces between words, so that's one reason <PRE> is frequently used.

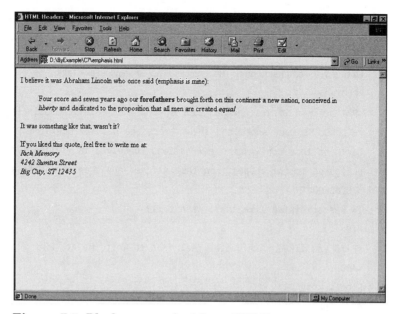

Figure 7.5: *Blockquote and address HTML tags.*

EXAMPLE

Consider the following example:

```
<P>Oh beautiful, for spacious skies,
For amber waves of grain.
For purple mountains' majesty,
Above the fruited plains.</P>
```

This is a familiar refrain, but it won't look so familiar in a browser if you leave it between paragraph tags. Instead, you can use the <PRE> tag to keep things exactly the way you want them:

```
<PRE>Oh beautiful, for spacious skies,
    For amber waves of grain.
For purple mountains' majesty,
    Above the fruited plains.</PRE>
```

In a browser, this will look exactly the way you want it to (see Figure 7.6).

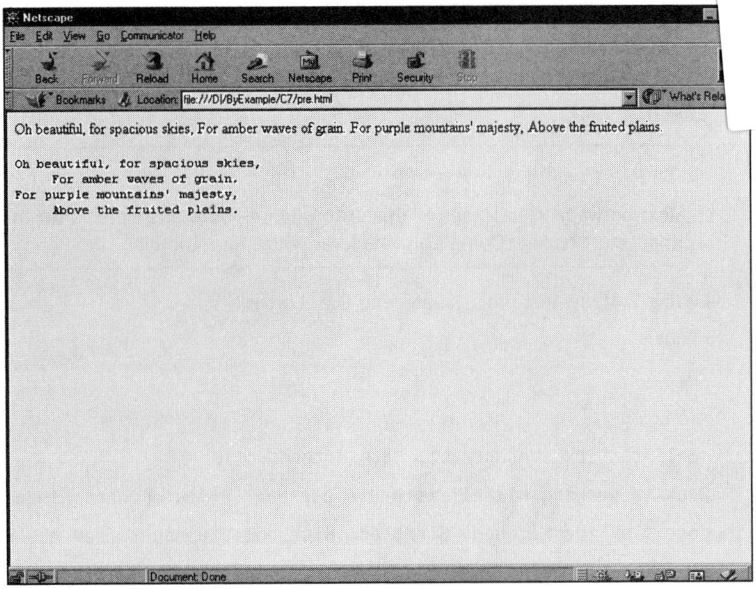

Figure 7.6: *Paragraph versus preformatted text.*

You may have noticed that preformatted text is in a monospaced font—and it will always be that way. Otherwise, the <PRE> tag works pretty much like the paragraph font, except that it lets you decide where the line breaks and spaces will appear. Look at the following example:

```
<PRE>I    simply want to make this <B>really</B> clear to you.
</PRE>
```

With this code, the browser will display this line in nearly exactly the same way as it would using the <P> tag, except that it will be in a monospaced font, and the extra spaces will appear as well.

NOTE

There is one potential drawback to the <PRE> tag. It doesn't allow the browser screen to wrap text automatically. Therefore, users must expand their browser window to view particularly long lines that you have placed within a <PRE> container. Just keep this in mind, and make sure that your lines of text are reasonably short so that all browsers can view them without scrolling.

Creating Your Own Layout with the <PRE> Tag

Let's take a look at a couple of different reasons why you might want to use the <PRE> tag in your HTML documents. Start by loading your template and choosing the Save As command in your text editor to save the file as pre_test.html or something similar.

Now between the body tags, let's create an example that uses some of the benefits of preformatting—the ability to center text and choose your own margins, for example. How? Let's format some screenplay dialogue (see Listing 7.4).

TIP

Text between <PRE> tags is easier to align if you press Enter after the opening tag and then start typing. Doing so will add an extra line, though.

Listing 7.4: pre_test.html: Create Your Own Layout

```
<BODY>
<P>
<TT>
<B>(Int) Rick's Apartment, Late Afternoon</B><BR>
Rick is busying himself with his personal computer when Linda walks through the
door from the kitchen. Startled, Rick bolts upright from his chair and swats
frantically at the keyboard trying to make something disappear. Linda moves
closer to the computer.</TT></P>
<PRE>


                    Linda
                     (confused)
          What were you doing?


                    Rick
          Just the finances.


                    Linda
          But you already printed checks
          last Sunday.


                    Rick
          I know. But Tuesday is when I, uh,
          enter my gambling debts. (Sighs deeply.)
          Honey, I'm in big trouble.
</PRE>
</BODY>
```

It takes a little tapping on the Spacebar, but with the <PRE> tag you can create some fairly elaborate layouts for getting your point across—especially when layout is just as important as the text itself. In a browser, this text comes out looking like a big-budget picture script (see Figure 7.7).

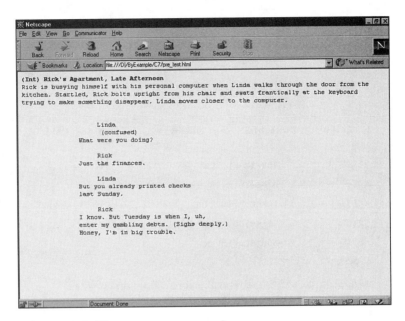

Figure 7.7: The <PRE> tag at work.

Using <PRE> for Spaces and Tables

In the same way that you created the film script using the <PRE> tag, you can also format a primitive table using the <PRE> tag along with some others.

TIP

One way to keep the columns in a table straight is to type your table first and then add emphasis tags afterward.

Load your template and save it as pre_tbl.html. Now enter Listing 7.5 between the body tags.

Listing 7.5: pre_tbl.html: Creating Spaces and Tables

```
<BODY>
<PRE>


</PRE>
<HR>
<H2>Price Per Item in Bulk Orders</H2>
<PRE>


Quantity        XJS100      RJS200      YJS50       MST3000


1-50            $40         $50         $75         $100
50-99           $35         $45         $70         $95
100-200         $30         $40         $65         $90
200+            $25         $35         $55         $75


</PRE>
<P>Prices do not include applicable sales taxes.</P>
</BODY>
```

You may need to play with the spacing a bit to line everything up. Save the HTML document and then choose the Open File command in your browser to proof it. Keep playing with it until it looks right.

TIP

If you use a more advanced text editor or word processor, fight the urge to use the Tab key to align <PRE> elements. Use the Spacebar instead. Tabs are not the same thing as multiple spaces!

Once you have everything aligned correctly, this is actually a fairly attractive and orderly little table (see Figure 7.8).

NOTE

You may be tempted to use <B> or another emphasis tag for the column heads in your table. However, you should realize that it is nearly impossible to align columns so that they will appear correctly in every browser when one row is bold and other rows are plain text. Different browsers make bold text a fraction wider than regular text, making the rows increasingly misaligned. Even if it looks good in your browser, chances are it won't look good in all of them.

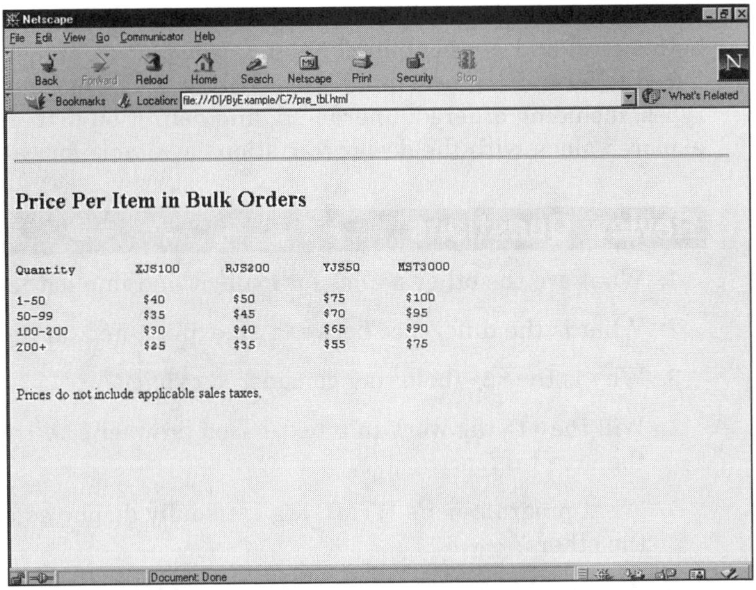

Figure 7.8: *Use the* <PRE> *tag to create a table.*

What's Next?

HTML 4 offers both explicit (physical) and implicit (logical) tags with which to mark up text. Explicit tags are designed to do something specific to the text, such as turn it bold or italic. If a browser can't do what's asked, it doesn't do anything.

Implicit tags are more general commands, such as Emphasis or Strong Emphasis. While most browsers will show these tags in a similar way, there's no specific rule. Each individual browser will display an implicit tag somehow, but not always in the same way that other browsers do it.

There are a number of implicit tags, many of which duplicate certain types of emphasis. These are good for internally documenting HTML documents, though, since the tags are generally designed for some specific task, such as displaying computer programming code or certain typographical elements.

The <PRE> tag is also a very useful tag, although it breaks some of the rules for other tags. It allows you to maintain the spaces and returns you've entered between the two tags. This lets you preformat your HTML documents so that tables and other elements are displayed correctly.

Now that you've learned how to manipulate blocks of text with emphasis, both logical and physical, implicit and explicit, in Chapter 8 you'll be introduced to formatting text into lists. HTML 4 provides three major lists types, including ordered, unordered, and definition lists. Each type will be explored along with the design variations available for each.

Review Questions

1. What are the other names for explicit and implicit tags?

2. What is the difference between an explicit and an implicit tag?

3. Why is the <B> (bold) tag considered explicit?

4. Will the <I> tag work in a text-based browser like Lynx? How about the <EM> tag?

5. What programmer's HTML tag is usually displayed differently from the others?

6. Why would you use a programmer's HTML tag?

7. Is it possible to have more than one paragraph of text in a single <BLOCKQUOTE> container?

8. What other common HTML tag is similar to the <PRE> tag?

9. Can you use other tags, such as <B> or <I>, within <PRE> containers?

Review Exercises

1. Create a document that uses all of the different implicit and explicit layout tags discussed, and note how your browser(s) render them. Also note what happens when you combine tags and view them in your browser(s).

2. What creates spaces in your browser? Create a document that uses multiple <BR> and <P> tags, and put returns between <PRE> tags to add blank lines to your document. See if your browser renders them differently. (Proper behavior is to collapse the extra white space with <BR> and <P>, although some browsers don't.)

3. Create a document using the <PRE> tag to work as an invoice or bill of sale, complete with aligned dollar values and a total. Remember not to use the Tab key, and avoid using emphasis tags like <B> or <EM> within your list.

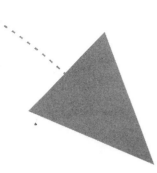

8

Displaying Text in Lists

You've probably heard that one of the best ways to communicate a great deal of information in a short amount of time is by using bulleted lists to convey the message. That philosophy was not lost on the early creators and designers of Web pages. Various tags allow for easy formatting of a number of styles of lists, including both bulleted and nonbulleted incarnations.

This chapter teaches you

- How to group items into unordered lists
- How to create lists ordered numerically, alphabetically, or by roman numerals
- How to use lists to introduce words or ideas and providing definitions for them
- How to manage multi-level lists

Using Lists in HTML

List tags, like paragraphs and preformatted text, are considered container tags. These list tags are responsible for taking chunks of text, divided into individual list item units, and presenting them in a certain style.

Most HTML lists are created following this form:

```
<LIST TYPE>
<ITEM> First item in list
<ITEM> Second item in list
<ITEM> Third item
</LIST TYPE>
```

Each of the items appears on its own line. The `<ITEM>` tag itself is generally responsible for inserting either a bullet or the appropriate number, depending on the type of list that's been defined. It's also possible that the `<ITEM>` tag could insert no special characters (bullets or otherwise), as is the case with definition listings.

You'll look at each type of list in the following sections. The basics to remember are to use the main container tags to define the list type and the individual item tags to announce each new list item.

Ordered and Unordered Lists

It might be better to think of these as numbered (ordered) and bulleted (unordered) lists, especially when we're talking about their use in HTML. The only drawback to that is the fact that the HTML codes for each suggest the ordered/unordered names. For numbered/ordered lists, the tag is `<OL>`, and for bulleted/unordered lists, the tag is `<UL>`. Confused yet? That's my job.

EXAMPLE

For either of these lists, a line item is designated with the empty tag `<LI>`. In the case of ordered lists, the `<LI>` tag inserts a number; for unordered lists, it inserts a bullet. Examples of both follow. This is an ordered list:

```
<OL>
<LI> Item number one.
<LI> Item number two.
<LI> Item number three.
</OL>
```

And here's an unordered list:

```
<UL>
<LI> First item.
```

```
<LI> Second item.
<LI> Third Item.
</UL>
```

Once you've got one of these under your belt, the other looks pretty familiar. To see how these look in a browser, check out Figure 8.1. (Note that I've added a line of text before each to make each list easier to identify.)

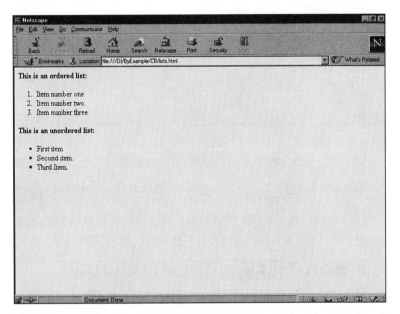

Figure 8.1: *The subtle differences between ordered and unordered lists.*

Changing List Styles

HTML 4 allows you to make changes to the default presentation of lists. Instead of bullets and numerals, you can use squares, letters, and more.

Changing the Unordered List Glyph

The default glyph, or character, used to delimit each list item is formally referred to as a *disc,* although most people simply call it a bullet. If you wish, you can use one of two other options: squares or unfilled circles.

To make the change, you only need to add a TYPE attribute to your <UL> tag:

```
<UL TYPE="square">
```

EXAMPLE

If we take that simple three-item list again and use squares, what you'll see will be similar to the first list in Figure 8.2.

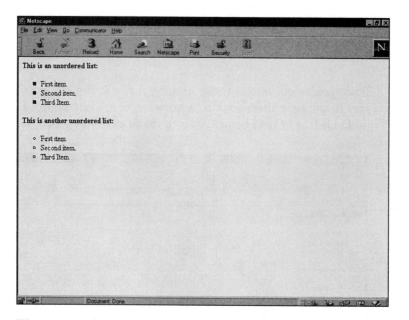

Figure 8.2: *An unordered list using squares instead of bullets.*

Using `circle` for the TYPE value instead of `square` results in the open or unfilled circle shown in the second list in Figure 8.2.

Replacing the Numbers in an Ordered List

Ordered lists have even more options than unordered lists do. A total of five options are available: Arabic numbers (the default), lower- or uppercase alphabet, and lower- or uppercase Roman numerals.

You make the change the same way you did with unordered lists—by using the TYPE attribute.

Table 8.1 lists the TYPE value to use and shows you how each will be displayed.

Table 8.1: TYPE *Values and Display Styles for Ordered Lists*

Type Value	Display Style
1	1, 2, 3
a	a, b, c
A	A, B, C
i	i, ii, iii
I	I, II, III

EXAMPLE

Changing the Values in an Ordered List

What happens if you don't want all your lists to start with the equivalent of number 1, or if you want to start with 5 and go to 10? HTML also lets you control this aspect of your list. To change the starting value, you'll need to add the START attribute to the opening <OL> tag, like this:

```
<OL START="100">
```

This line would start your list at the number 100.

TIP

If you've chosen to use an alphabetic or Roman-numeral list, your start values are still set using Arabic numbers. For example, to start a list with "e," you'd still use START="5".

EXAMPLE

If you want to change an individual list item's number, you modify the <LI> tag with a VALUE attribute. Taking our earlier example, if you've got a standard numbered list with five items, but you want the next item numbered 10 instead of 6, you'd type the following:

```
<LI VALUE="10">
```

The list then continues with 11, 12, and so on, as shown in Figure 8.3.

![Netscape browser window showing an ordered list]

```
 1. First item.
 2. Second item.
 3. Third Item.
 4. Fourth Item.
 5. Fifth Item.
10. Item number changed to ten.
11. Numbering continues with eleven.
12. Then twelve.
13. Then thirteen, etc.
```

Figure 8.3: *List numbers can be manipulated with the* VALUE *attribute on the* <LI> *tag.*

EXAMPLE

Adding Additional Formatting Within Lists

Different formatting within lists can offer some dramatically different results, and you should take some time to experiment. Load and save your template as a new HTML document, and enter Listing 8.1 (or similar experiments) within the body tags.

Listing 8.1: lists.html: Formatting Example

```
<BODY>

<P>The following are some of the things that little boys are made of:</P>

<UL>

<LI> Dirt

<LI> Snails

<LI> Puppy-dog <B>tails</B>

<LI> Worms

<LI> Various ramblings from <I>Boy Scout Magazine</I>

<LI> An affinity for volume controls

</UL>

<P> And, in order of importance, here are the things that little girls are
made of:</P>

<OL>

<LI>An instinctive ability to listen and reason. Although relational in their
logic, and often not as <I>spatial</I> and detached in their thinking, a
superior empathetic capability in general makes little girls better at conflict
resolution.

<LI> Outstanding memories. Little girls can remember things like addresses with
little or no difficulty. Consider this long lost professor of my aging mother
whose address she can still recall:<BR>

<ADDRESS>

1472 Wuthering Heights Circle<BR>

Poetsville, CT 31001<BR>

</ADDRESS>

She visited once, and his dogs were mean to her.</P>

<LI> The gift of <STRONG>Absolute control</STRONG> over all things sentient.

</OL>

</BODY>
```

Notice that, in every instance, only a new <LI> tag is capable of creating a new line in the list. Nearly any other type of HTML markup is possible within a given line item. Once you've saved this document, call it up in a browser and notice how it's formatted (see Figure 8.4).

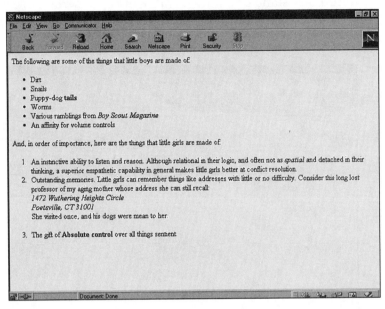

Figure 8.4: *Ordered and unordered lists with special HTML formatting.*

Definition Lists

Definitions are unique among all lists because they offer two levels of line items within the list structure—one for the defined term and one for the definition itself. This is useful in many different ways. Some designers like it for its consistent lack of bullets or numbering.

EXAMPLE

The tags for this list are the container tag <DL> (definition list) and two empty tags, <DT> (definition term) and <DD> (definition). The <DT> tag is designed (ideally) to fit on a single line of your Web page, but it will wrap to the beginning of the next line if necessary. The <DD> tag will accept a full paragraph of text, most often rendered with continuous indentation beneath the <DT> term. The following is an example of all three tags:

```
<DL>

<DT><B>hero</B> <I>(n.)</I>

<DD>A person admired for his or her brave or noble deeds.

<DT><B>hertz</B> <I>(n.)</I>

<DD>A unit used in the measurement of the frequency of electromagnetic waves
```

```
<DT><B>hex</B> <I>(n.)</I>
<DD>An evil spell or magical curse, generally cast by a witch.
</DL>
```

Notice that standard inline HTML markup is permissible within the boundaries of a definition list, and that using bold and italics for the defined terms adds a certain dictionary-like quality (see Figure 8.5).

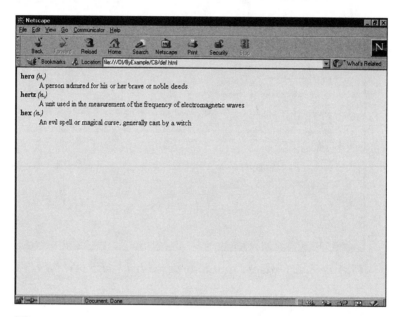

Figure 8.5: *A basic definition list.*

TIP

Not all browsers display definition lists in the same way, so adding spaces to <DT> items (to get them to line up with the <DD> text) is often a waste of time.

EXAMPLE

HTML Within Lists

With the definition list, there are many things you can accomplish with formatting. You can experiment with different HTML tags to see how they react within the list. Remember that within the <DL> and </DL> tags, the two data item tags, <DT> and <DD>, reign supreme. For instance, even a new paragraph within a <DD> tag will stay indented in most browsers.

Load your template and choose the Save As command to give the template a new name. Then type Listing 8.2 between the body tags. The result is shown in Figure 8.6.

Listing 8.2: lists2.html: HTML Within Lists

```
<BODY>
<H1>Computer Terms</H1>
<DL>
<DT><B>CPU</B>
<DD>Central Processing Unit. This is the "brain" of a computer, where
instructions created by the computers system software and application
software are carried out.
<DT><B>Hard Drive</B>
<DD>Sometimes called a <I>fixed drive</I>, this is a device (generally
mounted inside a computer's case) with spinning magnetic plates that is
designed to store computer data. When a file is "saved" to the hard drive, it
is available for accessing at a later time.<BR>
Most system software and application programs are also stored on the
computer's internal hard drive. When an applications name is typed or an icon is
accessed with a mouse, the application is loaded from the hard drive in RAM and
run by the system software.
<DT><B>Application Software</B>
<DD>Computers programs used to create or accomplish something on a computer, as
distinct from system software. Examples of computer application software might
include:<BR>
WordPerfect (a word processing application)<BR>
Microsoft Excel (a spreadsheet application)<BR>
QuarkXPress (a desktop publishing application)<BR>
Corel Draw (a computer graphics application)<BR>
</DL>
<BODY>
```

Using the <BR> tag allows you to create an impromptu list within the list, although everything remains indented because it's ultimately under the influence of the <DD> tag. The definition item tags (<DT> and <DD>) stay in effect until another instance of a definition item tag is encountered or until the </DL> tag ends the definition list.

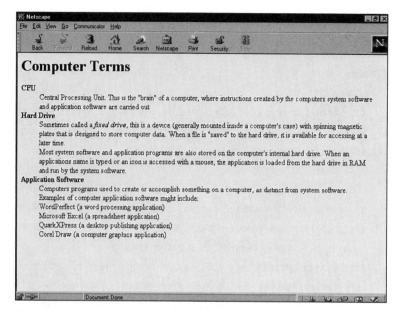

Figure 8.6: *Using extensive HTML formatting in a list.*

Nesting Tags and Combining List Types

Since most of your HTML lists can accept HTML tags within their list items, it stands to reason that you could potentially create lists within lists. In fact, creating a list and then creating another list as part of an item in that first list is how you can create an outline in HTML.

Nesting Tags

You might think of nesting tags as being similar to a set of food storage containers. The smallest one, with its lid on, fits inside the next larger container. You can then put the lid on the second container and place the entire thing in a third container that's even bigger. The same concept can apply here. In HTML, this means completing an HTML tag within the confines of another container tag. This could look something like the following:

```
<P>She was easily the most <EM>beautiful</EM> girl in the room.</P>
```

This is an example of correctly nesting the <EM> tag within a paragraph container.

With lists, things can get complicated. So it's best to remember the "nesting" concept when you begin to add lists within lists. As far as HTML is concerned, a nested list works as marked-up text within the previous list item. When the next list item is called for, HTML moves on.

EXAMPLE

Lists Within Lists

Let'slook at an example of a simple nested list:

```
<OL>
<LI>Introduction
<LI>Chapter One
    <OL>
    <LI> Section 1.1
    <LI> Section 1.2
    <LI> Section 1.3
    </OL>
<LI>Chapter Two
</OL>
```

TIP

It's a good idea to indent nested lists as shown in the example. The browser doesn't care—it's just easier for you (or other designers) to read in a text editor.

Notice that the nested list acts as a sublevel of the Chapter One list item. In this way, you can simulate an outline in HTML. Actually, the nested list is just HTML code that is part of the <LI>Chapter One list item. As you saw in Listing 8.2, you can use the <BR> tag to create a line break in a list element without moving on to the next list item. Following the same theory, an entire nested list works as if it's a single list item in the original list.

The following:

```
<OL>
<LI>Section Five<BR>
    This section discusses ducks, geese, finches and swans.
<LI>Section Six
</OL>
```

is essentially the same as this:

```
<OL>
<LI>Section Five
    <OL>
    <LI> Ducks
    <LI> Geese
    <LI> Finches
    <LI> Swans
    </OL>
```

```
<LI> Section Six
</OL>
```

In both cases, the nest HTML container is simply a continuation of the first list item. Both the text after the `<BR>` in the first example and the ordered list in the second example are part of the list item labeled Section Five. That list item is over when the next list item (Section Six) is put into effect (see Figure 8.7).

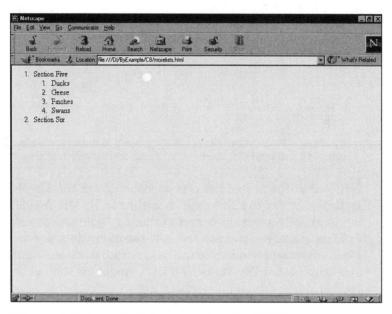

Figure 8.7: *In both of the examples, the HTML container is simply part of the list.*

EXAMPLE

Combining List Types

When nesting lists, it's also possible to nest different types of lists within one another. This is useful when you'd like to vary the types of bullets or numbers used in an outline form. For instance:

```
<OL>
<LI>Introduction
<LI>Company Financial Update
     <UL>
     <LI>First Quarter
     <LI>Second Quarter
     <LI>Third Quarter
```

```
        <LI>Fourth Quarter
        </UL>
<LI>Advertising Update
        <UL>
        <LI>Results of Newspaper Campaign
        <LI>Additions to Staff
        <LI>New Thoughts on Television
        </UL>
<LI>Human Resources Update
</OL>
```

There's nothing terribly difficult to learn here—just the added benefit of being able to nest different types of lists within others. You're still simply adding HTML markup code to items in the original list. This time, however, you have more control over how your outline looks (see Figure 8.8).

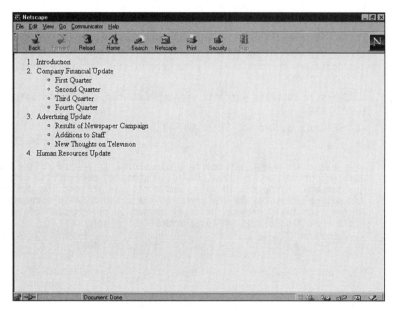

Figure 8.8: *Nesting different types of lists.*

EXAMPLE

Nesting Definition Lists

Although creating outlines is nice, more often you're interested in presenting actual information on your Web pages. Doing that in an outline form can often be helpful to your Web users. You have a number of different ways you can do this, including nesting paragraphs within ordered and unordered lists. Or you can just use definition lists.

Load your template and choose the Save As command to rename it. Then enter the following text between the body tags:

```
<BODY>

<H2>About Our Company</H2>

<OL>

<LI>Our Leaders

        <DL>

        <DT><B>Richard B. McCoy, CEO</B>

        <DD>  Little did Mr. McCoy know

that events in his family life that occurred while he was attending Harvard
Business School would lead to his choice of career.  As father to a newborn baby
girl, he realized that the current baby beds on the market didn't serve his
family well. After graduating from Harvard with his MBA, he set out to build a
better bed. His invention, the SleepMaker 3000, was an instant success. His
inventive spirit continues to influence and inspire our company to this day.

        <DT><B>Leslie R. Gerald, CFO</B>

        <DD>  Ms. Gerald,

a graduate of Northwestern University, joined our team in 1998 after a leading
e-widgets.com through a highly successful IPO. Her considerable experience in
e-commerce and

business-to-business extranet support make her a valuable asset to our
organization.

<DT><B>David W. Deacon, VP of Marketing</B>

        <DD>

Mr. Deacon has spent his entire professional life here in the Seattle area.
Joining our company in 1991, David spearheaded our initial efforts in bringing
the company to the Web in 1994, and continues to lead the design of our expand-
ing online presence. We are proud to acknowledge David's receipt of 1999's Man
of the Year award here in Seattle, earned in recognition ofover 500 volunteer
hours worked on behalf of local charities.

        </DL>

         <BR>
```

```
<LI>Employees of the Month
    <UL>
    <LI> January: Bill Cable, IS
    <LI> February: Janet Smiles, Marketing
    <LI> March: Rich Lewis, Finance
    <LI> April: Wendy Right, Vendor Relations
    <LI> May: Alice Cutless, Area Sales
    <LI> June: Dean Wesley, Training
    </UL>
</OL>
</BODY>
```

Combining different types of lists is a great way to organize your Web site in such a way that it's easy to get at interesting information. At the same time, it's still possible to present that information in many different ways using various list tags (see Figure 8.9).

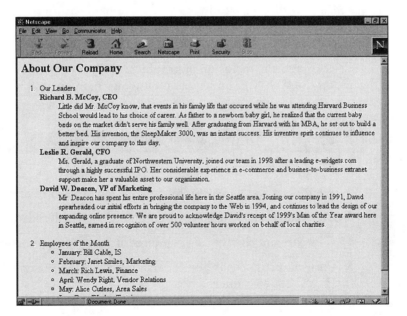

Figure 8.9: *Nesting and combining the various types of HTML lists.*

What's Next?

HTML lists are an effective way to communicate a great deal of information in a relatively small amount of space. HTML provides tags for both ordered (numbered) lists and unordered (bullet-style) lists. In addition to those, you can create unstructured lists using definition lists.

Ordered and unordered lists are easily the most commonly used. Definition lists are unique because they allow you to have two different types of list items within the lists—a term and its definition.

Both ordered and unordered lists can change the glyphs used to delimit each list item. Individual list item glyph values within ordered lists can also be adjusted.

All of these lists can be used together in what's called nesting, or creating lists within other lists. The definition list is especially good for this, because you can add all different types of lists (such as bullet and numbered lists) within the descriptions in your definition list.

It's also possible to nest different types of lists within numbered lists to create multilevel outlines in your HTML documents.

Next in Chapter 9, you'll begin to add considerable visual spice to your Web pages through the inclusion of graphics. We'll cover what types of graphics work on the Web, tips on how to create and manage graphics files, and an overview of a popular graphics editing tool.

Review Questions

1. What are the two basic tags in an HTML list?

2. What does a `<LI>` create, by default, when used in an unordered list?

3. Can you change the style of numbers in an ordered list?

4. How can you change an unordered list bullet from a disc to a square?

5. Can you use other inline HTML tags (such as `<B>` or `<EM>`) within HTML list containers?

6. What is unique about the definition list style?

7. Do definition lists have to be used for words and their definitions?

8. Which of these is an example of a nested list?

   A.

   ```
   <OL>
   <LI>Groceries<BR>
   ```

```
    Milk<BR>
    Soup<BR>
    Ice Cream<BR>
<LI>Other groceries
</OL>
```

B.
```
<OL>
<LI>Groceries
    <UL>
    <LI> Milk
    <LI> Soup
    <LI> Ice Cream
    </UL>
<LI>Other Groceries
</OL>
```

9. What type of HTML lists would you use to create an outline, the major points of which were numbered and the minor points of which used bullets?

Review Exercises

1. Create a seven-item ordered list using Roman numerals. After the fifth item, increase the next list item value by 5.

2. Within a definition list, use three inline container tags and a nested unordered list.

3. Beginning with an ordered list, create a list that nests both an unordered list and a definition list.

Adding Graphics to Your Web Pages

Now that you've seen the many ways you can add some character to your text—and use different tags to better communicate your ideas—it's time to jazz up your pages a little bit. Let's add some graphics!

First, though, you should know a couple of important things about placing graphics. Some of these considerations may seem a bit foreign to you, especially if you're a graphic designer or commercial artist. You have to think in a slightly different way about graphics for your HTML pages.

This chapter teaches you

- How to choose good sizes for your graphics
- How to choose a file type for your graphics
- How to create and manipulate graphics
- How to embed graphics in your Web pages

The Special Nature of Graphics on the Web

You may be comfortable using a program such as CorelDRAW! or Adobe Photoshop to create and manipulate graphics. You may already know the difference between a PICT file and a TIF file (and why that difference might be important). You may even know a lot about preparing graphics for professional printing or adding graphics to desktop publishing documents.

But if you've never done any design for the World Wide Web, there's also a good chance that you've never worried about one special graphics issue, even if you are a print design expert: How big is that graphics file you created? Aside from using the correct graphics format, this issue is the single most important consideration in graphical Web design.

The Size of Graphics Files

Why is the size of graphics files so important? Your Web users have to download your pages to view them, including all the graphics associated with the pages. Couple that fact with the Web speed issues discussed in Chapter 5, "What You Need for a Web Site," and the need for smaller graphics files becomes apparent.

The high-color, high-resolution graphics files that color printers and professional designers work with are generally measured in the number of megabytes of information required to create them. Each image can take up more space than is available on a floppy disk—or even the bulk of a zip disk! Often, special tapes and cartridges are required to transfer these files from the graphics shop to the printer.

A good average size for a Web graphic, on the other hand, is between 10 KB and 30 KB—about one to three percent of the size of those high-color, high-resolution graphics. This could be tough to get used to.

EXAMPLE

Watching Graphical Sites Download

Just to get a feel for how all this graphics stuff works, start your Web browser and Internet connection. Make sure that your browser has its preferences or options set so that it downloads graphics automatically.

Let's visit the Internet Explorer home page at Microsoft's Web site: `http://www.microsoft.com/windows/ie/default.htm`. If you have Internet Explorer available, go ahead and use that browser. Otherwise, use the browser of your choice.

Now, as the page downloads, watch the status bar at the bottom of your browser's window. You should be able to watch as your browser downloads the page and the various graphics. Your browser may even tell you how large each graphics file is as you're downloading.

Next, select an individual graphics file on the page, and save it to your hard drive. In Windows, right-click a graphic and then choose to save the graphic as a file (in Navigator or Internet Explorer), as shown in Figure 9.1. On a Macintosh, hold down the mouse button as you click the graphic, and then choose to save the graphic when the pop-up menu appears.

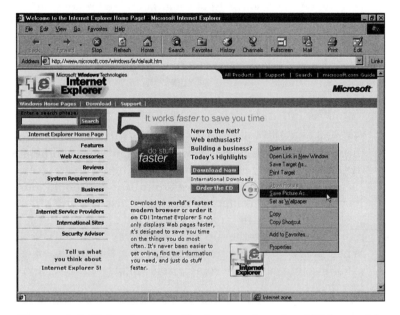

Figure 9.1: *Using Internet Explorer to download Web graphics.*

Finally, look at the file using Windows Explorer or Mac Finder. Check the graphic's file size. Notice how small the file is, and remember how long downloading it took. You'll have to be aware of these considerations when you create your Web graphics.

Picking Your Web Graphics File Type

The other thing that you need to concern yourself with is the file type that you will use for Web graphics. In general (at least currently), you can choose either of two file types: GIF or JPG. GIF (CompuServe Graphics Interchange Format) is the more popular among Web browsers, but JPG (sometimes abbreviated as JPEG, for Joint Photographic Experts Group) is gaining popularity and becoming more widely used.

Why have two standards? GIF and JPG bring different advantages to the table. Let's take a look.

GIF Format Graphics

Any graphical browser supports the display of GIF format files *inline,* meaning that the browser doesn't require a special viewer for these files. GIFs are compressed graphics, meaning that they tend to have smaller file sizes. That small file size is partially a result of being limited to a 256-color palette. GIF is also the file format of choice for creating transparent graphics—graphics that make the Web page appear to be the actual background of the GIF graphic (see the later section "Creating Transparent GIFs").

GIF files work well when you have large blocks of individual colors, as often occurs in images used for navigation, or text incorporated into graphics.

The JPG Format

Gaining on GIF in popularity is the JPG format. JPG graphics can be viewed in most graphical browsers without a special helper application. JPG graphics have the advantage of being better for graphics such as photographs that have more colors (up to 16.7 million, in most cases) than similar GIF files. The compression formula used for JPG files can cause problems if you have large blocks of color. It uses what's called a *lossy* format: It compresses the file by taking away some of the color information. When that occurs in large blocks of color, the process of expanding the graphic again can leave some pixels slightly off-color, a problem known as *artifacts*.

TIP

Here's a general rule of thumb to remember when you're faced with many colors or photographs: Choose JPG; otherwise, GIF should do fine.

The Future of Web Graphics Formats

In the spring of 1996, the World Wide Web Consortium (W3C) announced a working paper standard for a new graphics format—the Portable Network Graphic (PNG) file type. It was an enhancement on the current popular formats—GIF and JPG.

The PNG file format provides for high, lossless compression of graphics, even at the highest levels of "true-color" depths, allowing transmission of very clean, crisp graphics over the Web. This specification uses public-domain compression schemes, making the format easy to incorporate in graphics editing tools.

This format is designed to be highly machine-independent so that different types of computers and operating systems can easily deal with the creation and display of PNG graphics. The PNG format allows for transparency effects (like the GIF format). These graphics often display more quickly in browsers that display graphics progressively (a piece at a time as the graphic is being downloaded).

Although adoption of PNG has been slower than many hoped, it is making progress on the Web. You can expect many more browsers, graphics applications, and helpers to support this format in the future.

Creating and Manipulating Graphics

It's no secret that a lot of Web design has transitioned from manipulating text-based HTML documents to designing and integrating compelling graphics into Web pages. As the Web has become more commercial, its graphical content has become more professional. If you're not up to the task of creating professional graphics, don't worry too much; programs are available that will help you. Also, it's more important that graphics further the usefulness of the text. The graphics in and of themselves are not the point (though I'm sure some artists might argue over that one!). The point is to make your Web pages more exciting and informative.

It is a fact, however, that Web sites are leaping forward daily into very slick, graphical presentations of Web-based information. Commercial artists and designers are continuing to find new niches on the Web. If you're a skilled computer artist, congratulations; this is where you'll put your skills to use. If you're not, that's okay, too. Any Web designer needs to be able to manipulate and edit graphics in a program such as Adobe Photoshop or CorelDRAW!, but you don't necessarily have to create those graphics if that's not your forte.

Creating Graphics for the Web

As you get started with a program such as Photoshop or CorelDRAW!, keep in mind that the most important consideration in creating Web graphics is the file size. File size isn't generally the first consideration for creating print graphics; almost any print shop or prepress house will accept large storage cartridges or tapes that provide access to your huge full-color graphics. Not so on the Web. Your target is as small as possible—between 15 and 35 KB for larger files (those that are bigger on the screen).

You can come up with graphics to use on your Web pages in many ways. Eventually, any graphic that you use needs to be in a standard file format (for example, GIF or JPG) and relatively small. But how you come up with the final graphic has a lot to do with the information you're trying to communicate and with your skills as an artist. The following are some of the different ways you might come up with Web graphics:

- **Create graphics in a graphics application.** Many programs for both professional and amateur artists can output GIF- or JPG-format files for use on the Web. Among these programs are Adobe Photoshop, CorelDRAW!, Paint Shop Pro, and others.

TIP

Any graphics program, even Microsoft Paint, can create Web graphics, although you may need to use another program to change the graphic to an acceptable file format.

- **Download public-domain or royalty-free graphics.** Many sites on the Internet allow you to download icons, interface elements, and other graphics for your Web site. At the same time, public-domain clip art collections (such as those available on CD-ROM) can be useful for Web pages. (Just be sure to read the licensing agreement to see if you can use them on the Web.)

- **Use scanned photographs.** Using photographs (especially those that you've taken yourself) is a great way to come up with graphics for your Web pages. Unless you have access to scanning hardware, though, you may need to pay someone to scan the photos.

- **Use a digital camera.** Cameras are available that allow you to take photos that can be downloaded directly from the camera to your computer. Although some of this equipment can be very expensive, entry-level machines can be purchased for $200 or less, and those photos can easily be downloaded to your computer for eventual use on the Web.

- **Use PhotoCDs.** Many photo development shops can create digital files of your photographs (from standard 35mm film or negatives) and save those files in PhotoCD format. Most CD-ROM drives allow you to access these photos, which you can then change to GIF or JPG format and display on your Web pages.

Creating Graphics in Paint Shop Pro

EXAMPLE

A popular program for creating Web graphics in Windows 95/98/NT is Paint Shop Pro, which has the added advantage of being try-before-you-buy shareware. To download Paint Shop Pro, access the URL `http://www.jasc.com/psp6dl.html` with your Web browser, and find the hypermedia link for downloading the program for your particular version of Windows.

NOTE

As with any shareware program, you should register Paint Shop Pro (by sending in the requested fee) if you find it useful. The program will disable itself after a time if you haven't entered the appropriate registration codes.

Paint Shop Pro arrives as a self-installing .exe file. Locate the file using Windows Explorer, and then simply double-click it to launch the installation program. After installation is complete, start the program. You should see a window like the one shown in Figure 9.2.

Figure 9.2: *The basic Paint Shop Pro interface.*

You can use Paint Shop Pro to create a simple graphic, such as a logo or title, for your Web pages. Begin by using the File, New menu option to create a new image. Select a basic 400 wide by 200 tall dimension. Choose white from the Background color box, and then click OK. If you want to change the background color, you can easily do so using the flood-fill tool. That's the paint bucket icon on the menu bar that runs down the left side of the screen. To select the new color, right-click the upper-left square of the two color squares on the right side of the screen. A Recent Colors dialog box appears. Click the Other button. The color palette appears, as shown in Figure 9.3.

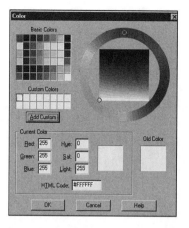

Figure 9.3: *Paint Shop Pro's color palette.*

Click the cursor anywhere in the ring of color to select a hue. You can adjust its intensity by clicking within the gradient square in the middle. Once you're happy with the color, click OK. Now you'll see the color you selected filling the color swatch square you first right-clicked.

Select the flood-fill tool by clicking the paint bucket icon in the toolbar on the left. Move the mouse cursor over the image canvas, and you'll see the cursor change to a bucket. One click inside the canvas, and it will be painted with the new color.

Now select the letter A just below the paint bucket, choose another color from the palette, and click anywhere within the graphics window. Type your text (your company name, for example) in the dialog box, as shown in Figure 9.4. Choose the Floating option in the Create As area of the dialog box so that you can move the text around to just the right spot within the canvas. Choose any other effects you want, and then click OK. Now you should be able to drag the text around the canvas. When you have the text arranged correctly, click anywhere in the canvas (other than within the text) to place the text permanently (see Figure 9.5).

Before you save this graphic, you should make it as physically small as possible so that it works well on your Web page. To cut the image down a bit, select Paint Shop Pro's rectangular selector tool (the dotted rectangle icon just below the four-way arrow icon). Click somewhere near the top-left corner of the text within the graphic (at the point where you want to create a new top-left corner for your cropped image), and drag the mouse pointer to the other side (bottom-right corner) of the text. When you release the mouse button, a thin box should appear around this smaller portion of your graphic. Choose the menu option Image, Crop to Selection, and the image is cropped to that size. If everything went well, you have a smaller graphic that is just as useful for your Web site.

Figure 9.4: *The Text Entry dialog box.*

Figure 9.5: *Creating a simple graphic.*

The last step is to save the graphic in a file format that's useful for the Web. Choose File, Save As. In the Save As dialog box that appears, you can select the file type from a drop-down list (see Figure 9.6). GIF will work best with this image, since it has large blocks of color. Type a filename and click OK.

Now you've created a graphic for use on your Web page. Use Windows Explorer or File Manager to check the file size. You want the file to be less than 20 KB—an ideal size for a Web page graphic. On my system, the result was just 3 KB!

Figure 9.6: *Saving your graphic in a Web-compatible format.*

Manipulating Web Graphics

After you decide what graphics to use, the next step is to manipulate and edit those graphics for best use on the Web. The preceding section discussed some of this manipulation (cropping and saving a graphic to make it as small as possible). The following are some other ways to use graphics applications to make your images lean, attractive, and useful:

- **Keep graphics small.** Creating smaller graphics in the first place, and using the cropping tool to take out backgrounds and extra space, are great ways to keep graphics to a manageable size.

- **Use fewer colors.** Many graphics applications allow you to decide how much color information should be included in the file, as shown in Figure 9.7. Do you want to use a possible 256 colors or millions of colors? The fewer colors you choose, the smaller your image file will be.

NOTE

Programs often describe the number of colors in a graphic using either a number or something called bit depth. An 8-bit graphic, for instance, offers 256 colors. How do you calculate these numbers? Two to the power of the bit depth is the number of possible colors (2^8 = 256 colors; 2^{16} = 65,536 colors).

- **Create thumbnail graphics.** At times, displaying a large graphic may be necessary, especially if your user chooses to view it. You can give users this option by creating thumbnail graphics in your graphics programs and then using the thumbnails as links to identical (but much larger) graphics files. This method allows you to create pages that contain many images, all of which are scaled down considerably (and, therefore, download more quickly). If a user wants to view one of the graphics at full size, he or she can simply click the thumbnail graphic.

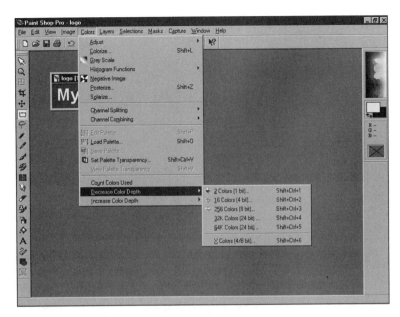

Figure 9.7: *Most graphics applications allow you to choose a color depth.*

NOTE

Avoid the temptation to use the HEIGHT and WIDTH attributes of the <IMG> tag to resize a graphic "on-the-fly." Although it can be convenient for the designer, the entire file still must be transferred across the Internet, and the display is often quite distorted, thereby negating the benefits that smaller thumbnail graphics offer in terms of down-loading speed and clarity.

EXAMPLE

Creating Thumbnails with LView Pro

Paint Shop Pro, Adobe Photoshop, and other image-editing tools do have the ability to resize and reformat graphics, but some designers like to use a tool designed specifically for that purpose. These specialized applications are also more lightweight, consuming fewer system resources.

LView Pro is just such an application. It has the convenience of being a shareware program. You can download LView by accessing the Web URL http://www.lview.com/downLViewPro.htm. Choose the version for your flavor of Windows, download it to your computer, install it in Windows, and start it.

To resize an image to create a thumbnail, follow these steps:

1. Choose File, Open. The Open dialog box appears.

2. In the Open dialog box, find the image you want to resize.

3. With the image open in a window on the desktop, choose Edit, Resize. The Resize Image dialog box, shown in Figure 9.8, appears.

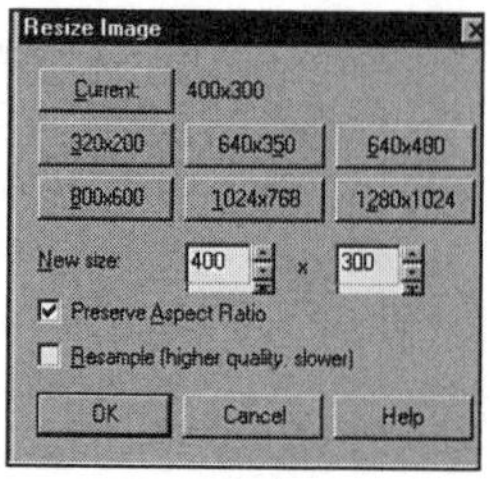

Figure 9.8: Resizing graphics in LView Pro for Windows.

4. You can use the slider controls or enter a new size for your thumbnails. A good rule is somewhere around 75 pixels wide (width is the first field after New size in the dialog box). If you have the Preserve Aspect Ratio box checked (it's on by default), changing the width also changes the height in order to preserve the image's aspect ratio.

5. When you have finished resizing, click OK.

TIP

If you plan to offer many thumbnails on one page, it's a good idea to make them a uniform width (or height) to keep the page orderly.

When you create thumbnails, you'll probably want to maintain the aspect ratio of the current graphic when resizing so that LView keeps the height and width of the new graphic at the same ratio as the original graphic, making the thumbnail smaller but similarly proportioned. Don't forget to save the new file with a slightly different name, using the appropriate file extension (.gif or .jpg).

TIP

Whenever an application gives you the choice, you should save GIF files as interlaced GIFs. This lets the graphics display faster in many browsers. Some software also offers the option for progressive JPGs, but not all Web browsers can display those, so it's best not to use it.

Creating Transparent GIFs

One very popular way to edit Web graphics is to create transparent GIFs. This process allows you to make one of the colors of your graphic (generally the background color) transparent so that the Web page's color scheme or background graphics show through (see Figure 9.9). Most often, it's used to give the illusion that the graphic is part of your Web page. You can use this method to add impact to your pages and to limit the size of your graphics by doing away with elaborate backgrounds.

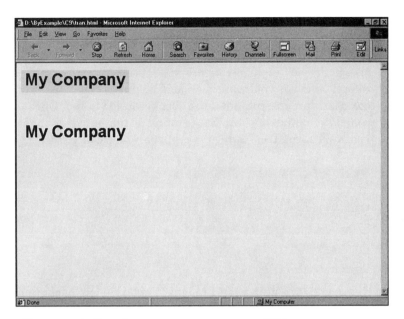

Figure 9.9: *Regular versus transparent GIFs.*

To be rendered with a transparent background, a GIF file must be saved in the GIF89a file format. This can be done with Paint Shop Pro, LView Pro, Transparency for the Mac, and many other programs. Saving a file in this format is simply a matter of deciding what color will be the transparent color when the GIF is displayed.

TIP

Giving the image in your transparent GIF a shadow (in a graphics application) enhances the appearance of a graphic floating directly over the page. The process of adding a shadow varies from graphics editor to graphics editor. In Paint Shop Pro, it's as simple as choosing the Image menu, then Effects, Drop Shadow.

EXAMPLE

Creating Transparent GIFs in Paint Shop Pro

One of the easiest ways to create a transparent GIF is to go back to Paint Shop Pro. Choose File, Open. In the Open dialog box that appears, open the GIF file that you want to change to a transparent GIF. Your image then appears in its own window.

Select Colors, Set Palette Transparency. You see the dialog box shown in Figure 9.10. I can simply select the Set the transparency value to the current background color option, provided the color palette still has that color selected as the background color. That is, if you've created an image with a yellow background, as I did, but have since changed the selected color to say, purple, when performing another operation, you need to be sure to change it back to yellow before attempting to apply transparency. Paint Shop Pro is not yet "smart" enough to deduce that the large yellow block of color is what you intended the "background" to be. Once the operation is complete, notice how the background of the image changes to a checkerboard pattern. That indicates transparency. Click OK.

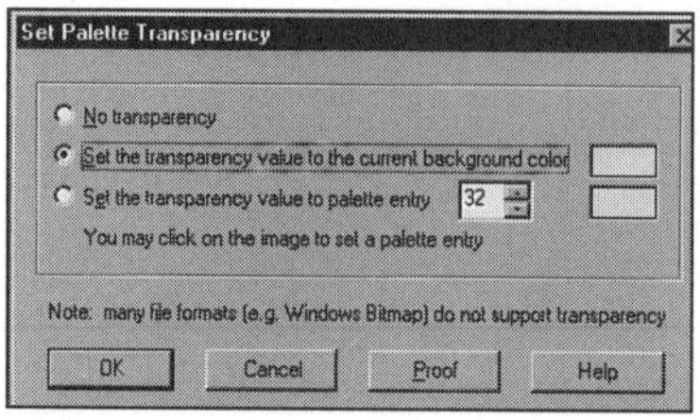

Figure 9.10: Paint Shop Pro, changing a yellow background to transparent.

Now choose File, Save As. Rename the file (or use the same name, if you want), and save it. The file should now appear in a Web browser as a transparent GIF.

Embedding Graphics in Web Pages

When your graphics are created, cropped, resized, and saved in the appropriate formats, you're ready to add them to your Web pages. To add graphics, you use an empty tag called the <IMG> (image) tag, which you insert into the body section of your HTML document as follows:

```
<IMG SRC="image URL">
```

or

```
<IMG SRC="path/filename">
```

SRC accepts the name of the file that you want to display, and *image URL* (or *path/filename*) is the absolute (full URL) or relative path (for a local file or a file in the current directory) to the image. As the first example shows, you can display on your page any graphics file that is generally available on the Internet, even if the file resides on a remote server. For graphics files, however, it is much more likely that the file is located on the local server, so a path and filename are sufficient.

You could enter the following text in a browser:

```
<HR>
<P>This is a test of the Image tag. Here is the image I want to display:</P>
<IMG SRC="image1.gif">
<HR>
```

In this case, `<IMG SRC="image1.gif">` is a relative-path URL, suggesting that the file image1.gif is located in the same directory as the HTML document. The result would be displayed by a browser as shown in Figure 9.11 (in this case, the nontransparent version of the image created earlier).

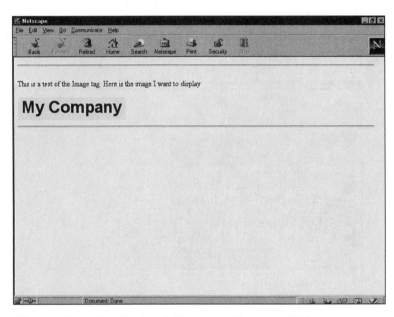

Figure 9.11: *Displaying inline graphics on a Web page.*

TIP

You'll learn more about absolute and relative URLs in Chapter 10, "Hypertext and Creating Links."

An absolute URL is essential if you are accessing an image on a remote site, as in the following (fictitious) example:

```
<IMG SRC="http://www.graphcom.com/pub/graphics/image1.gif">
```

Please realize that using a URL to a distant site on the Internet causes that site to be accessed every time this `<IMG>` tag is encountered on your page. Therefore, you should probably have some sort of arrangement with that Web site's system administrator before you link to a graphic on their server.

Adding Graphics to Other HTML Tags

You can add graphics links to HTML tags to do various things, including placing graphics next to text (within paragraphs) and even including graphics in lists. The following example displays the graphic flush with the left margin, and the bottom of the text that follows the image is aligned with the graphic's bottom edge:

```
<P><IMG SRC="sleepy.jpg" ALT="My cat Dizzy taking a nap"> My cat Dizzy loves to
take naps. In this photo, I caught her sleeping on the back of a recliner. </P>
```

Words that go beyond the end of the first line wrap below the image, as shown in Figure 9.12.

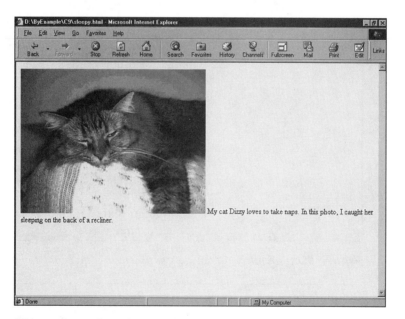

Figure 9.12: *Graphics within paragraph containers.*

The ALT Attribute

So far, most of the tags you've encountered have had only one attribute, if any.

The ALT attribute for the <IMG> tag is designed to accept text that describes the graphic, in case a particular browser can't display the graphic. Consider the plight of users who use Lynx or a similar text-based program to surf the Web (or users of graphical browsers that choose not to auto-load graphics). Because those users can't see the graphic, they'll want to know what they're missing.

The ALT attribute works this way:

```
<IMG SRC="image URL" ALT="Text description of graphic">
```

The following is an example:

```
<IMG SRC="image1.gif" ALT="Logo graphic">
```

For people whose browsers can't display the graphic, the ALT attribute tells them that the graphic exists and explains what the graphic is about.

TIP

Test your site with the Load Images option turned off so that you can see how your ALT text displays.

The ALIGN Attribute

<IMG> can accept another attribute that specifies how graphics appear relative to other elements (such as text or other graphics). Using the ALIGN attribute, you can align other elements to the top, middle, or bottom of the graphic. It follows this format:

```
<IMG SRC="image URL" ALIGN="direction">
```

NOTE

The ALIGN="BOTTOM" attribute isn't necessary, because it is the default setting for the <IMG> tag.

The ALIGN attribute is designed to align text that comes after a graphic with a certain part of the graphic. An image with the ALIGN attribute set to TOP, for example, has any subsequent text aligned with the top of the image, as in the following example:

```
<IMG SRC="image1.gif" ALIGN="TOP"> Descriptive text aligned to top.
```

Giving the <IMG> tag an ALIGN="MIDDLE" attribute forces subsequent text to begin in the middle of the graphic (see Figure 9.13):

```
<IMG SRC="image1.gif" ALIGN="MIDDLE"> Descriptive text aligned to middle.
```

Order among the attributes that you assign to an image tag is unimportant. In fact, because SRC="URL" is technically an attribute (although a required one), you can place the ALIGN or ALT attribute before the SRC information. Anywhere you put attributes, as long as they appear between the brackets of the <IMG> tag, is acceptable. However, if you're consistent, you'll be less likely to forget one.

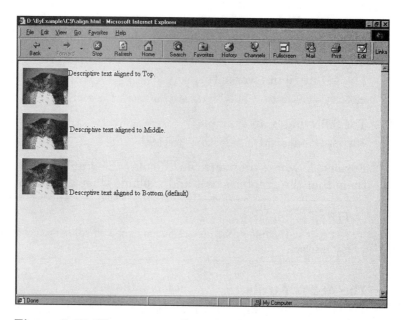

Figure 9.13: *The* `ALIGN` *attribute for the* `<IMG>` *tag.*

EXAMPLE

Adding Graphics to Your Web Site

Now that you've learned how to add images to your Web pages, you have almost doubled the things you can do on the Web. In this example, you will add graphics to a typical corporate Web page, using a couple of methods you've learned.

To start, you need to create some graphics for your home page. If you have a corporate logo and a scanner handy, go ahead and scan some graphics. Alternatively, you can use a graphics program to create, crop, and save your graphics as GIF or JPG files. While you're at it, you may want to create some of your GIFs as transparent GIFs.

Create a logo and a photo for use on the page. Name your GIFs logo.gif and photo.gif, or something similar. (If you have already created a Web site, feel free to name the files according to the organizational system you're using for the site. You can also use JPG graphics if you so desire.) Then load your HTML template, and save it as a new HTML document. Between the body tags, type something like the following example.

```
<!DOCTYPE HTML PUBLIC "-//W3C//DTD HTML 4.0 Transitional//EN">

<HTML>

<HEAD>

<TITLE>Welcome to Tech Support</TITLE>

<BODY>
```

```
<IMG SRC="support.gif" ALT="Tech Support">

<P><IMG SRC="dave.jpg" ALT="Photo of Chief Technician Dave Navarro" ALIGN="MID-
DLE" HSPACE=20> Hi, I'm Dave. Can we help you?

<P>Here's the place to come for any questions you may have about our products.
We specialize in researching even the toughest problems!</P>

<P>You can:

<UL>

<LI>Contact us by phone, at 941-555-1234

<LI>Email us, at <A HREF="mailto:support@foo.com">support@foo.com</A>

<LI>Read answers to our <A HREF="faq.html">Frequently Asked Questions</A>

<LI>Submit a <A HREF="report.html">problem report</A> over the Web.

</UL>

</BODY>

</HTML>
```

For the photo of the Chief Technician, the <IMG> tag has another attribute
in it: HSPACE. This provides some horizontal padding around the image,
measured in pixels. It helps separate the descriptive text from the image so
that they don't butt up against each other (see Figure 9.14).

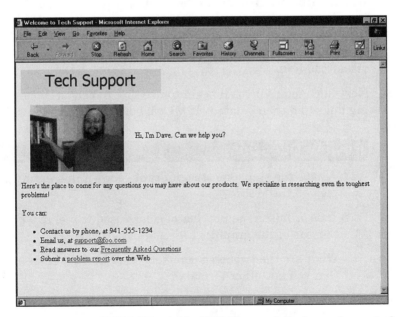

Figure 9.14: *HSPACE within HTML tags help keep elements from appearing crowded.*

Play with this example a little bit to get a feel for when you should place the <IMG> tag within another HTML container and when you can leave the tag out on its own. A page sometimes looks completely different, based only on where you place your image tags.

What's Next?

Creating and manipulating graphics for display on the World Wide Web is somewhat different from the procedures for many other media, because Web graphics files need to be much smaller. In general, the smaller a graphic, the fewer colors it uses; and the more compressed a file, the better the experience for the user. Web designers need to know how to use some fairly specialized graphics programs.

One of the most interesting manipulations of a Web graphic is the transparent GIF file, which makes the graphic seem to float above the Web page—or makes the Web page the actual background for the graphic. You need special techniques and programs to create such a file.

After you create some fast-loading, attractive graphics, placing them on your Web pages is fairly simple. All you need is the <IMG> tag, complete with a path and filename to the graphic. Our discussion of the <IMG> tag introduces something new for HTML tags: attributes. Various attributes for the <IMG> tag allow you to add text to a graphic (for text-based browsers); to align the text with the top, middle, or bottom of the graphic; and to provide visual padding.

Next in chapter 10 you'll begin to use the "hyper" of hypertext, by integrating links and their related HTML tags into your documents.

Review Questions

1. What's the single most significant concern in creating graphics for display on the Web?

2. True or false: The number of colors used to create a graphic can affect the size of the graphics file.

3. What are the two most common graphics formats used on the Web? Can you use other formats?

4. What does it mean when a graphics format (such as JPG) is lossy?

5. Name four ways that you can obtain graphics for your Web site.

6. What is the ideal size range for Web graphics?

7. What are thumbnail graphics?

8. When used with the <IMG> tag, what sort of command or HTML element is SRC?

9. What is the purpose of the ALT attribute?

10. True or false: The <IMG> tag automatically inserts a carriage return after displaying its graphic.

11. Why do you never have to set the ALIGN attribute to BOTTOM?

Review Exercises

1. Use your graphics program to save the same photograph as both a GIF and a JPG image. Then create a Web page that loads both. Note the differences in size and quality.

2. Create a GIF image and turn the background transparent with your graphics program (Paint Shop Pro, LView Pro, or Transparency for the Mac, among others). Load both the original and the transparent GIF into your browser (create a Web page if necessary), and notice the difference that transparency makes. Also note whether the file size changes.

3. Use the ALIGN attribute of an <IMG> tag to align another image to the top of the first image. Play with this feature, aligning images to TOP, MIDDLE, and BOTTOM.

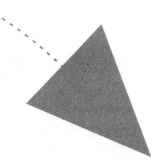

Hypertext and Creating Links

Now that you've seen in detail the ways you can mark up text for emphasis and add images to your Web pages, it's time to take the leap into making these pages useful on the World Wide Web by adding hypertext links.

This chapter teaches you the following:

- How to use the anchor tag for hypertext links
- How to create fragment links
- What relative URLs are and how to use them
- How to use the BASE tag
- How to create links to Internet services
- How to use the LINK tag

You'll see how URLs are useful for creating hypermedia links and links to other Internet services.

Using the <A> Tag

The basic link for creating hypertext and hypermedia links is the <A>, or anchor, tag. This tag is a container, and it requires an </A> to signal the end of the text, images, and HTML tags that are to be considered part of the hypertext link. Here's the basic format for a text link:

```
<A HREF="URL">Text describing link</A>
```

Be aware that although you'll use HREF with nearly every anchor tag you create, it's simply an attribute for the <A> tag. Displayed in a browser, the words *"Text describing link"* would appear underlined and usually in another color (on a color monitor) to indicate that clicking that text initiates the hypertext link.

The following is an example of a *relative* link:

```
<A HREF="products.html">Our Product Information</A>
```

"Relative" means that the server can find the page *relative* to the current document's location. If the products.html page in this example is in the same directory as the main index.html page, this link will allow the server to find the page.

However, if the HTML document you want to link to is located in another directory, or even elsewhere on the Internet, you simply need a more complete, *absolute* URL, such as the following:

```
<A HREF="http://www.foo.com/store/products.html">Our Product Information</A>
```

In either case, things end up looking the same in a browser (see Figure 10.1).

Fragment Links

Aside from creating hypertext links to documents on your local computer or elsewhere on the Internet, you can create links to other parts of the same document in which the link appears. These "fragment" links are useful for moving people to a new section that appears on the same Web page without forcing them to scroll down the entire page.

Doing this, though, requires two instances of the anchor tag: one that serves as the hypertext link and another that acts as a reference point for that link, following this format:

```
<A HREF="#SectionName">Link to another section of this document</A>
 ...additional content...
<A NAME="SectionName">Beginning of new section</A>
```

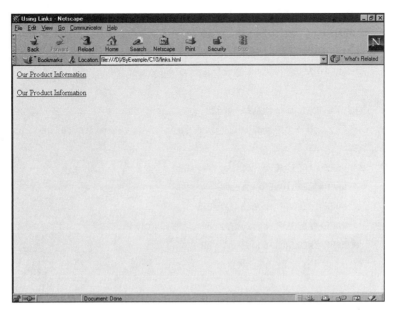

Figure 10.1: *The hypertext links you've created.*

Notice that the anchor tag that creates the hyperlink is similar to the anchor tags you have used previously. The only difference is the hash mark (#) at the beginning of the HREF text. This sign tells the anchor that it is looking for a section within the document, as opposed to an entire file.

The NAME attribute is used to create the actual section within the current HTML document. The text that the NAME attribute contains is relatively unimportant, and it won't be highlighted or underlined in any way when displayed by a browser. NAME is nothing more than an internal reference; without it, though, the link won't work.

NOTE

Remember to use the hash mark (#) only for the actual hypertext link, not the NAME anchor. Also, realize that the NAME text is case sensitive and that the associated HREF text should use the same case for all letters that NAME does. If the HREF calls for SectionONE and the NAME is actually SectionOne, the link will not work.

EXAMPLE

A More Effective Definition List

In Chapter 8, "Displaying Text in Lists," you worked with the definition list tags available for use in HTML, and in some cases, you actually used them for a list of definitions. You'll do that again in this section, but this time you'll use section links to move directly to the words that interest you.

Load the HTML template into your text editor, and choose the Save As command in your text editor to create a new file. In the body of your HTML document, type Listing 10.1 or something similar.

Listing 10.1: listlink.html: Creating a Definition List

```
<BODY>
<H2>The Definition List</H2>
<P>Click one of the following words to move to its definition in the list:
<BR>
<A HREF="#EPITHET">epithet</A><BR>
<A HREF="#EPITOME">epitome</A><BR>
<A HREF="#EPOCH">epoch</A><BR>
<A HREF="#EPOXY">epoxy</A><BR>
<A HREF="#EQUAL">equal</A><BR>
</P>
<HR>
<DL>
<DT><A NAME="EPITHET"><B>ep i thet</B></A>
<DD><EM>noun.</EM> a descriptive, often contemptuous word or phrase
<DT><A NAME="EPITOME"><B>ep it o me</B></A>
<DD><EM>noun.</EM> someone who embodies a particular quality
<DT><A NAME="EPOCH"><B>ep och</B></A>
<DD><EM>noun.</EM> a division in time; a period in history or geology
<DT><A NAME="EPOXY"><B>ep ox y</B></A>
<DD><EM>noun.</EM> a synthetic, heat-sensitive resin used in adhesives
<DT><A NAME="EQUAL"><B>e qual</B></A>
<DD><EM>adj.</EM> having the same quality or status; having enough strength,
courage, and so on.
<DD><EM>noun.</EM> a person or thing that is equal to another; a person
with similar rights or status
</DL>
</BODY>
```

In this example, clicking one of the words that appears as a hyperlink in the first section of the page moves the browser window down to that link's associated NAME anchor so that the definition becomes the focal point of the user's attention. Obviously, fragment links would be of greater use in a larger list. Consider the implications of turning an entire dictionary into HTML documents.

TIP

Resize your browser window so that the entire listlink.html document won't fit, generating a scrollbar. Then click one of the links. You can see the focus within the document shift down to the linked fragment.

Also notice that anchors can be placed within the confines of other HTML tags, as in the first paragraph container and in the example's definition lists. In general, anchor tags can be acted on by other HTML tags as though they were regular text. In the case of hyperlinked text, the underlining and change in color in graphical browsers take precedence, but the hyperlinked text also has any other qualities of the surrounding text (for example, indenting with the rest of the definition text or using an italic font style within <I> tags).

In Figure 10.2, notice which anchors cause the text to become a hyperlink and how the anchor tags respond within other container tags.

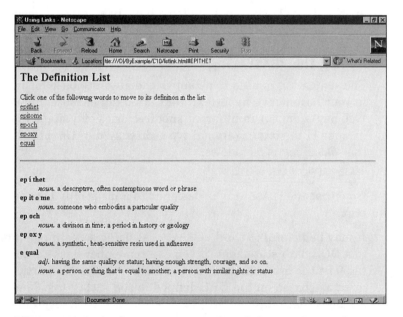

Figure 10.2: *Anchor tags are used to define and move between sections of an HTML document.*

Using Relative URLs

Go back and look at the hypertext links that we discussed at the beginning of this chapter (as opposed to the fragment links). In most cases, the URL referenced by the HREF attribute within the anchor tag needs to be an absolute URL, unless it refers to a file located in the same directory as the current HTML document.

But consider the case of a well-organized Web site, as set out in Chapter 5, "What You Need for a Web Site." That chapter discussed the fact that it's not always the best idea to drop all your Web site's files into the same directory, especially for large sites that contain many graphics or pages. How do you create links to files that may be on the same server but aren't in the same directory?

One obvious way is to use an absolute URL for every link in your Web site. If the current page is `http://www.foo.com/index.html` and you want to access a specific page that you organized into your products directory, you could simply create a link like the following, using an absolute URL:

```
<A HREF="http://www.foo.com/products/new.html>Our new products</A>
```

These absolute URLs can get rather tedious, not to mention the fact that if you happen to change the name of your Web server or move your site to another basic URL, you'll probably have to edit every page in your site to reflect the new URLs.

Adding the `<BASE>` Tag

The `<BASE>` tag is used to establish the absolute base for relative URLs used in your document's hypertext links. This tag is especially useful when your Web pages appear in different subdirectories of a single main directory, as in some of the organizational types discussed in Chapter 5. The format of the `<BASE>` tag is as follows:

```
<BASE HREF="absolute URL">
```

Note that the `<BASE>` tag is designed to appear only between the `<HEAD>` tags.

It may be helpful to think of `<BASE>` as doing something similar in function to a DOS path statement (if you can remember back that far!). The `<BASE>` tag tells the browser that relative URLs within this particular Web document are based on the URL defined in the `<BASE>` tag. The browser then assumes that relative URLs derive from the URL given in the `<BASE>` tag and not necessarily from the current directory of the HTML document.

Consider a document named `http://www.foo.com/products/list.html` that looks something like this:

```
<HEAD>
<TITLE>Page One</TITLE>
</HEAD>
<BODY>
```

```
<A HREF="index.html">Back to Index</A>
</BODY>
```

In this example, the browser tries to find a document named index.html in the products directory because the browser assumes that all relative addresses are derived from the current directory. Using the <BASE> tag, however, changes this example a bit, as follows:

```
<HEAD>
<BASE HREF="http://www.foo.com/">
<TITLE>Page One</TITLE>
</HEAD>
<BODY>
<A HREF="index.html">Back to Index</A>
</BODY>
```

Now the browser looks for the file index.html in the main directory of this server, regardless of where the current document is stored (such as in the products directory). The browser interprets the relative URL in the anchor tag as though the complete URL were http://www.foo.com/index.html.

TIP

If you plan to create a large Web site, you may want to add the <BASE> tag (complete with the base URL) to your HTML template file.

Using the <BASE> tag to point to your Web site's main directory allows you to create the different types of organization systems described in Chapter 5 by using relative URL statements to access HTML documents in different subdirectories.

EXAMPLE

A Hybrid-Style Web Site

Chapter 5 discussed the hybrid style of Web site organization, which allows you to put some common files (such as often-used graphics) in separate directories and to organize unique files with their related HTML pages.

In this example, you'll create an HTML document called products.html, located at the URL http://www.foo.com/products/products.html. Some of your graphics are maintained in a subdirectory of the main directory of this Web site; the subdirectory is called graphics/. You also have links to other pages in the main directory and in a subdirectory called about/.

For this example, you create only one Web page. To test the page, however, you should create a directory structure similar to the one indicated in the sample markup and include the files mentioned.

Begin by saving your template file as products.html. Then, in your text editor, enter Listing 10.2.

Listing 10.2: basetag.html: Creating a Directory Structure

```
<!DOCTYPE HTML PUBLIC "-//W3C//DTD HTML 4.0 Transitional//EN">
<HTML>
<HEAD>
<TITLE>Our Products</TITLE>
<BASE HREF="http://www.foo.com/">
</HEAD>
<BODY>
<IMG SRC="products/prod-banner.gif" ALT="Our Products">
<H2>Our Products</H2>
<P>Here's a listing of the various product types we have available. Click
the name of the product category for more information:</P>
<DL>
<DT>
<DD><IMG SRC="graphics/bullet.gif" ALT=""> <A HREF="products/pc-soft.html">
PC Software</A>
<DD><IMG SRC="graphics/bullet.gif" ALT=""> <A HREF="products/mac-soft.html">
Macintosh Software</A>
<DD><IMG SRC="graphics/bullet.gif" ALT=""> <A HREF="products/pc-hard.html">
PC Hardware</A>
<DD><IMG SRC="graphics/bullet.gif" ALT=""> <A HREF="products/mac-soft.html">
Macinotsh Hardware</A>

</DL>
<HR>
<A HREF="index.html">Return to Main</A>
</BODY>
</HTML>
```

Notice that all the hypertext link HREF commands are pointing to pages that are relative to the <BASE> URL, which is set for the main directory of the Web site. With <BASE> set, it's no longer appropriate to simply enter a filename for your relative URL, even if the file is in the current directory (for example, products/). If all goes well and all your references hold up, your page is displayed as shown in Figure 10.3.

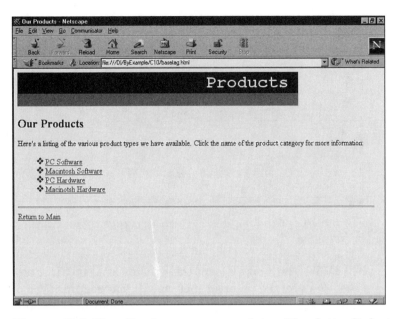

Figure 10.3: *Your Products page, complete with relative links to other parts of the Web site.*

NOTE

Notice that the <BASE> HREF also affects graphics placed with the <IMG> tag. Remember to use relative addresses for images that take the <BASE> address into account. Only HTTP documents and media objects are affected by <BASE>, though, and not other URL types (such as ftp:// and telnet://).

Creating Links to Other Internet Services

Here's where the real power of URLs comes into play. Remember how a URL can be used to describe almost any document or function that's available on the Internet? If something can be described in a URL, a hyperlink can be created for it. In the following section, you start with email.

Hyperlinks for Email Messages

Creating a hyperlinked email address is simple. Using the mailto: type of URL, you can create the following link:

```
<A HREF="mailto:books@webgeek.com">Send me e-mail</A>
```

In many graphical browsers, this URL often loads an email window that allows you to enter the subject and body of an email message and then send it via your Internet account (see Figure 10.4). Even many of the major online services support this hyperlink with their built-in email systems.

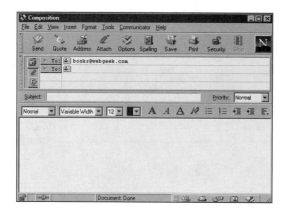

Figure 10.4: *Clicking a* `mailto:` *link brings up an email message window in Netscape.*

Not all Web browsers accept the `mailto:` style of URL, however, and most of those don't return an error message. If you use this type of link, you may want to warn users. Something like the following should work well for users of nongraphical browsers:

```
<P>If your browser supports email links, you can send me an
<A HREF="mailto:books@webgeek.com">e-mail message</A>.</P>
```

Other Internet Services

Using the various types of URLs discussed in Chapter 3, "How Web Browsers Work," you can create links to nearly all other types of Internet services as well. For Gopher sites, for example, a hypertext link might look like the following:

```
<A HREF="ftp://ftp.cdrom.com/">CDROM.com FTP site</A>
```

Most Web browsers can display FTP sites. In most cases, clicking an FTP link points the browser to the FTP site, and the FTP directory structure appears in the browser window.

You can create links that cause the Web browser to download a file from an FTP server, as follows:

```
<P>You can also <A HREF="ftp://ftp.foo.com/pub/newsoft.zip">download</A>
the latest version of our software.
```

When the connection to the FTP server has been negotiated, the file begins to download to the user's computer, as shown in Figure 10.5.

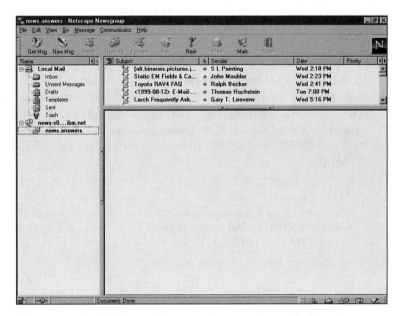

Figure 10.5. Netscape Navigator is downloading a file from an FTP server.

NOTE

Most browsers can accept hyperlinks only to anonymous FTP servers. You generally should not include in your HTML documents links to FTP servers that require user-names and passwords.

Most browsers have some mechanism (sometimes built into the browser window) for reading Usenet newsgroups. Some browsers launch a separate program to read Usenet groups. In either case, you can create a link like the following:

```
<A HREF="news:news.answers">Usenet Help Newsgroup</A>
```

This link loads whatever Usenet reading features the browser employs and displays the specified newsgroup, as shown in Figure 10.6. The news: URL type does not require a particular Internet server address to function. Each browser should be set up with its own links to the user's news server.

Figure 10.6: Netscape Communicator after a link to the newsgroup news.answers is clicked.

Other Links for the `<HEAD>` Tag

You can create a couple more tags in the `<HEAD>` section of your HTML documents. These tags have varying levels of real-world usefulness, so you may want to read this section quickly and refer to it again later if you have a question. The most useful is the `<LINK>` tag, featured here.

The `<LINK>` Tag

The `<LINK>` tag is designed to establish a hypertext relationship between the current document and another URL. Most of the time, the `<LINK>` tag does not create a clickable hypertext link in the user's Web viewer window. It's a little beyond the scope of this book, but programs can be written to take advantage of the `<LINK>` tag, such as a program that creates a toolbar that makes use of the relationship defined.

The `<LINK>` tag generally has either of the following formats:

```
<LINK HREF="URL" REL="relationship">
<LINK HREF="URL" REV="relationship">
```

For the most part, `<LINK>` is used to create an author-defined structure to other HTML documents on a Web site. The attribute REL, for example, defines a forward link for the HREF URL from the current document. Conversely, REV defines a reverse link between the current document and the HREFed URL.

The following are two examples of `<LINK>` statements:

```
<LINK HREF="http://www.foo.com/product3.html" REL="NEXT">
<LINK HREF="http://www.foo.com/product1.html" REV="PREVIOUS">
```

In the HTML 4.0 standard, these definitions are relatively irrelevant—at least publicly on the Web. You more commonly find these statements used within certain organizations (perhaps companies employing an intranet), especially for advanced Web-based documentation efforts and for efforts that use HTML and SGML together (as discussed in Chapter 1, "What Is HTML?").

TIP

You can find more information about `<LINK>` and the various values for REL/REV by reading the HTML 4.0 Recommendation at `http://www.w3.org/TR/REC-html40/struct/links.html#h-12.3`.

What's Next?

The <A> (anchor) tag is the basis for creating hyperlinks on your Web pages. This tag is fairly straightforward; you can use it in conjunction with other tags (such as definition lists) to make hypertext links easy to understand and presentable to the user.

You can also create links to other parts of the same document: relative links and links for special services, such as email. In the case of some of these links (especially relative links), you must seriously consider the way in which your Web site is organized.

The head section of your HTML page can accept several other link-related tags. To keep relative links in check, you can use the <BASE> tag. The <LINK> tag is used mainly for internal reference.

Next up in chapter 11, you'll continue to explore the abilities of linking in HTML by adding them to objects other than text.

Review Questions

1. Is HREF a tag or an attribute?

2. Do local links and distance links look any different when they are viewed in a browser?

3. What type of link is <A HREF="#intro">Intro</A>? Can you tell from the link what document will be accessed?

4. Is it possible to include HTML markup tags (such as emphasis tags) inside anchor tags?

5. What is the purpose of the <BASE> tag, and in what part of the HTML document does it appear?

6. True or false: The <BASE> tag's HREF attribute requires a relative URL.

7. Would the following link succeed? (Assume that the email address is correct.)

   <A HREF="mailto://buddy@aol.com">Mail me!</A>

8. What two attributes for the <LINK> tag are discussed in this chapter?

9. Does the <LINK> tag create a hypertext link in the browser window?

Review Exercises

1. Create a hypertext link that points to a section of another document. (Hint: Use the URL and a section name, like

`http://www.foo.com/products.html#clothing`). Don't forget the `NAME` anchor in the second document.

2. Using the `<BASE>` tag, change the following so that the URL and image `SRC` attribute are relative:

```
<BODY>
<IMG SRC="http://www.foo.com/images/logo.gif">
<P> Welcome to <A HREF="http://www.foo.com/about.html">BigCorp</A>
on the World Wide Web!</P>
</BODY>
```

3. Create a page about your hobbies and interests. (This might be a great About page for your personal Web site.) On the page, include links to interesting sites that coincide with your description. (For instance, if you like sports, you might create a link to `http://www.cnnsi.com/` for the benefit of your users.)

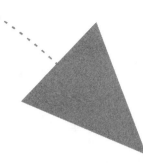

Using Links with Other HTML Tags

Creating links to other local and distance HTML documents is a relatively straightforward process, as shown in Chapter 10, "Hypertext and Creating Links." You also can include links within and together with other HTML tags to make them more interesting, better organized, and more accessible to your users.

As you read this chapter, it may strike you that very little new information about HTML is presented. That's done somewhat purposefully. The point of most of this chapter is simply to explore the various ways that hypertext links can be added to fully formatted HTML documents.

This chapter teaches you the following:

- How to integrate hypertext links more completely into your Web pages
- How to usse graphical links
- How to create menu bars using a series of images
- How to create links to multimedia presentations

Using Links with Block-Level HTML Tags

You can include the anchor tag (<A>) for hypertext links inside or with nearly any other block-level HTML tags. Entire sentences, paragraphs, and even lists and headers can be a single hypertext link. Although this would be unsightly and a bad design, it is possible.

You can also include links within nearly all other HTML container tags. Even emphasis tags, such as <EM> and <B>, can accept an entire anchor container within their confines; they still allow the hypertext link to be created and the descriptive text to be emphasized. The following section shows how this might work.

Emphasis Tags and Hyperlinks

The first, most obvious example of using emphasis tags and hyperlinks involves emphasizing the descriptive text of the link within the <A> tag itself. What if you need to create a link that is also the title of a book and that, as such, must be italicized? You could do this in either of the following ways:

```
<A HREF="book1.html"><I>The Young and the Dirty</I></A>
<I><A HREF="book2.html">The Old and the Unkempt</A></I>
```

Either method is acceptable, although the first probably makes a bit more sense to someone viewing your source document.

As usual, you must finish inside tags first and then close off outside tags. In the first example, the closing </I> tag should come before the </A> tag because the italics tag is the interior tag, and the <A> tag is acting as a container for the entire line. The <STRONG>, <BOLD>, and <TT> tags can be used the same way with hypertext links.

Hyperlinks can appear within the confines of any of the container tags that this book has described so far. The <PRE> tag, header tags, the special formatting tags (such as <ADDRESS>, <CITE>, and <CODE>), and the <P> tag can contain hyperlinks.

Hyperlinks in Context

This example shows you a few more ways to use emphasis tags with hyperlinks in an HTML document. For this example, give your HTML template a new name, and type Listing 11.1 between the <BODY> tags.

EXAMPLE

Listing 11.1: links.html: Creating Hyperlinks

```
<BODY>
<H2>Links</H2>
<ADDRESS>
Ann Navarro<BR>
Port Charlotte, FL<BR>
<A HREF="mailto:books@webgeek.com">books@webgeek.com</a><BR>
</ADDRESS>
<P>The HTML Writers Guild has a comprehensive
<A HREF="http://www.hwg.org/resources/">list of resources</A>
for HTML authors that you may find interesting.<BR>
<B>Yahoo!'s  <A HREF="http://dir.yahoo.com/new/"><I>What's New</I></A> keeps
you up to date on new Web sites being launched.</B></P>
<HR>
<P>The following table will lead you to some of my favorite links on a
variety of topics:
<PRE>
My Favorite Web Sites by Topic:
<B>Topic               Site</B>
Tech News     <A HREF="http://www.news.com">C¦Net's news.com</A>
Weather       <A HREF="http://www.weather.com">The Weather Channel/A>
Television    <A HREF="http://www.stargatesg-1.com">Showtime's Stargate SG-1
site</A>
</PRE>
</P>
<CITE>The opinions stated here do not reflect the preferences of
<A HREF="http://www.mcp.com">Macmillan Computer Publishing</A>.</CITE>
</BODY>
```

When displayed in a browser, all the links should appear properly formatted and ready for the user to click (see Figure 11.1).

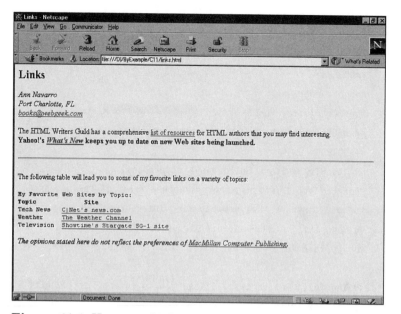

Figure 11.1: Hypertext links, formatted with other HTML tags.

Using Hypertext Links in HTML Lists

In Chapter 10, you saw an example of using the <DL> (definition list) tag to create a better organization for section links within a hypertext document. Like other types of HTML container tags, HTML lists can easily accept any sort of hypertext link as an <LI> (list item), <DT> (definition term), or <DD> (definition).

Any HTML list type that accepts the <LI> tag to create a new list item can include a hypertext link. An unordered (bullet-style) list can easily accept hypertext links by themselves, as the following example shows:

```
<UL>

<LI><A HREF="http://www.news.com">News.com</A>

<LI><A HREF="http://www.weather.com">The Weather Channel</A>

<LI><A HREF="http://www.stargatesg-1.com">Stargate SG-1</A>

</UL>
```

It can even accept hypertext links mixed with other text (see Figure 11.2):

```
<UL>

<LI>To see the latest in tech news, visit

<A HREF="http://www.news.com">News.com</A>.

<LI>For a look at your local forecast, visit
```

```
<A HREF="http://www.weather.com">The Weather Channel</A> before going out.
<LI>Science fiction fans often like to spend time at
<A HREF="http://www.stargatesg-1.com">Stargate SG-1</A>
</UL>
```

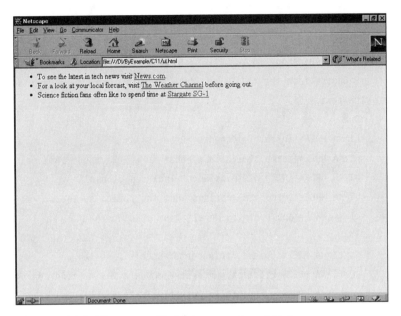

Figure 11.2: *Hypertext links in unordered lists.*

Adding hypertext links works just as easily with other HTML list types, including ordered (numbered) lists, menu lists, directory lists, and definition lists.

An HTML Table of Contents

EXAMPLE

One of the most common reasons for using a combination of HTML lists and hypertext links is to create a table of contents for a particularly long HTML site (or the HTML version of an academic thesis, scientific study, or book). Using nested HTML lists (like those that you created in Chapter 8, "Displaying Text in Lists"), you can add different levels of links under each subject heading in your outline.

Using your HTML template, create a new HTML document and enter Listing 11.2 or something similar. The results are shown in Figure 11.3.

Listing 11.2: listlink.html: HTML Table of Contents

```
<!DOCTYPE HTML PUBLIC "-//W3C//DTD HTML 4.0 Transitional//EN">
<HTML>
<HEAD>
<TITLE>Local Guide</TITLE>
</HEAD>
<BODY>
<H2>The Guidebook to Local Hangouts</H2>
<P>Choose from the following links to jump directly to that section of
the text:</P>
<OL>
<LI><A HREF="intro.html#thanks">Credits</A>
<LI><A HREF="intro.html#unique">What is unique about this guide?</A>
<LI><A HREF="intro.html#included">Included clubs</A>
<LI><A HREF="intro.html#ratings">How the rating system works</A>
<LI><A HREF="guide.html#general">Type of Club</A>
    <UL>
    <LI><A HREF="guide1.html#sports">Sports Bars</A>
    <LI><A HREF="guide1.html#country">Country (& Western) Bars</A>
    <LI><A HREF="guide.html#alternative">Alternative Bars</A>
    <LI><A HREF="guide.html#rock">Album/Hard Rock Clubs</A>
    <LI><A HREF="guide.html#jazz">Jazz & Classic Blues Bars</A>
    <LI><A HREF="guide.html#oldies">Big Band/Classical/Torchsong Bars</A>
    <LI><A HREF="guide.html#pool">Pool Halls</A>
    </UL>
<LI><A HREF="restaurant.html#general">Type of Restaurant</A>
</OL>
<BR>
</BODY>
</HTML>
```

A table of contents is a great excuse to use section tags, along with regular URLs, to access parts of remote documents. In the preceding example, the document guide.html contains information on all types of bars in the area, with each section being defined by an <A NAME=> tag. Using the tags enables your Web page users to access parts of the remote document directly.

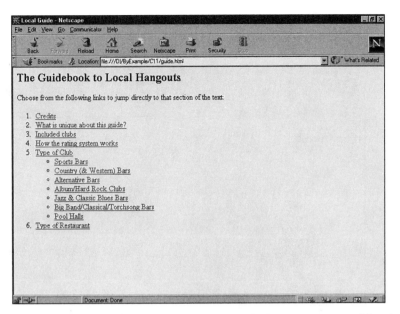

Figure 11.3: *Using lists and hypertext links to create a table of contents.*

Creating Graphical Links

Now you know that you can place a hypertext link inside nearly any other HTML container tag, and you know that different tags work well inside the anchor tag. What about graphics?

Graphics work as well as just about all other types of HTML tags. Simply by placing an <IMG> tag inside an anchor tag, you create a clickable image that can work in conjunction with the descriptive text in a link.

Consider the following example:

```
<A HREF="http://www.foo.com/"><IMG SRC="foocorp.gif"
ALT="Foo Corporation Logo"></A>
```

Notice that the example doesn't include any sort of descriptive text in the link. If a user's graphical viewer can support this type of image, the link displays the graphic with a colored border. Clicking the image sends the browser to the associated link. If the user isn't viewing this page with a graphical viewer, he sees the ALT text, which works as a hyperlink.

If you want, you can include text inside the anchor container, as follows:

```
<A HREF="http://www.foo.com/"> <IMG SRC="foocorp.gif"
ALT="Foo Corporation Logo">
Go to Foo Corporation's Web Site</A>
```

The descriptive text is displayed right next to the graphic image, and both the text and image are hyperlinks, as shown in Figure 11.4.

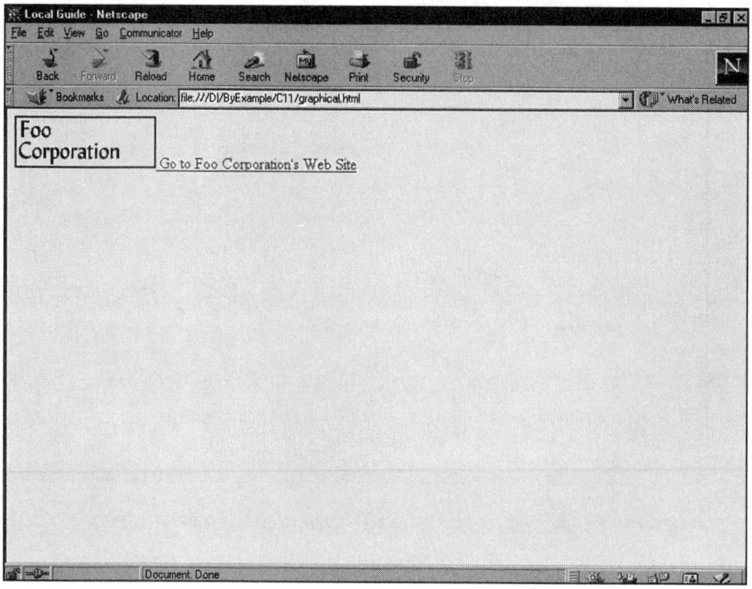

Figure 11.4: *A linked image with descriptive text that also serves as a link.*

A Graphical, Hyperlinked Listing

EXAMPLE

Another interesting use of lists and hypertext links features the <DL> list, with an interesting twist. This example throws in thumbnail versions of some graphics that suggest what the links access. The user can access a link by clicking the associated graphic.

This example shows a popular HTML menuing format: It gives you a low-bandwidth way to offer a visual reference for a database-style Web site. On a page such as this, you could include artwork, movie reviews, other Web sites, a company's products, a list of people, screen shots of computer programs, or just about anything else graphical.

Create a new HTML document from your template, and then enter text and tags according to the example shown in Listing 11.3.

Listing 11.3: linkmenu.html: Creating a Graphics Listing

```
<HTML>
<HEAD>
<TITLE>A menu of links</TITLE>
</HEAD>
<BODY>
```

```
<H2>Suggested Search and Directory Pages</H2>
<P>Ready to search the Net? Click the associated icon to jump to that particular
Web search page.</P>
<DL>
<DT><A HREF="http://www.yahoo.com"><IMG SRC="yahoo.gif" BORDER="0">
The Yahoo Directory</A>
<DD>Widely regarded as the earliest attempt to organize the Web, Yahoo! remains
a formidable directory of links to useful sites. Searching isn't as
comprehensive as some others, but the directory is often held to have great
quality of sites.
<DT><A HREF="http://www.lycos.com"><IMG SRC="lycos.gif" BORDER="0"> The Lycos
Search Engine</A>
<DD>Recently upgraded to include personalization, the Lycos site is often
considered one of the most comprehensive search engines around.
<DT><A HREF="http://www.excite.com"><IMG SRC="excite.gif" BORDER="0"> The Excite
Search Page</A>
<DD>Once considered Yahoo!'s main competitor, Excite has also diversified and
positions itself not only as a search tool, but as an entry portal for the Web
at large.
</DL>
</BODY>
</HTML>
```

The BORDER="0" attribute you see on each <IMG> tag removes the blue link border from around the images. Most Web users now recognize that you can click links, especially when the cursor changes as it hovers over the links. The presentation of this menu could be improved with tables, and the spacing could be improved by adding some more presentational markup, but you should get the general idea of using images to serve as links (see Figure 11.5).

EXAMPLE

A Clickable Graphic Menu Bar

Wrapping a hypertext anchor tag around a graphic allows you to do something else with graphical links: create clickable menu bars. You'll frequently see this style of interface on the Web. Menu bars are generally designed to allow you to access the most frequently sought pages or commands on a Web site. By lining up your graphical hyperlinks, you can create your own menu bars.

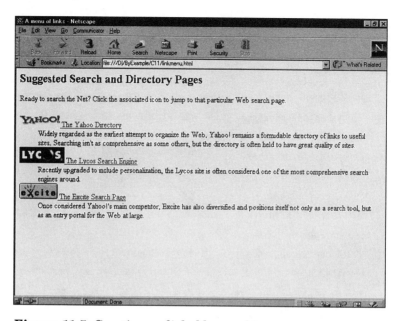

Figure 11.5: *Creating a clickable graphic menu.*

TIP

The key to a good menu bar is creating graphical buttons of uniform height. Some designers do this by creating one larger image and then breaking it into pieces using their image-editing software.

You start by creating a couple of button images in a graphics application. Save the images as GIF or JPEG files. Then create the menu bar in a new HTML file, as shown in Listing 11.4.

Listing 11.4: menubar.html: Creating a Graphical Menu Bar

```
<!DOCTYPE HTML PUBLIC "-//W3C//DTD HTML 4.0 Transitional//EN">
<HTML>
<HEAD>
<TITLE>A Sample Menu Bar</TITLE>
</HEAD>
<BODY>
<A HREF="feedback.html"><IMG SRC="feedback.gif" ALT="Give us Feedback"
BORDER="0"></A><A HREF="products.html"><IMG SRC="products.gif"
ALT="Our Products" BORDER="0"></A><A HREF="orders.html"><IMG SRC="orders.gif"
ALT="Place an Order" BORDER="0"></A><A HREF="support.html">
<IMG SRC="support.gif"
ALT="Get Support" BORDER="0"></A>
```

```
</BODY>
</HTML>
```

Notice that each graphic link is intentionally not on its own line. Although using separate lines would result in prettier code, some browsers *do* recognize the carriage return as a space, and you'd end up with a space between each image instead of a nice solid bar, as shown in Figure 11.6.

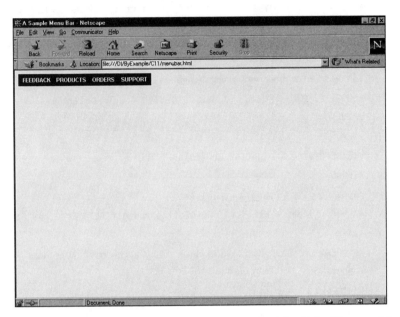

Figure 11.6: *A sample menu bar, created with clickable graphic links.*

Chapter 17, "Client-Side Image Maps" goes into further depth about creating a graphical interface for your Web site.

Custom Controls

The HTML isn't any different for this example, but it shows something else that you can do with graphical links: add custom controls (such as clickable arrows) to your Web site.

EXAMPLE

A good place to get started looking for some is with Yahoo!'s listing of icon sites: `http://dir.yahoo.com/Arts/Design_Arts/Graphic_Design/ Web_Page_Design_and_Layout/Graphics/Icons/`.

Suppose that you've decided you want to use directional arrows to lead visitors around your site. Start by either creating some arrow images that you want to use or downloading them from a public-domain graphics site on the Web. Then save your template as a new document and enter HTML text similar to Listing 11.5.

Listing 11.5: controls.html: Using Navigation Controls

```
<!DOCTYPE HTML PUBLIC "-//W3C//DTD HTML 4.0 Transitional//EN">
<HTML>
<HEAD>
<TITLE>Having Navigation Controls</TITLE>
</HEAD>
<BODY>
<A HREF="index.html"><IMG SRC="left-arrow.gif"ALT="Previous Page" HSPACE="10">
</A>
<A HREF="product2.html"><IMG SRC="right-arrow.gif" ALT="Next Page" ></A>
</BODY>
</HTML>
```

The HSPACE attribute in the first <IMG> tag surrounds the left-arrow image with 10 pixels worth of space measured horizontally. This results in a little "breathing room" between images. This example only places the arrows between the <BODY> tags. You probably have much more to say, but arrows tend to be attractive at the top of the page. Some people duplicate the arrows at the bottom of the page so that users can move on after reading everything.

It's important to realize that your pages will have to be fairly well organized for the arrows to be effective. If people are supposed to move through your site page by page, using arrows is a great idea. If your site is a little more relaxed, arrows may only confuse people. You can always use only the left arrow to provide a link back to your index or main page.

TIP

Also keep in mind that not everyone will come in to your site via the main page. Search engines now catalog nearly every page on a site, so there's no telling where a visitor might start out!

Using Hypermedia Links

You don't need to remember anything special about transferring multimedia files across the Internet, except for the fact that you need to use the correct transport protocol. In most cases, that just means using the `http://` protocol for transferring files that you expect the browser to hand off to a helper application.

For example, you could easily send a multimedia QuickTime movie from your Web page with the following link:

```
<A HREF="http://www.foo.com/videos/vacation.qt">Click to see my
vacation movie (218K)</A>
```

By the same token, you could use a relative link to the multimedia file by using the `<BASE>` tag or by putting the multimedia file in the same directory as the HTML document that includes the link, as follows:

```
<A HREF="vacation.qt">Click to see my vacation movie (218K)</A>
```

TIP

It's often considered good "netiquette" to include an estimate of the size of multimedia files so that users with slower modems can decide whether to spend time downloading the files.

Using what you've learned about clickable graphics, it's just as easy to include a small, single-frame graphic clip of your QuickTime movie in GIF or JPEG format to use as your link:

```
<A HREF="vacation.qt"><IMG SRC="vacation.jpg" ALT="My Vacation Movie">
(218K)</A>
```

Although you can send multimedia files by using the `ftp://` protocol, some browsers interpret this as an attempt to download the file to the user's computer without invoking the associated helper application (or without displaying the file using the browser's built-in capabilities).

Suppose that you have a graphics file that you want to display at full size in the browser window, instead of embedding the image in an HTML document. Create the following link:

```
<A HREF="http://www.foo.com/videos/photo.gif">Click here to see the full
512x240 image</A>
```

This link sends the graphic over the Web to the browser. The browser then attempts to display the full graphic in the browser window.

Now suppose that you use the FTP protocol instead, as shown in the following example:

```
<A HREF="ftp://ftp.foo.com/videos/photo.gif>Click here to see the full
512x240 image</A>
```

In most browsers, the user is prompted for a directory and filename to give the file when it arrives. The file is then saved to the user's hard drive but isn't displayed automatically.

In fact, such is the case with most multimedia files. The HTTP protocol suggests to the browser that it should display the file, if possible, or pass the file on to a helper application. The FTP protocol, on the other hand, causes some browsers to simply save the file to the hard drive.

NOTE

The FTP protocol doesn't always cause browsers to simply save the file. One notable exception is HTML documents themselves. Often, an FTP server can successfully serve HTML documents to a Web browser, which then displays the documents in the browser window.

What's Next?

This chapter took some of the things you've learned about hyperlinks, graphics, and hypermedia links and rolled them into one. Most of this material isn't new, but most of the ideas for using it are.

You can include hypertext links within most other HTML markup tags, or you can use HTML emphasis tags to mark up the descriptive text of most hypertext links. Remember to keep things organized and mark up your anchor text only for a good reason. Using lists, for example, you can create a table of contents that makes getting around a text-heavy site much easier.

When you put graphics and hypertext links together, ideas start to explode. You can create graphical menus, employ clickable menu bars, and add custom controls to your Web pages. Clickable graphics (especially thumbnail-style images) are among the easiest and most satisfying ways to enhance your Web site.

In Chapter 12, "Adding Tables to Your Documents," we'll move away from images and take another look at the structure of your content. HTML 4 provides complex functionality for presenting tabular data on the Web. You'll learn how to arrange and display a variety of information using these tags.

Review Questions

1. True or false: Like the <P> tag, the anchor (<A>) tag usually is displayed with a return after the closing </A> tag.

2. Can you mix hypertext and emphasis tags? If so, for what purpose?

3. What emphasis tag usually is redundant when it's used with an anchor tag?

4. Are any HTML list types incapable of accepting hypertext links as list items?

5. Is the following link correctly formatted? If so, what does it access?

```
<a href="chapter1.html#parttwo">Ch.1, Part II</A>
```

6. What might the following link be used for? Is this construct legal?

```
<A HREF="big-photo.gif"><IMG SRC="sm-photo.gif"></A>
```

7. What happens if a link uses the FTP protocol to transfer a multimedia file over the Web? Can the user still view or listen to the multimedia file?

Review Exercises

1. Create a "table of contents"-style page (using regular and section links) that loads a different document for each chapter or section of the document. For example, clicking the link Introduction would load the file intro.html into the browser window. Clicking the link Chapter 1.1 would load the link chapter1.html#section1, and so on.

2. Create a vertical (up-and-down) menu bar. (Hint: Use <BR> and graphics that are all the same width.) Can you get the images to touch (and appear seamless), as you can with a horizontal menu bar?

3. Using a <DL> (definition list) tag, create a "thumbnails" page of graphics (for a catalog, for instance). When users click one of the thumbnail graphics, take them to a product page with a larger graphic and a description of the product. Also, place a graphical button or arrow on the product page that lets them click to get back to the thumbnail view.

Part III

Interactive HTML

Adding Tables to Your Documents

HTML Forms

Form Design and Data Gathering with CGI Scripts

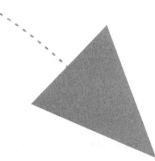

Adding Tables to Your Documents

Many chapters ago you learned to use the <PRE> tag to create preformatted tables that align your data and text for easy reading. The table functionality in HTML 4, however, takes you far beyond that. Tables are a great addition to any Web site—especially sites that need to offer a lot of information in an easy-to-read way.

HTML 4 even offers new features for tables that help text-based and speech-synthesizing browsers properly interpret tabular data. Let's take a closer look.

This chapter teaches you the following:

- The basic set of HTML tags used to structure tabular data

- How to enhance the visual presentation of tables using cell and content spacing or padding

- How to add images inside tables

Creating a Table

Tables work a lot like HTML list tags, in that you must use the table container tag to hold together a group of tags that define each individual row. The main container is the <TABLE> tag, which uses additional container tags for table rows <TR>) and table data (<TD>). Many tables also use an element for table headers (<TH>) that is generally used as the label for rows and columns. <CAPTION> provides a title for the entire table.

Tables have the following format:

```
<TABLE>
<CAPTION>Caption text for table</CAPTION>
<TR><TH>column1</TH><TH>column2</TH><TH>column3</TH></TR>
<TR><TD>row1data1</TD><TD>row1data2</TD><TD>row1data3</TD></TR>
<TR><TD>row2data1</TD><TD>row2data2</TD><TD>row2data3</TD></TR>
...
</TABLE>
```

EXAMPLE

Here's an example of a table using this format:

```
<TABLE>
<CAPTION>Team Members for 3-Person Basketball</CAPTION>
<TR><TH>Blue Team</TH><TH>Red Team</TH><TH>Green Team</TH></TR>
<TR><TD>Mike R.</TD><TD>Leslie M.</TD><TD>Rick G.</TD></TR>
<TR><TD>Julie M.</TD><TD>Walter R.</TD><TD>Dale W.</TD></TR>
<TR><TD>Bill H.</TD><TD>Jenny Q.</TD><TD>Fred B.</TD></TR>
</TABLE>
```

After you work with HTML list containers, it's fairly easy to make the jump to creating tables in HTML. You can see how this table looks in Figure 12.1.

The <TABLE> Tag

The <TABLE> tag is actually a rather complex creature, at least insofar as it can accept many different attributes. Some of the attributes are more useful than others, so let's look at the most useful of them as they currently stand:

- **WIDTH** Sets the relative or absolute width of your table in the browser window. Values can be either percentages, as in WIDTH="50%", or absolute values. With absolute values, the value is a number of pixels. Relative widths work best because they fill the same proportion of the available "screen real estate," regardless of the resolution any given user has set for her monitor.

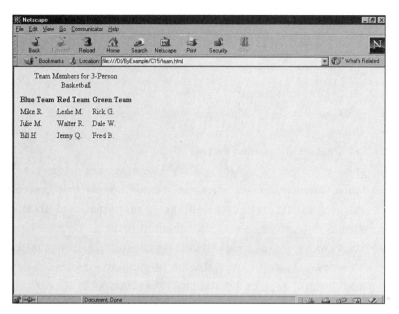

Figure 12.1: *A simple table in HTML.*

- **COLS**   Specifies the number of columns in your table, allowing the browser to draw the table as it downloads and to specify different behavior or presentation for the cells within a given column.

- **BORDER**   Defines the width of the border surrounding the table. The default value is 1 (pixel).

- **CELLSPACING**   Tells the browser how much space to include between the walls of the table and between individual cells. Think of this one as how big the "internal borders" of the table are. (The value is a number in pixels.)

- **CELLPADDING**   Tells the browser how much space to give data elements away from the walls of the cell. (The value is a number in pixels.)

It is definitely not necessary to use all of these attributes for your table—in fact, the simple table example earlier didn't use any of them. Often, however, they will come in handy.

Experimenting with Table Attributes

This is another fairly freeform example. Let's look at the difference between a plain table and a table embellished with a few attributes. Insert Listing 12.1 in a new HTML document.

EXAMPLE

Listing 12.1: badtable.html: Creating a Plain Table

```
<!DOCTYPE HTML PUBLIC "-//W3C//DTD HTML 4.0 Transitional//EN">
<HTML>
<HEAD>
<TITLE>BigCorp's Computer Systems</TITLE>
</HEAD>
<BODY>
<H2> BigCorp's Computer Systems </H2>
<P>We use only the highest quality components and software for all of our
Wintel computer systems. Plus, if you don't see a configuration you like,
call (or email) and let us know. We'll custom build to please!</P>
<TABLE>
<CAPTION>BigCorp's Computer Systems and Specifications</CAPTION>
<TR><TH>System 1</TH><TH>System 2</TH><TH>System 3</TH></TR>
<TR><TD>Intel Celeron 300 MHZ CPU</TD><TD>AMD K6-2 450 MHZ CPU</TD><TD>Intel
PIII 366 MHZ CPU</TD></TR>
<TR><TD>32 MB RAM</TD><TD>64 MB RAM</TD><TD>64 MB RAM</TD></TR>
<TR><TD>4.6 GB HD</TD><TD>13.2 GB HD</TD><TD>27.1 GB HD</TD></TR>
<TR><TD>56.7 Modem</TD><TD>56.7 Modem</TD><TD>ISDN Modem</TD></TR>
<TR><TD>desktop case</TD><TD>minitower case</TD><TD>tower case</TD></TR>
<TR><TD>Windows 98</TD><TD>Windows 98</TD><TD>Windows NT 4.0</TD></TR>
</TABLE>
</BODY>
```

Now, take a quick glance at how this looks in a browser (see Figure 12.2).

The first time we tried a simple table, it communicated its data well, but this one is fairly ineffective because everything is lined up so poorly. Using just the attributes mentioned, though, you can change this table so that it looks better to the user and is easier to read.

All that needs to change is the first <TABLE> tag:

```
<TABLE BORDER ="1" CELLSPACING="3" CELLPADDING="3">
```

That makes for a much nicer-looking table, complete with borders and lines for cells and a comfortable amount of spacing to separate cell data elements from one another (see Figure 12.3).

The rest of this example is up to you. Play with CELLSPACING and CELLPADDING without a border, for instance, or increase all values out of proportion. See the range of what's available to help you choose how to format your tables in the future.

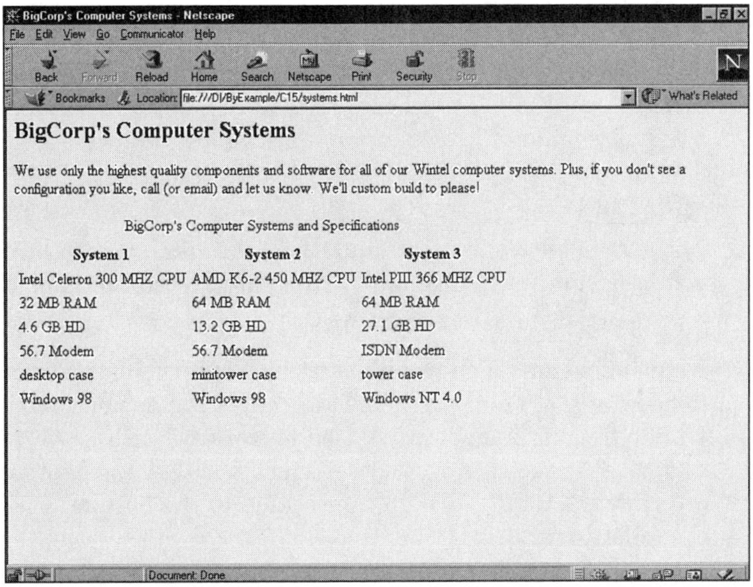

Figure 12.2: *A simple table, without attributes, can be difficult to read.*

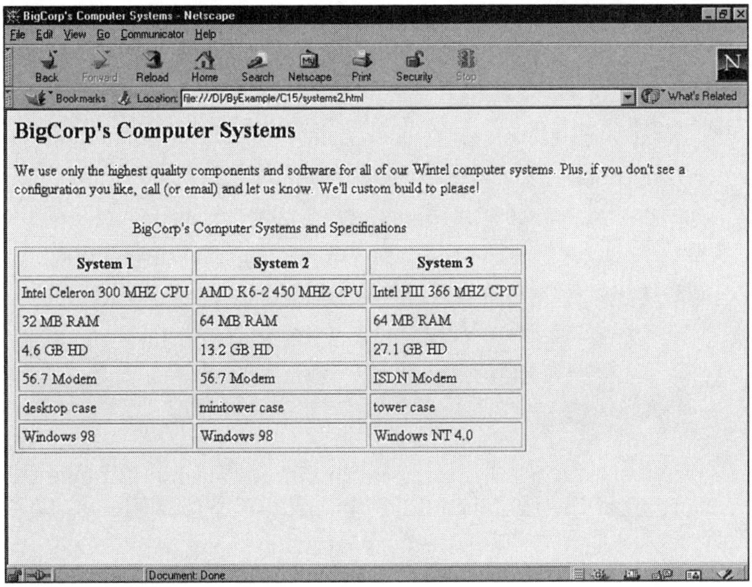

Figure 12.3: *Look how nice the table looks with spacing and borders.*

Captions, Table Headers, and Table Data

To round out your tables, you have the other basic tags to examine. You've already successfully used <CAPTION>, <TR>, and <TD>, but each has its own attributes and abilities that you need to know about.

<CAPTION>

The <CAPTION> tag is a container for reasons that may be obvious: it allows you to nest other HTML tags within the description. For instance:

```
<CAPTION><B>Table 3.1 from the book <I>Life in El Salvador</I></B></CAPTION>
```

Inline elements, such as emphasis and other font treatments, are possible inside the <CAPTION> tags. The <CAPTION> tag has one attribute, ALIGN. Unlike the alignment you're used to working with, <CAPTION> alignment is vertical. In other words, it determines whether the caption appears above or below the table. To align the caption to the bottom, for instance, enter the following:

```
<CAPTION ALIGN="BOTTOM">Table of Common Foods</CAPTION>
```

The <CAPTION> tag, when used, must be the first tag just inside the <TABLE> tag. You must use ALIGN if you want to put the caption at the bottom of the table. Otherwise, it will appear at the top, according to its default.

Let's create an entire table and use the ALIGN attribute to make the caption appear at the bottom:

```
<H2>Favorite Ice Cream Flavors</H2>
```

EXAMPLE

```
<TABLE BORDER="1">
<CAPTION ALIGN="BOTTOM">Data from the <I>New Jersey Times</I></CAPTION>
<TR><TH>Date</TH><TH>Chocolate</TH><TH>Vanilla</TH></TR>
<TR><TH>1970</TH><TD>50%</TD><TD>50%</TD></TR>
<TR><TH>1980</TH><TD>76%</TD><TD>24%</TD></TR>
<TR><TH>1990</TH><TD>40%</TD><TD>60%</TD></TR>
</TABLE>
```

When the browser interprets this table, it should place the caption at the bottom of the table, centered horizontally (see Figure 12.4).

Table Rows

Individual table rows (>> tag><TR>) can acan also accept the ALIGN attribute. It is used to determine how text will appear (horizontally) in each

EXAMPLE of the row's cells. For instance:

```
<TR ALIGN="CENTER"><TH>Date</TH><TH>Chocolate</TH><TH>Vanilla</TH></TR>
<TR ALIGN="CENTER"><TH>1970</TH><TD>50%</TD><TD>50%</TD></TR>
```

```
<TR ALIGN="CENTER"><TH>1980</TH><TD>76%</TD><TD>24%</TD></TR>

<TR ALIGN="CENTER"><TH>1990</TH><TD>40%</TD><TD>60%</TD></TR>
```

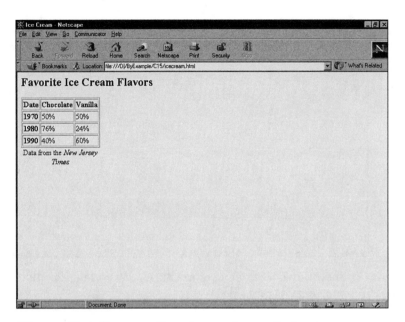

Figure 12.4: *You can align the caption to the bottom.*

Here, I've added the ALIGN attribute (with a value of CENTER) to the rows in the previous example. Notice now that all cells align data horizontally to the center (see Figure 12.5). This ALIGN attribute can also accept LEFT and RIGHT.

A second alignment method is also available in table rows: the VALIGN attribute for vertical alignment. This attribute accepts values of TOP, BOTTOM, and MIDDLE.

Table Data and Rows

The actual table content is placed within individual table cells using the <TD> tag. TD stands for table data.

Aside from accepting nearly any type of HTML markup tags, <TD> tags have four common attributes. These are ALIGN, VALIGN, COLSPAN, and ROWSPAN. If you were to add all these attributes, a typical <TD> tag would be formatted like this:

```
<TD ALIGN="direction" VALIGN="direction" COLSPAN="number" ROWSPAN="number">
```

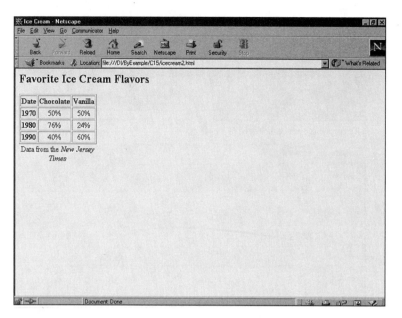

Figure 12.5: *This table uses the* ALIGN *attribute with* <TR>. *(Compare this figure to Figure 12.4.)*

EXAMPLE

ALIGN is used to align the data within the cell horizontally, accepting values of LEFT, RIGHT, and CENTER. Note that ALIGN is redundant when used with the ALIGN attribute of <TR>, unless it is used to override the <TR ALIGN=> setting.

VALIGN is used to align the data vertically within cells. Possible values are TOP, BOTTOM, and MIDDLE.

COLSPAN and ROWSPAN are used to force a cell to span more than one column or row, respectively. An example of this might be the following:

```
<TABLE BORDER="1">
<TR><TH>Student</TH><TH>Test 1</TH><TH>Test 2</TH><TH>Average</TH>
<TR><TH>Mike M.</TH><TD>100</TD><TD>75</TD><TD ROWSPAN="3">N/A</TD>
<TR><TH>Susan T.</TH><TD>80</TD><TD>95</TD>
<TR><TH>Bill Y.</TH><TD COLSPAN="2">Dropped Course</TD>
</TABLE>
```

Viewed in a browser, the table looks like Figure 12.6.

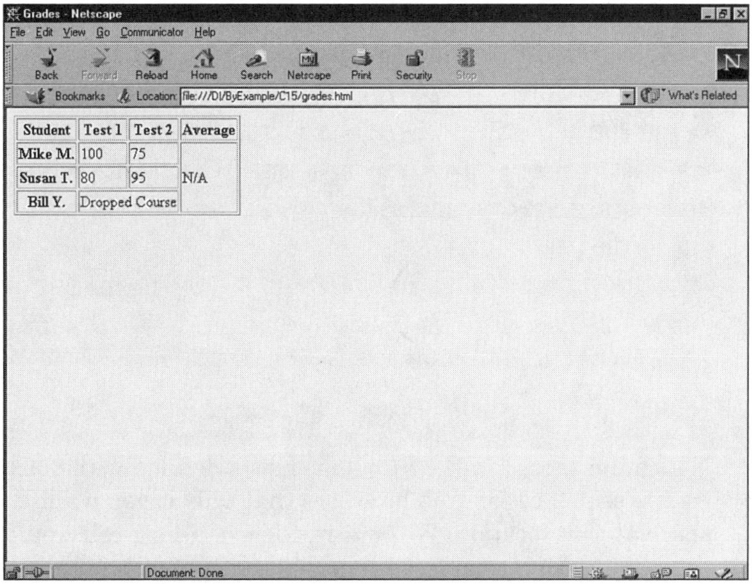

Figure 12.6: Using COLSPAN *and* ROWSPAN *in a table.*

EXAMPLE

An Events Calendar

One interesting way to use a table is to create a calendar. This is possible with what you now know about attributes for tables and table elements. Let's create a calendar for March 2000. We'll also throw in some hypertext links that would (presumably) be used to note events planned for those days. Enter Listing 12.2 in a new HTML document.

Listing 12.2: events.html: Using HTML Tables to Create a Calendar

```
<BODY>
<H2>Coming Events</H2>
<P>Click any of the days highlighted in the calendar to read about the event
scheduled for that day.</P>
<TABLE BORDER="1" WIDTH="75%">
<CAPTION>BigCorp's Calendar of Events - March 2000</CAPTION>
<TR ALIGN="CENTER"><TH>Sun</TH><TH>Mon</TH><TH>Tue</TH><TH>Wed</TH><TH>Thu</TH>
<TH>Fri</TH><TH>Sat</TH>
<TR ALIGN="CENTER"><TD COLSPAN="3"> </TD><TD>1</TD><TD>2</TD><TD>3</TD>
<TD>4</TD></TR>
<TR ALIGN="CENTER"><TD>5</TD><TD>6</TD><TD>7</TD><TD>8</TD><TD>9</TD>
<TD>10</TD><TD><A HREF="nov11.html">11</A></TD></TR>
```

continues

Listing 12.2: continued

```
<TR ALIGN="CENTER"><TD>12</TD><TD>13</TD><TD>
<A HREF="nov14.html">14</A></TD><TD>15</TD><TD>16</TD><TD>
<A HREF="nov17.html">17</A></TD><TD>18</TD></TR>
<TR ALIGN="CENTER"><TD>19</TD><TD><A HREF="nov20.html">20</A></TD><TD>21</TD>
<TD>22</TD><TD>23</TD><TD>24</TD>
<TD>25</TD></TR>
<TR ALIGN="CENTER"><TD>26</TD><TD>27</TD><TD>28</TD><TD>29</TD>
<TD>30</TD><TD>31</TD></TR>
</TABLE>
</BODY>
```

Notice the   in the <TD> tag that is defined with COLSPAN? This is an escape sequence for Web browsers that tells it you want a non line-breaking space at that location. Without it, the extra-long cell wouldn't be rendered correctly (with a complete border) because there's nothing in that cell. With it, this table looks like a calendar (see Figure 12.7).

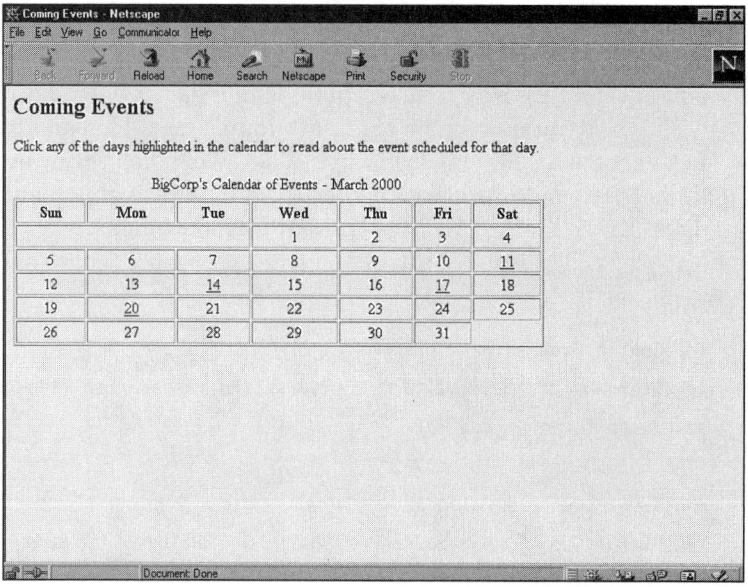

Figure 12.7: Creating a calendar with HTML table tags.

Product Details

One thing that hasn't really been touched on so far is the possibility of including images in tables. It's definitely possible, and it's just about as easy as anything else you've done with tables.

In this example, let's create a product details table for a couple of books published by Macmillan Computer Publishing. With liberal use of the ALIGN and VALIGN attributes, this table should come out looking rather pretty. Insert Listing 12.3 into a new HTML document.

Listing 12.3: aligntbl.html: Using ALIGN and VALIGN with Images in an HTML Table

```
<BODY>
<H2>New Releases</H2>
<P>The following table will tell you a little more about some of MCP's recent
titles.</P>
<HR>
<TABLE BORDER CELLSPACING="2" CELLPADDING="2">
<CAPTION>New Releases</CAPTION>
<TR ALIGN="CENTER"><TH>Cover Photo</TH><TH>Title</TH><TH>Series</TH>
<TH>User Level</TH></TR>
<TR ALIGN="CENTER"><TD VALIGN="MIDDLE"><IMG SRC="fixing.jpg"></TD><TD><A
HREF="fixing.html">
Complete Idiot's Guide to Fixing Your #$%@ PC</A></TD>
<TD ROWSPAN="2">Complete Idiot's Guide</TD><TD ROWSPAN="2">New/Casual</TD></TR>
<TR ALIGN="CENTER"><TD VALIGN="MIDDLE"><IMG SRC="webtv.jpg"></TD><TD><A
HREF="webtv.html">
Complete Idiot's Guide to Surfing the Internet with WebTV</A></TD></TR>
<TR ALIGN="CENTER"><TD VALIGN="MIDDLE"><IMG SRC="vb.jpg"></TD><TD><A
HREF="vb.html">
Practical Visual Basic 6</A></TD><TD>Practical...</TD><TD>Accomplished</TD></TR>
</TABLE>
</BODY>
```

Graphics look very nice in tables, and they work well to enliven what would otherwise be drier, text-heavy information (such as computer specs). I've offered some creative uses of attributes in this example, and I think it was worth it (see Figure 12.8).

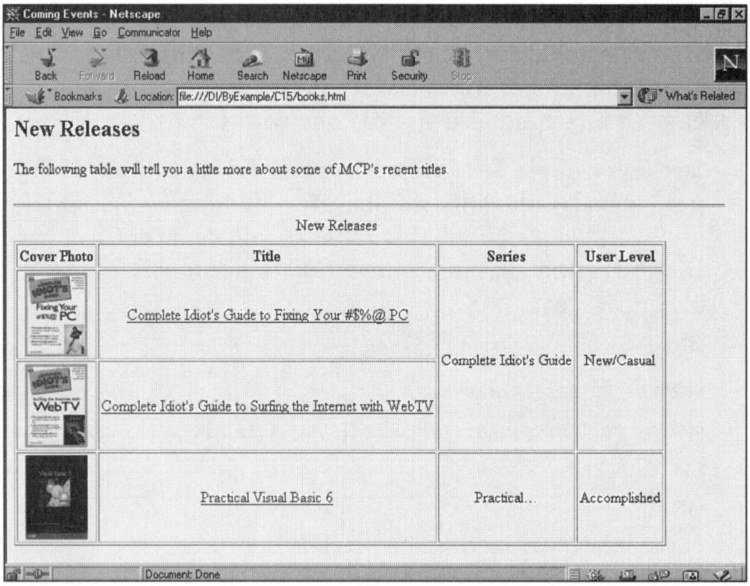

Figure 12.8: *A very complete custom HTML table.*

What's Next?

Tables are an incredible leap over the <PRE> tag for formatting HTML text. The basic tags—<TABLE>, <CAPTION>, <TR>, <TD>, and <TH>—give you everything you need to build an impressive, easy-to-read table for data elements.

Building on those tags, you can add formatting to rows, cells, and individual text. You can also add just about any conceivable type of HTML markup to your table data. You can even include graphics and hypertext links to take tables to a higher level.

Next up in Chapter 13, "HTML Forms," we'll move beyond Web pages that simply present information to your visitors and into pages that can actually collect information from them. HTML has a collection of tags used to create forms. Users can enter text, choose from a set of options using checkboxes, and select options from familiar "pull-down" lists. You'll learn how to construct these forms and gather the information submitted by the visitor.

Review Questions

1. In what unit is the number value measured in the attribute definition WIDTH="500" for the <TABLE> tag?

2. What's the difference between the attributes CELLPADDING and CELLSPACING?

3. True or false: You must always define a value for the BORDER attribute to the <TABLE> tag.

4. If I had the following example, where would the <CAPTION> text appear relative to the table?

```
<TABLE>
<CAPTION>My favorite foods</CAPTION>
<TR><TH>Soup</TH><TD>Chicken Noodle</TD>
<TR><TH>Salad</TH><TD>Tossed Green</TD>
</TABLE>
```

5. Is it possible to ALIGN all of the data cells in a particular row using the <TR> tag?

6. What happens in the following example?

```
<TD>Ted David<BR>Mike Rogers<BR>Bill Howell</TD>
```

7. Which is used for horizontal alignment when used as an attribute to the <TD> tag, ALIGN or VALIGN?

8. What possible reason could there be to force a <TD ALIGN> tag definition to override a <TR ALIGN> tag?

Review Exercises

1. Create a caption, aligned to the bottom of the table, that includes an image. Does it work correctly?

2. Create a table that uses images as the column headers.

3. Create a table of "thumbnail" images, with a small image, a description of the image, and the image's filename in each row. Make each image clickable so that a larger image appears (on a new page) when the user clicks the thumbnail.

4. Create a table with no visible border (BORDER="0"). With this kind of table, it's possible to lay out very intricate pages with text and graphics aligned to the left or right of the page. Use the table to place a paragraph of text on the left side of the page and three clickable graphics on the right side. (Hint: Use ROWSPAN on the paragraph's cell.)

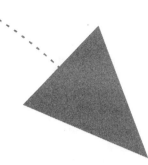

HTML Forms

The next set of HTML tags is designed to allow you to enhance the interactivity of your Web pages by increasing your ability to request information from users. Using the forms tags, you can ask users to enter text information, choose from menus, mark checkboxes, make choices from radio buttons, and then send that information to the Web server for processing.

The idea behind a Web form is simple: It allows you to accept information or answers from your users with varying levels of guidance. Users can be asked to type answers, choose their answers from a list of possibilities you create, or even be limited to choosing one answer from a number of options that you specify.

That data is then passed on to the Web server, which hands it to a script, or small program, designed to act on the data and (in most cases) create an HTML page in response. In order to deal with forms data, you need to understand a little something about scripting, or programming, for a Web server—or know someone who does. Although learning to program is beyond the scope of this book, we'll look at how these scripts work in Chapter 14, "Form Design and Data Gathering with CGI Scripts."

NOTE

Most Web server scripts are written in Perl, C, or UNIX shell scripts. If your Web server is Windows-based, however, you may have other options. Some Windows Web servers can accept Visual Basic applications as CGI scripts (not to be confused with Microsoft's new Visual Basic Script language).

This chapter teaches you the following:

- How a form is able to pass data back to the site owner

- What tags are used to create common input features

- How to match the data you want to collect with the correct input control

- How to send form data using email

Creating the Form

In an HTML document, forms are set between the <FORM> container tags. The <FORM> container works as follows:

```
<FORM METHOD="how_to_send" ACTION="URL of script">
...form data...
</FORM>
```

Notice that the <FORM> tag takes two attributes: METHOD and ACTION. The METHOD attribute accepts either POST or GET as its value. POST is by far the more popular because it allows for a greater amount of data to be sent. GET is a little easier for Web programmers to deal with and is best used with single responses, such as a single textbox.

The second attribute is ACTION, which simply accepts the URL for the script that will process the data from your form. Most often the script is stored in a directory called bin/ or cgi-bin/ located on your Web server.

EXAMPLE

Here's an example of the <FORM> tag:

```
<FORM METHOD="POST" ACTION="http://www.foo.com/cgi-bin/register.cgi">
</FORM>
```

As with any HTML container tag, this implementation of the <FORM> tag has actually created a complete form (just as <P> and </P> are a complete paragraph). Unfortunately, our complete form doesn't do anything yet, so it's not terribly useful.

NOTE

You can't nest forms within one another. You need to add the end tag </FORM> for the first form before creating another one in the same document. Generally, browsers will ignore any new occurrences of the <FORM> tag because the purpose of the tag is to tell the browser how to submit data to the server, and different parts of the form can't be submitted in different ways.

EXAMPLE

A Simple Form Application

Let's take a quick look at a form that's been created by someone else—one that many Web enthusiasts have encountered at one time or another. Load your Web browser and point it to http://www.m-w.com/.

This is the WWWebster page, an online dictionary and thesaurus offered by Merriam-Webster. Your next step is to view the source of this document. From your Web browser, select Edit, View Document Source. You'll need to scroll down a bit to get past the table code, but soon you'll see the opening <FORM> tag, and you'll know you're in the right spot. What you see will look something like Figure 13.1.

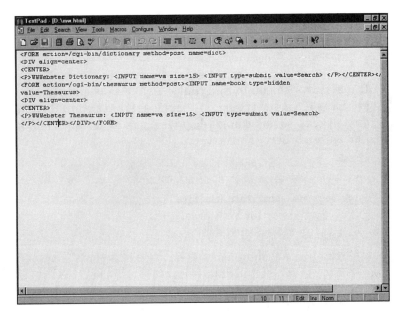

Figure 13.1: *An example of an HTML form available on the Web.*

NOTE

If you're not sure how to "view source," look at your browser's menu options. In Netscape 4.7 for Windows, there's a View menu item right on the menu bar.

Notice a couple of things here. The <FORM> tag at WWWebster is using the ACTION and METHOD attributes that were discussed. ACTION is accessing a script called dictionary found in the cgi-bin/ directory of the Web server. The METHOD used is POST.

TIP

Although you shouldn't copy others' work, don't forget that you can always use the View Source command to learn how something was done on the Web. Just be sure to be respectful of the intellectual property rights and copyrights of others.

Text Fields and Attributes

One of the more common uses for forms is to accept multiple lines of text from a user, perhaps for feedback, bug reports, or other uses. To do this, use the <TEXTAREA> tag within your form. You can set this tag to control the number of rows and columns it displays, although it will generally accept as many characters as the user wants to enter. It takes the following form:

```
<TEXTAREA NAME="variable_name" ROWS="number" COLS="number">
default text
</TEXTAREA>
```

EXAMPLE

It may surprise you to find that `<TEXTAREA>` is a container tag because it just puts a box for typing on the page. What's contained in the tag is the default text, so you can guide your users by letting them know what you'd like entered there. For instance:

```
<FORM>
<TEXTAREA NAME="comments" ROWS="4" COLS="40">
Enter comments about this Web site.
Good or Bad.
</TEXTAREA>
</FORM>
```

The default text appears in the textbox just as typed. Notice in Figure 13.2 that text inside the `<TEXTAREA>` tag works like `<PRE>` formatted text. Any returns or spaces you add to the text are displayed in the browser window.

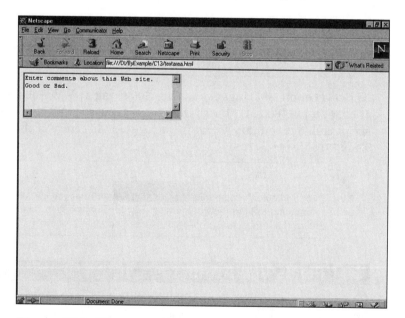

Figure 13.2: *The* `<TEXTAREA>` *tag in action.*

The NAME attribute is a variable name for this string of text. It gets passed on to your processing script on the Web server. ROWS and COLS can accept different numbers to change the size of the text area box, but you should take care that the majority of browsers can see the entire box onscreen.

It's best to limit COLS to 80 and ROWS to something like 24 (the typical size for a text-based computer screen). But it's up to you.

EXAMPLE

A Web-Based Feedback Form

I mentioned before that <TEXTAREA> is commonly used to gather feedback from your Web users. To create a small form to do just that, save your default template as a new HTML document and enter the following:

```
<BODY>
<H3>Feedback Form</H3>
<P>Please take a moment to tell us what you thought of the Web site.<BR>
Your Feedback is appreciated!</P>
<FORM METHOD="POST" ACTION="cgi-bin/feedback">
Enter your comments below:<BR>
<TEXTAREA NAME="comments" ROWS="10" COLS="70">
Dear BigCorp:
</TEXTAREA>
</FORM>
</BODY>
```

You can see how this looks in Figure 13.3. Notice in the example that some descriptive text is enclosed inside the <FORM> tag but outside of the <TEXTAREA> tag. This is completely legal; it just lets you explain what the purpose of the text area is.

You may have realized that there's something lacking in this sample form. There's no way to submit the user's entry! You'll get to that in the next section, when I discuss the tag for form entry.

The <INPUT> Tag

Our next tag for HTML forms gives you the opportunity to be a bit more picky about the type of input you'll accept from the user. The <INPUT> tag has this format:

```
<INPUT TYPE="type_of_input" NAME="variable" SIZE="number" MAXLENGTH="number">
```

Technically, the only required attributes are TYPE and NAME. Some other "types" of the <INPUT> tag also accept the attribute VALUE. First let's look at the different types of <INPUT>.

NOTE

By the way, notice that <INPUT> is an empty tag. There's no </INPUT> element.

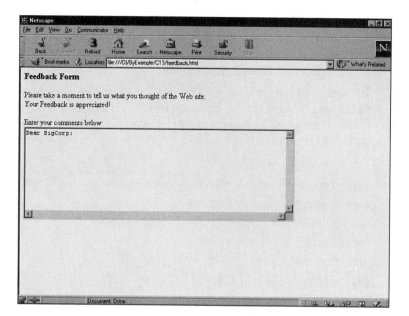

Figure 13.3: *A sample text area HTML form.*

TEXT

The first possible value for the TYPE attribute is TEXT, which creates a single-line textbox of a length you choose. Note that the length of the box and the maximum length entered by the user can be set separately. It's possible to have a box longer (or, more often, shorter) than the maximum number of characters you allow to be entered. Here's an example of a textbox:

```
Last name: <INPUT TYPE="TEXT" NAME="LastName" SIZE="40" MAXLENGTH="40">
```

When appropriately entered between <FORM> tags, this <INPUT> yields a box similar to Figure 13.4. If you want, you can use the attribute VALUE to give the textbox a default entry, as in the following example:

```
Type of Computer: <INPUT TYPE="TEXT" NAME="computer" SIZE="50" MAXLENGTH="50"
VALUE="Pentium">
```

PASSWORD

The PASSWORD option is nearly identical to the TEXT option, except that, when letters are typed, it displays asterisks or something similar (chosen by the browser) to keep the words from being read. A sample password box could be the following:

```
Enter Password: <INPUT TYPE="PASSWORD" NAME="password" SIZE="25" MAXLENGTH="25">
```

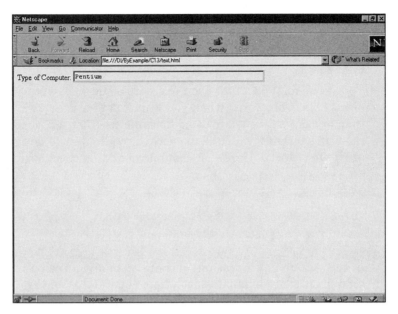

Figure 13.4: *Using the* TEXT *option with the* TYPE *attribute.*

When characters are typed into this textbox, they appear onscreen as shown in Figure 13.5.

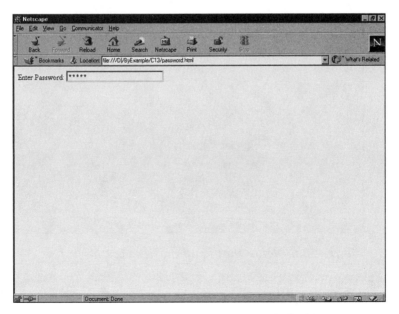

Figure 13.5: PASSWORD *hides text from people looking over your user's shoulder.*

Recognize that the text is still stored as the text typed by the user—not as asterisks or other masking characters.

EXAMPLE

CHECKBOX

This value for TYPE allows you to create a checkbox-style interface for your form. This is best used when you want to allow your visitor to choose more than one option. You can also determine whether a checkbox will already be checked (so that it must be unchecked by the user, if desired) by using the attribute CHECKED. Here's an example of adding checkboxes to a form:

```
Type of computer(s) you own:<BR>
<INPUT TYPE="CHECKBOX" NAME="P3" CHECKED> Pentium III
<INPUT TYPE="CHECKBOX" NAME="P2"> Pentium II
<INPUT TYPE="CHECKBOX" NAME="Macintosh"> Macintosh
```

In this example, it's possible to check as many of the options as are presented. CHECKBOX evaluates each item separately from any others. Figure 13.6 illustrates how CHECKBOX is displayed in a browser.

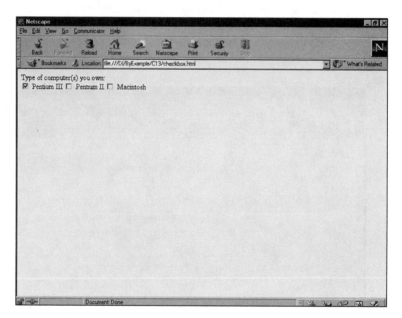

Figure 13.6: *Notice that Pentium III is prechecked.*

RADIO

Like CHECKBOX, RADIO is designed to offer your user a choice from predetermined options. Unlike CHECKBOX, however, RADIO is designed to accept only one response from among its options. RADIO uses the same attributes and basic format as CHECKBOX.

EXAMPLE

RADIO requires that you use the VALUE attribute and that the NAME attribute be the same for all the \<INPUT\> tags that are intended for the same group. VALUE, on the other hand, should be different for each choice. For instance, look at the following example:

```
Choose the computer type you use most often:<BR>
<INPUT TYPE="RADIO" NAME="Computer" VALUE="P" CHECKED> Pentium
<INPUT TYPE="RADIO" NAME="Computer" VALUE="4"> 486-Series PC
<INPUT TYPE="RADIO" NAME="Computer" VALUE="M"> Macintosh
<INPUT TYPE="RADIO" NAME="Computer" VALUE="O"> Other
```

With RADIO, it's important to assign a default value because it's possible that the user will simply skip the entry altogether. Although the user can't check more than one, she can check none. So, choose the most common value and set it as CHECKED, just so that the form-processing script doesn't have trouble.

It's also important to notice that the value of the NAME attribute is the same for each radio button. This is necessary to allow the script to know that each one belongs to the same radio button group.

HIDDEN

This \<INPUT\> type technically isn't "input" at all. Rather, it's designed to pass some sort of value along to the Web server and script. It's generally used to send a keyword, validation number, or some other kind of string to the script so that the script knows it's being accessed by a valid (or just a particular) Web page. The \<INPUT TYPE="Hidden"\> tag takes the attributes NAME and VALUE.

NOTE

This isn't terribly covert because an intrepid user could simply choose View Source to see the value of the hidden field. It's more useful from a programmer's standpoint. For instance, on a large Web site, the hidden value might tell a multipurpose script which particular form (among many) is sending the data so that the script knows how to process the data.

EXAMPLE

RESET

The <INPUT> tag has built into it the ability to clear an HTML form. RESET simply creates a push button (named with the VALUE string) that resets all the elements in that particular FORM to their default values (erasing anything that the user has entered). Here's an example:

```
<INPUT TYPE="RESET">
```

With a VALUE statement, you could enter the following:

```
<INPUT TYPE="RESET" VALUE="Reset the Form">
```

The results are shown in Figure 13.7.

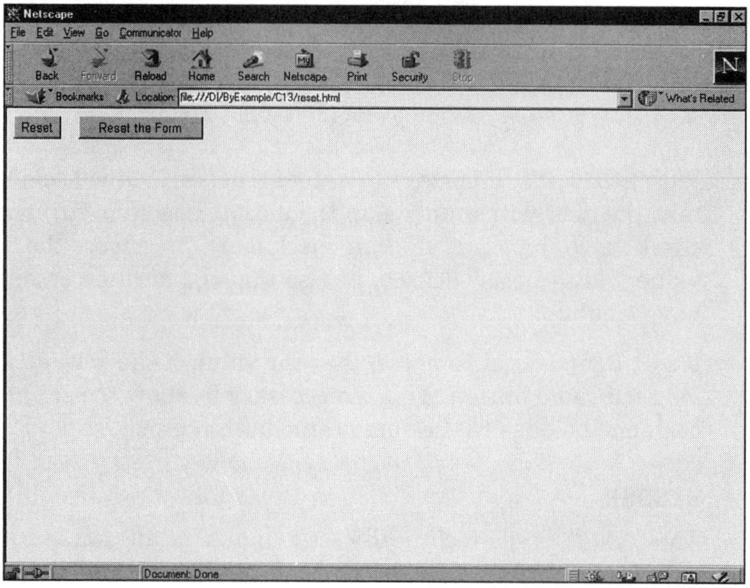

Figure 13.7: *Default and* VALUE-*attributed Reset buttons.*

SUBMIT

The <INPUT> tag also has a type that automatically submits the data that's been entered into the HTML form. The SUBMIT type accepts only the attribute VALUE, which can be used to rename the button. Otherwise, the only purpose of the Submit button is to send off all the other form information that's been entered by your user. See the following two examples, shown in Figure 13.8:

```
<INPUT TYPE="SUBMIT">
```

```
<INPUT TYPE="SUBMIT" VALUE="Send it in!">
```

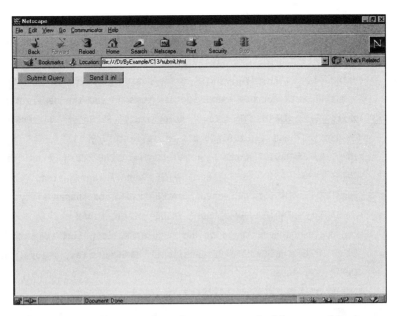

Figure 13.8: *The complete form as seen in Netscape Navigator.*

You can use just about anything you want for the VALUE, although it's best to remember that really small words, such as OK, don't look great as buttons.

A More Complete Form

Along with all the other <INPUT> types, now you've finally got a way to submit data. So, let's create a more involved form that includes some of these examples—a subscription form.

EXAMPLE

Save your HTML template to create a new document. Then, enter something similar to Listing 13.1.

Listing 13.1: sub-form.html: Creating a Complete Form

```
<BODY>
<H2>Subscribe to CorpWorld</H2>
<P>Interested in receiving daily email updates of all the latest exploits of
BigCorp? Well, now you can. And, best of all, it's free! Just fill out this form
and submit it by clicking the "Send it In" button. We'll put you on our mailing
list, and you'll receive your first email in 3-5 days.</P>
<FORM METHOD="Send" ACTION="http://www.fakecorp.com/cgi-bin/subscribe.cgi">
Please complete all of the following:<BR>
```

continues

Listing 13.1: continued

```
First Name: <INPUT TYPE="Text" Name="first" SIZE="25" MAXLENGTH="24"><BR>
Last Name:  <INPUT TYPE="Text" Name="last" SIZE="35" MAXLENGTH="34"><BR>
Business:   <INPUT TYPE="Text" Name="business" SIZE="50" MAXLENGTH="49"><BR>
We must have a correct email address to send you the newsletter:<BR>
Email:      <INPUT TYPE="Text" Name="email" SIZE="50" MAXLENGTH="49"><BR>
How did you hear about BigCorp's email letter?<BR>
<INPUT TYPE="RADIO" NAME="hear" VALUE="web" CHECKED>Here on the Web
<INPUT TYPE="RADIO" NAME="hear" VALUE="mag">In a magazine
<INPUT TYPE="RADIO" NAME="hear" VALUE="paper">Newspaper story
<INPUT TYPE="RADIO" NAME="hear" VALUE="other">Other
<BR> Would you care to be on our regular mailing list?<BR>
<INPUT TYPE="CHECKBOX" NAME="snailmail" CHECKED> Yes, I love junk mail<BR>
<INPUT TYPE="RESET">
<INPUT TYPE="SUBMIT" VALUE="Send it in!">
</FORM>
</BODY>
```

Figure 13.9 shows how this looks on a Web page. (You'll get to straightening everything out and making it look great in Chapter 14.)

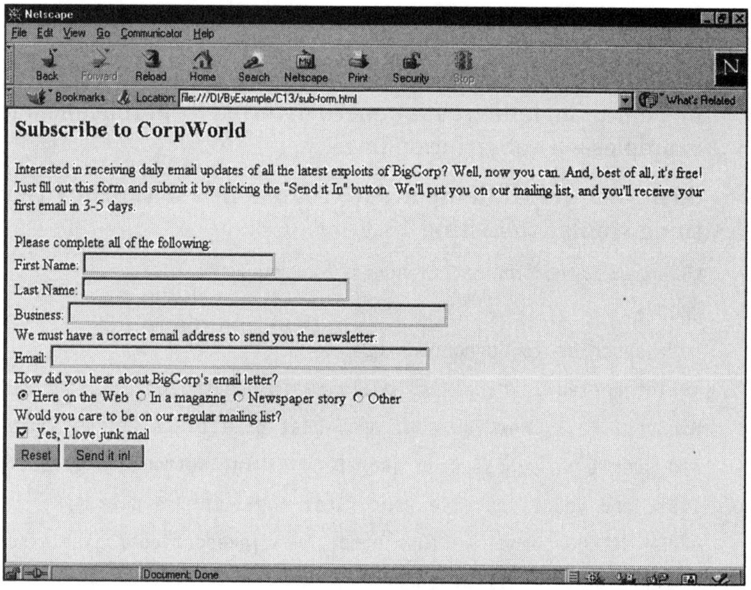

Figure 13.9: *Creating a Submit button.*

Creating Pop-Up and Scrolling Menus

The last types of input that you can offer to users of your Web page revolve around the <SELECT> tag, which can be used to create different types of pop-up and scrolling menus. This is another element designed specifically to let users make a choice; they can't enter their own text. The <SELECT> tag requires a NAME attribute and allows you to decide how many options to display at once with the SIZE attribute.

Using <SELECT>

Note that, like <TEXTAREA>, <SELECT> is a container tag. Options are placed between the two <SELECT> tags, each with a particular VALUE that gets associated with <SELECT>'s NAME attribute when chosen. The following is the basic format:

```
<SELECT NAME="variable">
<OPTION VALUE="value"> Menu text
<OPTION VALUE="value"> Menu text

...

</SELECT>
```

EXAMPLE

The value can be anything you want to pass on to the Web server and associated script for processing. An example might be the following:

```
Choose your favorite food:
<SELECT NAME="food">
<OPTION VALUE="ital"> Italian
<OPTION VALUE="texm"> TexMex
<OPTION VALUE="stek"> SteakHouse
<OPTION VALUE="chin"> Chinese
</SELECT>
```

You can also use the SIZE attribute to display the menu in its entirety. Simply change the first line of the example to the following:

```
<SELECT NAME="food" SIZE="4">
```

Both examples are shown in Figure 13.10.

In the first example, selecting the menu item with the mouse cursor causes the menu to pop up on the page. The user can then select from the choices. In the second example, the user must click the desired item.

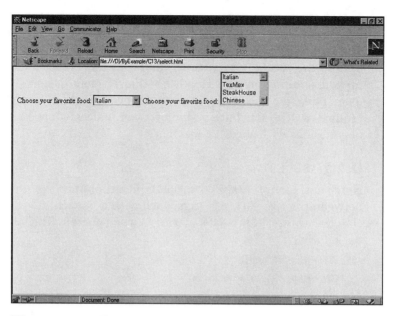

Figure 13.10: *Two* <SELECT> *menus—a pop-up and a fixed.*

EXAMPLE

Allowing More Than One Selection

One more attribute for the <SELECT> tag allows the user to select more than one option from the menu. Using the MULTIPLE attribute forces the menu to display in its entirety, regardless of the SIZE attribute. An example might be the following (the result appears in Figure 13.11):

```
What type of cars does your family own (select as many as apply)?
<SELECT NAME="cars" MULTIPLE>
<OPTION VALUE="sedan"> Sedan
<OPTION VALUE="coupe"> Coupe
<OPTION VALUE="mivan"> Minivan
<OPTION VALUE="covan"> Conversion Van
<OPTION VALUE="statn"> Stationwagon
<OPTION VALUE="sport"> SUV (4x4)
<OPTION VALUE="truck"> Other Truck
</SELECT>
```

EXAMPLE

An Order Form

With all these possibilities for the form, you can manage some fairly complete data entry interfaces for users. Consider this one: an online order form. Used in conjunction with a secure Web site, this form could be used to process purchase orders over the Internet.

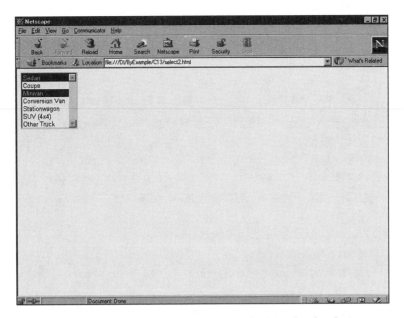

Figure 13.11: *A* <SELECT> *menu can allow multiple choices.*

Save your template as a new HTML file and enter Listing 13.2's sample text between the <BODY> tags.

Listing 13.2: order-form.html: Creating an Order Form

```
<BODY>

<H3>Online Order Form</H3>

<P>Please enter your name, billing address and shipping address. Please
don't forget the order number from our online catalog listings. Thanks for
shopping BigCorp!</P>

<FORM METHOD="POST" ACTION="http://www.fakecorp.com/cgi-bin/order.cgi">


Please enter a full name and address for BILLING purposes:<BR>
First Name: <INPUT TYPE="TEXT" NAME="first" SIZE="25" MAXLENGTH="25"><BR>
Last Name: <INPUT TYPE="TEXT" NAME="last" SIZE="35" MAXLENGTH="35"><BR>
Address: <INPUT TYPE="TEXT" NAME="address" SIZE="60" MAXLENGTH="60"><BR>
City: <INPUT TYPE="TEXT" NAME="city" SIZE="25" MAXLENGTH="25">
State: <INPUT TYPE="TEXT" NAME="state" SIZE="3" MAXLENGTH="3">
ZIP: <INPUT TYPE="TEXT" NAME="zip" SIZE="10" MAXLENGTH="10"><BR>
<HR>
```

continues

Listing 13.2: continued

```
<INPUT TYPE="CHECKBOX" NAME="same_add"> Check if Shipping Address is
different from Mailing Address

<TEXTAREA NAME="ship_add" ROWS="3" COLS="60" >Enter shipping
address here if different from above.
</TEXTAREA>
<HR>
Please enter the code for the product you wish to purchase: <INPUT TYPE=
"TEXT" NAME="ProdNum" SIZE="7" MAXLENGTH="7">

How would you like to pay for this?<BR>
<SELECT NAME="credit">
<OPTION VALUE="mast"> MasterCard
<OPTION VALUE="visa"> Visa
<OPTION VALUE="amex"> American Express
<OPTION VALUE="disc"> Discover
</SELECT>
Please enter the card number: <INPUT TYPE="TEXT" NAME="CardNum" SIZE="17"
MAXLENGTH="17"><BR>
Expiration date (01/99): <INPUT TYPE="TEXT" NAME="ExpDate" SIZE="6"
MAXLENGTH="6"><HR>
<BR>
Please take care that everything is filled out correctly, then click "Submit
Order." If you'd like, you can select the "Reset" button to start again.
Clicking the "Submit Order" button will send your order to BigCorp and your
credit card will be charged.<BR>
<INPUT TYPE="reset">
<BR>
<INPUT TYPE="submit" VALUE="Submit Order">
</FORM>
</BODY>
```

Here, you've taken advantage of most of the options available to you for forms (see Figure 13.12). Note that if the checkbox for Check if Shipping Address Is Different from Mailing Address is left unchecked, you can assume (in the processing script) that this text area can be ignored.

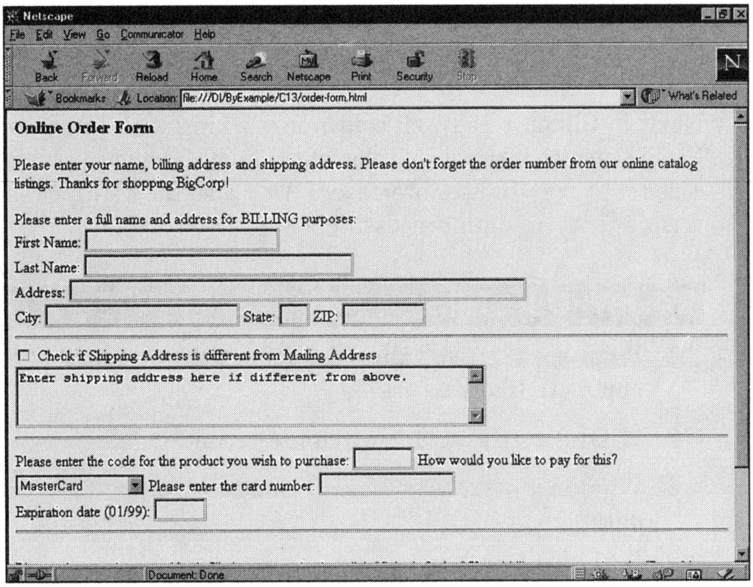

Figure 13.12: *The completed Web order form.*

Once the user clicks the Submit Order button, the script on your Web server takes over. The script should be designed to accept the data, add it to your internal order-processing database (if appropriate), and respond to the submission with an HTML page confirming the order and offering any additional help or instructions. Then, hopefully, the product will ship on time!

What's Next?

HTML forms are a powerful way to add interactivity to your Web site. They can be used to elicit information, responses, memberships, or even product orders from your users. They can also be used as an interface for data retrieval.

The basic elements of a form are the <FORM> tag itself, along with a number of different types of form elements, including <INPUT>, <SELECT>, and <TEXTAREA>. Each of these have their own attributes, values, and special cases.

<TEXTAREA> creates a relatively free-form text entry area where comments, messages, and other feedback can be typed by the user. <INPUT> allows for a number of different types of interaction with the user, including single-line textboxes, radio button interfaces, checkboxes, and special buttons for resetting forms or sending in the form data.

<SELECT> types allow you to control how users respond by offering them access to menu listings. Menus can be either pop-up or scrolling, giving the user the ability to make a single choice or multiple choices from each menu.

Next, in Chapter 14, we'll continue working with forms and their design. You'll learn to integrate tables within your forms to create visually organized and easy-to-use interfaces. We'll also take a quick look at using CGI scripts for form data processing.

Review Questions

1. What are the two values for the <FORM> attribute METHOD? Which are you more likely to use?

2. What does the ACTION attribute accept?

3. What is a <TEXTAREA> form element used for? How does the user enter data?

4. <TEXTAREA> is a container tag. What does it contain?

5. Why sort of element is TYPE as it relates to the <INPUT> tag?

6. Aside from how they look, what's the major difference between checkboxes and radio buttons?

7. How do you define a checkbox or radio button as the default value?

8. How do you tell an HTML form to send its data to the Web server?

9. What type of interface element does the <SELECT> tag display?

10. If you use the attribute MULTIPLE with the <SELECT> tag, what happens to the way the menu displays?

Review Exercises

1. Create a simple form that lets your user send you an email message. (Hint: You can use the mailto: type of URL to actually cause the form to mail the form data to your email account.)

2. Create a form that offers the following choices in a pop-up menu, a series of radio buttons, and a list of checkboxes. Make a different value the default in each. The choices are North, South, East, and West.

3. Using a Select menu, create two different menus for the following items. Make one a pop-up menu and the other a scrolling menu. The choices are Life, Liberty, Happiness, Death, and Taxes.

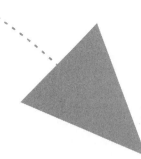

Form Design and Data Gathering with CGI Scripts

Now that you've seen how to create the basic form tags, let's put that knowledge together with some of the HTML tags you've already learned and make your forms more intuitive, attractive, and meaningful to the user. You'll also look at how data is transferred to the Web server and how your scripts need to be written to deal with the data.

This chapter teaches you the following:

- How to plan your form's design

- How to separate input controls into logical groups

- How to improve the presentation of your Web pages with tables and lists

- The basics of of CGI scripts

Form Design Issues

Central to the idea of form design is making the form easy for users to understand and inviting enough that they follow through and fill it out. The less incentive you have for them to fill out the form, the less likely they are to try. A clean, short form is more likely to entice users than a long, confusing one.

There are a few rules you should consider when building your forms so that they're easier and more effective for users:

- **Use other HTML tags to make things clear.** You can use <BR>, <HR>, and paragraph tags to set apart different "chunks" of your form, while <B>, <I>, and even <PRE> can be used to make the form easier to read.

- **Keep your forms short.** This isn't always possible, but when your forms are long, it's important to use some visual grouping to break them up a bit. If forms have smaller sections, they're easier on the eye.

- **Use intuitive design.** Common sense is sometimes the key to a good form. For instance, putting the Submit button in the middle of the form will keep people from filling out the rest of it. Often, it's best to use <SELECT>, radio buttons, and checkboxes to keep your users from guessing what type of information you want.

- **Warn users of unsecured transactions.** You should tell your users whether your Web server is secure and how they can make sure that the connection is current. If you ask for a credit card or similar personal information over an unsecured connection, let them know that, too.

Sound simple enough? Let's move on to some of the specifics of this advice and get these form tags to work.

Line Breaks

Unlike text-oriented HTML, your best friend in form design is not the paragraph tag; it's the line-break tag. This is because you want to directly affect the layout of the forms instead of leaving it up to the browser. Therefore, you've got to be a little more proactive. You'll end up with a lot of line-break tags before your form is through.

Consider the following example:

EXAMPLE

```
<FORM>

<B>Enter your name and phone number</B>
```

```
First Name: <INPUT TYPE="TEXT" NAME="first" SIZE="30">
Last Name: <INPUT TYPE="TEXT" NAME="last" SIZE="40">
Phone: <INPUT TYPE="TEXT" NAME="phone" SIZE="12">
</FORM>
```

Figure 14.1 illustrates how this would appear in a browser.

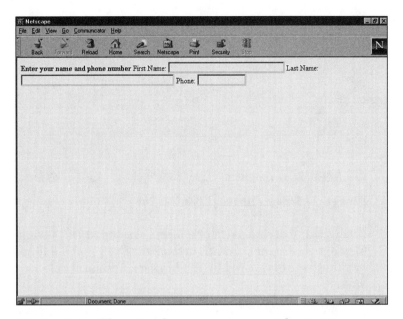

Figure 14.1: *These text boxes were input without*
 tags.

It doesn't look terribly clean, does it? To get each text box on a separate line and thus make the form more pleasing to the eye, we need to add the <BR> tag:

```
<FORM>
<B>Enter your name and phone number</B><BR>
First Name: <INPUT TYPE="TEXT" NAME="first" SIZE="30"><BR>
Last Name: <INPUT TYPE="TEXT" NAME="last" SIZE="40"><BR>
Phone: <INPUT TYPE="TEXT" NAME="phone" SIZE="12"><BR>
</FORM>
```

Adding <BR> forces each subsequent text box to the next line. This is a more attractive form, and the <BR> tags make it easier for the user to understand (see Figure 14.2).

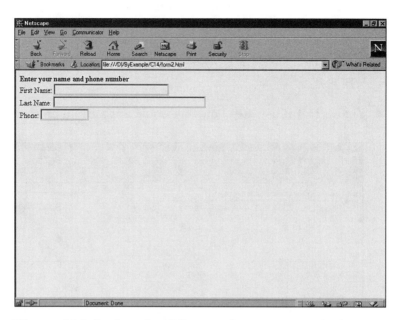

Figure 14.2: *Look at the difference the*
 tag makes!

Note, then, that the parts of a form (like the <INPUT> empty tag) work a lot like text in a regular HTML document. Even if you add returns while typing, they're still ignored by the browser. You need <BR> tags to create new lines.

Also notice the use of instructional text for these text boxes, which was put in boldface for the example. This is another important tenet of form design—using emphasis tags to make things clear. Most of your forms will need instructions throughout, just like any paper-based form. It's a good idea to standardize your instructions, using bold or italic tags to make them stand out from your other text.

EXAMPLE

Horizontal Lines

Along that same line of thought, not only should you use instructional text, but you might also choose to break your form into smaller chunks by using the <HR> tag. Start with Listing 14.1, which uses <BR> and emphasis tags.

Listing 14.1:.html: Our Example So Far

```
<FORM>

<B>Enter your name and phone number</B><BR>

First Name: <INPUT TYPE="TEXT" NAME="first" SIZE="30"><BR>

Last Name: <INPUT TYPE="TEXT" NAME="last" SIZE="40"><BR>

Phone: <INPUT TYPE="TEXT" NAME="phone" SIZE="12"><BR>
```

```
<B>Enter your mailing address</B><BR>

Address: <INPUT TYPE="TEXT" NAME="address" SIZE="50"><BR>

City: <INPUT TYPE="TEXT" NAME="city" SIZE="25">

State: <INPUT TYPE="TEXT" NAME="state" SIZE="2">

Zip: <INPUT TYPE="TEXT" NAME="zip" SIZE="7"><BR>

<B>Enter your email address</B><BR>

Email: <INPUT TYPE="TEXT" NAME="email" SIZE="45"><BR>

<B>Enter your comments below:</B><BR>

<TEXTAREA NAME="comments" ROWS="5" COLS="40">

Dear Customer Support,

</TEXTAREA>

</FORM>
```

Viewed in a browser, this form is easier for the user to understand, with instructions in bold and textboxes where you'd expect them (see Figure 14.3).

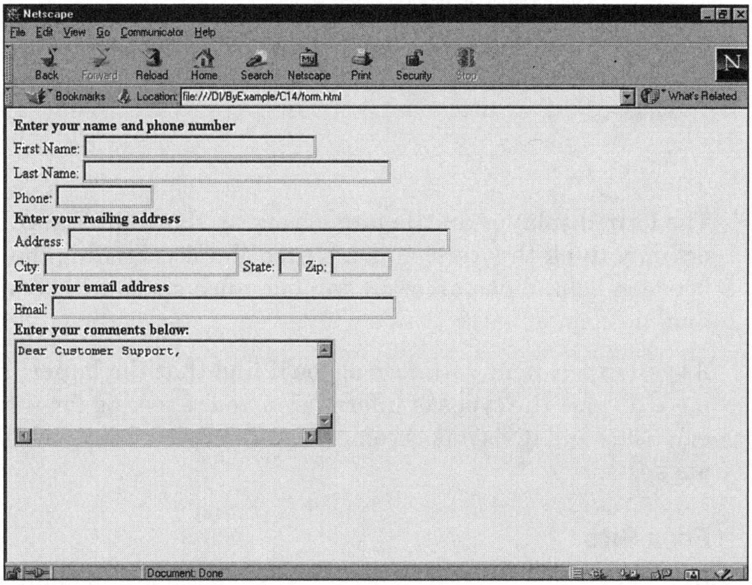

Figure 14.3: *Adding emphasis.*

There's still more you can do. By placing <HR> tags in your form, you make it clear that new instructions are coming up or that the form has reached the next logical chunk of entry. The <HR> tag simply makes the form easier to look at because it guides the user through the different parts of the form. In Listing 14.2, you add <HR> tags at the logical breaks.

EXAMPLE

Listing 14.2: form3.html: Adding <HR> to the Form

```
<FORM>
<B>Enter your name and phone number</B><BR>
First Name: <INPUT TYPE="TEXT" NAME="first" SIZE="30"><BR>
Last Name: <INPUT TYPE="TEXT" NAME="last" SIZE="40"><BR>
Phone: <INPUT TYPE="TEXT" NAME="phone" SIZE="12"><BR>
<HR>
<B>Enter your mailing address</B><BR>
Address: <INPUT TYPE="TEXT" NAME="address" SIZE="50"><BR>
City: <INPUT TYPE="TEXT" NAME="city" SIZE="25">
State: <INPUT TYPE="TEXT" NAME="state" SIZE="2">
Zip: <INPUT TYPE="TEXT" NAME="zip" SIZE="7"><BR>
<HR>
<B>Enter your email address</B><BR>
Email: <INPUT TYPE="TEXT" NAME="email" SIZE="45"><BR>
<HR>
<B>Enter your comments below:</B><BR>
<TEXTAREA NAME="comments" ROWS="5" COLS="40">
Dear Customer Support,
</TEXTAREA>
</FORM>
```

The form display is a little larger now, as shown in Figure 14.4. Some viewers may think this version is a bit too chunky. Finding the right balance between helpful demarcation and too much space will be up to you in your final design.

As you experiment with forms, you'll find that the larger the form—and the more diverse the types of information you're asking for—the more useful emphasis and divisions become in guiding your user's eye to the appropriate spots.

EXAMPLE

Fix-a-Site

In this example, we'll start with a site that offers the bulk of the form elements you've learned but none of the spacing and layout tips just discussed. It's just a plain little form. You'll go through it and change the way it looks to try to make it more intuitive and attractive.

Of course, there aren't any truly right answers when talking about aesthetics. By the end of this example, see if you agree with the changes made.

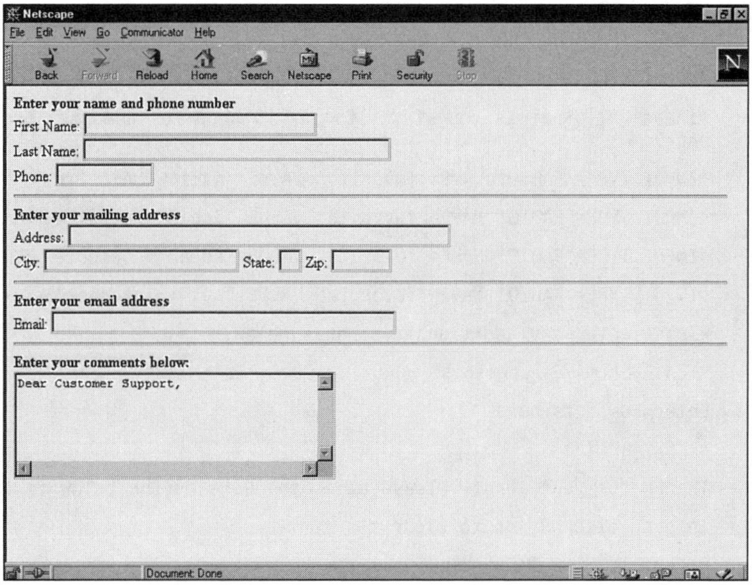

Figure 14.4: *Adding <HR> tags to clearly define each new section of the form.*

The HTML for your form is shown in Listing 14.3.

Listing 14.3: old-form.html: Making a Form Look Better

```
<BODY>

<H2>Customer Survey</H2>

<P>Please fill out the following form, including your personal information, to
help us better serve you. None of the addresses or other information in these
forms will be sold without your permission. Thank You!</P>

<HR>

<FORM METHOD="POST" ACTION="http://www.foo.com/cgi-bin/csurvey">

Enter your name and address:

Name: <INPUT TYPE="TEXT" NAME="name" SIZE="60">

Address: <INPUT TYPE="TEXT" NAME="address" SIZE="60">

City: <INPUT TYPE="TEXT" NAME="city" SIZE="25"> State: <INPUT TYPE="TEXT"

NAME="state" SIZE="2"> Zip: <INPUT TYPE="TEXT" NAME="zip" SIZE="5">

Phone: <INPUT TYPE="TEXT" NAME="city" SIZE="12">

Please check the type of computer you own:

<INPUT TYPE="CHECKBOX" NAME="pentium"> Pentium

<INPUT TYPE="CHECKBOX" NAME="P2"> Pentium II

<INPUT TYPE="CHECKBOX" NAME="P3"> Pentium III
```

continues

Listing 14.3: continued

```
<INPUT TYPE="CHECKBOX" NAME="mac"> Mac

<INPUT TYPE="CHECKBOX" NAME="NT"> Please check if your computer runs

Windows NT. What is your favorite way to shop for computer products (choose
one)?

<INPUT TYPE="RADIO" NAME="favorite" VALUE="mail"> Mail Order Catalog

<INPUT TYPE="RADIO" NAME="favorite" VALUE="local"> Local Computer Store

<INPUT TYPE="RADIO" NAME="favorite" VALUE="super"> Computer Superstore

<INPUT TYPE="RADIO" NAME="favorite" VALUE="net"> Internet/World Wide Web

Please enter any additional comments below:

<TEXTAREA NAME="comments" ROWS="5" COLS="70">

Enter comments here

</TEXTAREA>

Thanks for your input. Please click the Done button below to send us your

info or click Reset to clear the form.

<INPUT TYPE="SUBMIT" VALUE="Done">

<INPUT TYPE="RESET">

</FORM>

</BODY>
```

Figure 14.5 shows how this looks in a browser.

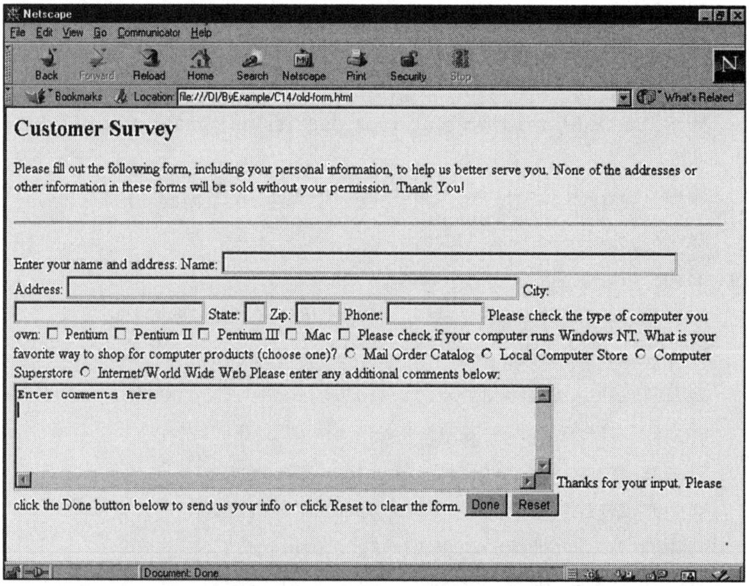

Figure 14.5: *The initial attempt at the customer feedback form.*

Now, let's pull this thing apart a bit and make some changes. It's a fairly logical organization, so you should be able to figure out what the major portions are. The first segment is the address section, which currently looks like this:

```
Enter your name and address:
Name: <INPUT TYPE="TEXT" NAME="name" SIZE="60">
Address: <INPUT TYPE="TEXT" NAME="address" SIZE="60">
City: <INPUT TYPE="TEXT" NAME="city" SIZE="25">
State: <INPUT TYPE="TEXT" NAME="state" SIZE="2">
Zip: <INPUT TYPE="TEXT" NAME="zip" SIZE="5">
Phone: <INPUT TYPE="TEXT" NAME="city" SIZE="12">
```

EXAMPLE

All this really needs is a little help in the presentation with some extra markup:

```
<B>Enter your name and address:</B><BR>
Name: <INPUT TYPE="TEXT" NAME="name" SIZE="60"><BR>
Address: <INPUT TYPE="TEXT" NAME="address" SIZE="60"><BR>
City: <INPUT TYPE="TEXT" NAME="city" SIZE="25">
State: <INPUT TYPE="TEXT" NAME="state" SIZE="3" MAXLENGTH="2">
Zip: <INPUT TYPE="TEXT" NAME="zip" SIZE="5"><BR>
Phone: <INPUT TYPE="TEXT" NAME="city" SIZE="12"><BR>
<HR>
```

Some designers feel that it's also a good idea to set the size of your textbox a little larger than the MAXLENGTH. That way, the user can still see all the text that he entered but encounter "resistance" as it fills the textbox. It could be considered a visual reinforcement of the limit. In this case, though, we're really only concerned with the State textbox; we want the user to enter the two-character state code. By setting the MAXLENGTH attribute to two, you can control that value, yet still leave the other elements open without artificial limits, to allow for longer names and addresses.

The next segment is the computer-related questions. It might seem like two pieces, but let's use the idea of putting them in the same section of the form, because they are similar and don't take up much space. Here's the original code for this section:

```
Please check the type of computer you own:
<INPUT TYPE="CHECKBOX" NAME="pentium"> Pentium
<INPUT TYPE="CHECKBOX" NAME="P2"> Pentium II
<INPUT TYPE="CHECKBOX" NAME="P3"> Pentium III
<INPUT TYPE="CHECKBOX" NAME="mac"> Mac
```

```
<INPUT TYPE="CHECKBOX" NAME="NT"> Please check if your computer runs

Windows NT. What is your favorite way to shop for computer products

(choose one)?

<INPUT TYPE="RADIO" NAME="favorite" VALUE="mail"> Mail Order Catalog

<INPUT TYPE="RADIO" NAME="favorite" VALUE="local"> Local Computer Store

<INPUT TYPE="RADIO" NAME="favorite" VALUE="super"> Computer Superstore

<INPUT TYPE="RADIO" NAME="favorite" VALUE="net"> Internet/World Wide Web
```

EXAMPLE

How can you fix this? You need to be more specific about where the checkboxes and radio buttons end and how they are allowed to wrap with the browser screen (using <BR>). As with regular sentences, these questions can be further broken up using paragraph tags:

```
<P><B>Please check the type of computer you own:</B><BR>

<INPUT TYPE="CHECKBOX" NAME="pentium"> Pentium

<INPUT TYPE="CHECKBOX" NAME="P2"> Pentium II

<INPUT TYPE="CHECKBOX" NAME="P3"> Pentium III

<INPUT TYPE="CHECKBOX" NAME="mac"> Mac

<P><INPUT TYPE="CHECKBOX" NAME="NT"> <B>Please check if your computer runs

Windows NT.</B>

<P><B>What is your favorite way to shop for computer products (choose one)?</B>

<BR>

<INPUT TYPE="RADIO" NAME="favorite" VALUE="mail"> Mail Order Catalog<BR>

<INPUT TYPE="RADIO" NAME="favorite" VALUE="local"> Local Computer Store<BR>

<INPUT TYPE="RADIO" NAME="favorite" VALUE="super"> Computer Superstore<BR>

<INPUT TYPE="RADIO" NAME="favorite" VALUE="net"> Internet/World Wide Web<BR>

<HR>
```

The three questions were separated into paragraphs, with an <HR> tag added at the bottom, because this would be one section. Also notice that the radio buttons all got <BR> tags, while we left the checkboxes as they were. Why? Because it's always best to save space (by leaving the checkboxes on one line). However, counting the characters in the descriptions of the radio buttons tells us that a single line of radio buttons would be well over 80 characters long, and that's likely to wrap oddly in the browser window.

The final segment currently looks like this:

```
Please enter any additional comments below:

<TEXTAREA NAME="comments" ROWS="5" COLS="70">

Enter comments here

</TEXTAREA>
```

Thanks for your input. Please click the Done button below to send us your
info or click Reset to clear the form.

```
<INPUT TYPE="RESET">
<INPUT TYPE="SUBMIT" VALUE="Done">
```

EXAMPLE

These tags need only minor touch-ups. Let's separate the form control buttons from the comment window and add some formatting:

```
<P><B>Please enter any additional comments below:</B><BR>
<TEXTAREA NAME="comments" ROWS="5" COLS="70">
Enter comments here
</TEXTAREA>
<P>Thanks for your input. Please click the Done button below to send us your
info or click Reset to clear the form.<P>
<INPUT TYPE="RESET"><BR>
<INPUT TYPE="SUBMIT" VALUE="Done">
```

Then, you close the form tags, and you're done. How does it look in a browser now? Take a look at Figure 14.6.

![Screenshot of a web browser window titled "D:\ByExample\C14\new-form.html - Microsoft Internet Explorer" showing the customer service survey form. The form includes: "Enter your name and address:" with fields for Name, Address, City, State, Zip, and Phone. "Please check the type of computer you own:" with checkboxes for Pentium, Pentium II, Pentium III, Mac. "Please check if your computer runs Windows NT." checkbox. "What is your favorite way to shop for computer products (choose one)?" with radio buttons for Mail Order Catalog, Local Computer Store, Computer Superstore, Internet/World Wide Web. "Please enter any additional comments below:" with a text area containing "Enter comments here". "Thanks for your input. Please click the Done button below to send us your info or click Reset to clear the form." with Done and Reset buttons.]

Figure 14.6: *Our masterpiece of a customer service survey.*

Other Tags for Form Formatting

You've used <P>, <BR>, and <HR> tags to space things and offer logical breaks for your forms. But what about other issues, such as aligning form elements? You can turn to <TABLE> tags and HTML list tags for that.

When using tables, not only can you neatly line up text boxes and rows of checkboxes or radio buttons, but you can condense the layout of your forms into columnar presentation where appropriate, as well as mixing several techniques to get a professional-looking page that rivals many print layouts.

Using Tables with Forms

One of the most annoying parts of setting up a form so far has been the inability to line up textbox fields as they go down the page. For instance, whenever the Name: and Address: fields have been used in examples, they always look a little ragged.

One nifty solution is to use tables within your <FORM> elements. If we create a two-column table in which the left column contains the labels for each input and the right column contains the input controls, we'll get a nicely aligned layout.

Let's start by taking a look at this basic form:

```
<FORM>
Favorite Book: <INPUT TYPE="TEXT" NAME="book" SIZE="40"><BR>
Best Food: <INPUT TYPE="TEXT" NAME="food" SIZE="30"><BR>
Favorite Music Group: <INPUT TYPE="TEXT" NAME="music" SIZE="40"><BR>
Personal Quote: <INPUT TYPE="TEXT" NAME="quote" SIZE="60"><BR>
</FORM>
```

Displayed in a browser, this looks like Figure 14.7.

To improve this situation, you can add <TABLE> tags and format them yourself:

```
<FORM>
<TABLE>
<TR>
<TD>Favorite Book:</TD>
<TD><INPUT TYPE="TEXT" NAME="book" SIZE="40"></TD>
```

```
</TR>
<TR>
<TD>Best Food:</TD>
<TD><INPUT TYPE="TEXT" NAME="food" SIZE="30"></TD>
</TR>
<TR>
<TD>Favorite Music Group:</TD>
<TD><INPUT TYPE="TEXT" NAME="music" SIZE="40"></TD>
</TR>
<TR>
<TD>Personal Quote:</TD>
<TD><INPUT TYPE="TEXT" NAME="quote" SIZE="60"></TD>
</TABLE>
</FORM>
```

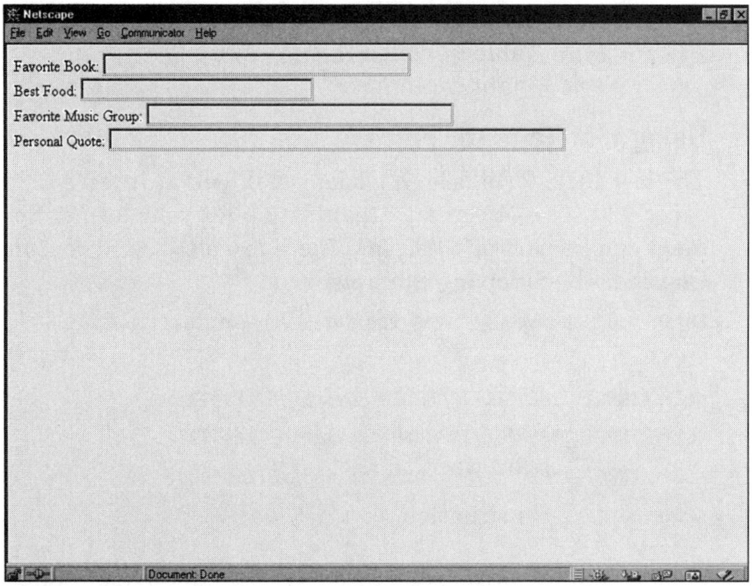

Figure 14.7: *Ragged textboxes in a form.*

The results are shown in Figure 14.8.

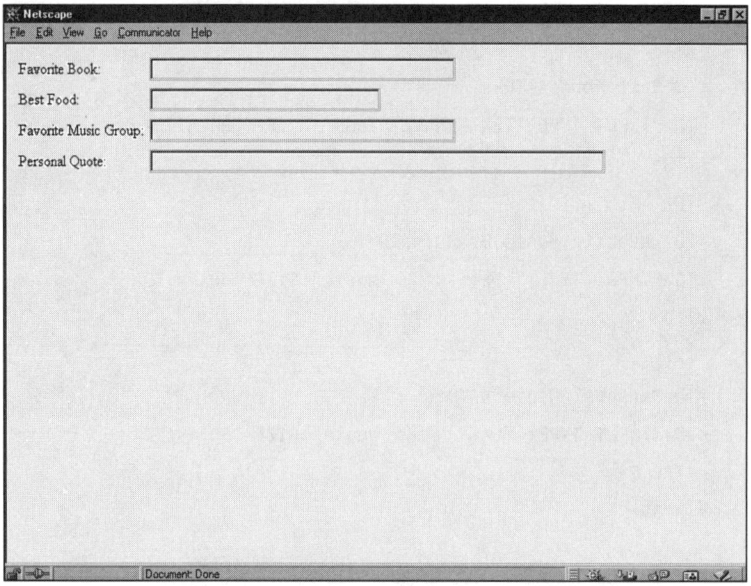

Figure 14.8: *A much cleaner-looking form.*

Using List Tags for Forms

The last little form design tricks you'll look at involve using the list tags—especially <OL>—to create organization for your forms. Nearly any form element can be part of a list, and there are often good reasons to use them. Consider the following example:

```
Enter your guesses for the top three movies this week: <BR>
<OL>
<LI> <INPUT TYPE="TEXT" NAME="movie1" SIZE="40">
<LI> <INPUT TYPE="TEXT" NAME="movie2" SIZE="40">
<LI> <INPUT TYPE="TEXT" NAME="movie3" SIZE="40">
</OL>
```

Seen through a browser, each entry is numbered, eliminating the need for individual descriptive text (see Figure 14.9).

Customer Service Revisited

EXAMPLE

Let's see if you can do an even better job with the customer service form you created earlier in this chapter. Now you have the opportunity to clean up some of those textboxes and other segments. Listing 14.4 shows the example as it stands (recall that Figure 14.6 showed this same form in a browser).

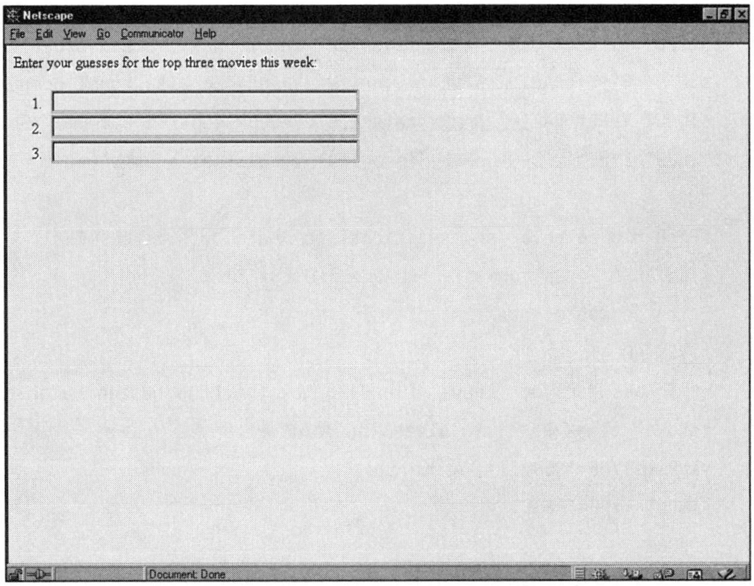

Figure 14.9: *You can use an ordered list for your form.*

Listing 14.4: survey.html: Customer Service Form

```
<FORM>
<B>Enter your name and address:</B><BR>
Name: <INPUT TYPE="TEXT" NAME="name" SIZE="60"><BR>
Address: <INPUT TYPE="TEXT" NAME="address" SIZE="60"><BR>
City: <INPUT TYPE="TEXT" NAME="city" SIZE="25">
State: <INPUT TYPE="TEXT" NAME="state" SIZE="3" MAXLENGTH="2">
Zip: <INPUT TYPE="TEXT" NAME="zip" SIZE="5"><BR>
Phone: <INPUT TYPE="TEXT" NAME="city" SIZE="12"><BR>
<HR>
<P><B>Please check the type of computer you own:</B><BR>
<INPUT TYPE="CHECKBOX" NAME="pentium"> Pentium
<INPUT TYPE="CHECKBOX" NAME="P2"> Pentium II
<INPUT TYPE="CHECKBOX" NAME="P3"> Pentium III
<INPUT TYPE="CHECKBOX" NAME="mac"> Mac
<P><INPUT TYPE="CHECKBOX" NAME="NT"> <B>Please check if your computer runs
Windows NT.</B>
<P><B>What is your favorite way to shop for computer products (choose one)?</B>
<BR>
```

continues

Listing 14.4: continued

```
<INPUT TYPE="RADIO" NAME="favorite" VALUE="mail"> Mail Order Catalog<BR>
<INPUT TYPE="RADIO" NAME="favorite" VALUE="local"> Local Computer Store<BR>
<INPUT TYPE="RADIO" NAME="favorite" VALUE="super"> Computer Superstore<BR>
<INPUT TYPE="RADIO" NAME="favorite" VALUE="net"> Internet/World Wide Web<BR>
<HR>
<P><B>Please enter any additional comments below:</B><BR>
<TEXTAREA NAME="comments" ROWS="2" COLS="70">
Enter comments here
</TEXTAREA>
<P>Thanks for your input. Please click the Done button below to send us your
info or click Reset to clear the form.<P>
<INPUT TYPE="SUBMIT" VALUE="Done">
<INPUT TYPE="RESET">
</FORM>
```

Clearly, the first segment can benefit from a <TABLE> so that you can line up those address lines. We'll also close up some of the lines by placing the City and State boxes in one row and the Zip and Phone boxes in the next row. You might notice that because you're using a table, you no longer need the <BR> tag to end some of the lines, as in the following code:

```
<P><B>Enter your name and address:</B></P>
<TABLE BORDER="0">
<TR>
<TD>Name:</TD>
<TD><INPUT TYPE="TEXT" NAME="name" SIZE="60"></TD>
</TR>
<TR>
<TD>Address:</TD>
<TD><INPUT TYPE="TEXT" NAME="address" SIZE="60"></TD>
</TR>
<TR>
<TD>City:</TD>
<TD>INPUT TYPE="TEXT" NAME="city" SIZE="25"> State:
<INPUT TYPE="TEXT" NAME="state" SIZE="3" MAXLENGTH="2"></TD>
</TR>
<TR>
```

```
<TD>Zip:</TD>
<TD><INPUT TYPE="TEXT" NAME="zip" SIZE="5">
Phone:
<INPUT TYPE="TEXT" NAME="city" SIZE="12"></TD>
</TR>
</TABLE>
<HR>
```

EXAMPLE

What else can you do? Let's put the second segment in list format. You could use a <UL>-style list for the series of radio buttons, although the current setup does just about the same thing. You probably shouldn't change the checkboxes because they're already formatted to appear on one line. The following code includes these changes:

```
<P><B>Please check the type of computer you own:</B><BR>
<INPUT TYPE="CHECKBOX" NAME="pentium"> Pentium
<INPUT TYPE="CHECKBOX" NAME="P2"> Pentium II
<INPUT TYPE="CHECKBOX" NAME="P3"> Pentium III
<INPUT TYPE="CHECKBOX" NAME="mac"> Mac
<P><INPUT TYPE="CHECKBOX" NAME="NT"> <B>Please check if your computer runs
Windows NT.</B>
<P><B>What is your favorite way to shop for computer products (choose one)?</B>
<BR>
<UL>
<LI><INPUT TYPE="RADIO" NAME="favorite" VALUE="mail"> Mail Order Catalog
<LI><INPUT TYPE="RADIO" NAME="favorite" VALUE="local"> Local Computer Store
<LI><INPUT TYPE="RADIO" NAME="favorite" VALUE="super"> Computer Superstore
<LI><INPUT TYPE="RADIO" NAME="favorite" VALUE="net"> Internet/World Wide Web
</UL>
<HR>
```

Notice that the <BR> tags at the end of each radio button entry are no longer required because each <LI> tag automatically appears on its own line.

The rest of the form can pretty much stand on its own. See how the whole thing looks in a browser in Figure 14.10.

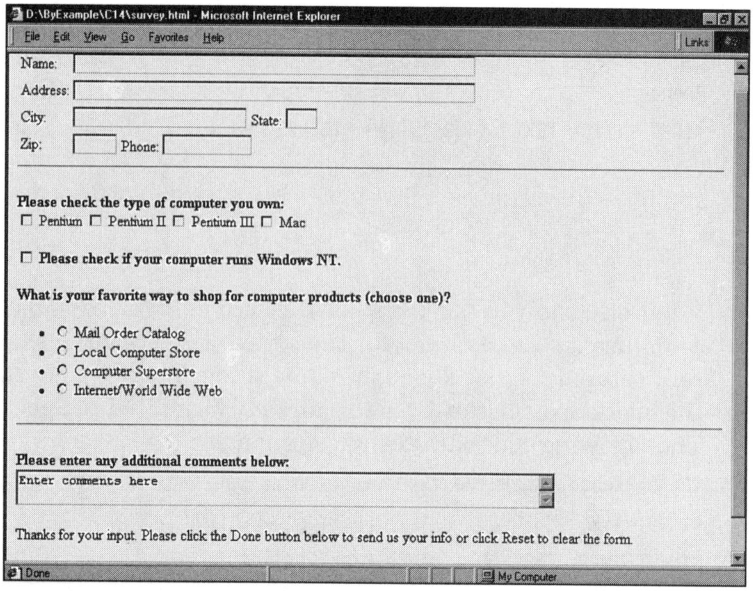

***Figure 14.10:** Our customer service form, now complete.*

CGI-BIN Scripts and Dealing with Form Data

Before we finish discussing HTML forms, we should touch on how data is passed to the Web server and how your script needs to be written to handle this data. First, we should start with a quick discussion of CGI-BIN scripts.

Using CGI-BIN Scripts

For the most part, CGI-BIN scripts are designed to receive values from your user, store or process them in some manner, and then create HTML code programmatically (or on the fly) by way of response. Scripts are most often used to handle form data but can also be used to add things such as "hit" counters and variable images (different images that appear at different times).

A URL to a script can be used just about anywhere you might use a URL to another document, a hypermedia file, or an image. In a hypertext link, for instance, you might use a script that chooses a "random" Web page to return, as in the following:

```
<A HREF="/cgi-bin/random.pl">Click me for a surprise Web page!</A>
```

Actually creating the scripts is a little beyond the scope of this book. Most of the time, CGI-BIN scripts are written in Perl, C, Visual Basic, or any number of other scripting languages. If you're a programmer, I recommend looking into a book that seriously discusses the ins and outs of CGI programming. Creating scripts can be complicated but rewarding—especially if you have access to your Web server and aspire to be a Webmaster as well as an HTML designer.

TIP

Look into Que's *Special Edition Using CGI* for an in-depth discussion of CGI scripts and programming.

In the case of forms, you've already seen that you call the CGI-BIN script in the <FORM> tag using the ACTION attribute. Once the script receives the data, it then needs to use that data to create an HTML "results" page, which is sent back to the browser.

Receiving Form Data

You may recall from Chapter 13, "HTML Forms," that there are two different methods to pass data to the script you've created. The two methods, GET and POST, cause data to be sent in different ways.

The type of method used to send the data is stored in an environment variable on the Web server called REQUEST_METHOD. The GET method simply appends your form data to the URL and sends it to the server. Most servers will then store this data in another environment variable called QUERY_STRING. This string is generally limited to less than one kilobyte of data (approximately 1,000 characters), which explains why it's not being used very much anymore.

The POST method causes the length of the data string to be stored in a variable called CONTENT_LENGTH, while the data itself is redirected to stdin (standard in). In effect, the data is made to appear to your script or program that it was typed into the server using a typical keyboard. Your script must then be designed to parse that input.

TIP

I'd let a program do your parsing for you. cgi-bin.pl is the Perl library for this. Other languages have their own publicly available modules to use as well.

Generally speaking, programs that do this for you are already available. There are actually two steps to receiving the input: *decoding* and *parsing*. Data sent from your Web browser is encoded to avoid data loss—essentially by turning spaces into plus signs (+) and nontext characters (like !) into a percent sign (%) and a hexadecimal code.

Once you've worked through the decoding process, you're left with a text input that follows this format (where the ampersand simply separates each pairing of name and value):

NAME1=VALUE1&NAME2=VALUE2&...

An example of this is the following:

`ADDRESS=1234 MAIN ST&CITY=DALLAS&STATE=TX`

EXAMPLE

If you're not using a parsing program or library (which, ideally, would allow you to simply reassign the values in this file to variables in your script), your script will need to accept this data, strip the ampersands, and reassign the values to appropriate variables.

Your Script's Output

Outputis much easier. Because `stdout` (standard out) is redirected to the HTML browser, you simply need to use `print` (Perl and other languages), `lprint` (the C language), or similar commands that print directly to the screen (or terminal or console). You use the `print` command to output HTML codes, just as if you were using your text editor.

Here's a short snippet of a Perl script to do just that:

```
print "Content-type: text\html\n\n";
print "<HTML>\n<HEAD><TITLE>Response</TITLE></HEAD>\n"
print "<BODY>\n<H2>Success</H2>\n<P>Thank you for your submission<P>\n"
print "<P>Click <A HREF="index.html">here</A> to go back <P>\n</BODY>\n</HTML>"
```

EXAMPLE

In a number of programming languages, \n is the newline character, which simply feeds a return to standard out. Otherwise, this should seem (and look) rather familiar (see Figure 14.11). It's just HTML!

What's Next?

Form design is something of an art *and* a science. It's important that forms look good and be easy for the user to follow if they are to be effective. There are some general rules you can follow for form design, and using other HTML commands you've learned previously, you can make your forms very easy to read. That, in turn, makes users more likely to use them.

It's also important for Web designers to have some idea of how forms send their data to the Web server and the associated script—even if they don't intend to create the scripts themselves. A designer with almost any programming experience will find it fairly easy to manage data-gathering scripts from her Web site.

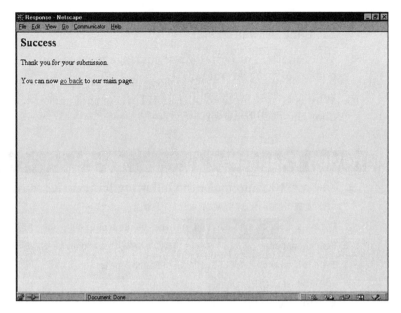

Figure 14.11: The results of the snippet of Perl scripting.

Next up in Chapter 15, "Frames," we'll jump head-first into user interface design with a discussion of the HTML <FRAME> elements. This relatively new addition to HTML allows the designer to divide the Web browser window into discrete units that can act as their own miniature "browser within a browser."

Review Questions

1. Why is the <BR> tag more effective than the <P> tag for individual lines of forms?

2. Is it possible to use HTML tags (such as <B> and <I>) within the confines of a <FORM> tag? What about just plain text?

3. What are segments of form elements?

4. What do <P> tags offer you that help break up sections of form elements? Why not just use multiple <BR> tags?

5. How can you get checkboxes and radio buttons to appear on a single line on your Web page?

6. What does MAXLENGTH do for <INPUT TYPE="TEXT">-style form elements? How is this error-checking?

7. What does the <TABLE> tag allow you to do with forms? Do you "lose" by using the <TABLE> tag?

8. How can <OL> lists keep you from having to add descriptive text to each line of your form?

9. What method of form data transfer is more popular? Why? Which is easier for programmers?

10. Why is it so simple to output HTML with a server-based script? What does the Web browser "act like"?

Review Exercises

1. Use a <TABLE> to make the following form easier to read:

```
<FORM METHOD="POST" ACTION="/cgi-bin/searcher">
Enter a Search phrase and a type of search (AND, OR, NOT).
Search phrase: <INPUT TYPE="TEXT" NAME="SearchFor" SIZE=38>
Type of search: <SELECT NAME="SearchType">
<OPTION SELECTED VALUE="and"> AND
<OPTION VALUE="or"> OR
<OPTION VALUE="not"> NOT
</SELECT>
<INPUT TYPE="submit" NAME="Submit" VALUE="Start the Search">
</FORM>
```

2. Create a form that allows the user to subscribe to a fictional magazine. Include different segments for name and address, demographic information, and a credit card number. Also use layout and HTML emphasis to make it clear to the user what information is required and what information is optional.

3. If you understand how to program in Perl, C, or another CGI scripting language and you have access to your Web server (so that you can place the script in the cgi-bin directory), create a script that accepts the value from the following simple form and outputs the appropriate HTML coded text:

```
<FORM METHOD="POST" ACTION="/cgi-bin/picker">
How would you like the next page to appear?<BR>
<SELECT NAME="Appear">
<OPTION SELECTED VALUE="bold"> bold
<OPTION VALUE="ital"> italics
<OPTION VALUE="list"> in an HTML list
</SELECT>
<INPUT TYPE="submit" NAME="Submit" VALUE="Create the Page">
</FORM>
```

Part IV

Page Layout and Formatting

Frames

Images, Multimedia Objects, and Background Graphics

Client-Side Image Maps

Enhancing Your Pages with Style Sheets

Validating Your HTML

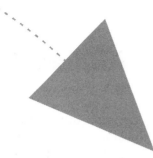

Frames

Love them or hate them, frames have certainly made their presence known on the Web. The idea began as an innovation by Netscape, and then frames caught on in other browsers with the introduction of Microsoft Internet Explorer 3.0 in 1996. It took much longer, however, for them to finally make it into the HTML Recommendations, first officially appearing in HTML 4.

Frames aren't overwhelmingly difficult to add to your pages, but they do require a slight shift in thought. They may seem similar to tables at first. However, instead of dividing content only visually, frames actually separate your screen real estate into mini browsers all their own, each displaying a unique URL.

This chapter teaches you the following:

- How frames change the user interface
- How to divide up screen real estate using the <FRAMESET> tags
- How to create a navigation system with frames

The Idea Behind Frames

Netscape frames are basically another way you can create a unique interface for your Web site. By dividing the page into different parts—each of which can be updated separately—you can offer a number of different interface elements. Even a simple use of the frame specification lets you add navigational interface graphics or a corporate logo to a site, while the rest of your page scrolls beneath it (see Figure 15.1).

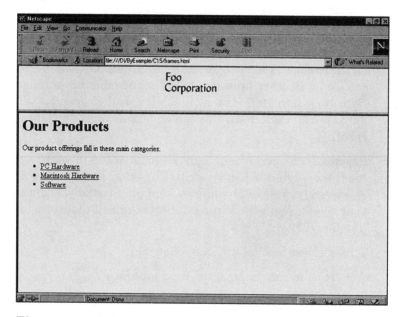

Figure 15.1: *A basic frames interface.*

Frames are most frequently used for the following effects:

- **Table of Contents (TOC)**   By placing the TOC in a "column" on your Web page, people can click around your site or your documentation pages without being forced to constantly move "back" to the contents page. Instead, users simply click a new content level in the static frame.

- **Fixed interface elements**   As mentioned previously, you can force logos, search tools, and other information to stay in one fixed portion of the screen, while the rest of your document scrolls in another frame.

Creating Frames

Probably the most unique HTML-style tag so far is the <FRAMESET> tag. This container is required for frames-style pages, but it also replaces the <BODY> tag on these pages. Therefore, when you use frames, you're committed to using them completely: You can't just add frames to part of your page. On a typical page, <FRAMESET> is added like this:

```
<HTML>
<HEAD>
...HEAD markup...
</HEAD>
<FRAMESET>
...Frames and other HTML markup...
</FRAMESET>
</HTML>
```

The <FRAMESET> tag has two major attributes: ROWS and COLS. Both attributes accept either numerical values (size in pixels), percentages, or a combination of both. The value * can also be used to suggest that a particular row or column should take up the rest of the page. The number of rows or columns is suggested by the number of values you give the attribute. These attributes take the following format:

```
<FRAMESET ROWS="numbers,percentages,*" COLS="numbers,percentages,*">
```

An example like the following creates two rows—one 50 pixels long and another row that takes up the rest of the page:

```
<FRAMESET ROWS="50,*">
```

EXAMPLE

This would be useful for a page that displays a fixed map or graphic at the top.

The following example creates a Web interface with two columns: one on the leftmost 25 percent of the screen and another on the other 75 percent:

```
<FRAMESET COLS="25%,75%">
```

EXAMPLE

This would be a good way to set up a documentation (or FAQ) site that offered contents in the first frame and actual text and examples in the second, larger frame.

Expanding your options, you can mix rows within columns (or vice versa) within the same <FRAMESET>. For instance, the following creates a page with two columns and two rows:

EXAMPLE

```
<FRAMESET COLS="25%,75%"ROWS="50, *">

...frame details...

   </FRAMESET>
```

As before, the screen is divided into two columns, one taking up 25% of the available space and the other 75%. The definition for rows is a bit different. The top-most row occupies exactly 50 pixels worth of space. The second row fills all remaining space below that. Although this doesn't display anything in and of itself, it creates logical breaks in the page that look like Figure 15.2.

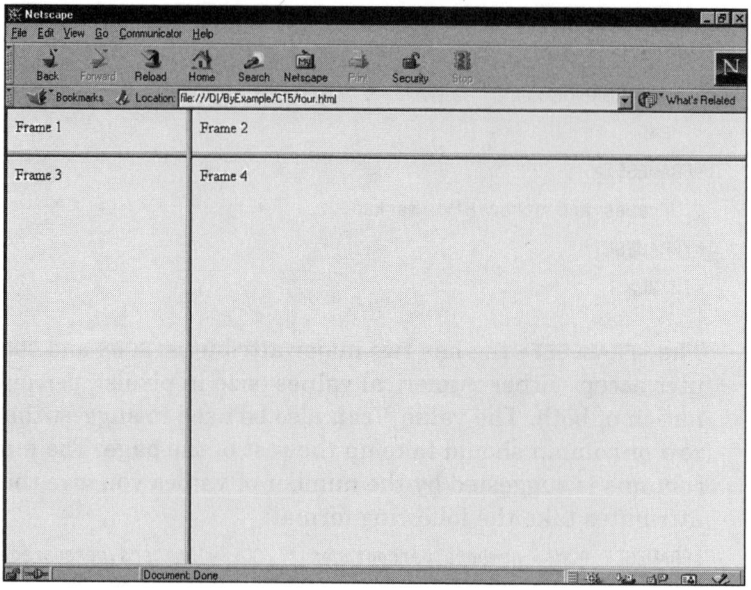

Figure 15.2: *Mixed rows and columns.*

The <FRAME> Tag

The <FRAME> tag is used within the <FRAMESET> container to determine what will actually appear in a particular frame. Each <FRAME> tag is an empty tag—not unlike the <LI> tags you add to HTML lists. It's simply there, within the <FRAMESET> container, to determine what URL or name is associated with the particular frame it defines. It takes the following format:

```
<FRAMESET COLS/ROWS="numbers">

<FRAME SRC="URL" NAME="string">

...

</FRAMESET>
```

The SRC attribute is used to tell the frame what URL should be loaded in that frame. For instance, the following creates two frame rows—one that loads the URL index.html at the top of the Web page and one that loads the URL help.html at the bottom of the page (see Figure 15.3):

```
<FRAMESET ROWS="50%,50%">
<FRAME SRC="index.html">
<FRAME SRC="help.html">
</FRAMESET>
```

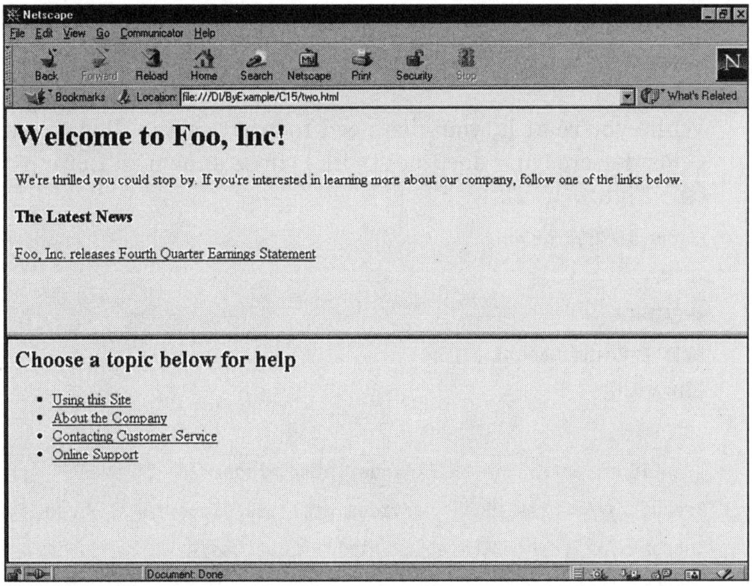

Figure 15.3: *The* <FRAME> *tag assigns URLs to each frame window.*

By using the <FRAME> tag, you create what's known as a frame window. Each window corresponds to a "row" or "column" definition in the <FRAMESET> tag, but nothing is drawn or displayed until an appropriate <FRAME> tag is used to define each individual window.

A Simple Frame Document

EXAMPLE

You'll essentially create the same document shown in Figure 15.3, but you should feel free to play with the numbers a bit to see how different percentages and even different attributes to <FRAMESET> change how the page displays. Enter Listing 15.1 in your text editor.

Listing 15.1: simpleframe.html: Simple Frame Document

```
<!DOCTYPE HTML PUBLIC "-//W3C//DTD HTML 4.0 Frameset//EN">
<HTML>
<HEAD>
<TITLE>Frame Example</TITLE>
```

continues

Listing 15.1: continued

```
</HEAD>
<FRAMESET ROWS="25%,75%">
<FRAME SRC="menu.html">
<FRAME SRC="help.html">
</FRAMESET>
</HTML>
```

While you're at it, you also need to create some files to put in those frames. Consider creating documents like those shown in Listings 15.2 and 15.3 (see Figure 15.4).

Listing 15.2: menu.html

```
<HTML>
<HEAD>
<TITLE>Frame Menu</TITLE>
</HEAD>
<BODY>
<P ALIGN="center"><A HREF="index.html">Index</A> ¦ <A HREF="products.html">
Products</A> ¦ <A HREF="services.html">Services</A> ¦ <A HREF="support.html">
Support</A> ¦ <A HREF="about.html">About Us</A>
</BODY>
</HTML>
```

Listing 15.3: help.html

```
<HTML>
<HEAD>
<TITLE>Frame Menu</TITLE>
</HEAD>
<BODY>
<H2>Choose a topic below for help</H2>
<UL>
<LI><a href="1.html">Using this Site</A>
<LI><A HREF="2.html">About the Company</A>
<LI><A HREF="3.html">Contacting Customer Service</A>
<LI><A HREF="4.html">Online Support</A>
</UL>
</BODY>
</HTML>
```

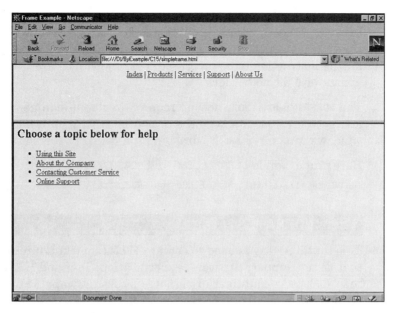

Figure 15.4: *Loading separate HTML documents into a frame-based page.*

If you'd like to experiment further, try changing the <FRAMESET> tag in Listing 15.1 to the following:

```
<FRAMESET COLS="25%,75%">
```

Or, change the percentages to see how that affects your layout.

Attributes for <FRAME>

Aside from SRC, the <FRAME> tag can accept the attributes NAME, MARGINWIDTH, MARGINHEIGHT, SCROLLING, FRAMEBORDER, and NORESIZE. All of these except NAME are appearance-oriented. Let's deal with those first and come back to NAME in a moment.

MARGINWIDTH and MARGINHEIGHT are used to control the right/left margins and the top/bottom margins of the text and graphics within a frame, respectively. Each takes a numerical value in pixels. For example:

```
<FRAME SRC="text.html" MARGINWIDTH="5" MARGINHEIGHT="5">
```

This creates a five-pixel border between the contents of text.html and the frame edges.

SCROLLING can accept the values yes, no, and auto. It's used to determine whether scrollbars will appear in the frame window. The default value is auto, and this is probably the best to use in most cases. Since users have different screen resolutions and available browser window space, even short documents sometimes need to be scrolled.

The FRAMEBORDER attribute is used to control the appearance of borders between the defined frames. When more than one frame shares a border, the values of FRAMEBORDER within each individual <FRAME> tag must match for the instruction to be processed. Possible values are 1 for borders to appear or 0 for no borders.

The NORESIZE attribute doesn't require a value assignment. (It's a Boolean attribute.) It's used to keep the user from resizing a frame window. (Frame windows can be resized by dragging the frame in the viewer window.)

Here's an example of SCROLLING and NORESIZE:

```
<FRAME SRC="text.html" SCROLLING="yes" NORESIZE>
```

The <NOFRAMES> Tag

This container tag is used to contain HTML markup intended for browsers that do not support the frames specification. Text and HTML tags inside the <NOFRAMES> container are ignored by frames-capable browsers. All others should generally ignore the other frames tags (which they won't recognize) and display the text between the <NOFRAMES> tags. The following is an example:

```
<FRAMESET ROWS="25%,75%">
<FRAME SRC="menu.html">
<FRAME SRC="index.html">
<NOFRAMES>
<P>This page requires a frames-capable browser to view. If you'd prefer,
you can access our <a href="noframes.html">unframed version</a>
to view this information without the frames interface.</P>
</NOFRAMES>
</FRAMESET>
```

EXAMPLE

Frames and No Frames

Now, we'll create another example, this time using the attributes and additional tags you've seen since the previous example. Create a new HTML document and enter Listing 15.4. (Use your own HTML document names for <FRAME SRC> if desired.)

Listing 15.4: frames2.html: Frames and No Frames

```
<HTML>
<HEAD>
<TTLE>Frames Example #2</TITLE>
</HEAD>
```

```
<FRAMESET COLS="25%,75%">
<NOFRAMES>
<P>If you are seeing this message, then your browser isn't capable of viewing
frames. Please access our <A HREF="plain.html">unframed</A> Web pages.</P>
<P>If you like, you can go directly to these pages in our site:
<UL>
<LI><A HREF="products.html">Product pages</A>
<LI><A HREF="support.html">Support pages</A>
<LI><A HREF="help.html">Help page</A>
</UL>
</NOFRAMES>
<FRAME SRC="index.html" MARGINWIDTH="5" MARGINHEIGHT="2" SCROLLING="no">
<FRAME SRC="info.html" MARGINWIDTH="5" MARGINHEIGHT="2" NORESIZE>
</FRAMESET>
</HTML>
```

Notice that you've used the attribute NORESIZE with the <FRAME> tags for the
second column. What's interesting about this is that it forces the first column to also be nonresizable because the columns share a common frame
border (see Figure 15.5). This is the case with any <FRAME> tag.

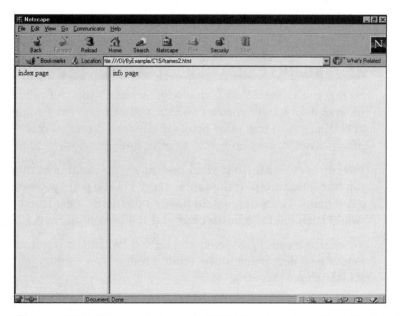

Figure 15.5: *The* <FRAME> *and* <NOFRAME> *tags in action. Notice that the
frame border can't be moved (resized).*

Experiment with different values for the <FRAME> attributes and see what makes a big difference in terms of margins, scrolling, and resizing. Also, if you have access to a browser that isn't frames-capable, load the page and see how the <NOFRAMES> markup looks (see Figure 15.6).

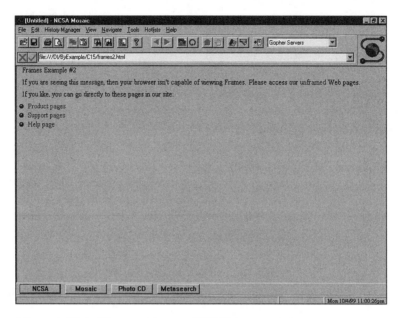

Figure 15.6: The <NOFRAMES> *HTML message.*

Targeting Frame Windows

So far, you've seen that frame windows offer you the cability to load URLs independent of one another so that you can present two (or more) different HTML pages in the same browser window. What good is this to you? In many cases, it may be useful to offer multiple documents at once.

For instance, with what you know now, you could use frames to add a button bar image map to the top of every HTML page you create. That would get tedious: Each link would have to point to a new frame document that would then load the button bar and the next document.

What if you could just leave the button bar in the top frame window and load a new document in the other window? You can do just that if you know a little about targeting.

The NAME Attribute

First, you need to name your frame windows; at least, you have to name
the windows you might want to change. This is accomplished with the NAME
attribute to the <FRAME> tag, which takes the following format:

```
<FRAME SRC="original URL" NAME="window-name">
```

EXAMPLE

This shouldn't look too foreign to you because it's a little like the way that
the NAME attribute works for <A NAME> links. Once the frame window has a
distinct name, you can access it directly from other frame windows. An
example of this is the following:

```
<FRAME SRC="index.html" NAME="main-viewer">
```

Although you can pretty much name your frame window anything you
want, there is one restriction: You can't start the name with an underscore
character (_). If you do, the name will be ignored. There's a good reason for
that. The underscore is used to signal a number of reserved target names.
You'll get to those after you learn how to target regular browser windows.

Targeting Frame Windows

With your frame successfully named, you're ready to target the name with
a hypertext link. This is accomplished with the TARGET attribute to a typical
<A> anchor tag. It follows this format:

```
<A HREF="new-URL" TARGET="window-name">link text</A>
```

EXAMPLE

The new-URL is the new document that you want to have appear in the
frame window. The window-name is the same name that you used to name
the frame windows with the NAME attribute to the <FRAME> tag. An example
is the following:

```
<A HREF="products.html" TARGET="main-viewer">View Products</A>
```

A Reason to Use Frames

Now, you finally have a good excuse for using frames. Let's create a document with two frames (in rows). In the top frame, you can put a quick
HTML menu of possibilities. In the second frame, put most of the information from your Web site. That's where you'll display the actual pages you've
created. The top frame will just be for static controls.

This will take two different listings, and both need to be complete Web documents (see Listings 15.5 and 15.6).

Listing 15.5: control2.html: Links for the Top Frame

```
<HTML>
<HEAD>
<TITLE>Controls</TITLE>
</HEAD>
<BODY>
<DIV ALIGN="CENTER">
<A HREF="index.html" TARGET="big-window">Index Page</A> ¦
<A HREF="products.html" TARGET="big-window">Products</A> ¦
<A HREF="service.html" TARGET="big-window">Customer Service</A> ¦
<A HREF="support.html" TARGET="big-window">Tech Support</A> ¦
<A HREF="about.html" TARGET="big-window">About Us</A>
</DIV>
</BODY>
</HTML>
```

That's the control document (save it as control2.html). Now, you'll create
the main frame document that will contain both this control document (at
the top) and whatever other documents it feels like tossing at the other
frame, called big-window.

Listing 15.6: frames3.html: The Frames Document

```
<HTML>
<HEAD>
<TITLE>Foo Inc World</TITLE>
</HEAD>
<FRAMESET ROWS="10%,90%">
<FRAME SRC="control2.html" SCROLLING="no" NORESIZE>
<FRAME SRC="help.html" NAME="big-window">
</FRAMESET>
</HTML>
```

Save the second file as frames.html. It's the one you'll load in your browser
window. Notice that you've told the second frame (the one named big-window) to load help.html initially. Although an empty frame is possible, you
generally don't want to do that; things work better with a default page in
every frame. You've also chosen certain attributes for the first frame. That's
just personal preference, but I'd rather have my viewers resize their
browser window to see all of the controls, so I won't allow that window to
scroll.

Finally, you can load frames.html in Netscape (see Figure 15.7). If all goes well, you should be able to click the menu items in the top frame and change the content in the bottom one!

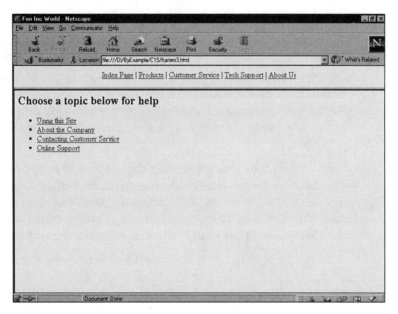

Figure 15.7: *At the top, it's always control2.html, but below, it's an ever-changing URL.*

Reserved Targets

Here's why you can't give frame windows a name that starts with an underscore. All reserved target names start with an underscore, which signals to the browser that they should treat this link in a special way. The following are some examples:

- `TARGET="_blank"`   The URL specified in this link will always be loaded in a new blank browser window.

- `TARGET="_self"`   This is used to force a link to load in the same window that it's clicked in.

- TARGET="_parent" This causes the document to load in the current window's parent—generally, the frame window immediately preceding it in the <FRAMESET> definition. If no parent exists, it acts like "_self".

- TARGET="_top" The document is loaded in the topmost frame of the current browser window.

Basically, these magic targets are designed to let you break out of the current <FRAMESET> structure in some way. Experiment with them to see how you can move around to different windows.

What's Next?

Frames provide designers with a way to load multiple Web pages in a single browser window. Creating frames requires a few new tags, including the <FRAMESET> container and the <FRAME> empty tag. <FRAMESET> containers can be nested to create columns within rows for multiple frame windows on a single page.

Dealing with frames also introduces the concept of *targeting,* which means naming frame windows and using the attribute TARGET to point anchor tags toward the named window. With targeting, however, comes the power of frames. With these two concepts, you can create detailed, elegant interfaces for your Web pages that really help you convey much information quickly.

Next up in Chapter 16, we'll start working with images and move into multimedia objects, allowing you to add more visual excitement to your Web pages.

Review Questions

1. What makes <FRAMESET> unique among the tags you've learned about so far?

2. True or false: A single <FRAMESET> can create either rows or columns for your page, but not both.

3. What does this page look like in a browser?

   ```
   <HTML>
   <HEAD>
   <TITLE>Test</TITLE>
   </HEAD>
   <FRAMESET COLS="25%, 75%">
   <FRAMESET ROWS="100%">
   </FRAMESET>
   ```

```
<FRAMESET ROWS="50%, *">
</FRAMESET>
</FRAMESET>
</HTML>
```

4. What's the default setting for the SCROLLING attribute to the <FRAME> tag?

5. Why does text between <NOFRAMES> appear in nonframe browsers but not in frame-capable browsers?

6. What is the one rule for naming frame windows with the NAME attribute to the <FRAME> tag?

7. Aside from the anchor tag, what two other tags can accept the TARGET attribute?

8. True or false: Reserved targets are shortcuts for more complicated TARGET statements.

Review Exercises

1. Create a frames document with two frames—one for a fixed image map interface and the other to act as a target for the pages of a Web site. Create the image map so that it targets the main frame window with new pages from the site.

2. Now, put the client-side image map at the bottom 10 percent of the page, with the Web site pages targeted at the top.

3. Using clickable graphics, create an interface in a frame window along the left side of your page. On the right side, display the pages that are loaded by the form buttons. Make sure each clickable graphic appears below the one before it.

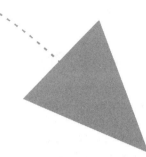

16

Images, Multimedia Objects, and Background Graphics

It is, perhaps, appropriate homage to the turbulent nature of HTML that the title of this chapter changed three times during the development of the first edition of this book, between its conception and its final form. Initially conceived to discuss the <FIG> tag of the HTML 3 specification, it became clear that the HTML Working Group was going in another direction. At the same time, the <IMG> tag has been expanded somewhat to offer control over layout, and new tags were developed to handle page components that were more than just still pictures.

This chapter teaches you the following:

- How to use the <IMG> tag
- How to insert multimedia objects into your Web pages
- How to choose a background color
- How to use images as page backgrounds

More Visual Control with `<IMG>`

For the most part, today's graphical browsers seem to agree that the ALIGN attribute for the `<IMG>` tag is here to stay. As you learned in Chapter 9, "Adding Graphics to Your Web Pages," the `<IMG>` tag is useful for both graphical and nongraphical browsers because it allows for the text-only ALT attribute, which can explain your graphics to users who can't see them.

The ALIGN attribute allows more control over the display of the graphic and whether text will wrap around it. Its general format is the following:

```
<IMG SRC="URL" ALT="text description" ALIGN="Direction">
```

Appropriate values for the ALIGN attribute include TOP, MIDDLE, BOTTOM, LEFT, and RIGHT. It's important to remember that for all ALIGN attributes, the direction refers to where text will be displayed *in relation to the graphic image*—not the other way around. In essence, you're using this attribute to align text to the graphic—not to align the graphic to anything in particular.

EXAMPLE

Consider the following example. Without the ALIGN attribute, you could render a graphic as the following:

```
<P>I just thought you might be interested in seeing this photo I've edited for
myself in PhotoShop. <IMG SRC="image1.gif" ALT="My Graphic"> I was actually a
bit surprised at how easy it was to manipulate. I'm no artist, but there are
enough filters and special effects in PhotoShop that I can do some pretty neat
tricks with it, even though I don't really know what I'm doing!</P>
```

The following is the same example, except that the ALIGN attribute is set to LEFT:

```
<P>I just thought you might be interested in seeing this photo I've edited for
myself in PhotoShop. <IMG SRC="image1.gif" ALT="My Graphic" ALIGN="Left"> I was
actually a bit surprised at how easy it was to manipulate. I'm no artist, but
there are enough filters and special effects in PhotoShop that I can do some
pretty neat tricks with it, even though I don't really know what I'm doing!</P>
```

Figure 16.1 shows you how these appear in a typical graphical browser. Interesting, isn't it?

As you can see, the ALIGN="LEFT" attribute forces this image to be displayed to the left of the text and allows text to wrap above and below it on the page. Without it, the image is displayed inline. (When a graphic is displayed inline, it appears at the exact point in the text that the `<IMG>` tag appears.)

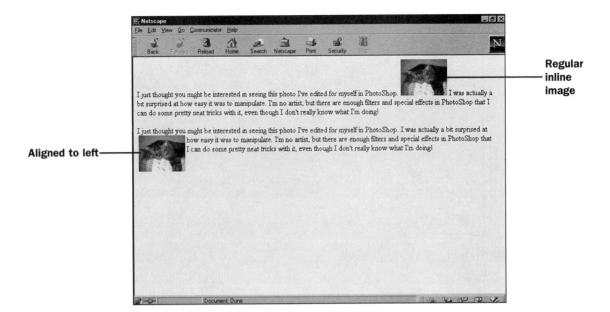

Regular inline image

Aligned to left

Figure 16.1: *Using the* ALIGN *attribute with the* <IMG> *tag.*

TIP

Aligning to the LEFT and RIGHT is most effective when the graphic is embedded in a long paragraph of text to achieve a "text-wrap" feel.

EXAMPLE

Aligning to the RIGHT works in a similar way:

```
<P>I just thought you might be interested in seeing this graphic I've created
for myself in PhotoShop. <IMG SRC="image1.gif" ALT="My Graphic" ALIGN="RIGHT">
I was actually a bit surprised at how easy it was to create. I'm not an artist,
but there are enough filters and special effects in PhotoShop that it makes it
possible for me to create something this professional looking without being
absolutely sure of what I'm doing!</P>
```

The graphic is lined up with the right border of the browser window (see Figure 16.2). It's flexible with that window, so dragging the window to make it larger or smaller would affect where the image would appear relative to the text.

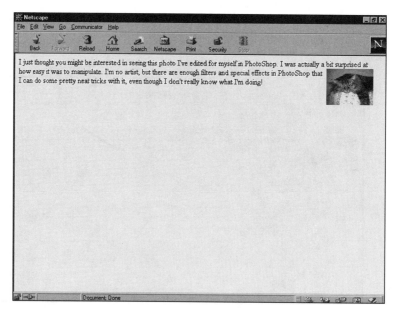

Figure 16.2: ALIGN *to* RIGHT.

EXAMPLE

Magazine-Style Presentation

One of the nicer things about gaining this kind of control over your graphics is the options it gives you to present a long page of text in a way that's a little more pleasing to the eye—by breaking it up with graphics. This example is an article I've written for a local magazine. Also notice the advantage in putting this particular article in HTML form: You can add hypertext links where appropriate.

Start with a fresh HTML document (from your template) and enter something similar to Listing 16.1 between the <BODY> tags.

Listing 16.1: story.html: Using ALIGN for HTML Page Layout

```
<BODY>
<P>By mixing alignments, you can create a more interesting layout for your pages
that incorporate both text and images. This is a technique you'll frequently see
in magazines and newspapers.

<P>To demonstrate, I'll tell you a little bit more about my cat Dizzy.
<IMG SRC="small.jpg" ALIGN="RIGHT" ALT="Dizzy Snoozing">You've met her already
in previous chapters, where we caught her snoozing on the back of a recliner.
Like most cats, one of Dizzy's favorite activities is napping. The recliner is
obviously a favorite spot, as is one of the patio chairs out on the lanai, and
underneath a coffee table in the living room where she thinks she's in a little
```

```
cave.

<P>Speaking of caves, Dizzy loves to jump into open boxes, drawers, bags, and
anything else where she can feel like she's hiding.
<IMG SRC="cave.jpg" ALIGN="LEFT" ALT="Dizzy in a cave">One day, I walked by the
guest room and noticed a strange lump in the quilt. I peered at it, and realized
that Dizzy had dug herself a cave in the bed! She didn't realize, at first, that
she was visible from the side when I snapped this picture.

<P>Pets sure are fun, aren't they?
</BODY>
```

It's a little hit-or-miss because some of how the graphics will appear is based on the size of the browser window. Check out Figure 16.3.

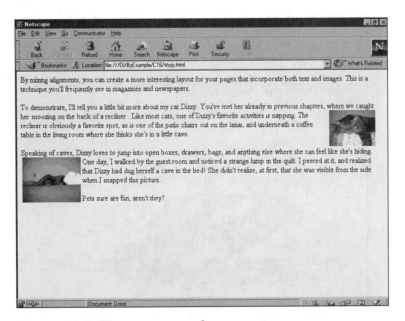

Figure 16.3: *The* ALIGN *example.*

Inserting Multimedia Objects

One of the biggest obstacles facing multimedia authors is the lack of consensus between browsers on what tags should be used to insert those components into your Web pages. HTML 3 started working with <INSERT>, which was dropped. Then Netscape came up with <EMBED>, which many designers were quick to adopt, but which never made it into HTML 4. Then the W3C chose <OBJECT> for HTML 4, which hasn't made it into some of the browsers! So what's a designer to do? Improvise!

Some video clips can be placed in the page using the <IMG> tag. Other objects, such as Java applets, actually have their own tags. Many more fun items, such as Shockwave presentations and Flash animations, make use of plug-ins and helper applications.

While I generally hate to suggest that you use tags that aren't in the HTML 4 specification, when it comes to some multimedia objects, it's the only way to go until browsers start supporting the <OBJECT> tag with any consistency.

First, let's look at how the specification is supposed to work, after which you can see what steps you may want to take to support one browser or another.

EXAMPLE

Let's take our first look at <OBJECT> by reviewing the code used to include a Macromedia Flash presentation on a Web site. My friends at Nerdygirl.com have an interesting splash screen made with Flash, as shown in Figure 16.4. (A *splash screen* is the initial screen at a Web site's "front door.")

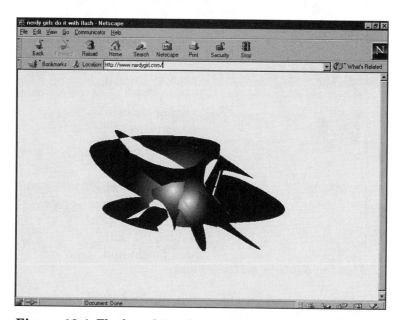

Figure 16.4: *Flash multimedia presentations are incorporated using the* <OBJECT> *tag.*

The following HTML code was used on this Web page:

```
<OBJECT CLASSID ="clsid:D27CDB6E-AE6D-11cf-96B8-444553540000"
CODEBASE="swflash.cab#version=4,0,0,0" ID="ngirl" "
```

```
WIDTH="100% "HEIGHT="100%"><param name="Movie" value="assets/ngirl4.swf">
param name="Loop" value="False">
<param name="Play" value="True"><param name="BGColor" value="ffffff">
<param name="Quality"
value="AutoHIGH"><param name="Scale" value="ShowAll">
<param name="SAlign" value="L"><param name="Base"
value="http://www.nerdygirl.com/"><param name="Menu" value="True">
<embed src="assets/ngirl4.swf" width=100%
height=100% name="ngirl" loop="false" play="true" bgcolor="ffffff"
quality="AutoLow" scale="ShowAll" align="L"
base="http://www.nerdygirl.com/" menu="true"></object><noembed>You might
consider a more talented
browser.<br><a href="index2.html">Try this</a>.</noembed>
```

Don't let this intimidate you. Considered piece by piece, these tags are no harder than any others you've worked with so far. To begin, we have the <OBJECT> tag. It acts as a container for the multimedia object itself and any other information that will be needed by the helper application or plug-in used to display it.

The <OBJECT> tag has five attributes in this example:

```
<OBJECT CLASSID ="clsid:D27CDB6E-AE6D-11cf-96B8-444553540000"
CODEBASE="swflash.cab#version=4,0,0,0" ID="ngirl" WIDTH="100%" "HEIGHT="100%">
```

The CLASSID attribute is a string of characters provided by Macromedia (the makers of the Flash authoring software). This tells the browser plug-in some details about the object it's going to load. You don't really need to worry about any more than copying it correctly if you use a Flash object.

The CODEBASE attribute tells the browser which version of Flash was used to create this object so that the right plug-in can be loaded. ID is a unique name given to the object by the page author. WIDTH and HEIGHT work as they do for regular images. In this case, the author wants to make sure that the object is presented at its normal height and width within the page, so she uses values of 100%.

The next tag we find inside the <OBJECT> container is a <PARAM> tag:

```
<param name="Movie" value="assets/ngirl4.swf">
```

PARAM stands for *parameter,* which is sort of a fancy way of saying "details." The <PARAM> tag has an attribute of NAME, which the author uses to give it a unique identity (much like the NAME attribute on a <META> tag). The value in this case is the URL for the movie's source file.

The <PARAM> tag is used to offer additional parameters to the <INSERT> tag—information such as how many times to play a movie clip. The <PARAM> tag takes elements NAME and VALUE, which work a little like they do for certain table tags. Unfortunately, each different type of multimedia file requires different NAME and VALUE values, so you have to seek those out from the creator of the particular object type you want to send.

Additional information about whether the movie should play more than once (LOOP), whether it should start automatically (PLAY), what background color it should have, and so on is stored in additional <PARAM> tags.

Finally, the last tag within the <OBJECT> container is the <EMBED> tag. This is where we start moving away from the HTML 4 specification. Since some browsers don't yet properly support <OBJECT> but do support <EMBED>, most multimedia authors make accommodations for them when creating their pages. Including the <EMBED> tag within the <OBJECT> container allows a browser that does understand <OBJECT> to go about its business undisturbed (and without launching a second instance of the multimedia object). Also, it allows a browser that doesn't understand <OBJECT> to see the <EMBED> tag and load the multimedia that way.

Notice that the <EMBED> tag has attributes that coincide with most of the <PARAM> tags found inside the <OBJECT> container:

```
<EMBED SRC="assets/ngirl4.swf" WIDTH="100%" HEIGHT="100%" NAME="ngirl"
LOOP="false" PLAY="true" BGCOLOR="ffffff" QUALITY="AutoLow" SCALE="ShowAll"
ALIGN="L" BASE="http://www.nerdygirl.com/" MENU="true">
```

Finally, to be as complete as possible in your multimedia presentation, you can use the <NOEMBED> tag to provide details or guidance for those people using browsers that don't understand both <OBJECT> and <EMBED>.

<NOEMBED> acts as a container that can hold links and most other HTML markup. One option many designers use is to provide a link to either a browser that can handle the multimedia object desired or to a newer browser's plug-in page, in cases such as with Shockwave and Flash, where the browser can easily handle the multimedia file if it has the correct plug-in.

Changing Your Page's Background Look

Let's face it: Sometimes, a plain white background can be a bit boring. This really isn't news or just related to Web pages. People have been experimenting with how their documents look for years. The popularity and proliferation of colored papers, newsletters with borders, and the variety of styles in which books and magazines are printed give testament to our love of color.

HTML 4 lets you choose between both solid colors and images to be used to subtly (or sometimes not so subtly!) enhance your pages. First we'll take a look at changing the color from basic white to any hue you can imagine.

Choosing a Background Color

The toughest part of using background colors, other than choosing one, is determining the necessary color code to use in the <BODY> tag.

Background color is set using the BGCOLOR attribute:

```
<BODY BGCOLOR="white">
```

Unfortunately, only 16 colors have universally recognized names that can be used as I did in this example. All the other possible colors need to be referenced using their hexadecimal color value.

If you've had any art training at all, you might remember that all colors are made up of a mixture of red, green, and blue (often abbreviated as RGB). Traditional computer graphics software often shows these values using numerals between 0 and 255, as shown in Figure 16.5.

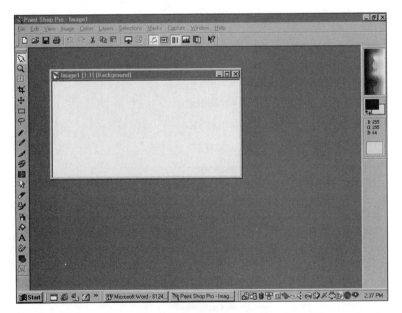

Figure 16.5: *Paint Shop Pro shows us that the yellow color is composed of a full saturation of red and green (as shown by the 255 values) and a partial saturation of blue.*

If we were to write white using the 0 to 255 values, it would be the full saturation of red, green, and blue, or 255, 255, 255.

Hexadecimal values, then, are the representation of the color's makeup of red, blue, and green, expressed in hexadecimal notation. Hexidecimal is the base-16 numbering system. (We normally count in base-10.)

> **NOTE**
>
> Don't panic just yet. You won't be required to learn how to count in base-16. Instead, just be aware that it's an easy way for computers to deal with the RGB color mixture.

Changing white into hexadecimal is easy, as long as you know what the base-16 equivalent of 255 is: the characters FF. So to represent white in hexadecimal (or "hex"), you simply write #FFFFFF. The # character (hash mark) is used to let the computer know that the six characters that follow are indeed a color code.

Table 16.1 lists 16 colors that have English names and their corresponding hexadecimal values.

Table 16.1: Color Hexadecimal Values

Color Name	Hexadecimal Value
Aqua	#00FFFF
Black	#000000
Blue	#0000FF
Fuchsia	#FF00FF
Gray	#808080
Green	#008000
Lime	#00FF00
Maroon	#800000
Navy	#000080
Olive	#808000
Purple	#800080
Red	#FF0000
Silver	#C0C0C0
Teal	#008080
White	#FFFFFF
Yellow	#FFFF00

CAUTION

It's important to note in these color values that the 0 character is the number zero (0), not the capital letter O. If you use the capital O character, the browser will likely give you unintended results!

You can find additional hexadecimal color values in charts and interactive tools online or by using software programs that were written to help you convert them. Try these URLs for more information:

- **The Palette Man**   An interactive color-selection tool online at `http://www.paletteman.com`.

- **ColorMix**   Another online tool that explains the process of dithering colors to come up with more combinations. See it at `http://www.colormix.com`.

- **Victor Engel's Browser Safe Palette**   A color chart that looks good even on low-color-resolution systems at `http://the-light.com/netcol.html`.

Using Images for a Page Background

In addition to solid-colored backgrounds, designers have the option of using GIF or JPG images for backgrounds. The trick to this is twofold: finding an image subtle enough that your text isn't obscured, making it unreadable, and finding an image that will tile well.

EXAMPLE

Tiling is the process of a graphic's being displayed more than once, essentially repeating from left to right and top to bottom. As long as there is Web page content to be displayed horizontally that is beyond the width of the graphic, it will tile from left to right. Likewise, as long as there is Web page content to be displayed vertically, the graphic will tile from top to bottom. Figure 16.6 is a small graphic that will be used in this manner. Figure 16.7 shows that same graphic tiled several times in each direction.

As with the solid background color, a background image is set using an attribute on the BODY tag; this time it's BACKGROUND. The value is the URL for the image file:

```
<BODY BACKGROUND="my-background-image.gif">
```

Figure 16.7: *The smaller the graphic, the more times it will tile in a Web page.*

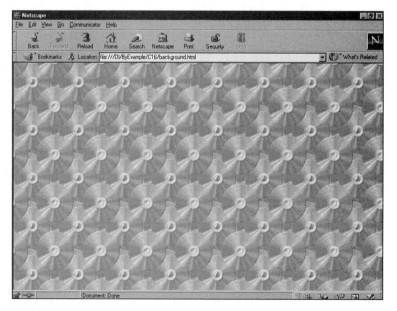

Figure 16.7: *The single image, tiled repeatedly.*

Background Images Versus Inline Images

There are three major differences to remember when working with background images versus inline images:

- The image URL is named in the <BODY> tag, using the BACKGROUND attribute. It does not have its own <IMG> tag.

- Background images can't take an ALT attribute.

- There are no HEIGHT and WIDTH attributes for the background.

What's Next?

The turbulent world of HTML offers several different ways to add graphical interest to your pages. You've re-examined the <IMG> tag discussed previously, adding attributes for alignment, image size, and alternative text. The alignment attributes are powerful in that they not only align the image in relation to the browser window, but they also allow text to wrap around the graphics themselves.

The <OBJECT> tag is a relatively new addition to HTML, designed to make it easier to add multimedia elements to Web pages. Unfortunately, even today's most popular browsers don't always understand it, necessitating the use of <EMBED> as a backup.

Finally, HTML offers the option of changing the color used for the background of Web pages and even incorporating images in place of solid color. The key is to use both background colors and graphics that don't interfere with the text color of the user's browser, which is usually set to black by default.

Next up in Chapter 17, we'll further explore the capabilities of images on your Web pages with the introduction of client-side image maps. This handy feature lets you create multiple "hot zones" for links within a single image, providing easy navigation tools even within a complex or non linear visual design.

Review Questions

1. What direction does the ALIGN attribute control when used on the <IMG> tag?

2. True or false: The ALIGN attribute for the <IMG> tag forces text to be aligned relative to the image.

3. What word describes the way that graphics are placed (relative to text) when the ALIGN attribute isn't used?

4. Why is <OBJECT> considered the "correct" way of incorporating multimedia objects in your Web pages?

5. If <OBJECT> is correct, why did you learn how to use <EMBED>?

6. What is the <NOEMBED> tag used for? How does it differ from <OBJECT>?

7. What can the <NOEMBED> container hold?

8. Do you need to learn to count in hexadecimal to use background colors in your Web page?

9. What does tiling mean?

Review Exercises

1. Use the ALIGN attribute with an image map graphic. Does it work correctly?

2. Again using ALIGN, test a small image and a long paragraph of text. Experiment a bit by placing the <IMG> tag at different points in the text. Does the image alignment vary according to where you place the tag? Also try this experiment without the ALIGN attribute to see how <IMG> appears when it's an inline graphic.

3. Test your browser's support of the <OBJECT> tag by using it to add a QuickTime or AVI movie to an HTML document.

4. Try adding different graphics as a background image on your Web page. See what kind of graphics work best behind text and which make reading difficult.

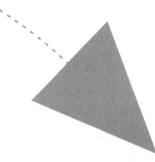

Client-Side Image Maps

Until this point, any images that you've used in creating navigation menus have been *linear*, that is, a series of images lined up horizontally, or perhaps stacked vertically within a table. As nice as these designs can be, they do tend to get rather predictable.

An interesting innovation, then, came in the ability to use a single image and to map portions of it to correspond to different URLs. The technology became known as *image maps*.

This chapter teaches you the following:

- How client-side image maps work

- How to plot and shape hot zones

- How to use software tools to create image maps

- Considerations to take into account as you design your image maps

What's a Client-Side Image Map?

You've probably heard of client/server technology, even if you aren't sure what it means. Essentially, client/server describes the relationship between computers on the Internet (and elsewhere in computer networking), which of course is just a giant network of computers. In most cases on the Web, for instance, the server is the Web server. The client is the Web browser program you use to access information on that server.

Back in the early days of HTML, image maps were nearly all server-side image maps, in that they required a special map server program to determine what coordinates on the screen matched up with what URLs. These mapped areas are referred to as *hot zones*. Instead of having your browser send a URL to the Web server, the map server program sent it.

Client-side image maps don't require a special map server to determine where the user clicked and what URL should be accessed. Instead, if properly marked up by the Web designer, a client-side image map is interpreted by the browser itself, which simply loads the URL as if a regular hypertext link were clicked. This clearly requires a client-side–aware browser such as Netscape Navigator, Microsoft Internet Explorer, Opera, or most other graphical browsers.

Advantages of Client-Side Image Maps

The inherent advantages of using client-side image maps are considerable. First, they do away with the need for extra files and programs on the Web server, which should be a great relief to nonprogramming Web designers. Client-side maps are just more HTML markup—and no CGI-BIN programming.

Related to that is the control that client-side maps offer you. As a designer, you're not forced to deal with your Web administrator to offer image maps to your users. If you don't think that's a big deal, think of what you might have to do to get the server administrators from the major online services to do that for you (such as AOL's member pages).

Finally, client-side maps don't require a Web server—or the HTTP protocol—at all. In fact, they don't even have to be on the Internet. It will become more and more common to see non-Web applications for HTML in the future (like CD-ROM–based HTML archives) where a Web server isn't part of the picture. With client-side maps, you don't need a server to create an interface.

The Various Shapes of Hot Zones

This section briefly defines the shapes of hot zones. Hot zones can be in any of the following shapes:

- **Rect (rectangle)**   This shape requires two points: the upper-left coordinates and the lower-right coordinates.

- **Circle**   To create a circular region, you need coordinates for a center point and an edge point. The circle is then computed with that radius.

- **Point**   A point requires only one coordinate. The map server software decides which point the mouse pointer was closest to when the shape was clicked (provided that the click didn't occur in another hot zone).

- **Poly (polygon)**   You can use up to 100 sets of coordinates to determine all the vertices for the polygon region.

- **Default**   Any part of the graphic that is not included in another hot zone is considered to be part of the default region, as long as no point zones are defined. If a point is defined, default is redundant because the map server will evaluate any click (outside of a hot zone) and choose the nearest point.

Figure 17.1 is the home page of the Stanford Linear Accelerator's Virtual Visitor Center. Notice the 13 options across the top: nine colored balls with text descriptions of the site's sections and four more traditional button images for site tools.

The map definition is set as a series of rectangles that outline each option. Careful placement of the rectangles will get them lined up so that visitors can click nearly anywhere on each text line or colored ball and get to where they wanted to go.

EXAMPLE

Creating a Map Definition File

There is one basic rule for creating image maps: Keep it simple! Take a look at your graphic. If *you* were going to click on a portion of it, where would you click? Have a friend look at it, and see if she goes for the same spot. Remember that if you use bullets or other graphical elements paired with text within your image, some people tend to click the bullet, and others tend to click the text. Make sure both pieces are within the same hot zone.

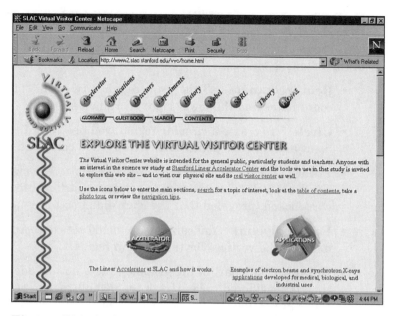

Figure 17.1: *An image map at work on the Web.*

EXAMPLE

Creating a Client-Side Image Map

As I mentioned earlier, one of the easiest ways to create an image map is to use one of many popular software tools designed to do just that. In this example, we'll use Web Hotspots 4.01 for Windows. Have your image and a new file based on your HTML template ready to go.

To begin, launch the program, choose File, Open, and open the image you want to use as your map (see Figure 17.2). Pick something easy to work with, such as a map where you can place hotspots over cities or a long bar that's visually divided into segments.

The image will open in the main editing window. Choose the shape of your first hotspot from the toolbar on the left. I'll use a square. Click the upper-left corner of what will be your rectangle, and then drag the mouse down and to the right until the spot is big enough. (Of course, you don't have to start in the upper-right corner; you can work in any direction.) When you release the mouse button, a dotted outline appears around your hotspot, and you can edit the URL that corresponds to it (see Figure 17.3).

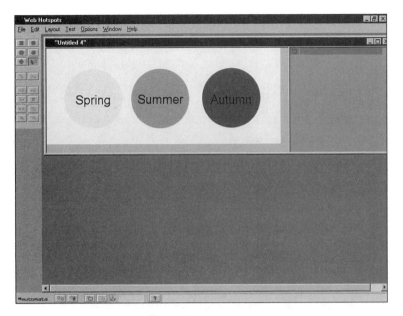

Figure 17.2: *The image map editing tool interface.*

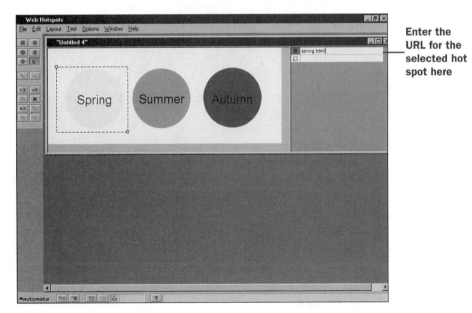

Enter the URL for the selected hot spot here

Figure 17.3: *Creating a new hotspot.*

Continue working in the same manner until you've set each hotspot needed. When finished, choose File, Save. Locate your HTML file in the Save Imagemap Into dialog, shown in Figure 17.4, and click Save.

Figure 17.4: *Choose the HTML file where the image map should be saved.*

A second dialog for implementation options appears, asking for the URL for the image's SRC attribute, the name of the map (they all have one), and the ALT text to use for the entire map. Enter the details as appropriate, and click OK.

Looking in my HTML file, I found the following new code added to it:

```
<MAP NAME="nav-map">

<AREA HREF="autumn.html" SHAPE="RECT" COORDS="327,41,482,174">

<AREA HREF="summer.html" SHAPE="CIRCLE" COORDS="243,106,74">

<AREA HREF="spring.html" SHAPE="RECT" COORDS="18,39,171,175">

</MAP>

<img src="map.gif" border=0 NAME="nav-map" WIDTH="500" HEIGHT="200"

USEMAP="#nav-map" ALT="Navigation Map - Spring, Summer, and Autumn">
```

In the next section, we'll take a closer look at each new element and attribute found in these tags.

Adding a Client-Side Map to Your Web Page

As you can see from the code produced by Web Hotspots, client-side maps require two different sections of code—the <IMG> tag and a new tag, the <MAP> container.

The <IMG> Tag

Although it comes second in our code sample, let's look at the <IMG> tag first. To create a client-side image map, you need to add the new attribute USEMAP, as follows:

```
<IMG SRC="map.gif" USEMAP="#nav-map">
```

Notice that USEMAP accepts a fragment-style hyperlink. That's how you can store the map definition information in the same HTML document. Here's the complete example:

```
<IMG SRC="map-name.gif" USEMAP="#nav-map" BORDER="0" NAME="nav-map" WIDTH="500"
HEIGHT="200" ALT="Navigation Map - Spring, Summer, and Autumn">
```

TIP

As with all images, be complete with your image map tag. Set your border value to 0 if you don't want the entire map wrapped in a link border, always use the actual height and width values, and provide alternative text.

That's all you need in order to display the image and tell the browser that this is a client-side image map. Now, you need to create the definition that the browser will use for that map.

The <MAP> Tag

The <MAP> tag is a container tag that is referenced using the fragment-style NAME attribute. Inside the <MAP> container, you use the <AREA> tag to define each hot zone for the client-side map. Here's how it works:

```
<MAP NAME="name">
<AREA SHAPE="shape1" COORDS="coordinate numbers" HREF="URL"
ALT="alternative text">
<AREA SHAPE="shape2" COORDS="coordinate numbers" HREF="URL"
ALT="alternative text">
...
</MAP>
```

Notice that most of the information for each <AREA> tag can be automatically generated by a map-editing tool, but you can do this by hand. Suppose that you don't have an editing tool, and you need to plot the coordinates. Open your map image in a regular graphics-editing tool, such as Paint Shop Pro, and you'll be able to find the coordinates.

First, let's take a closer look at the <AREA> tag.

The <AREA> Tag

There are only three basic shapes. (Remember this when you use your map-editing program to determine coordinates.) The SHAPE attribute is used to accept these values. The numbers are given to the COORD attribute. The three basic shapes are as follows:

- **RECT**   The rectangular hot zone requires four coordinates: the top-left corner and the bottom-right corner. An example would be 1,0,55,54, which places the left at pixel 1, the top at pixel 0, the right at 55, and the bottom at 54.

- **CIRCLE**   A circular zone requires three different coordinates: center-x, center-y, and a radius. An example might be 20,20,5, which would represent a circle with its center at 20,20 and a radius of 5 pixels.

- **POLYGON**   For a polygon, each vertex requires a pair of points as its definition. (This is nearly the same as is created by most map definition programs.) A COORD value of 1,2,55,56,1,99 would create a polygon (triangle) with a vertex at 1,2, a second one at 55,56, and a third at 1,99.

The HREF attribute is used to give the appropriate URL for each hot zone. If no URL is desired, the attribute NOHREF can be used to make a particular hot zone useless.

EXAMPLE

Mapping Coordinates by Hand

Use the selection tool to select an area of the image that represents the first hotspot you want to create (see Figure 17.5). Don't release the mouse button. Look at the status bar, and notice the numbers in parentheses. The first set represents the coordinates where you first placed the mouse and clicked. The second set represents the current position of the mouse. The four numbers together represent the coordinates of a rectangle: your hotspot! Copy those numbers down, and use them in your first shape:

```
<AREA SHAPE="rect" COORDS="27,40,174,173" HREF="spring.html"
ALT="Our Spring Collection">
```

Creating a circle is a bit trickier without a mapping program or an image editor that doesn't give these exact coordinates. (I've found that Paint Shop Pro doesn't, but CorelDRAW! does. Check your program as we did in creating the rectangle.) You need the coordinates of the exact center of the circle, plus the radius. You can find these numbers by creating a square selection and finding its midpoint. From our previous selection, that would be 174 minus 27 (the two x coordinates) divided by 2 to get half the width, which is 73.5 (in this case, rounding to 74 or 73 is fine). Do the same with the height (173–40 = 133 / 2 = 66.5), and you have a midpoint of 74, 67. (Note that our original wasn't a perfect square, so if you used this, your circle would be a bit off.) The radius, then, is simply half the square's width.

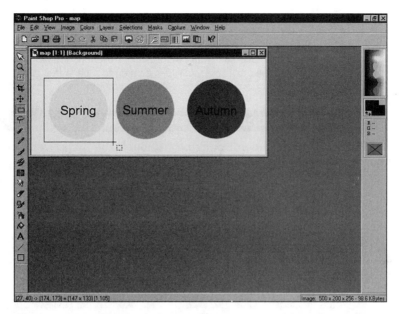

Figure 17.5: *Checking for coordinates.*

EXAMPLE

Here are three different examples of <AREA> tags:

```
<AREA SHAPE="RECT" COORDS="0,0,49,49" HREF="about_me.html"ALT="About Me">
<AREA SHAPE="CIRCLE" COORDS="75,49,10" HREF="resume.html"ALT="My resume">
<AREA SHAPE="POLYGON" COORDS="50,0,65,0,80,10,65,20,50,20" HREF="fun.html"
ALT="How I have fun">
```

To complete our image map sample, we'll create two more <AREA> tags, one for each additional hotspot. Here is the final result:

```
<MAP NAME="nav-map">
<AREA HREF="autumn.html" SHAPE="RECT" COORDS="327,41,482,174"
ALT="Our Autumn Collection">
<AREA HREF="summer.html" SHAPE="CIRCLE" COORDS="243,106,74"
ALT="Our Summer Collection">
<AREA HREF="spring.html" SHAPE="RECT" COORDS="18,39,171,175"
ALT="Our Spring Collection">
</MAP>
<img src="map.gif" border=0 NAME="nav-map" WIDTH="500" HEIGHT="200"
USEMAP="#nav-map" ALT="Navigation Map - Spring, Summer, and Autumn">
```

TIP

With all maps, but especially those created by hand, review the final coordinates and test each map to make sure your hotspots don't overlap. Two hotspots covering the same points will lead to some users being taken to a page they didn't select!

Design Choices for Image Maps

I probably should point out that although the maps we've been working with in this chapter have been rather linear—that is, they go straight across from left to right—that's not required. Indeed, some of the best image maps are distinctly nonlinear, using curves, a patchwork effect, and other layout devices that bring visual excitement to the page.

EXAMPLE

Figure 17.6 illustrates how random placement of images can still provide very workable links. Each individual graphic within the bounds of the dotted line is a hotspot.

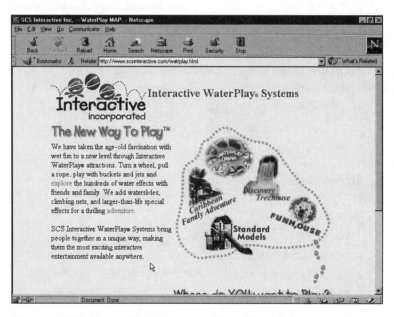

Figure 17.6: Irregular layouts work well with image maps.

Other, more predictable patterns may also be used, while still being nonlinear in form, such as the graceful curves shown in the map in Figure 17.7.

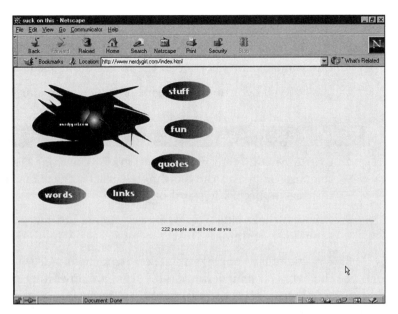

Figure 17.7: *Smooth curves within an image map.*

What's Next?

Client-side image maps have become the standard for providing links within larger graphics. Coordinates of clickable areas are mapped to the graphic, creating what's known as hotspots.

Creating a client-side map can be made much easier if you use a map-editing program to determine the appropriate coordinates for your particular graphic. With that information, you can create the <MAP> container element, which includes the information relevant to each hot zone.

You should keep the hot zone shapes fairly uncomplicated for client-side maps because there are only three shapes to work with, and the hot zone coordinates must be entered by hand.

Next up in Chapter 18, we'll take a look at one of the Web's newer technologies: Cascading Style Sheets, or CSS. The W3C is responsible for the design of this language, which allows designers more robust control over the presentational elements of the Web page designs.

Review Questions

1. Which attribute of the <IMG> tag is used to create a link to the client-side map data? What tag is used to contain that data?

2. What are the three shapes for client-side hotspots?

3. What purpose does the ALT attribute serve for the <AREA> tag?

4. Can you leave any portion of the image unmapped?

5. How do you determine the coordinates for a circular hotspot?

Review Exercises

1. Create two different map definitions for the same graphic, and then compare them. Are the coordinates exactly the same? If not, what are the most appropriate coordinates?

2. Create a client-side map with overlapping hot zones (as defined in your <MAP> container). Test it in a browser. What happens?

3. Using a fairly simple graphic, create a client-side image map without the help of a map definition file from a map-editing program. Use simple shapes and try to estimate the appropriate coordinates for hot zones.

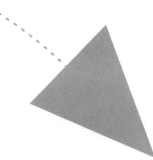

Enhancing Your Pages with Style Sheets

You'll remember that back in the first few chapters of this book, we spent a lot of time talking about what HTML is and isn't. Remember that the purpose of HTML is described in its name: It is the Hypertext Markup Language. It's not a programming language, nor a layout and design language, but a markup language.

In the earliest versions of HTML, we had only structural elements available, containers like <BODY>, <P>, and <A> tags for links. The presentation of these elements depended on how the programmer who created the browser decided to display them.

As the Web gained popularity, designers suggested tags for handling the visual side of documents, such as alignment, color choices, and more. You've been using those tags in the examples provided in most of the chapters before this one and with good results. So why do we need to use something else?

One of the initial selling points of the Web is still a very important factor today. Web pages need to be able to be displayed on any type of computer, from desktop workstations to laptops, PDAs, hand-held computers, speech readers, cell phones, and any other type of device we haven't yet thought of. If we provide detailed presentation information directly in the HTML markup, we increase the chances that one of those devices may not be able to display the document.

Style sheets, then, provide a means to separate the presentation from the structure of the document. The presentation details can be stored in a separate portion of the same file, via the <HEAD> element, or even in an external file, formally known as the *style sheet*.

This chapter teaches you the following:

- The syntax used for CSS style declarations
- What properties can be adjusted using CSS

- How to change colors using style sheets
- The rules of inheritance

A Basic Style Declaration

The easiest way to start including style information in your Web pages is to use the container tag <STYLE>, which appears in the document's <HEAD> container. Within the <STYLE> container, individual style "rules" are written that operate on whatever element you choose.

EXAMPLE

For example, let's create a <STYLE> container that will tell the browser to render <H1> tags in green, to center paragraph tags, and to add blue coloring to <I> tags. To do that, we would write the following:

```
<STYLE TYPE="text/css">
<!--
H1 {color:green}
P {text-align:center}
I {color:blue}
-->
</STYLE>
```

The first thing you'll notice is that the <STYLE> tag has an attribute of TYPE. The value is "text/css", which tells the browser that the data is stored in ASCII text form (versus a binary file or some other storage format) and that it is written in CSS, or *cascading style sheets*. CSS is one flavor of style sheet. Others are being developed, but none are yet as popular or widely deployed as CSS.

Next, the contents of the <STYLE> container are bounded by an HTML comment. This helps prevent any browser that doesn't understand style sheets from trying to display the style rules as regular content.

Finally, each style rule is presented on its own line (just for easy readability). The rules' syntax is a little different from what you're used to seeing. Take a look at the rule for <P> again:

```
P {text-align:center}
```

If we had written that rule using HTML and the ALIGN attribute, it would have looked like this:

```
<P ALIGN="center">
```

You'll see that the same information is presented, just in a different manner. In the language of style sheets, the element you're operating on is known as the *selector*. The rule—that is, the portion enclosed in braces—is known as the *declaration*.

For our purposes, what's important to remember is that the element is written first, without the HTML brackets, and then the style property along with its value in braces, separated by a colon (versus an attribute's being separated from its value by an equals sign, =).

Start with a fresh HTML document (from your template) and enter something similar to Listing 18.1 between the <BODY> tags, with the style rules placed in a <STYLE> container in the document <HEAD>.

EXAMPLE

Listing 18.1: style1.html: A Few Basic Style Rules

```
<HTML>
<HEAD>
<STYLE TYPE="text/css">
<!--
H1 {color:green}
P {text-align:center}
I {color:blue}
-->
</STYLE>
</HEAD>
<BODY>
<H1>This is my heading</H1>
<P>My paragraph is aligned to the center</P>
<P>I can add <I>italicized text</I> that will be blue</P>
</BODY>
</HTML>
```

Figure 18.1 shows the results in a CSS-compliant Web browser (Netscape Navigator 4.5 for Windows 98).

Essential Style Properties

There are literally hundreds of possible style properties that you can apply to various elements in your HTML pages. The definitive source for properties is, of course, the W3C CSS specification, which can be found at http://www.w3.org/Style/, along with lots of other helpful hints and articles. In this section, I'll try to highlight the ones that most designers will use frequently.

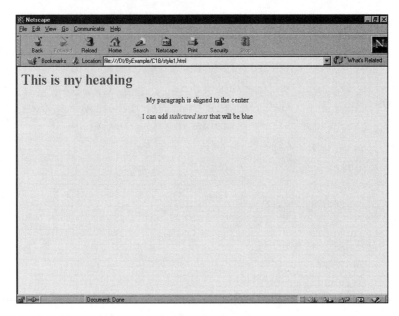

Figure 18.1: *A basic style sheet at work.*

Five major styles present you with a multitude of choices for fonts, as shown in Table 18.1.

Table 18.1: Five Major Style Properties

Style Property	Values
font-family	Font names, such as Arial, Helvetica, and Courier, or generic font types such as sans-serif
font-size	Keywords (small, medium, large, and so on), relative sizes (2 for twice the size, -1 for half, and so on), or percentages (50% for half the base size, and so on)
font-style	Normal, italic, oblique
font-variant	Small caps
font-weight	Bold

EXAMPLE

Font Properties

In this example, you'll incorporate four of the font properties you've learned.

Start with a fresh HTML document (from your template) and enter something similar to Listing 18.2 between the <BODY> tags, with the style rules placed in a <STYLE> container in the document <HEAD>.

Listing 18.2: fonts.html: An Experiment in Font Styles

```
<HTML>
<HEAD>
<STYLE TYPE="text/css">
<!--
H1 {font-family:Arial}
H2 {font-variant:oblique}
BLOCKQUOTE {font-variant:small-caps}
STRONG {font-size:150%}
EM {font-weight:bold}
-->
</STYLE>
</HEAD>
<BODY>
<H1>H1 tags have the font-family Arial</H1>
<P>We did not set a style for P tags, so they are written in
normal text.</P>
<H2>The H2 tag has an oblique font-variant, even though it's not displayed
here.</H2>
<P>Next is the blockquote</P>
<BLOCKQUOTE>Which is displayed in the small-caps font-variant</BLOCKQUOTE>
<P>Finally, <STRONG>Strong text is 150% larger</STRONG>, but <EM>emphasized
text</EM> has bold added to it.</P>
</BODY>
</HTML>
```

EXAMPLE

Text Properties

In this example, you will see three common text properties at work. Table 18.2 outlines each of them.

Table 18.2: Three Common Text Properties

Style Property	Values
text-align	Center, left, justify, right
text-decoration	Strikethrough, underline
text-indent	Number in specified unit (pixels, percent, inches, and so on)

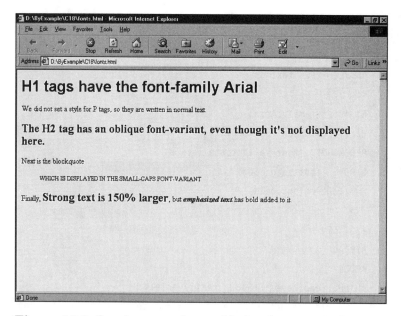

Figure 18.2: *Our font experiment. Notice that even in Internet Explorer 5.0,* `font-variant` *isn't supported.*

The `text-indent` property is one that many designers have been clamoring for, because it allows them to indent the contents of container elements without resorting to abuses of tags whose default presentation includes an indent but doesn't include "bare" text (such as using a `UL` tag without `LI` tags to contain the content).

Start with a fresh HTML document (from your template) and enter something similar to Listing 18.3 between the `<BODY>` tags, with the style rules placed in a `<STYLE>` container in the document `<HEAD>`.

Listing 18.3: textstyle.html

```
<HTML>
<HEAD>
<STYLE TYPE="text/css">
<!--
H1 {text-decoration:underline}
H2 {text-align:center}
P {text-indent: 30px}
-->
</STYLE>
</HEAD>
<BODY>
```

```
<H1>H1 tags have a text-decoration of underline</H1>
<P>Paragraph text is indented by 30 pixels, which is abbreviated as "px" in the
style sheet.</P>
<H2>The H2 tag is centered using the text-align:center style rule.</H2>
<P>Here's another paragraph, that's also been indented.</P>
</BODY>
</HTML>
```

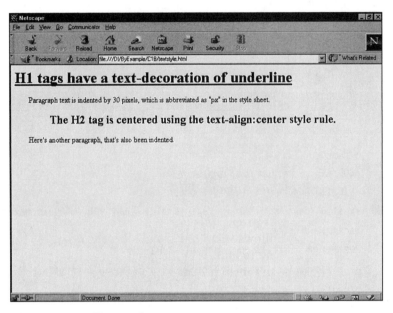

Figure 18.3: Text styles.

EXAMPLE

Color Properties

In this example, you will use the three major color and background properties available to you in CSS. Table 18.3 provides the details.

Table 18.3: The Three Major Color and Background Properties

Style Property	Values
background-color	Color name, rgb, hex
background-image	URL
color	Color name, rgb, hex

To put these to work, start with a fresh HTML document (from your template) and enter something similar to Listing 18.4 between the <BODY> tags, with the style rules placed in a <STYLE> container in the document <HEAD>. Figure 18.4 shows the results.

Listing 18.4: colorstyle.html

```
<HTML>
<HEAD>
<STYLE TYPE="text/css">
<!--
H1 {color:green}
H2 {color:blue}
BODY {background-image:URL(bar.gif)}
EM {background-color:yellow}
-->
</STYLE>
</HEAD>
<BODY>
<H1 align=center>H1 tags are green </H1>
<P align=center>Paragraph text is plain, but <EM>emphasis text</EM> has a yellow
background color</P>
<H2 align=center>H2 tags are blue</H2>
<P align=center>The entire body has a background image.</P>
</BODY>
</HTML>
```

Notice the special format of the background-image style rule. You will always see URL immediately after the colon and then the actual URL, either relative or absolute, in parentheses. In this case, I chose a relative URL because I stored the image in the same directory as my HTML file.

Inherited Styles

One of the truly timesaving devices built into CSS is the concept of inheritance. Just as you inherit physical traits from your parents, HTML tags can inherit style traits from other tags.

EXAMPLE

Consider the behavior of the following HTML, shown in Figure 18.5:

```
<H2><FONT color="red">This <EM>heading</EM> is red</FONT></H2>
```

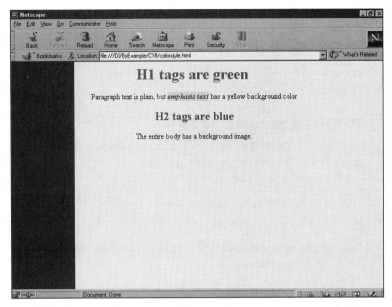

Figure 18.4: *Color options using CSS.*

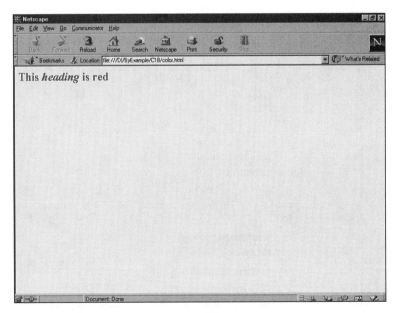

Figure 18.5: *Several nested HTML tags.*

The emphasis tag can be said to have inherited both the color red from the <FONT> tag and the heading status from the <H2> tag. Inheritance, then, simply means that a child element (one nested inside another) is given the same traits as the parent element (the outer tag).

The same idea applies in CSS. If we gave all <P> tags a blue color using the following CSS rule

```
P {color:blue}
```

an <EM> or <STRONG> tag inside that <P> would also have its contents be blue in color.

Overriding an Inherited Style

Inevitably, there will be times when you don't want all child elements to have the same traits as their parents, so you'll need to override the inherited style of a few tags. Luckily, with CSS that's an easy thing to do.

EXAMPLE

Let's look at the color sample again:

```
P {color:blue}
```

Let's incorporate it into a Web page that has the following code (see Figure 18.6 for the results):

```
<P>This is a bunch of nonsense text. We're just filling up space so we can see
our cascading style sheets in action. <EM>This phrase is emphasized</EM> while
this one is not. Let's see how it looks.</P>
```

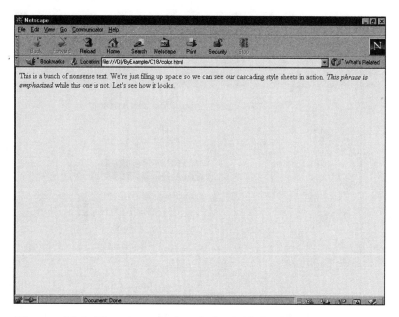

Figure 18.6: *The* <EM> *tag has inherited the blue* <P> *color.*

Although the <EM> tag does italicize the text, the text doesn't stand out very well. Your eyes are drawn a bit more to the color instead. So to make it really stand out, let's override the color designation for this one particular <EM> tag. You do that by setting a style property within the <EM> tag itself:

```
<EM style="color:red">
```

The results are shown in Figure 18.7.

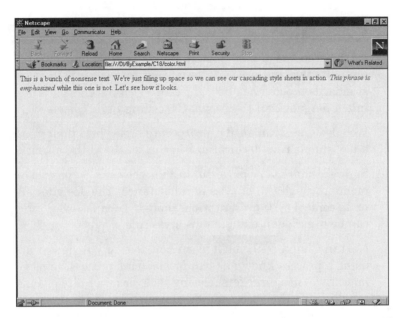

Figure 18.7: *The style rule applied within the* <EM> *tag overrides the parent tag color selection.*

Resources for Style Sheets

As you can see from the examples in this chapter, CSS can be very easy to incorporate in your Web pages. However, that doesn't mean that it's not very powerful or that you can't create very complex designs using it. To further explore the possibilities available with CSS, you may find the following Web sites helpful:

- **W3C Core Styles**   Eight different looks created expressly for you to use while learning CSS.
  http://www.w3.org/StyleSheets/Core/

- **WebMonkey's Style Sheet Reference**   Lots of detailed information on which properties work in which browsers.
  http://www.hotwired.com/webmonkey/stylesheets/reference/

- **Cnet's Builder.com** A whole production section devoted to style sheet issues.
  `http://home.cnet.com/category/0,10000,0-7258,00.html`

- **Web Review's Master Grid** A detailed "who supports what" grid of CSS rules and browsers.
  `http://webreview.com/pub/guides/style/mastergrid.html`

What's Next?

As the Web has gained popularity, HTML has undergone changes that have brought style and presentational tags into the language. Recent work in the standards process has brought those visual items back out of HTML and into a language all their own: Cascading Style Sheets.

Web designers can easily incorporate styles into their documents by making a few simple rule declarations in the <HEAD> of the document.

Style rules are very powerful in that they can be passed on to child elements through the process of inheritance. The designer still retains ultimate control over presentation, though, because even inherited style traits can be overridden using a new style rule.

Next in Chapter 19, you'll learn how to easily review your HTML for errors using a process known as *validation*. This process helps you catch any missing quotes, brackets, closing tags, or other bits of HTML markup that could impact the successful display of your page.

Review Questions

1. What must the value of the <STYLE> tag's TYPE attribute be when writing CSS?

2. True or false: Style rules can only be placed in an external style sheet document.

3. What does the C in CSS stand for?

4. Is "italic" a font-family, font-variant, or font-style property?

5. What are three popular units for measuring screen distances in CSS rules?

6. What is different about the background-image property?

7. True or false: If a <P> tag had a style rule for color:blue, the <UL> that appeared next would also be blue in color by inheritance.

Review Exercises

1. Create a Web page that uses each of the font and text properties listed in this chapter. View it in at least two different browsers. Which properties are supported in one browser but not the other? Are any not supported at all?

2. Can you think of a use for `background-image` other than in the `<BODY>` tag? If you can, does your browser support its use? (Hint: Look at Web Review's master grid.)

3. Create a Web document using CSS that you find particularly pleasing to the eye. Then view it with a non-CSS-enabled browser. What, if anything, do you feel is missing? Is the same information presented to you?

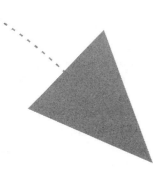

Validating Your HTML

Now that you've worked your way through more than a dozen chapters, learning all kinds of new HTML tags, have you wondered at all what would happen if you made mistakes in your HTML? Surely everyone does—even I do. Is there any way to prevent silly mistakes from making us look bad when we put files on the Web? Luckily, there is, and it's called the process of *validation*.

This chapter teaches you the following:

- Why you should care about valid HTML
- What tools you can use to check your work
- How to interpret error reports
- How to validate CSS markup

Why Write Valid HTML?

When you write a letter, you spell-check it. Many word processors today even have "grammar checkers" that alert you when you've written in the passive voice or misplaced your modifiers. As with any other document you create for public consumption, every Web designer wants to be sure that he hasn't made any little mistakes that might detract from his work.

Similar to word-processing tools, an HTML validator can tell you that you left off a required closing tag, forgot to completely quote your color values, or any other little oversight or error that might make your pages render funny. The process of validating takes only a few seconds, so why not validate all your pages?

The W3C HTML Validation Service

Considered to be the "best of the best" in many circles because it comes right from the source, the W3C provides its own validation service using the actual DTDs (document type definitions) published as part of the HTML Recommendations. The service is found at http://validator.w3.org (see Figure 19.1).

NOTE

If you'll recall back to Chapter 6, "Creating a Web Page and Entering Text," the document type definition is what made up part of the <DOCTYPE> tag. The DTD is the file that defines all the rules for the specific version of HTML you are using in your pages.

The interface is pretty straightforward. Type in the URL of the page you want to validate in the Location box, and then click the Validate this URI button and wait for the results. If your site passes, you'll see a screen similar to Figure 19.2 (the results of validating the HTML Writers Guild home page, at http://www.hwg.org).

How the Validator Works

The W3C HTML Validation Service provides an SGML-based validation. If you'll think back to Chapter 1, "What Is HTML?" we talked briefly about SGML and how HTML is viewed as a subset of that more complicated and powerful language. The very strict rules of SGML pertain to structural integrity: Are all the tags that must be in your document actually there? Are there tags in places where they're not allowed? Have you tried to misnest tags anywhere? Those are the types of errors the SGML-based validator will find.

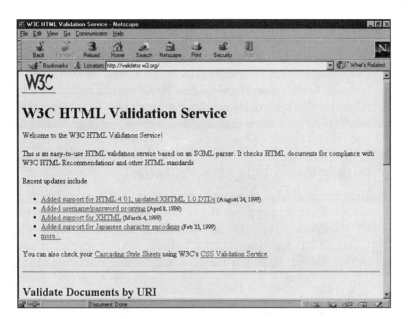

Figure 19.1: *The W3C HTML Validation Service.*

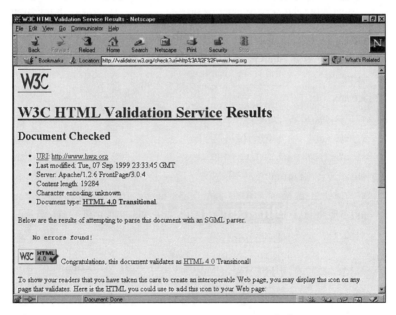

Figure 19.2: `http://www.hwg.org` *passes validation.*

It begins by reading the <DOCTYPE> tag you now always include at the top of every HTML page you write. Based on that <DOCTYPE>, it retrieves the corresponding DTD. If you're using a standard HTML 4 doctype, it simply grabs it off the W3C server where it's stored. It then *parses* the file (in essence, "reads thoroughly") and looks for the details we just mentioned. If it runs into an error, it makes a note as to what it was and where it occurred, and it then continues. If errors are found, they're displayed for you on the results page.

Finding Errors Using the Validator

To get a good idea of how the validator works, you'll need to create an HTML file that purposefully contains at least one error. Start with a fresh HTML document (from your template) and enter something similar to Listing 19.1 between the <BODY> tags, paying special attention to the errors in this listing. Save the file as invalid.html, and upload it to your Web site.

NOTE

The W3C HTML Validator Service only works with HTML files that have already been uploaded to the Web. They can be stored on password-protected Web servers to prevent casual visitors from stumbling across pages that aren't quite ready for "prime time," but the service must be able to access the page on a real Web server.

Listing 19.1: An Invalid HTML File

```
<!DOCTYPE HTML PUBLIC "-//W3C//DTD HTML 4.0 Transitional//EN">
<HTML>
<HEAD>
<TITLE>My HTML Page
</HEAD>
<BODY>
<H1>First Heading</H2>
<P>This is a sample HTML page that purposefully contains a few errors. We will
use this page to learn more about how the W3C HTML Validation Service works.
</BODY>
```

When you've uploaded the file, open your Web browser and visit http://validator.w3.org. Enter the URL for the invalid.html file in the Location box, and submit the page for validation. Your results page should look similar to Figure 19.3.

Finally:

```
Error at line 7:
  <H1>
      start tag was here
```

Again, the validator is pointing out where it picked up the opening <H1>, so this isn't really a new error.

Now, to be sure you've caught all the errors, upload valid.html to your Web site and validate it. If you caught everything, you'll get a No errors found! report back, as shown in Figure 19.4. If so, congratulate yourself on a job well done. If not, review what the validator tells you, remembering to look at the tags right before the error if the report doesn't make much sense (like the "error" on line 8 reported for invalid.html).

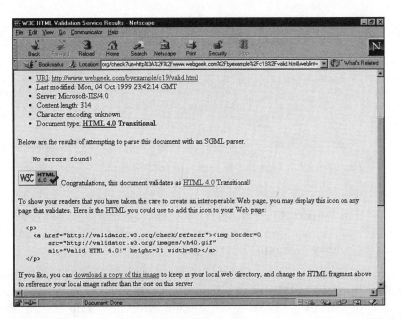

Figure 19.4: *We passed with flying colors, so we can now add the validator icon!*

The W3C has provided a nifty icon that you can use to show everyone that your pages are valid HTML. The HTML for this icon is provided on the results page (see Figure 19.4). Just cut and paste right into your document to proudly show that you've paid careful attention to your work.

Another Look at Your Source Code

When you first visited the W3C Validator site, you may have noticed a checkbox option below the Location field that said Include Weblint results, along with several other options (see Figure 19.5).

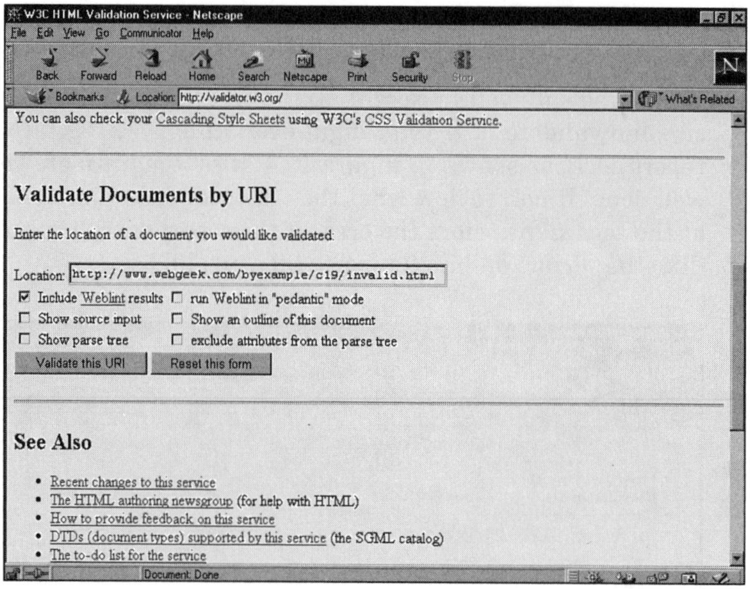

Figure 19.5: Opt to get picky with Weblint.

Weblint is designed as a heuristic validator. Not only will it pick up errors in construct, like the SGML-based validator will, but it will also point out what it has been programmed to recognize as potential stylistic or interoperability problems.

Let's take another look at the output of the validator by checking the invalid.html file again. This time, select the Include Weblint results checkbox before submitting the file for validation. Your results should look something like Figure 19.6.

You can see that Weblint picked up three errors. Not only did it find the two that the standard validator did (no closing </TITLE> and the mismatched closing </H2>), but it also pointed out that we forgot the closing </HTML> tag. Why didn't the primary validator see this?

Actually, it did. But the closing </HTML> tag is optional, according to the HTML 4 Transitional DTD. Therefore, the validator didn't mark that as an error.

EXAMPLE

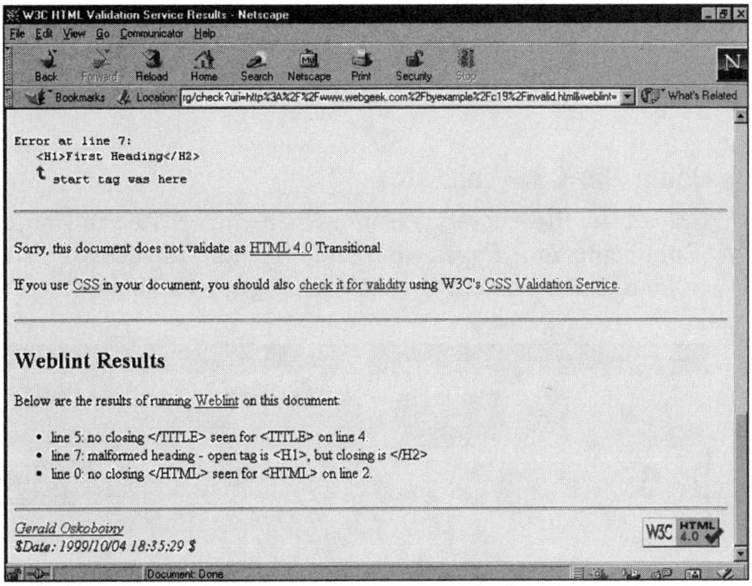

Figure 19.6: *Validator results with Weblint turned on.*

Weblint, on the other hand, is pointing out that while it may be valid to leave off the </HTML> tag, it's not very good form, so it's probably not a bad idea to go ahead and fix that in the valid.html file.

NOTE

The validator can make use of quite a few DTDs other than the three flavors of HTML 4. For a complete list, look at http://validator.w3.org/sgml-lib/catalog.

TIP

If you want to get *really* picky, run the validator with Weblint in "pedantic" mode. Your results will be "hyper"-correct!

Validating Style

The W3C HTML Validation Service was such a hit that when CSS started to be accepted by the HTML authoring public, there was a demand for a tool that could check the validity of CSS style rules much as the validator checked HTML tag syntax.

The W3C took on the project and came up with the aptly named W3C CSS Validation Service. You can find it online at http://jigsaw.w3.org/css-validator/.

Unlike the HTML validator, the CSS Validation Service provides three options for checking your work: by URI (as with the HTML service), by cutting and pasting your code into a form's text area, or by uploading the file itself.

Using the CSS Validator

Upload the file colorstyle.html, which you created in Chapter 18, "Enhancing Your Pages with Style Sheets," to your Web site. Choose to validate the document by URI (see Figure 19.7).

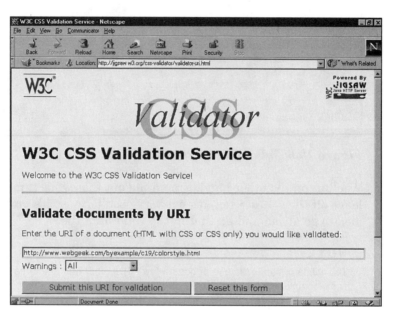

Figure 19.7: Using the CSS Validator by URI.

If it was written exactly as the sample listing was, you'll get a passing mark! (See Figure 19.8.)

Notice that the top of the results page has three "warnings" provided by the service. These are rather like the Weblint comments: They're not errors that render your CSS invalid, but suggestions that might increase the chances of your page being displayed as you intended. In this case, the warnings were reported as the following:

```
Line: 7 Level: 1 You have no background-color with your color : H1

Line: 8 Level: 1 You have no background-color with your color: H2

Line 10: Level: 1 You have no color with your background-color : EM
```

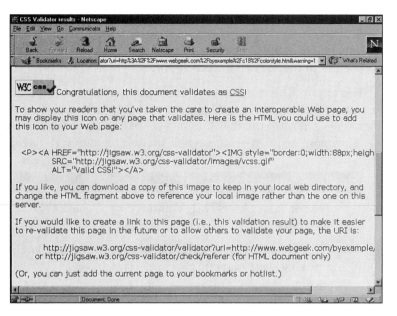

Figure 19.8: *The CSS code passes muster.*

CSS not only allows you to set a color for the text in the <H1> and <H2> tags as we did, but it also lets you set a background color to go along with the primary object color. It's not required. If it's not present, the background color defaults to the overall page background. However, if you wanted to, you could declare it.

The same thing applies to the primary color declaration for <EM> (otherwise known as the "foreground" color). Since we didn't explicitly state it, it picked up the color from the main <P> color.

If you wish, you can go back and add these rules to your page and then run it through the validator again to see what happens.

What's Next?

Validation is an important tool in every Web designer's arsenal. Checking your work using the validator should become as critical to you as running the spell-checker on your word processor. Slight typos or other errors of oversight can cause your pages to render in unexpected ways. The validator is a quick and easy way to catch these problems before they turn away visitors to your Web site.

The W3C HTML Validation Service provides an SGML-based validator for HTML markup and access to the heuristic-style Weblint validator. Weblint can pick up issues that may be "bad form" while still technically valid HTML.

In addition to the HTML Validation Service, the W3C also provides a tool for validating CSS style sheets. You have the option of validating by URI, as with the HTML validator, or you can cut and paste into a form or upload the file to the service for processing.

Next up in Chapter 20, you'll be introduced to two popular Web scripting and programming languages: Java and JavaScript. Despite their similar names, they are distinct languages created by different companies. You'll learn how to incorporate each of them into your Web pages.

Review Questions

1. True or false: An HTML Validator spell-checks the text content of your Web page.

2. Which tag in your HTML file tells the validator how to proceed in checking your markup?

3. Can the validator check markup that uses an Internet Explorer–specific DTD?

4. What does it mean to be an SGML-based validator?

5. True or false: Every "error" reported by the validator is a unique instance of something that's wrong with your code.

6. Where should you look for a problem if the error being reported doesn't seem to make any sense?

7. When are you allowed to use the W3C validator icon?

8. What is a heuristic validator?

9. Are all Weblint's errors truly about invalid markup?

10. Which methods can be used to check your CSS using the W3C CSS validator service?

Review Exercises

1. Run one of your favorite sites through the W3C HTML Validation Service. Does it pass? If not, can you tell why?

2. Upload and check the files you created in Chapter 12 and see if you created valid work. If there's a problem, can you see where it is and fix it?

3. Create a full Web page using both HTML and CSS. Validate it, fixing any errors presented, until it passes both services. Upload it to the Web proudly bearing both validation icons.

Part V

Internet Programming and Advanced Web Technologies

Using Java and JavaScript

JavaScript Objects and Functions

Adding Portable Documents to Web Sites

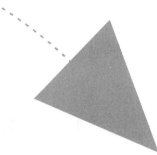

Using Java and JavaScript

We should start this chapter by making a distinction between Java and JavaScript. Java is an object-oriented, compiled (at runtime), full-fledged programming language that many people find similar to C++. It is designed for the more-advanced programmer. Its strength is its ability to run in a *virtual machine* that is run within Java-enabled Web browsers. Java, then, is similar to the programming languages used to build full-fledged applications, sometimes referred to as *applets,* that can be run on PCs, Macs, and UNIX machines. It's well-suited for the Internet because it can run on any of these different computing platforms, but it is not necessarily exclusive to the Web.

JavaScript, on the other hand, is a less-complex, interpreted scripting language similar to Perl, Visual Basic Scripting, and similar languages. JavaScript is similar in some ways to Java beyond their names, but it doesn't require the programmer to understand or implement complicated object-oriented syntax or worry about programming issues such as variable typing and object hierarchies.

In fact, Java and JavaScript are different enough that you can think of them with different titles, depending on your ability. It's convenient to think of creating programs in Java as programming, and you can refer to creating scripts in JavaScript as scripting or authoring.

NOTE

Java programming is outside of the scope of this book. (I suggest *Java 2 by Example* or *Special Edition Using Java 2* from Que.) In this chapter, you'll learn about the tags used to add existing Java programs to your HTML pages, and then you'll look at the basics of JavaScript authoring.

This chapter teaches you the following:

- How to use the <APPLET> tag to add Java to your Web pages
- How to plan for browsers that don't support Java

- The basics of JavaScript

- How to use functions and declarations

Adding Java Applications to Your Web Pages

There are two basic ways to add Java applets (programs) to your Web pages. The first started as a proprietary extension added to the Netscape Navigator browser. This quickly caught on with the other browser development companies. For a while, at least, this was to be the preferred way of adding applets. The other method uses HTML 4's <OBJECT> tag, which still suffers from the uneven support you found out about in Chapter 16, "Images, Multimedia Objects, and Background Graphics."

The <APPLET> Tag

This first method adds the container tag <APPLET>. Along with the <APPLET> tag is the <PARAM> tag, used to offer certain parameters to the browser concerning the applet (like the speed at which something should display, initialize, and so on). You'll remember the <PARAM> tags from our first discussion of <OBJECT> in Chapter 16. The <APPLET> tag itself accepts the attributes CODE, CODEBASE, HEIGHT, and WIDTH.

An <APPLET> tag follows this general format:

```
<APPLET CODEBASE="applet_path_URL" CODE="appletFile.class" WIDTH="number"
HEIGHT="number">
<PARAM NAME="attributeName" VALUE="string/number">
...
Alternative text for display in non-Java browsers
</APPLET>
```

CODEBASE is the path (in URL form) to the directory on your server containing the Java applet. CODE takes the name of the applet. This file always ends in .class to indicate that it's a compiled Java class. CODE should always be just the filename because CODEBASE is used to find the path to the Java applet.

TIP

Notice that CODEBASE and CODE work together to create a complete URL. So, for a relative URL, CODEBASE isn't required if the applet is in the same directory as the Web page.

The WIDTH and HEIGHT attributes accept the number in pixels for the Java applet on your Web page.

EXAMPLE

An example of the first line of <APPLET> would be the following:

```
<APPLET CODEBASE="http://www.foo.com/applets/" CODE="clock.class"
HEIGHT="300" WIDTH="300">
```

<PARAM> is a bit easier to use than it may seem. It essentially creates a variable, assigns a value, and passes it to the Java applet. The applet must be written to understand the parameter's name and value. NAME is used to create the parameter's name; it should be expected by the applet. VALUE is used to assign the value to that particular parameter. It could be a number, a bit of text, or even a command that causes the applet to work in a particular way.

NOTE

Understanding the <PARAM> tag might enable you to use freeware/shareware Java applets on your own pages. By passing your own parameters to general-purpose applets, you may find them useful for your particular Web site.

A simple <PARAM> tag is the following:

```
<PARAM NAME="Speed" VALUE="5">
```

In this case, the Java applet will have to recognize and know what to do with a variable named Speed with a value of 5.

The alternative HTML code in the <APPLET> container allows you to offer HTML text to browsers that aren't Java-enabled. A Java-aware browser will ignore the markup (and display the applet window instead), while non-Java browsers will ignore everything but the markup. So an example would be the following:

```
<APPLET CODE="game.class" HEIGHT="20" WIDTH="20">
<P>You need a <I>Java-aware</I> browser to play this game!</P>
</APPLET>
```

This will display the text instead of the applet when it encounters a browser that doesn't support Java.

EXAMPLE

Adding Java Applets

This example is designed to do two things: reinforce the ways you can add Java applets to your Web pages and test your browser for Java capabilities. If your browser supports Java, it will be interesting to see which method it prefers for adding Java applets.

To begin, create a new HTML page, and add the code in Listing 20.1.

Listing 20.1: java.html: Adding Java Applets to a Web Page

```
<BODY>

<H3>This applet has been added using the APPLET tag:</H3>

<APPLET CODEBASE="classes" CODE="JavaClock.class" WIDTH="150" HEIGHT="150">

<PARAM  NAME="delay"    VALUE="100">

<PARAM  NAME="link"     VALUE="http://java.sun.com/">

<PARAM  NAME="border"   VALUE="5">

<PARAM  NAME="nradius"  VALUE="80">

<PARAM  NAME="cfont"    VALUE="TimesRoman¦BOLD¦18">


<PARAM  NAME="bgcolor"  VALUE="ffffff">

<PARAM  NAME="shcolor"  VALUE="ff0000">

<PARAM  NAME="mhcolor"  VALUE="00ff00">

<PARAM  NAME="hhcolor"  VALUE="0000ff">


<PARAM  NAME="ccolor"   VALUE="dddddd">

<PARAM  NAME="ncolor"   VALUE="000000">

</APPLET>


<H3>This applet was added using the OBJECT tag:</H3>

<OBJECT CLASSID="Java:JavaClock.class"

        CODEBASE="classes"

        WIDTH="150"

        HEIGHT="150"

        ALIGN="LEFT">

<OBJECT>

</BODY>
```

Save this file as java.html. To get this to work correctly, you'll need a Java applet. You can use an applet provided by Sun Microsystems as a demo, which is on the included CD-ROM. Make sure it's in the same directory as java.html. Then load the page in your browser to test it (see Figure 20.1).

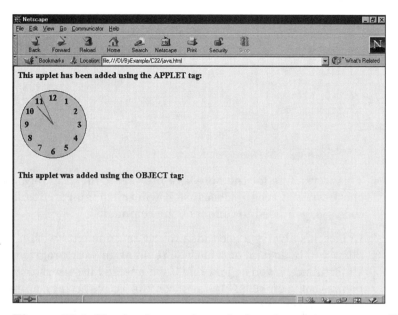

Figure 20.1: *Here's what works and what doesn't in my copy of Netscape Navigator 4.6 .*

Creating JavaScript in Your Web Pages

Now let's move on to JavaScript, the smaller Java-like scripting language available in Netscape Navigator and other programs. Unlike Java, JavaScript is generally written right into HTML pages. You'll start with how to add JavaScript code to a Web page, and then you'll look at how these programs are created.

The <SCRIPT> Tag

The <SCRIPT> tag is used to add JavaScript commands to your HTML pages. <SCRIPT> is a container tag that can accept the attribute LANGUAGE, which allows you to specify the scripting language used (JavaScript is generally the default). Here's how it works:

```
<SCRIPT LANGUAGE="lang_name">

script code

</SCRIPT>
```

Hiding Code

While it's possible that old browsers (those that don't recognize JavaScript) will just skip over the <SCRIPT> tag, it's also possible that the browser will attempt to interpret your script commands or other text as HTML markup.

To keep this from happening, you can embed the script commands in HTML comments. You might try something using the HTML comment tags like the following:

```
<SCRIPT>
<!--
script commands
-->
</SCRIPT>
```

This works fine for the non-Java browser. Unfortunately, JavaScript will choke when it sees --> because it will try to interpret that as scripting code. So, you need to comment the comment.

In fact, it's always a good idea to create comments within your script that allow you to document what you're doing in your programming. Unfortunately, you've just told Java-enabled browsers that HTML comments (between <SCRIPT> tags) contain active script commands. So, how can you add comments for the benefit of the script? Like this:

```
<SCRIPT>
<!--
script command     // One-line comment
...script commands...
/* Unlimited-length comments must be
ended with */
// comment to end hiding -->
</SCRIPT>
```

It looks like you can fill a decent-sized page with nothing but comments, doesn't it? Notice that you've solved the HTML comment problem with a single-line JavaScript comment. Single-line comments start with two forward slashes and must physically fit on a single line, with a return at the end. Multiline comments can be enclosed between an opening comment element (/*) and a closing comment element (*/).

EXAMPLE

Writing a Hello World Program in JavaScript

Although you haven't learned how to do anything with a script yet, I'll throw one quick command at you for the purpose of getting your first JavaScript page to work. It's document.write, and it's something called a *method* in JavaScript. It's basically a piece of code that does something automatically. In this case, it prints text to your Web page.

Create a new HTML document, and enter Listing 20.2.

Listing 20.2: hiworld.html: "Hello World" JavaScript Document

```
<HTML>
<HEAD>
<TITLE>Hello World JavaScript Example</TITLE>
</HEAD>
<BODY>
<H3>The following text is script generated:</H3>
<SCRIPT LANGUAGE="JavaScript">
<!--
/* Our script only requires
one quick statement! */
document.write("Hello World!") // Prints words to Web document
// end hiding -->
</SCRIPT>
</BODY>
</HTML>
```

Save this document, and then load it into the browser of your choice. If your browser is capable of dealing with JavaScript, your output should look something like Figure 20.2. If it isn't, you'll just see the header text.

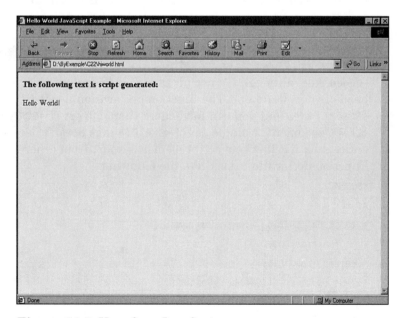

Figure 20.2: *Your first JavaScript program.*

TIP

If your browser can't see the JavaScript example, I suggest getting the latest copy of Netscape Navigator or Microsoft Internet Explorer for testing your work in this chapter.

Functions

The basic building block of a script in JavaScript is the *function*. A function is basically a "mini-program." It performs a distinct computing task. Functions start by being "passed" a particular value, either through user input or from another segment of the overall script; they work with that value to make something else happen   the distinct computing task it was designed to perform   and then "return" a new value to the body, or main portion of your program.

In JavaScript, there are two times you need to work with functions. First, you need to declare the function. This means that you're defining how the function will work. The browser, when it loads a page, will make note of the different functions that you may use in your script.

The second step is to call the function in the body of your script. Generally, your script will be just a series of function calls. There isn't a whole lot of calculating done in the body of your script. You send a value out to a function to be computed and then receive the results back in the body of your script.

Declaring Your Functions

A good rule, although it's not necessary, is to declare your functions in the head of your document. The function declaration needs to appear between <SCRIPT> tags, but you can have more than one set of <SCRIPT> tags in an HTML document. A single set of <SCRIPT> tags doesn't necessarily define an entire script; it just sets script elements apart from other HTML tags. Function declarations look like the following:

```
<SCRIPT>

<!--

   function function_name(value_name) {

   ...function code...

   return (new_value)

}

// end hiding -->

</SCRIPT>
```

The *value_name* for the function is just the variable name that you assign to the passed value for the duration of the function. When the body of your JavaScript document calls this function, it will generally send along a value. When that value gets to the function, it needs a name. If the function is designed to perform simple math, for instance, you might call the passed value *old_num*. Also, notice that the entire calculating part of the function is between braces.

EXAMPLE

An example of a function declaration might be the following:

```
<SCRIPT>
<!--
   function get_square(old_num) {
   new_num = (old_num * old_num)
   return (new_num)
}
// end hiding -->
</SCRIPT>
```

In this example, you've created a function called `get_square` that accepts a value, names it `old_num`, squares that value, and assigns it to a variable named `new_num`. At least, that's what the function is supposed to do. It won't do this yet because this is just a declaration. It doesn't even know what actual values to work with until you call the function.

Calling a Function

You call the function from the body of your script, which is generally in the body of the document. It doesn't really matter where you declare functions (although, as mentioned, it's best to declare them between the <HEAD> tags), but it is best to put the function calls of your script close to the parts of your document where they're needed (this will become more obvious as you work with JavaScript). A function call is basically formatted like the following (and it always appears between <SCRIPT> tags):

function_name(value);

EXAMPLE

In this function call, the *function_name* should be the same function name that you used in the function declaration, while the *value* can be anything you want to pass to the function. In the previous example, this value was to be renamed *old_num* and then squared. So, it would make sense to put a number in the parentheses of that particular function call. In fact, you can put almost anything in the parentheses—a variable name, an actual number, or a string of text—as long as the function is designed to accept such a value. For instance, the get_square function will work equally well if you use this.

```
number = 5;
num_squared = get_square (number);
```

or this:

```
num_squared = get_square (5);
```

By the way, if something looks strange to you here, it might be the way I'm naming variables—especially if the last time you did any programming was a number of years ago. The following would work just as easily:

```
x = 5;
y = get_square (x);
```

Does that make you more comfortable?

Remember, though, that you should pass a value that the function expects. If you pass a string of text to a function designed to perform math functions, you won't get anything useful.

Also notice that, in the previous three examples, the function is on the right side of an assignment, represented by the equals sign. This may take a little leap of thought, but JavaScript does two things with function calls. First, the call is used to pass a value to the function. Then, when the function returns a value, it "takes the place" of the original function call.

EXAMPLE

Look at the following example:

```
num_squared = get_square (5);
```

After the math of the get_square function is completed and the value is returned, the entire function call (get_square (5)) is given a value of 25. This, in turn, is assigned to the variable num_squared.

EXAMPLE

Calling All Declarations

You know enough now to build a fairly simple little script. You'll use document.write again, with a function declaration and a function call. In this script, you'll do some simple math and track the results in your browser window.

Create a new HTML document and enter Listing 20.3.

Listing 20.3: simpmath.html: Using JavaScript for Simple Math

```
<HTML>
<HEAD>
<TITLE>Simple Math</TITLE>
<SCRIPT>
<!--
  function simple_math(num) {
  document.write("The call passed ",num," to the function.<BR>");
  new_num = num * 2;         // multiply the value by 2
  document.write(num, " * 2 equals ",new_num,"<BR>");
  return new_num;            // return new_num to the function call
}
// end hiding -->
</SCRIPT>
</HEAD>
<BODY>
<H3>Let's watch some simple math:</H3>
<SCRIPT>
<!--
  x = 5;
  document.write("The starting number is ",x,"<BR>");
  new_x = simple_math(x);
  document.write("The function returned the number ",new_x,"<BR>");
// end hiding -->
</SCRIPT>
</BODY>
</HTML>
```

That's pretty much it. Notice that document.write lets you track the progress of your number as it moves from the function call through the function itself and back down to the main part of your script. You can see this work by focusing on the order of the output shown in Figure 20.3.

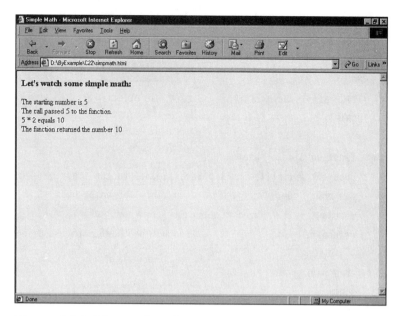

Figure 20.3: *The results of your script.*

Handling Events

Well, you've created a complete script, but it can't do much. That's because the strength of JavaScript, more than anything else, is in *event handling*. In other words, it's best at responding to something a user does on your page. This is generally done in response to some HTML tag. Here's the basic format for an event handler:

```
<TAG event_handler="JavaScript code">
```

`<TAG>` can be just about any form or hyperlink tag. Most other tags don't have the ability to accept input from the user. The `event_handler` is the browser's code for some action by the user. The `JavaScript code` will most often be a function call.

EXAMPLE

For instance, you could use an input textbox to send data to a function you've written, as with the following code:

```
<INPUT TYPE="text" NAME="number" SIZE="4">
<INPUT TYPE="button" NAME="Calculate" onClick="result =
compute(this.form.number.value)">
```

In this example, you're responding to the event created when the user clicks the Input button. When that happens, the value `this.form.number.value` is sent to a function called `compute`. Notice that the variable `this.form.number.value` is JavaScript's object-oriented way of storing the value of the textbox named `number` in the first statement.

Returning Values

Let's dig a little deeper into how the object-oriented storage thing works. Your average object is usually just a bunch of grouped variables. For instance, a typical browser has a JavaScript object called `this`, which (in our example) means "variables for this page." Within `this` is a subcategory called `form`, which means "the form variables." So, the name `this.form` is basically where "the form variables for this page" are stored.

NOTE

Actually, `this` is a special keyword in JavaScript used to refer to the current object. In the case of our example, the current object is, in fact, where the "variables for this page" are stored. We'll discuss the correct use of `this` a bit more in Chapter 21, "JavaScript Objects and Functions."

When you use the `NAME` attribute to an `<INPUT>` tag, you're creating another variable within this object. For instance, `NAME="mynumber"` creates `this.form.mynumber`. The value of this variable is stored at `this.form.mynumber.value`.

EXAMPLE

Let's look at that last example again:

```
<INPUT TYPE="text" NAME="number" SIZE="4">

<INPUT TYPE="button" NAME="Calculate" onClick="result =
compute(this.form.number.value)">
```

Now, the neat trick here is that you don't necessarily have to pass the specific value to a function in order to use it. All you need to do is send the name of the object that you want the function to concentrate on. That way, it can deal with more than one value from that object.

Consider this: You've just gathered `this.form.number.value` from the textbox. Now, you want to send it to a function. You can make the function call like this:

```
<INPUT TYPE="button" NAME="Calculate" onClick="result = compute(this.form)">
```

You've also cleverly designed the function to work with this value. So, your function will look something like the following:

```
function compute(form) {
  new_number = form.number.value;
  new_number = new_number * 2;
  return (new_number);
}
```

The function receives what's known as a *pointer* to the object responsible for storing information about this page. Once the function has its hands on that pointer (which the function calls from), it can access data within that function by using the object variable scheme, as in form.number.value. Get it?

This gets even cooler. If the function knows the pointer to the data storage object, it can also create new variables within that object. So, you can change a few more things:

EXAMPLE

```
<INPUT TYPE="text" NAME="number" SIZE="4">
<INPUT TYPE="button" NAME="Calculate" Value="Click Me"
onClick="compute(this.form)">
<INPUT TYPE="text" NAME="result" SIZE="8">
```

Now (in the second line), you're just telling the browser to run the compute() function when the Calculate button is clicked. But you're not assigning the function to a value. So how do you get an answer for your user? By using the object pointer. Here's the new function:

```
function compute(form) {
  new_number = form.number.value;
  form.result.value = new_number * 2;
  return;
}
```

In line three of the function declaration, notice the new variable form.result.value. What happens now is that the function call sets the function in motion and passes it the object pointer. The function creates its own new variable within the object, called result, and gives it a new value. When the function returns, the next line of script is activated. That line is the following:

```
<INPUT TYPE="text" NAME="result" SIZE="8">
```

Notice the NAME. Because there's already a value assigned to this NAME, that value will be displayed in the textbox (just as if it were default text). In your case, it happens to be the answer (see Figure 20.4). Here's the complete code again:

```
<HTML>
<HEAD>
<TITLE>Compute A Number</TITLE>
<SCRIPT LANGUAGE="JavaScript">
<!--
function compute(form) {
```

```
  new_number = form.number.value;
  form.result.value = new_number * 2;
  return;
}
// -->
</SCRIPT>
</HEAD>
<BODY>
<FORM>
<INPUT TYPE="text" NAME="number" SIZE="4">
<INPUT TYPE="button" NAME="Calculate" Value="Click Me"
onClick="compute(this.form)">
<INPUT TYPE="text" NAME="result" SIZE="8">
</FORM>
</BODY>
</HTML>
```

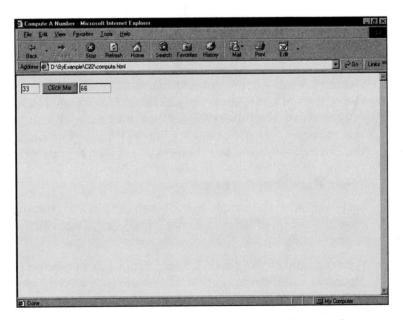

Figure 20.4: *Your textbox script, complete with a result.*

Possible Events

A typical browser will recognize a number of different events. You can write handlers for them. Even the simplest handler should call a function you've declared previously and then elegantly return to that point in the Web document. Table 20.1 shows you some of the events for which there are associated handlers (according Netscape Navigator's documentation).

Table 20.1: Events and Their Event Handlers

Event	What It Means	Event Handler
blur	User moves input focus from form box	onBlur
click	User clicks form element or link	onClick
change	User changes a form value	onChange
focus	User gives a form box input focus	onFocus
load	User loads the page in the Navigator	onLoad
mouseover	User moves mouse over a link	onMouseOver
select	User selects form input field	onSelect
submit	User submits a form	onSubmit
unload	User exits the page	onUnload

You can probably figure out what most of these do from the table. It should also make you realize how scriptable your Web page really is. For instance, you can create alert dialog boxes that tell your user that a particular field is required or that it needs to be filled with a certain number of characters. You can even say good-bye to users as they leave your page.

EXAMPLE

Event Handling, Part One

Let's start with the simple event I just mentioned: creating an alert to say good-bye. As an added bonus, you'll learn how to create an alert box, which is simply a dialog box that requires your user to click OK to clear the box.

You may want to use an HTML document you've created previously. Any document will do. Add Listing 20.4 to the body of your page.

Listing 20.4: events1.html: Handling a Simple Event

```
<HTML>
<HEAD>
<TITLE>Saying Goodbye</TITLE>
</HEAD>
<BODY>
```

```
<A HREF="anylink.html" onClick="alert('you are about to go to anylink.html,
click to continue')">Click me</A>
</BODY>
</HTML>
```

Notice that this forces you to use the single-quote character for the alert text because we've set up the alert inside the link rather than using a JavaScript function that's declared in the <HEAD> area. Your results should look something like Figure 20.5.

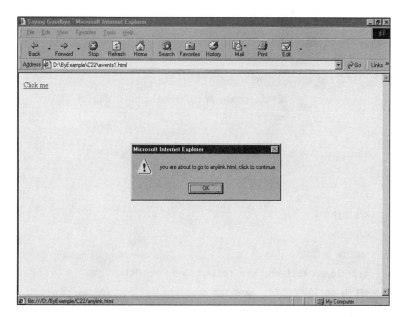

Figure 20.5: *Before the current link is followed, this alert will appear.*

EXAMPLE

Event Handling, Part Two

Now let's use event handling for something a little more complex and perhaps useful. One of the best uses of event handling is verifying form data. You can use JavaScript to hand off your data object pointer to a function, which can then take a close look at what your user has entered and determine whether it's correct.

We'll try it for a ZIP code. You're simply going to make sure that the user has entered five numbers. Enter Listing 20.5 into a new HTML document.

Listing 20.5: events2.html: Verifying Form Data with JavaScript

```
<HTML>
<HEAD>
<TITLE>Data Checking</TITLE>
<SCRIPT>
<!--
  function zip_check (form) {
  zip_str = form.Zip.value;
  if (zip_str == "") {
     alert("Please enter a five digit number for your Zip code");
     return;
     }
  if (zip_str.length != 5) {
     alert ("Your Zip code entry should be 5 digits");
     return;
     }
  return;
  }
// end hiding -->
</SCRIPT>
</HEAD>
<BODY>
<H3>Please fill out the following form:</H3>
<FORM ACTION="http://www.fakecorp.com/cgi-bin/address_form">
<PRE>
Name:    <INPUT TYPE="TEXT" SIZE="50" NAME="Name">
Address: <INPUT TYPE="TEXT" SIZE="60" NAME="Address">
City:    <INPUT TYPE="TEXT" SIZE="30" NAME="City">
State:   <INPUT TYPE="TEXT" SIZE="2" NAME="State">
Zip:     <INPUT TYPE="TEXT" SIZE="5" NAME="Zip"
            onChange = "zip_check(this.form)">
Email:   <INPUT TYPE="TEXT" SIZE="40" Name="Email">
<INPUT TYPE="SUBMIT" VALUE="Send it" onClick = "zip_check(this.form)">
</FORM>
```

```
</BODY>
</HTML>
```

This event-handling script checks an entry in the Zip box, using the onChange handler to determine when the user has moved on from Zip's textbox (by either pressing Tab or clicking another textbox). Notice that it's a good idea to place the Zip textbox before the Email box because the user could just click the Submit button and skip past your error check.

Also, by adding the onClick event to the Submit button, you can catch users if they happen to skip the Zip box completely. Now, you've double-checked their entry.

I've also cheated and introduced another new method. In the function declarations, you may have noticed the following line:

```
if (zip_str.length != 5) {
```

variable.length is a method that allows you to determine the length of any variable in JavaScript. Because JavaScript does no *variable typing* (it doesn't explicitly require you to say "this is a number" or "this is text"), any variable can be treated as a string. In this case, even though the Zip code could be interpreted as a number, zip_str.length tells you how many characters long it is.

The preceding snippet could be expressed as "If the length of zip_str does not equal 5, then...." Note that != is the "does not equal" comparison. Similarly, == is the "does equal" comparison. Look at the following snippet from the braces' function declaration:

```
if (zip_str == "") {
```

This could be read as "If zip_str equals nothing, then...." If the condition (zip_str == "") is true, the code specified by the braces is performed.

CAUTION

Be very careful that you use == for comparisons and = for assignments. If you accidentally type (zip_str = ""), that means "Make zip_str equal nothing." You've made it so that the condition is always true because it's an assignment.

You'll learn more about conditions and JavaScript methods in the next chapter. For now, let's just see this script in action in Figure 20.6.

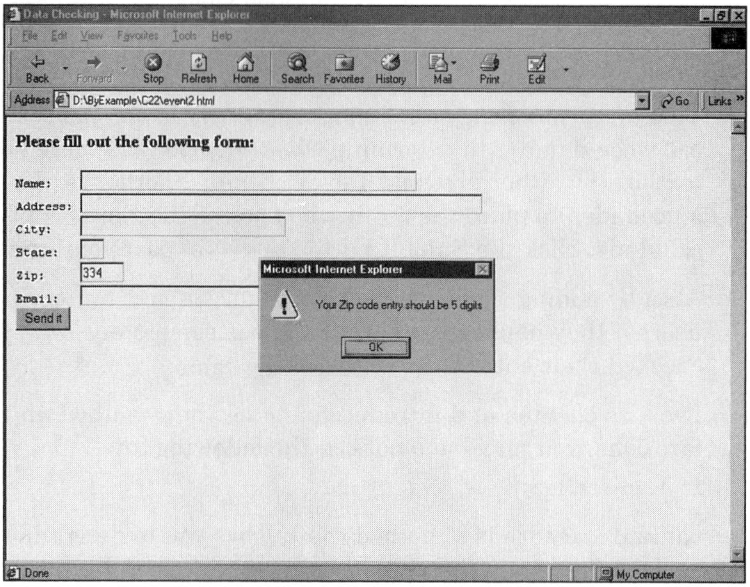

Figure 20.6: *Error checking with JavaScript.*

What's Next?

Java and JavaScript are distinct entities. Java is a sophisticated, full-fledged programming language, and JavaScript is a smaller, easier-to-grasp scripting language.

There are two ways to add Java applets to your Web pages. The first, using the <APPLET> tag, was the original solution used when Java first hit the Web. The second is the <OBJECT> tag, HTML 4's all-purpose tag for adding multimedia and applet files to HTML documents.

JavaScript can be added directly to your HTML pages, fitting between <SCRIPT> tags. Script code should be hidden between HTML comment tags to keep it from being interpreted by non-JavaScript browsers.

There are two basic parts to any JavaScript script: the function definitions and the function calls. Function definitions should be in the head of your HTML document, while function calls can appear anywhere you want in the <BODY> of your document. Function calls can also appear as event handlers in certain HTML tags. One of the strengths of JavaScript is error checking for HTML forms.

Getting serious about JavaScript authoring requires an understanding of the object-oriented methods used to store variables related to your page. You can then pass pointers to these data objects to your functions, which allows you to work with more than one variable at once, creating scripts that accomplish more.

Next in Chapter 21, we'll take an even closer look at JavaScript. The specifics of objects and functions will be covered, along with several samples you can implement right in your browser.

Review Questions

1. Which tag, `<APPLET>` or `<OBJECT>`, was the first way to add Java applets?

2. Can Java applets be stored in the same directory as your HTML pages?

3. What is the `<PARAM>` tag used for with `<APPLET>` and `<OBJECT>`?

4. What attribute can the `<SCRIPT>` tag accept?

5. What do you call the type of JavaScript command that `document.write` represents?

6. In the following function declaration, where does the value for `number` come from?

   ```
   function add_two (number) {
   ```

7. What's wrong with the following script?

   ```
   <SCRIPT LANGUAGE="JavaScript">

   <!--

   document.write("Hi!")

   -->

   </SCRIPT>
   ```

8. What is the purpose of an event handler? What's an event?

9. True or false: If a function call sends the value `this.form`, the function declaration must call the value form, as in `calculate (form)`.

10. What is the full object hierarchy-style name for the value created by `<INPUT NAME="city">`?

11. Why is a blur event called that?

12. What method can be used to determine the length of a variable string?

Review Exercises

1. Write a JavaScript script (and the HTML page) that asks for the user's name and then tells her how many characters are in her name.

2. Write a script and page that display an alert dialog box when the user clicks an anchor link.

3. Now, write a script that pops up an alert when the user clicks the link, but doesn't move him to a new HTML document or part of an HTML document. (For instance, clicking the word hypertext brings up an alert with the definition of hypertext.)

4. Write a script that pops up an alert when the user touches a graphic with the mouse pointer. (Hint: Make it a clickable graphic. Suggestion: Use a picture of a person, and make the alert say "Stop touching me; I'm ticklish" or something similar.)

5. Write a script that determines whether a number entered in a textbox is "798."

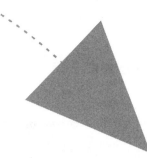

JavaScript Objects and Functions

In the preceding chapter, you learned enough JavaScript to accomplish some pretty impressive things, such as error checking on forms, creating alert messages, and performing simple functions like math. In this chapter, you'll get a little deeper into how JavaScript and Netscape Navigator store values for scripting. Then you'll learn how you can use this knowledge to do even more sophisticated things with JavaScript.

This chapter assumes that you have some experience with computer programming languages. JavaScript is a fairly simple scripting language for the "initiated," but this chapter may be less than useful if you've had no exposure to programming or script authoring concepts.

This chapter teaches you the following:

- The Object Model
- How to work with the JavaScript operators
- How to use math objects

The JavaScript Object Model

An *object,* for the purposes of this discussion, is basically a collection of properties. Often these properties are variables, but they can also be functions or JavaScript methods. Properties within objects are accessed using the following notation:

```
objectName.propertyName
```

For instance, if you created an object called myComputer, you might have properties called diskspace, monitor, and cdspeed. You could assign values to those properties like this:

```
myComputer.diskspace = "9.6 GB"

myComputer.monitor = "17-inch VGA"

myComputer.cdspeed = "24x"
```

What we've basically done is assign values to variables that happen to all be associated with one another because they're part of my computer (and myComputer). So, you could pass this object to a function using the following function call:

```
<SCRIPT>

printSpec (myComputer);

</SCRIPT>
```

Then you could use the pointer to that object to access each of the individual variables:

```
<SCRIPT>

function printSpec (computer) {

   document.write ("Disk space = " + computer.diskspace + "<BR>">);

   document.write ("Monitor = " + computer.monitor + "<BR>");

   document.write ("CD Speed = " + computer.cdspeed + "<BR>");

   return;

   }

</SCRIPT>
```

Methods

Methods, then, are basically functions associated with objects. For instance, one of the methods we've used quite a bit is document.write, which is really just a function provided by JavaScript that allows you to write HTML code to the current document.

Notice that write is the function, and document is the associated object. Netscape Navigator and other JavaScript browsers define certain basic objects, such as document, that are designed to make it easier for you to deal with the document or window in question. You'll learn about some of those standard objects later in this chapter.

You can even create your own methods by simply assigning a function name to an object variable, following this format:

```
object.methodname = function_name
```

Creating New Objects

You may remember that you used the keyword this for an object reference in the last chapter. JavaScript offers you the special keyword this, which acts as a placeholder. It's used to represent the current object involved in a function call. An example is the following:

```
<FORM NAME="MyForm">
<INPUT TYPE="Text" NAME="first" onClick="check(this)">
</FORM>
```

This code sends a pointer to the current object to the function check. In this case, the actual object is document.myform.first, but the keyword this can be used here because it's clear what the current object is.

That's part of how you create your own objects. It's done in two steps. First, you need to define a function that outlines the basic object you'd like to create. This is your own personal object definition for this new type of object.

EXAMPLE

For instance, if you wanted to create a data object that could be used to describe a person, you might use the following function:

```
function person(name, height, weight, age) {
    this.name = name;
    this.height = height;
    this.weight = weight;
    this.age = age;
}
```

Notice the use of this. In the case of this example, this refers to the object that's being created by another keyword, new. Using new is the second step in creating your new object. The following is an example:

```
stan = new person("Stan", 5.11, 210, 35) ;
```

The keyword new creates a new object. It also tells the object-creating function person that the name of this new object will be stan. So, when the function is called, stan will replace this, and the assignment will work like this:

```
stan.name = "Stan";
stan.height = 5.11;
stan.weight = 210;
stan.age = 35;
```

Of course, you won't see any of this happen, but it's now possible for you to access this data just like a regular object, as in the following:

```
document.write("Stan's age is: ",stan.age);
```

EXAMPLE

Creating New Objects and Methods

In this example, you'll create a script that not only creates a new object but also creates a method within that object. The object will be designed to hold data concerning a user's purchase. The method will be designed to generate a total of what is owed. You can use HTML form tags to allow the user to enter the information.

You start by defining all your functions in the head of the document and then creating the form in the body. Create a new HTML document, and enter Listing 21.1.

Listing 21.1: method.html: Creating Objects and Methods

```
<HTML>
<HEAD>
<TITLE>Customer Purchases</TITLE>
<SCRIPT>
<!--
function customer (val1, val2, val3) {
    this.item1 = val1;
    this.item2 = val2;
    this.item3 = val3;
    this.getsum = getsum;
    }
function getsum (form) {
    var total = 0
    total = this.item1 + this.item2 + this.item3;
    form.Sum.value = total;
}
```

```
// -->
</SCRIPT>
</HEAD>
<BODY>
<H3> The amount of each puchase is: </H3>
<PRE>
Purchase 1:    $5
Purchase 2:    $10
Purchase 3:    $12
</PRE>
<SCRIPT>
<!--
cust1 = new customer (5, 10, 12);
// -->
</SCRIPT>
<FORM NAME="form1">
<INPUT TYPE="BUTTON" NAME="Total" VALUE="Get Total" onClick="cust1.getsum
(this.form)">
<INPUT TYPE="TEXT" NAME="Sum" SIZE="12">
</FORM>
</BODY>
</HTML>
```

Notice first that the function that defines the object, called customer, uses the keyword this to reference its individual properties. When the new object is created, it's called cust1, and the new keyword passes that name to the object creator. So, in the onClick statement, you can then call the object's properties using cust1, as in cust1.item1 or cust1.getsum.

In fact, cust1.getsum is a special case: It's the method you're creating in this example. All you have to do is assign the function getsum as a property of your object, and then you can call it using object notation, as in cust1.getsum (this.form). Notice that the function getsum() is designed to accept a pointer to form data. See Figure 21.1 for an example of how this will look in a browser.

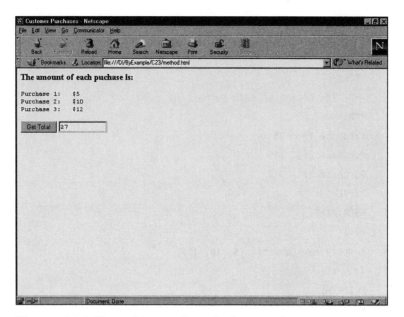

Figure 21.1: *Your object and method example.*

JavaScript Statements

If you have any experience with programming languages, you'll be familiar with JavaScript's small set of statements. JavaScript includes the conditional statement if...else and the loop statements for, while, break, and continue. You'll also get to know some of the associated JavaScript operators.

TIP

Remember that, in most cases, you'll use these statements in functions. These are the commands in JavaScript that you'll use to actually process data.

The key to many of these statements is called the *condition,* which is simply a bit of JavaScript code that needs to be evaluated before your script decides what to do next. So, before you look at JavaScript statements, let's look at the conditions and operators that JavaScript recognizes.

Comparison Operators and Conditions

Conditions are generally enclosed in parentheses, and they are always a snippet of code that is designed to evaluate as true or false. For instance, the following is a conditional statement:

```
(x == 1)
```

If x equals 1, this condition is valid.

This is why it's important to recognize and use the correct operators for conditions. For instance, an *assignment* always evaluates to true, so the condition

```
(errorLevel = 1)
```

is always true because it's an assignment. Although it may seem to make sense to use an equals sign in this instance, you actually need to use the comparison operator == for this condition. Table 21.1 lists the comparison operators.

Table 21.1: Comparison Operators in JavaScript

Operator	Meaning	Example	Is True When...
==	Equals	x == y	x equals y
!=	Not equal to	x != y	x is not equal to y
>	Greater than	x > y	x is greater than y
<	Less than	x < y	x is less than y
>=	Greater than or equal to	x >= y	x is greater than or equal to y
<=	Less than or equal to	x <= y	x is less than or equal to y

So, you have a number of different ways to create conditions by using comparisons. Realize, too, that conditions are not necessarily limited to numerical expressions. For instance, look at the following:

```
(carName != "Ford")
```

This will return the value false if the variable carName has the value of the string Ford.

EXAMPLE

Boolean Operators

The other operators common to conditional statements are the Boolean operators. In English, these operators are AND, OR, and NOT. In JavaScript, AND is &&, OR is ¦¦, and NOT is !. Here's an example of a condition that uses the AND operator:

```
((x == 5) && (y == 6))
```

This condition evaluates to true only if each individual comparison is true. If either comparison is false—or both comparisons are false—the entire conditional statement is false.

EXAMPLE

This conditional statement uses the OR operator:

```
((x == 5) || (y == 6))
```

In this case, if either of the conditions is true, the entire statement is true. The statement is false only if both of the conditions are false.

EXAMPLE

Finally, the NOT operator changes the result of an expression. Assuming that x == 5, you can create the following conditional:

```
(!(x == 5))
```

NOT simply reverses the result of the conditional statement. In this example, the entire condition is false because (x == 5) is true, and the NOT operator reverses that.

if…else

So, how do you put these conditional statements and operators to use? JavaScript offers the if…else conditional statement as a way to create either/or situations in your script. The basic construct is as follows:

```
if (condition) {
  script statements }
else {
  other statements }
```

EXAMPLE

The condition can be any JavaScript that evaluates to either true or false. The statements can be any valid JavaScript statements. For example:

```
if (x == 1) {
    document.write("X equals 1!");
    return;
    }
    else {
    x = x + 1;
    }
```

EXAMPLE

The else and related statements are not required if you simply want the if statements to be skipped and the rest of the function to be executed. An example might be the following:

```
if (errorLevel == 1) {
    return (false);
    }
```

In this case, if the condition is false (that is, if errorLevel does not equal 1), the rest of the function executes. If it is true, the function ends.

Loop Statements

The next two statement types are used to create loops—script elements that repeat until a condition is met. These loop statements are `for` and `while`.

A `for` loop follows this basic construct:

```
for (initial_assignment; condition; increment) {
    JavaScript statements
    }
```

EXAMPLE

You'll generally start a `for` loop by initializing your *counter* variable. Then, you'll evaluate the counter to see whether it's reached a certain level. If it hasn't, the loop will perform the enclosed statements and increment your counter. If the counter has reached your predetermined value, the `for` loop ends. For example:

```
for (x=0; x<10; x=x+1) {
   y = 2 * x;
   document.write ("Two times ",x," equals ",y,"<BR>");
   }
```

You start by initializing a counter variable (x=1) and then evaluating the counter in a conditional statement (x<10). If the condition is true, the loop will perform the enclosed scripting. Then, it will increment the counter—in this case, add 1 to it. When the counter reaches 10 in your example, the loop will end.

The `while` loop is similar to the `for` loop, except that it offers a little more freedom. `while` is used for a great variety of conditions. The basic construct is as follows:

```
while (condition) {
   JavaScript statements
   }
```

EXAMPLE

As long as the condition evaluates to true, the loop will continue. An example is the following:

```
x = 0;
while (x <= 5) {
   x = x +1;
   document.write (X now equals ",x,"<BR>")
   }
```

As long as the condition remains true, the `while` statement will continue to evaluate. In fact, the risk with `while` statements is that they can be infinite if the expression never evaluates to false. A common mistake is the following:

```
while (x=5) {
  x = x +1;
  document.write (X now equals ",x,"<BR>")
  }
```

The condition is actually an assignment, so it will always evaluate to true. In this example, the loop would continue indefinitely, and the output would always be X now equals 6.

break and continue

Two other keywords, `break` and `continue`, can be used in `for` or `while` loops to change the way the loop operates when certain conditions occur. Note that both of these are generally used with an `if` statement.

EXAMPLE

Here's an example of `break`:

```
for (x=0; x < 10; x=x+1) {
    z = 35;
    y = z / x;
    if (y == 7)
        break;
    }
```

`break` will terminate the loop when encountered. In this example, the loop is terminated when x is equal to 5 because 35 divided by 5 is 7. When the condition (y == 7) evaluates to true, the loop stops, and you move on to the next script element.

EXAMPLE

`continue` is basically used to skip a particular increment. For instance:

```
while (x < 10) {
    x = x +1;
    if (x == 5)
        continue;
    y = y + x;
    }
```

In this case, when the condition (x == 5) evaluates to true, the `continue` statement will cause the loop to move directly back to the `while` statement,

```
Your Number: <INPUT TYPE="TEXT" NAME="number" SIZE="3">
<INPUT TYPE="Button" VALUE="Submit Number" onClick="countTen
(this.form.number.value, this.form)">
<HR>
<H4> The result: </H4>
<TEXTAREA NAME="results" COLS="60" ROWS="10"></TEXTAREA><BR>
<INPUT TYPE="RESET" VALUE="Clear Form">
</FORM>
</BODY>
</HTML>
```

This may take some wading through, but it works—and it should eventually make sense.

Starting in the body of the document, the form requests a number from the user. When the user enters that number and clicks the Submit Number button, that number's value and a pointer to the form object are sent to the function declaration.

The first `if` statement determines whether the number is between 0 and 20. If it isn't, an alert is shown, and the user is asked to enter another number. If it is between 0 and 20, you move on to the `while` statement.

The `while` statement will loop only until the value of your number reaches 10. If the value is not currently 10, the `if...then` statement will determine whether you need to increment or decrement the number to move it toward 10. It then prints the statement, incrementing or decrementing the number while at the same time adding the text string to the form's `results` property.

When the function returns, there's a new value for the TEXTAREA named `results`. So, those strings are printed, and you can see what the script did to move the original number toward 10 (see Figure 21.2).

> **NOTE**
>
> This example introduces two miscellaneous scripting ideas. First, notice that you can use an addition sign (+) to piece together a string. `"You and " + "me"` results in the string `"You and me"`. Also notice the carriage return character `\r\n`. This carriage return varies from platform to platform. Windows uses `\r\n`; UNIX and Macs use `\n`. (When you have to choose one, the Windows style works best.) In Chapter 25, "HTML Examples," you'll look at slightly more complicated examples that format correctly on all platforms.

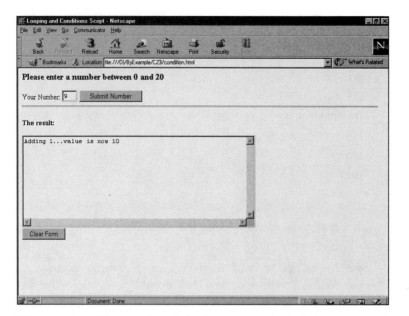

Figure 21.2: *The results of the looping and conditions example.*

Built-In Objects

In authoring scripts, there are a number of things you're likely to do repeatedly. Instead of forcing you to write your own functions and create your own objects to achieve this, JavaScript includes some of these often-used calls in the language itself. The built-in objects tend to store useful values or offer convenient methods. The functions usually perform some fairly intensive calculating that you'll often need to use.

The `string` Object

Let's talk about two major built-in objects available to you in JavaScript. The first is the `string` object, which helps you manipulate your strings. The second object, the `Math` object, holds certain constant values for you to use in your script and methods that make it a little easier to perform some mathematical functions.

The first object, `string`, is interesting if only for the fact that you don't actually have to use the notation `string.property` to use it. In fact, any string you create is a string object. You can create a string as simply as this:

```
mystring = "Here's a string"
```

The string variable `mystring` can now be treated as a `string` object. For instance, to get a value for the length of a `string` object, you can use the following assignment:

```
stringlen = mystring.length
```

When you create a string (and JavaScript makes it a `string` object), the value of its length is stored in the property `length`. It also associates certain methods with the object, such as `toUpperCase`. You could change a string to all uppercase letters with the following line:

```
mystring = mystring.toUpperCase
```

If the string had the value `Here is a string`, this assignment would change it to `HERE IS A STRING`. Table 21.2 shows some of the other methods available with `string` objects.

Table 21.2: Methods for JavaScript `string` Objects

Method	Works...	Example
anchor	Between `<A NAME=>` tags	`mystring.anchor` (*section_name*)
big	Between `<BIG>` tags	`mystring.big()`
blink	Between `<BLINK>` tags	`mystring.blink()`
bold	Between `<B>` tags	`mystring.bold()`
charAt	By choosing single letter at index	`mystring.charAt(2)`
fixed	Between `<TT>` tags	`mystring.fixed()`
fontcolor	Between `<FONT COLOR=>` tags	`mystring.fontcolor("red")`
fontsize	Between `<FONT SIZE=>` tags	`mystring.fontsize(2)`
indexOf	By finding index of certain letter	`mystring.indexOf("w")`
italics	Between `<I>` tags	`mystring.italics()`
lastIndexOf	By finding occurrence before indexOf	`mystring.lastIndexOf("w")`
link	Between `<A HREF=>` tags	`mystring.link` (`"http://www.foo.com"`)
small	Between `<SMALL>` tags	`mystring.small()`
strike	Between `<STRIKE>` tags	`mystring.strike()`

continues

Table 21.2: continued

Method	Works...	Example
sub	Between <SUB> tags	mystring.sub()
substring	By choosing part of a string	mystring.substring (0,7)
sup	Between <SUP> tags	mystring.sup()
toLowerCase	By changing string to lowercase	mystring.toLowerCase()
toUpperCase	By changing string to uppercase	mystring.toUpperCase()

Most of these methods should be fairly self-explanatory: They allow you to use the method to create and print text as if it were between HTML tags. For instance, the following two script lines have the same results:

```
document.write("<BIG>" + mystring + "</BIG>");

document.write(mystring.big);
```

Some of the other tags take some explaining—especially those that deal with indexes. Every string is "indexed" from left to right, starting with the value 0. So, in the following string, the characters are indexed according to the numbers that appear under them:

```
Howdy, boy
0123456789
```

In this case, using the method howdystring.charAt(4) would return the value y. You could also use the method howdystring.indexOf("y"), which would return the value 4.

EXAMPLE

Talking Decimals

Let's see how this string stuff can be useful. What you'll do is a little bit of math involving decimal numbers, known to programmers as *floats* because they include a floating decimal point. The problem is that, when you use dollars-and-cents decimals, you can get in trouble with JavaScript because it tends to return as many decimal places as possible. This is actually a bug (of sorts) in certain Netscape versions, and it may be changed some time in the future. In the meantime, you'll need to use these string methods to display things correctly.

Create a new HTML page and enter Listing 21.3.

Listing 21.3: strings.html: Numbers as Strings in JavaScript

```
<HTML>

<HEAD>

<TITLE> Doin' Decimals </TITLE>
```

```
<SCRIPT>
<!--
 function sumValues (val1, val2, val3, form) {
    sum = val1 + val2 + val3;
    form.total.value = sum;
    return;
    }
 function findPoint (form) {
    tot = form.total.value;
    var point_idx = tot.indexOf(".");
    form.results.value = tot.substring (0,point_idx+3);
    return;
    }
// -->
</SCRIPT>
</HEAD>
<BODY>
<H3> The Sum of Your Purchases is:</H3>
<SCRIPT>
<!--
var pur1 = 4.95;
var pur2 = 10.95;
var pur3 = 12.50;
// -->
</SCRIPT>
<FORM>
<INPUT TYPE="Button" VALUE="Click to Compute" onCLICK="sumValues
(pur1, pur2, pur3, this.form)"><BR>
<INPUT TYPE="Text" NAME="total" SIZE="10"><BR>
<INPUT TYPE="Button" VALUE="Click to Cut" onClick="findPoint (this.form)"><BR>
<INPUT TYPE="Text" NAME="results" SIZE="10"><BR>
</FORM>
</BODY>
</HTML>
```

There are two things to notice here. First, when you use the `substring` method, you need to add 3 to the index of the decimal point because the values for `substring` tell the method where to start (that is, index 0) and how far to go (that is, `point_idx + 3`). For example:

```
mystring.substring (0, 7)
```

This doesn't mean "Get all the characters and index 0 through index 7." What it really means is "Get seven characters, starting with index 0." Because it's counting from zero, it will stop gathering characters at index 6.

Number two is simple: There's a problem with this script. It doesn't round the value. In fact, using exactly the numbers in this example, the total cheats you of nearly a full cent (see Figure 21.3). Use this exact script for a million transactions, and you have the potential to loose $10,000! You'll look at rounding in the next example.

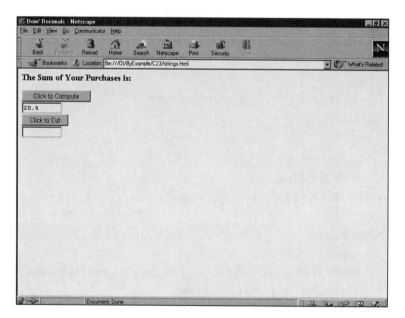

Figure 21.3: *Taking a substring of a calculated value.*

The `Math` Object

The `Math` object basically just holds some useful constants and methods for mathematical calculations. The `Math` object's properties are mathematical constants such as e, pi, and log10e (log, base 10, of e). You can use these by simply adding the name as `Math`'s property, as in the following example:

```
var pi_value = Math.PI;
area = Math.PI*(r*r);
```

Table 21.3 shows you the various properties for `Math`.

Table 21.3: Properties for the `Math` *Object*

Property	Value
`.PI`	Pi (approximately 3.1416)
`.E`	e, Euler's constant (approximately 2.718)
`.LN2`	Natural log of 2 (approximately 0.693)
`.LN10`	Natural log of 10 (approximately 2.302)
`.LOG10E`	Base 10 log of e (approximately 0.434)
`.SQRT1_2`	Square root of 1/2 (approximately 0.707)
`.SQRT2`	Square root of 2 (approximately 1.414)

The `Math` object's methods are called like any other methods. For instance, the arc sine of a variable can be found by using the following:

```
Math.asin(your_num);
```

Table 21.4 shows the methods for the `Math` object.

Table 21.4: Methods for the `Math` *Object*

Method	Result	Format
`.abs`	Absolute value	`Math.abs` (*number*)
`.acos`	Arc cosine (in radians)	`Math.acos` (*number*)
`.asin`	Arc sine (in radians)	`Math.asin` (*number*)
`.atan`	Arc tangent (in rads)	`Math.atan` (*number*)
`.cos`	Cosine	`Math.cos` (*num_radians*)
`.sin`	Sine	`Math.sin` (*num_radians*)
`.tan`	Tangent	`Math.tan` (*num_radians*)
`.ceil`	Least integer >= number	`Math.ceil` (*number*)
`.floor`	Greatest int <= number	`Math.floor` (*number*)
`.exp`	e to power of number	`Math.exp` (*number*)
`.log`	Natural log of number	`Math.log` (*number*)
`.pow`	Base to exponent power	`Math.pow` (*base, exponent*)
`.max`	Greater of two numbers	`Math.max` (*num, num*)
`.min`	Lesser of two numbers	`Math.min` (*num, num*)
`.round`	Round to nearest integer	`Math.round` (*number*)
`.sqrt`	Square root of number	`Math.sqrt` (*number*)

Rounding for Dollars

With the newly learned `Math.round` method, maybe you can get that last example to round dollars correctly. Create a new HTML document and enter Listing 21.4 (or make changes on the last example, using Save As to change the name).

Listing 21.4: rounded.html: Rounding Decimal Numbers in JavaScript

```
<HTML>

<HEAD>

<TITLE> Rounding for Dollars </TITLE>

<SCRIPT>

<!--

 function sumValues (val1, val2, val3, form) {

   sum = Math.round ((val1 + val2 + val3)*100);

   form.total.value = sum * .01;

   return;

   }

 function roundTotal (form) {

   var tot = form.total.value;

   var sub_total = Math.round (tot * 100);

   tot_str = "" + sub_total;

   var point_idx = tot.indexOf(".");

   result_str = "";

   y = 0;

   x = 0;

   while (x <= (point_idx+2)) {

      if (x == point_idx && y == 0) {

         result_str += ".";

         y = 1;

      }

      else {

         result_str += tot_str.charAt(x);

         x++;

      }

   }

   form.results.value = result_str;

   // form.results.value = totstr.substring (0,point_idx+3);

   return;

   }
```

```
// -->
</SCRIPT>
</HEAD>
<BODY>
<H3> The Sum of Your Purchases is:</H3>
<SCRIPT>
<!--
var pur1 = 4.96;
var pur2 = 11.13;
var pur3 = 13.15;
// -->
</SCRIPT>
<FORM>
<INPUT TYPE="Button" VALUE="Click to Compute" onCLICK="sumValues
(pur1, pur2, pur3, this.form)"><BR>
<INPUT TYPE="Text" NAME="total" SIZE="10"><BR>
<INPUT TYPE="Button" VALUE="Click to Round" onClick="roundTotal (this.form)"><BR>
<INPUT TYPE="Text" NAME="results" SIZE="10"><BR>
</FORM>
</BODY>
</HTML>
```

JavaScript does weird things with math, so it's difficult to make this work exactly right. Here's my logic: Your values are passed to sumValues as before, and the same answer appears in the first textbox. (This is already weird because adding numbers shouldn't give you this odd answer. Unfortunately, this is the kind of trouble you run into with decimal math on computers.)

When you click the second button, the form is sent to roundTotal, and a subtotal is generated by multiplying the total by 100 and rounding (remember, Math.round rounds to the nearest integer). The subtotal is turned into a string, and then the while loop is implemented to find the right place for the decimal point and is replaced in the rounded number. Why not just multiply by .01? Good idea, except that you'd get a weird floating-point number again, and you'd have to start over again!

Take special note that the following line turns tot_str into a string variable with the value sub_total:

```
tot_str = "" + sub_total;
```

The alternative is the following:

```
tot_str = sub_total;
```

This assignment would make `tot_str` a numerical variable, which wouldn't work in the subsequent `while` loop. Figure 21.4 shows the whole thing in action.

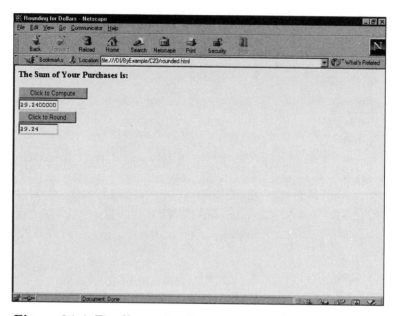

Figure 21.4: *Finally, you've done some rounding.*

Thoughts on JavaScript

Although JavaScript is a fairly easy language, it still can become very involved, and there's no way you can cover the entire thing in a few chapters. If you'd like to learn more about JavaScript, I suggest starting with the JavaScript Authoring Guide by Netscape Corporation at `http://home.netscape.com/eng/mozilla/3.0/handbook/javascript/index.html`. If you don't have any programming experience, you might be better off picking up a book designed to teach you JavaScript from the ground up. Both *Special Edition Using JavaScript* and *JavaScript by Example* are excellent titles from Que.

JavaScript is a very powerful way to make your Web site client-side in that it allows you to actually compute and process without the help of a Web server and special handling (like that required for CGI-BIN scripts). Even more powerful for this purpose are full-fledged Java applets. You may be able to find some that will help you do what you want on your page without much programming at all.

What's Next?

Once you get deeper into the JavaScript object model, you can start to see a number of easier ways to accomplish advanced scripting issues. Objects can have both properties (variables) and methods (functions) associated with them. The ability to store a number of associated values and function calls in one object makes it easier to group data and work with calculations in JavaScript.

JavaScript also includes a number of keywords and statements for creating if...else and looping statements. Using these takes some understanding of the comparison operators used in JavaScript, as well as a look at the assignment operators. These operators, which can be either binary or unary, can be used to increment, decrement, multiply, assign, and compare values or strings.

Loops can then be used to calculate something a number of times until a condition changes. You can also use the BREAK or CONTINUE statements to perform special commands when a certain condition within a loop is encountered.

JavaScript includes some of its own built-in objects, including those for math and strings. Both have properties and methods associated with them that make many common calculations easier.

Next in Chapter 22, "Adding Portable Documents to Web Sites," we'll take a look at placing entire documents onto the Web, in a non-HTML, yet still portable format.

Review Questions

1. How can you assign the property at_bats (with a value of 25) to the object player2? (Assume that the object already exists.)

2. If document is an object, what is write in document.write?

3. What is substituted for the keyword this in an object definition when a new object is created?

4. True or false: Assigning a new method to an existing object requires the new keyword.

5. What's the difference between (x == 1) and (x = 1)? Which of these always evaluates to true?

6. What happens if you don't include an `else` statement with an `if` condition and the `if` condition is `false`?

7. Consider the following:

```
for (x=0; x<5; ++x) {
    y = x;
}
```

The first time this loop executes, what is the value of y?

8. In the following example, what is the final value of y?

```
for (x=0; x<5; x++) {
  if (x == 4)
     continue;
  y += x;
}
```

9. How can you piece two strings together?

10. What string method would you use to create a link to a new HTML document?

Review Exercises

1. Create a new object function called `player` that creates the properties `name`, `hits`, `strikeouts`, `atbats`, and `homeruns`.

2. Add a method to the preceding object definition that computes the batter's batting average (`hits` divided by `atbats`). (Baseball enthusiasts will please excuse the crudity of this model.)

3. Write a script that defines a new `player` object and outputs the batter's average in a form textbox.

4. Write a script that defines a new `player` object and allows the user to enter the `name`, `hits`, `strikeouts`, `atbats`, and `homeruns` values in a text form. Then compute the average and print the player's name and stats to a form text area.

NOTE

There's something you need to know for this example. The built-in function `parseInt` (`string_variable`, `10`) can be used to change a string to an integer. The parameters for this function are the name of the string variable and the base numbering system you want to use (that is, `10` for base 10 or decimal numbers). This is an important step because form values are always strings.

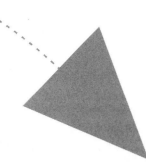

Adding Portable Documents to Web Sites

Even with all the advances that have occurred over the years, up to and including HTML 4, you still don't always have the minute control over presentation that you sometimes need. By design, HTML isn't a layout language. Instead, it concentrates on structure and offers suggestions for presentation.

For most people and in most cases, that's not a problem, but consider this example. What if you were setting up a Web page for the IRS? With the complex, computer-readable forms that the IRS must distribute to taxpayers, HTML just wouldn't be able to cut it. For the answer to this example—and any others where forms, newsletters, instruction sheets, legal documents, or any other published material needs to be delivered completely intact—we must turn to portable document formats.

This chapter teaches you the following:

- What portable documents are
- Adobe's Portable Document Format (PDF)
- How to create your own portable documents
- How to use Rich Text Format

What Are Portable Documents?

Portable Document Format (PDF) is actually a file format (like GIF or MPEG) created and used by the Adobe Acrobat system. The Acrobat system is probably the most widely known (and Internet-pervasive) method for distributing portable documents. Based on Adobe's PostScript technology, certain Adobe products are capable of generating PDF files, which can then be viewed by Web helper applications and plug-ins (see Figure 22.1).

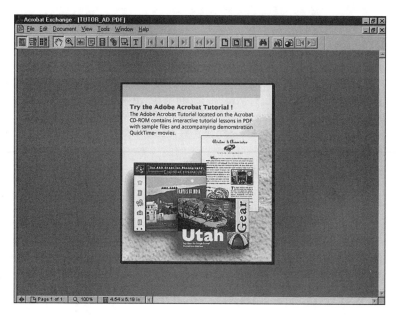

Figure 22.1: Viewing an Adobe PDF file.

In more general terms, portable documents refer to any sort of technology that allows you to distribute documents intact to users without relying on the "machine-dependent" nature of HTML. In other words, these are documents that can be viewed by the user, but only in one way—they cannot be reformatted to fit the needs of the user's Web browsing program or machine.

Although they are more sophisticated than this, you can almost think of portable documents as just big graphics files. Most of these documents don't allow the user to alter them in any way, although a growing trend is

fed back to the Web browser, which then retrieves the associated Web document or multimedia file. This allows great flexibility in combining the freedom of the Web with a file format other than HTML through which you can access URLs (see Figure 22.4).

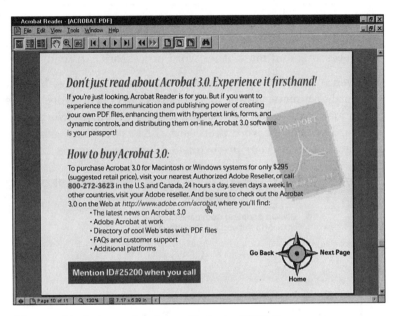

Figure 22.4: *Accessing hyperlinks in PDF documents.*

Other plug-ins give Acrobat the ability to play inline movies, animations, sounds, and other multimedia files in a way that's similar to newer plug-in technology for Web browsers.

NOTE

The plug-ins discussed here are for the Adobe Acrobat program itself—not for Netscape Navigator or another Web browser.

Creating Your Own PDFs

If high-end PDF applications aren't quite your style, you can still use other programs you have hanging around as substitute PDF files. Most of these file formats don't allow for the inclusion of graphics and don't give you much control over fonts, but the more sophisticated PDF formats do. At the same time, however, they do give you control over things such as centering, text size, hard returns, font appearance (bold, italic, and underlined), and similar attributes.

NOTE

PDF formats are designed to appear exactly the same on different computer platforms. These makeshift PDFs (like Microsoft Word documents, discussed next) will generally have slight differences from platform to platform and version to version.

For instance, Microsoft Word documents are an easy way to distribute documents on the Web because Word tends to be one of the most popular word processors, and most other word processors can read Word's .doc files.

Even if a user's word processor can't read .doc files, Microsoft offers a free Word document viewer for Windows users. The Word Viewer is designed to do just that—allow your users to view and print Word documents. Without Word or another word processor, they can't do any editing, but they can view and print your preformatted form (see Figure 22.5).

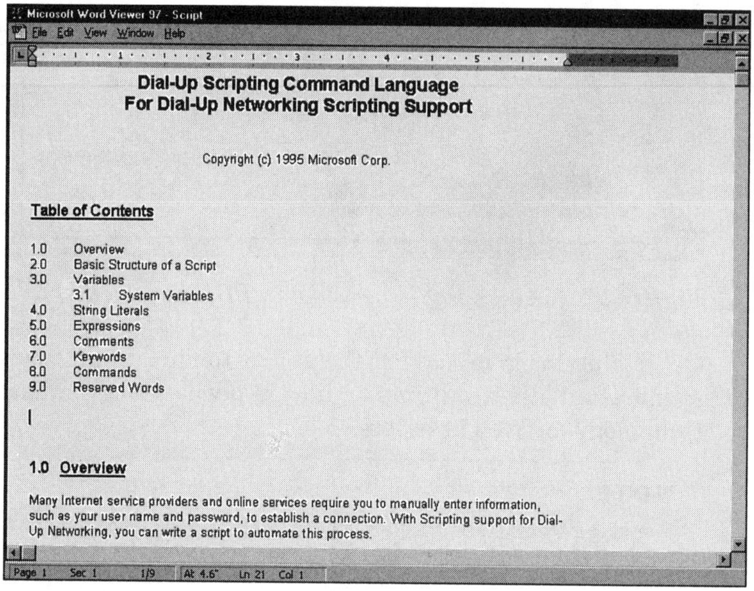

Figure 22.5: Using the Microsoft Word Viewer.

TIP

The Word viewer can be downloaded from `http://officeupdate.microsoft.com/2000/downloadDetails/wd97vwr32.htm`. You might want to let your users know this if you offer Word documents for downloading.

Creating the Word Document

Fortunately, there's nothing special you need to do to create a Word document for viewing on the Internet. The only requirement is that you use Microsoft Word to create the document (or a word processor that can save in Microsoft Word for Windows 2.0 and above or Word for Mac 4.0 and above formats). Save the file with a .doc extension, just as Windows and DOS users normally would.

TIP

Windows 95/98 users can use WordPad to create, view, and edit Word documents.

EXAMPLE

Then, you can make it available as a hyperlink on your Web site, just as with any other multimedia file, as in the following example:

```
Download the file in <A HREF="file.doc> MS Word format </A>.
```

Using Rich Text Format

Another interesting way to distribute formatted documents on the Web is by using the Rich Text Format (RTF). RTF is a Microsoft file format that's designed to be more sophisticated than plain ASCII text but less proprietary and complicated than word processing document types. Most word processors can create, view, print, and save documents in this format.

EXAMPLE

To make RTF format files available on your Web site, first save your document in your word processor as an RTF file with the extension .rtf. From there, all you have to do is include it in a hypertext link, like in the following:

```
<A HREF="myfile.rtf">Here's a copy of my special RTF file.</A>
```

EXAMPLE

Creating a Portable Word File

If you have Microsoft Word, WordPad, or any word processor that can save files in Microsoft Word for Windows 2.0 or above format, enter Listing 22.1 in a new Word document.

Listing 22.1: A Portable Microsoft Word File

```
Printable Order Form
The following information is required to complete your order in as timely
a fashion as possible.
First Name:
Last Name:
Street Address:
```

continues

Listing 22.1: continued

```
City:
State:
Zip:
Daytime Phone Number:
Evening Phone Number:
Credit Card Number:
Expiration Date:
Signature:
If you prefer, please enclose a check for $43.95US ($39.95 and $4.00 shipping).
Please mail this order form to:
Foo, Inc.
Attn: Order Processing
001 Tallest Building
Metropolis, USA 10001
Copyright 1999 Foo, Inc. Please allow 4-6 weeks delivery.
```

Microsoft Word or your word processor offers you the freedom to alter this form with font size, emphasis, and even centering. For instance, I'm going to center the title of this page, make it slightly bigger than the rest of the form, and bold it. I'm also going to boldface the "most required" information on the form so that users will see what's most important. I'll make the small print at the bottom of the page even smaller. The results are shown in Figure 22.6.

TIP

Use common fonts (such as Times, Courier, and Helvetica) when creating these documents so that nearly any Microsoft Word user can view them just as you create them.

What's Next?

In some instances, HTML simply doesn't give you enough control over the documents you distribute on the Web. Whether you simply want your "corporate image" to remain intact or whether you need to transmit format-dependent forms for official use, you can use portable documents when HTML won't work.

Adobe Acrobat is easily the most popular PDF format, and adding these documents to your Web pages is as simple as creating a hypermedia link. Acrobat files can be read with the free Acrobat viewer program for most computer platforms. If you include Acrobat or any other formats, you'll need to correctly set the MIME type for your server. You'll also want to point your user to the correct Web site for downloading the appropriate viewer software.

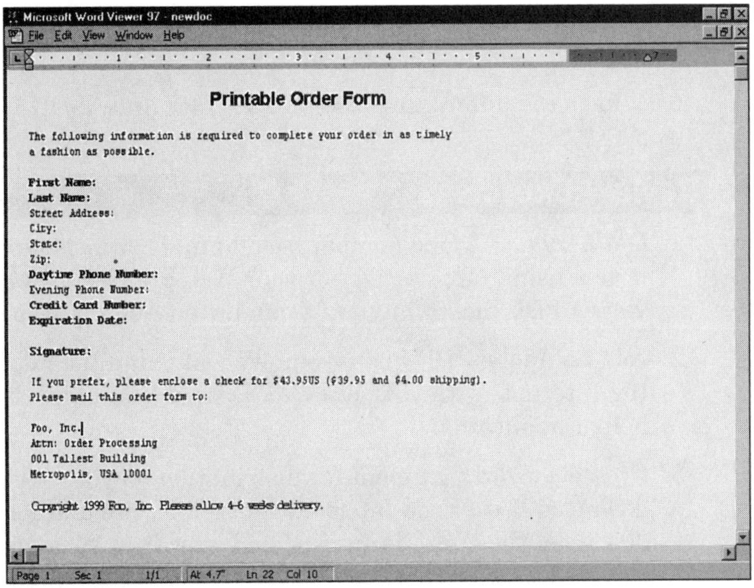

Figure 22.6: *My new "portable" Microsoft Word form.*

The "poor man's" portable document format might just be Microsoft Word files or even Rich Text Format (RTF) files. Both of these formats are widely supported by Microsoft and other word processing products. Microsoft even offers a Word Viewer program free on the Web. While control is not as rich as with true PDFs, these are good, inexpensive substitutes for documents that are still more reliably rendered than HTML.

In the next two chapters, we'll explore two popular and freely available tools for creating HTML documents: Netscape Composer, covered in Chapter 23, and Microsoft FrontPage Express, covered in Chapter 24. These programs are known as "WYSIWYG" tools, which stands for "What You See Is What You Get," a more graphical means of composing your HTML. These two chapters will take a look at how easy they are to use and what kind of output they create.

Review Questions

1. True or false: PDFs give you increased control over the physical appearance of your documents.

2. Can Adobe Acrobat files be used as hypertext documents?

3. Which PDF is the most popular on the Web?

4. In most cases, how are PDFs handled by the user's Web browser?

5. To use Microsoft Word files as PDFs, which version of Word should you save your documents in?

6. What's the difference between RTF files and ASCII files?

Review Exercises

1. Get a copy of Adobe Acrobat from `http://www.adobe.com` and configure it as a helper application for your Web browser. Now, download and view a PDF file. (Many are available on Adobe's Web site.)

2. Add an Adobe PDF file to your Web site, and then download it (over the Internet) with your browser. Does it load properly into the Acrobat helper application?

3. Create a Word document for distribution on your Web site, and then download it over the Internet. If possible, use a different computer to download the Word document, and view it in Word or the Word viewer. Does it look any different?

Part VI

HTML Editors and Tools

Creating HTML Documents with Netscape Composer

Using Microsoft FrontPage Express

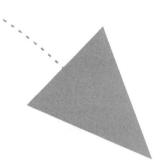

Creating HTML Documents with Netscape Composer

Up until now, all the HTML page creation you've done has been with a standard text editor and a Web browser for viewing. That isn't the only way to go. In this chapter and the next few chapters, you'll learn about some of the programs that allow you to create documents without handcrafting each tag. Keep in mind, however, that authoring aides don't replace a solid knowledge of HTML, which is why I'm just now introducing you to them. In most cases, you'll need to carefully review the HTML output of these programs for completeness and an accurate reflection of your intentions. None of them are sophisticated enough at this time for you to wholly ignore the tags.

In this chapter, you'll learn specifically about Netscape Communicator, the full-featured Netscape offering that includes Netscape Composer, an HTML authoring tool. This editor allows you to create HTML documents in a what-you-see-is-what-you-get (WYSIWYG) environment.

This chapter teaches you the following:

- Why you might choose a WYSIWYG tool instead of hand coding
- How to work with the Composer interface
- What Composer is doing "under the hood"
- How to create tables with Composer

Why Edit by Hand at All?

I wouldn't be surprised if you were wondering why I bothered to write an entire book about editing HTML by hand when tools like Netscape Composer exist. It's not quite that simple, as I alluded to in the introduction.

First, without a pretty solid knowledge of how HTML works, using many HTML editors could get you into trouble. Some are particularly bad about giving you options in their menus and toolbars without making it clear what standard, if any, they adhere to. Browser-isms abound in these tools, something the unwary and underinformed HTML author won't know to be concerned about.

Although it's true that many people find writing basic HTML in these editors to be easier and more convenient than using a plain text editor, I feel strongly that you should know what you're doing and understand what's happening behind the scenes. Having read this book, you know how HTML tags work and how to validate your results. If using a tool like Netscape Composer helps you get some portions of your work done more quickly, by all means, use it. Chances are you'll still need to get your hands dirty with HTML to make your pages the best they can be.

Editing HTML with Netscape Composer

To launch the Netscape Composer HTML Editor, choose File, New, Blank Page from within Netscape Navigator, or select the Netscape Composer item from your Start menu. What appears next is the Netscape Composer HTML Editor (see Figure 23.1). From here, you can simply begin typing your HTML document.

TIP

Choosing From Template or From Wizard in the New Document menu gives you access to templates and guides designed by Netscape to make Web document creation easier, if somewhat generic looking.

The Netscape Composer Editor is designed to be used much like a standard word processor. Notice that the toolbar across the top has options for making text bold, italic, or underlined. You can choose different font sizes and styles and even insert images and create hyperlink anchors simply by pressing buttons. It's easy to create a basic HTML page using just the toolbar.

For instance, to create a header for your page, enter the text for the header as follows:

```
Welcome to my Page
```

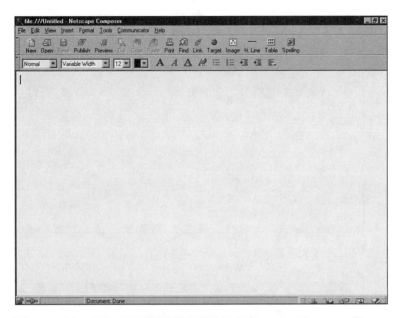

Figure 23.1: *The WYSIWYG HTML Editor in Netscape Composer.*

Then, highlight the text by dragging the mouse pointer from one end to the other. Using the Format menu, choose Heading, and then choose the number corresponding to the heading level you want to use, say, 1 (see Figure 23.2). The text will change in the editor window to suggest the new "look" of your text.

Notice too, that you can use the pull-down menu (select-box) to perform the same action (see Figure 23.3).

Of course, like a good word processor, you can also choose to change the text to a heading level first and then type. For instance, use that same pull-down menu to change the appearance to Normal, and then click the menu button for Italics. Now, back in the Netscape Editor window, type some text such as the following:

```
Copyright 1999. Do not duplicate without permission.
```

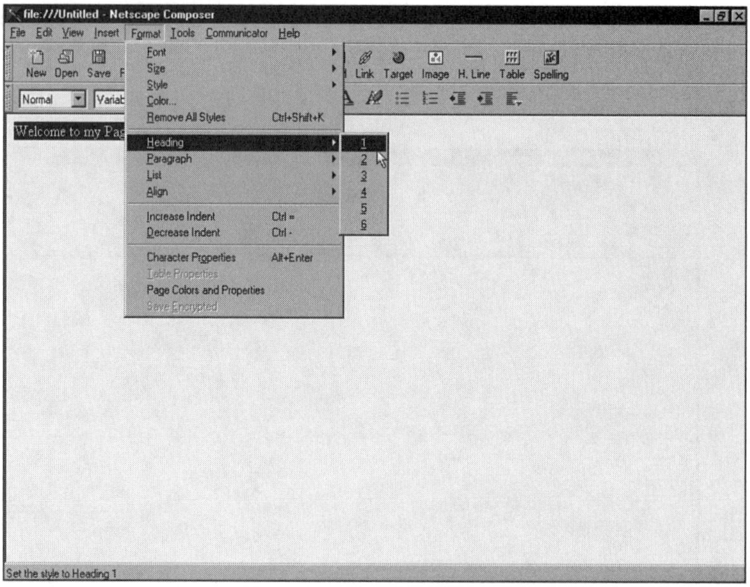

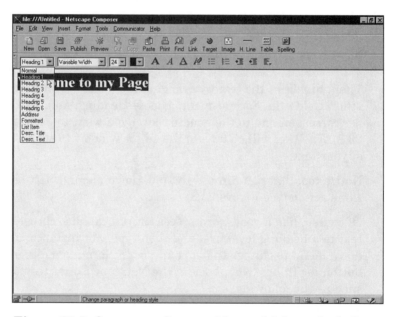

Figure 23.2: *Setting a heading in Netscape Composer.*

Figure 23.3: *Composer often provides multiple methods for accomplishing similar tasks.*

Notice that it comes out looking just as if it were between <I> tags (see Figure 23.4).

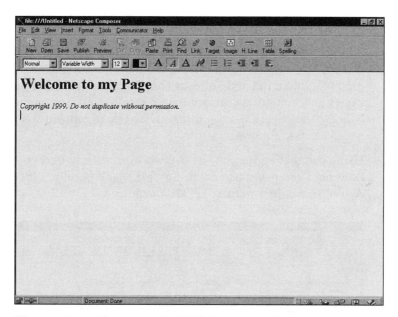

Figure 23.4: *Changing the HTML types before typing.*

In fact, that's exactly what Composer is doing—it's putting your text between HTML tags. To prove it, try the following example.

Checking Under the Hood

In this example, you'll create a simple HTML document in Netscape Composer. Then, you'll take a look at it with your trusty text editor. You'll see that all Composer is really doing is basic HTML markup; it just has a fancy interface.

Enter Listing 23.1 into a new document in Composer.

Listing 23.1: composer-test.html: A Sample Netscape Composer Document

```
Products

All of our products here at Foo, Inc. are designed with the consumer in mind.
It's more important to us that you be happy with our products and services than
it is that we make a profit. If we can make money, so much the better, but we
like to think of ourselves as a charitable organization.

The following is a list of our more popular product lines:

Fine Jewelry

Luxury Automobiles

Cruises and Exotic Vacations

Deforestation Services

Chemical Pollutants

Indoor Mall Construction
```

With that entered, there's some formatting you should do. For instance, highlight the word "Product" and change it to a heading (perhaps Heading 1) using one of the techniques described earlier. Then, change text in the document to bold or italics using the appropriate buttons. Make the list of products into a list style of your choosing. Then, select File, Save As and save the document as composer-test.html. You'll be prompted to select a title for the page. Do so, and then click OK to continue. Now is when you see Composer's secret.

Using the text editor you've been working with in earlier chapters, open the document composer-test.html. Anything look familiar? (See Figure 23.5.) Again, this is just regular HTML markup.

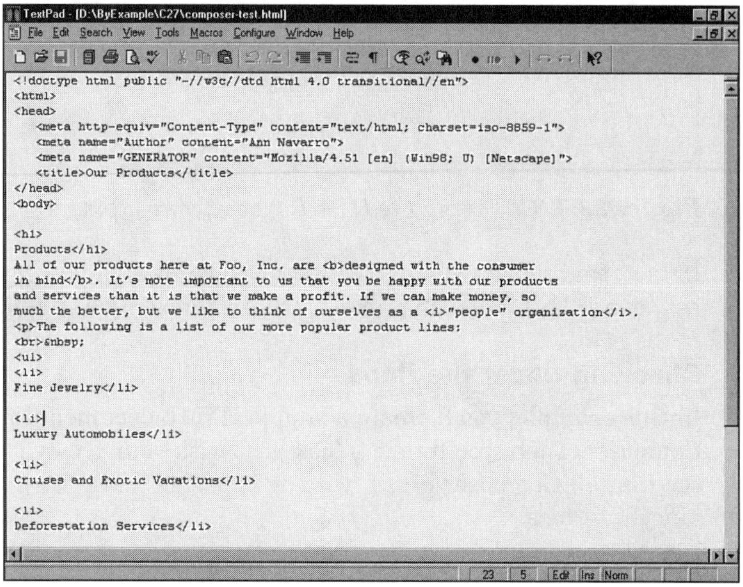

Figure 23.5: *Netscape Composer creates traditional HTML documents.*

Notice anything else about the source code for this document? The one place where Composer does "fall down," as it were, is in the <DOCTYPE> tag. I give Netscape credit for having Composer insert one (many editors don't even bother), but remember what we discussed about the <DOCTYPE> tag back in Chapter 6? It's case-sensitive. The all-lowercase presentation provided by Composer won't work. You'll need to edit the <DOCTYPE> tag accordingly.

Inserting a Line Break

This one isn't quite as obvious from the outset. It's clear that Netscape Composer creates new <P> paragraph tags whenever you hit Enter in the Editor window (except when <P> is inappropriate, as with list elements). How do you create a <BR> tag?

EXAMPLE

Just press Shift+Enter on your keyboard. That's all there is to it. For instance, try entering the following:

```
How do I love thee?
```

Press Shift+Enter, and then enter the following:

```
Let me count the ways.
```

If you were to view this in your text editor, you'd see that the <BR> tag has been inserted where you hit Shift+Enter.

NOTE

If you experiment with this, you may find that just hitting Enter can also generate a <BR> tag. However, to be certain you generate <BR> rather than a new <P>, use the Shift+Enter method.

Hyperlinks, Images, and Head Elements

Of course, Composer allows you to add both hyperlinks and images to your documents. Both are accomplished through commands in the Insert menu or through the icons in the toolbar. You can also create clickable images rather easily.

Adding Hyperlinks

Adding a typical hypermedia or hypertext link is just about as easy as regular markup in Composer. Simply highlight the text, choose Insert, Link from the menu (or click the Link icon button), and you're presented with the Character Properties dialog box (see Figure 23.6). Make sure that the Link tab is selected. Now you can either enter the name of the URL to the linked document (or file), or you can use the Browse File button to find the file on your hard drive.

NOTE

If you're currently not working with files resident on the Web server, remember that you'll need the correct relative path to your files (once they're on the Web server) in this dialog box. So, take special care when using the Browse File button.

When you've completed entering the URL and clicked OK, the highlighted text will act as a link in your Web document.

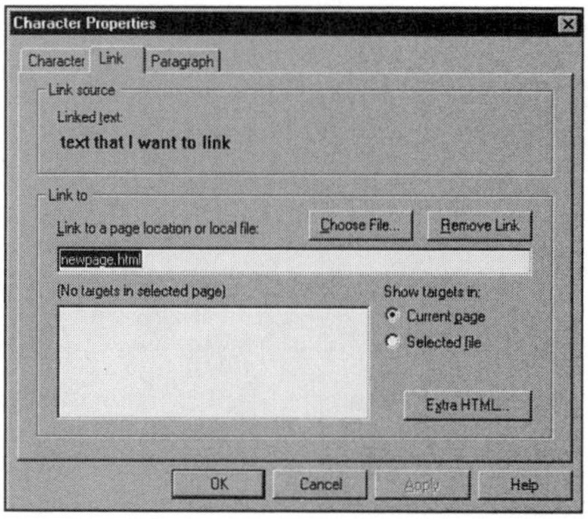

Figure 23.6: The Character Properties dialog box.

Adding Images

To add an image file to your document, place your cursor at the point in the editor where you would like the image to appear. Choose Insert, Image. (You can also click the Insert Image icon on the toolbar.) The Image Properties dialog box should appear with the Image tab selected (see Figure 23.7). In this dialog box, enter the URL to the graphic that you want to include, or, you can use the Browse button to find the file.

NOTE

With images, using the Browse button actually causes the graphic file to be copied to the current directory. If this isn't what you want, check the Copy Image to the Document's Location check box at the bottom of the dialog to turn this feature off. You should also enter absolute URLs in the Image File Name field when using graphics already on the Web (or in specific directories on your own Web server).

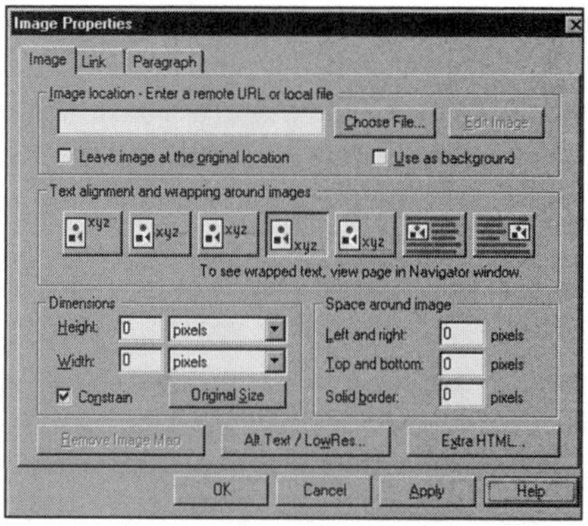

Figure 23.7: The Image Properties dialog.

Now, as you can see, this dialog box is pretty sophisticated, and you have some more choices to make. First, you can use the Text Alignment section of the Image Properties dialog box to decide how text will be aligned relative to the graphic. In the Dimensions section, specify the true height and width for the image. In the Space Around Image section, you can decide how much space to put between the image and surrounding text.

Remember that valid HTML 4 requires that every image use the ALT attribute. Click the Alt Text/LowRes button near the bottom of the Image Properties dialog to activate the Alternate Image Properties dialog box. Enter the text that best acts as an alternative to your image. The concept of a "low-res" graphic isn't standard, so we won't be using that option. Clicking OK returns you to the main Image Properties dialog box.

Finally, if you want this image to serve as a link, click the Link tab and enter a URL in the Link To section.

The Easy Road to Tables

If HTML authors had to pick one segment of HTML that is made significantly easier by WYSIWYG tools like Composer, I suspect the vast majority would choose tables. Let's face it, endless `<TR></TR>` and `<TD></TD>` tags, with all the content in between, can get confusing, if not just tiring. Composer offers several solutions for tables that make the process much easier.

Start by entering the following comma-delimited lists into a new Composer document as shown:

```
one, two, buckle my shoe
three, four, shut the door
```

Highlight the text using your mouse, then choose Tools, Tableize, By Commas (see Figure 23.8).Composer then divides your data by line and by comma. Each line is wrapped in a table row container `<TR>`, and each segment of the line divided by commas is a table cell `<TD>`. Save the file as table1.html, and then open it using your regular text editor. You should see something like Figure 23.9.

Notice that Composer has chosen several default values for you: cellpadding, cellspacing, and table border. To change these, you're pretty much stuck with editing the source by hand. However, using the next table creation method allows you to set these options from the start.

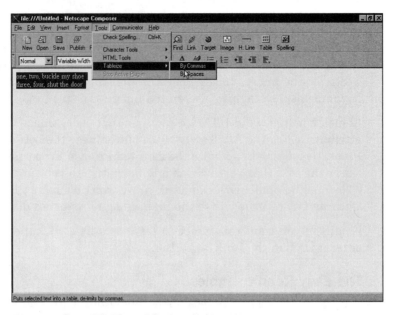

Figure 23.8: *"Tableize" by commas.*

```
<!doctype html public "-//w3c//dtd html 4.0 transitional//en">
<html>
<head>
    <meta http-equiv="Content-Type" content="text/html; charset=iso-8859-1">
    <meta name="Author" content="Ann Navarro">
    <meta name="GENERATOR" content="Mozilla/4.51 [en] (Win98; U) [Netscape]">
    <title>Table Test</title>
</head>
<body>
 
<table BORDER=3 CELLSPACING=3 CELLPADDING=3 >
<tr>
<td>one</td>

<td>two</td>

<td>buckle my shoe</td>
</tr>

<tr>
<td>three</td>

<td>four</td>

<td>shut the door</td>
</tr>
</table>

</body>
</html>
```

Figure 23.9: *The resulting table HTML.*

Click the Table icon from the icon bar. This will bring up the New Table Properties dialog box (see Figure 23.10).

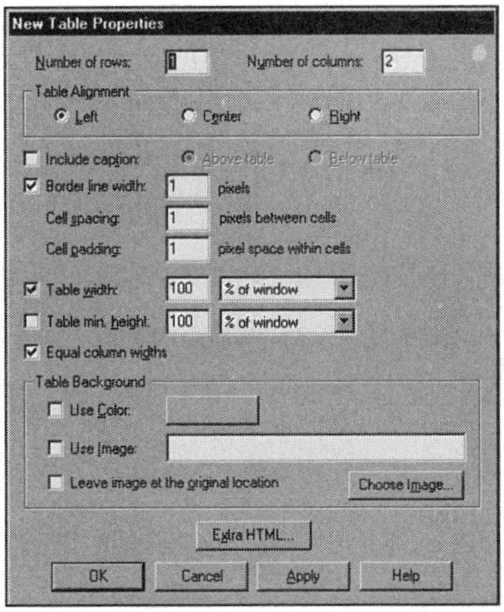

Figure 23.10: The New Table Properties dialog box.

Notice that you haven't yet written the text content for your table, so the dialog doesn't automatically know how many rows and columns you want. You'll need to plan and enter these values by hand. Enter 2 rows and 3 columns. Set the other choices as you desire (keeping in mind that options such as Table Minimum Height aren't valid HTML 4). When you're satisfied with the table parameters, click OK, and your empty table will be rendered on the page (see Figure 23.11)

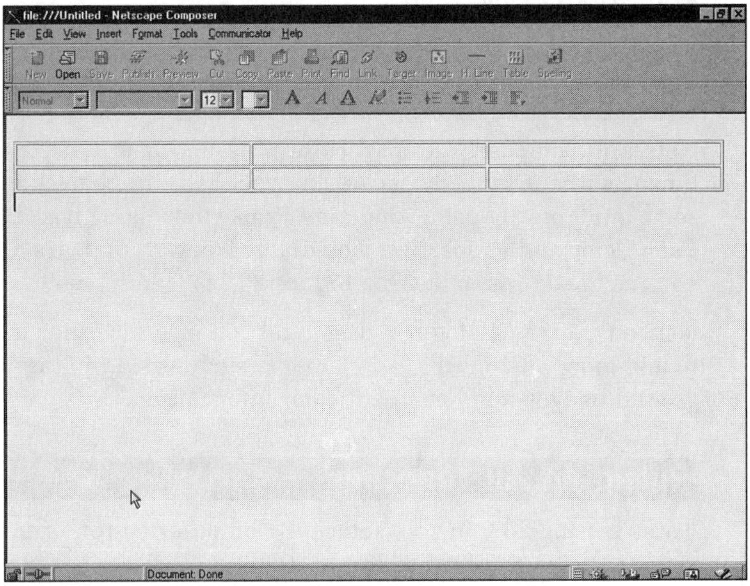

Figure 23.11: The resulting empty table.

Type the following items, starting in the upper-left table cell and pressing the Tab key to move left to right (and top to bottom) within the table:

`Windows,Mac, Unix, IBM, Dell, Gateway`

The final table should look like Figure 23.12.

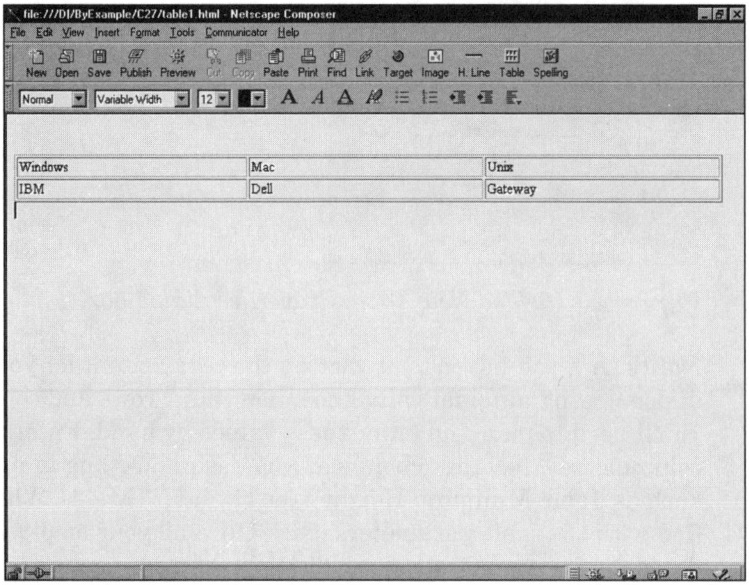

Figure 23.12: Your completed table.

Editing the Head

Netscape Composer automatically adds <HEAD> and <BODY> tags to your document without initially consulting you. You can go back and edit them with some guidance by using the Page Properties dialog box. Choose Format, Page Color and Properties. The dialog box that appears allows you to enter various head properties (see Figure 23.13).

Notice that this dialog box uses a tabbed interface that will also allow you to add more advanced head elements such as <META> tags, as well as background images and document color information.

Putting it All Together

Enter Listing 23.2 in the Netscape Composer editor, or use the document you created in the first example.

EXAMPLE

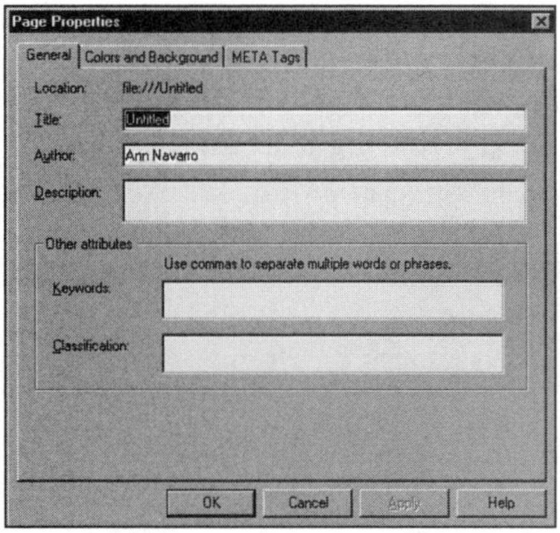

Figure 23.13: *Adding information to the document's head.*

Listing 23.2: version2.html: Advanced Editing in Netscape Composer

Products

All of our products here at Foo, Inc. are designed with the consumer in mind.
It's more important to us that you be happy with our products and services than
it is that we make a profit. If we can make money, so much the better, but we
like to think of ourselves as a charitable organization.

The following is a list of our more popular product lines:

Fine Jewelry

Luxury Automobiles

Cruises and Exotic Vacations

Deforestation Services

Chemical Pollutants

Indoor Mall Construction

If you've already turned the product lines into list items, great. If not, highlight them all, and then choose List Item from the pull-down menu in the
button bar.

Now, select each product-line name individually and give each a hypertext
link. Click the Link button in the button bar or choose Insert, Link from
the menu. In the Links dialog box, enter a URL for your link, or click
Browse to choose a local file. Click OK to change the text to a link.

Next, you'll enter a graphic (use anything handy). Find a good place in your
document for it, and then click the Image button or choose Insert, Image. In
the Image tab of the Properties dialog box, give a URL or path for the
image, or choose to Browse for the graphic file. If you'd like this image to be
clickable, choose the Link tab and then enter a URL.

Finally, choose Properties, Document. In the Document Properties dialog, give your document a title and enter any other information you feel like giving (name, description, and so on). Click OK, and as far as this example is concerned, you're done. Try viewing it in the Netscape Browser (see Figure 23.14).

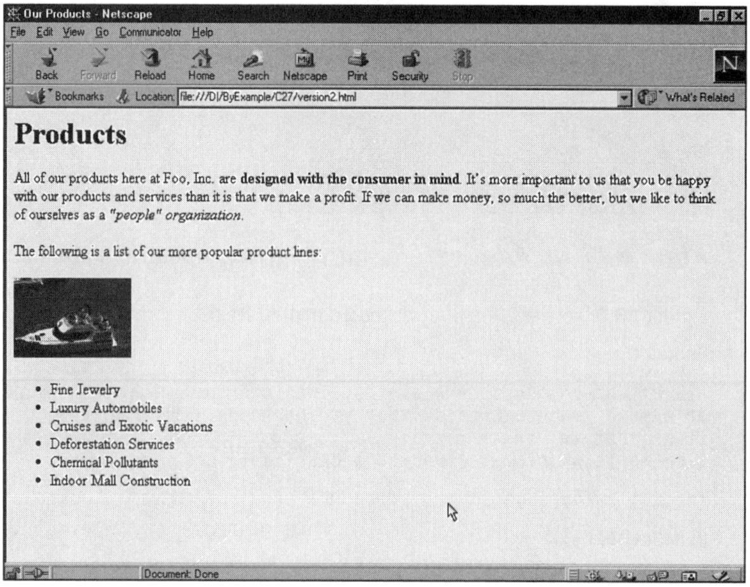

Figure 23.14: *The final product in Navigator.*

What's Next?

You've spent most of this book learning about raw HTML—how to create Web documents using nothing more than a text editor. More and more programs are appearing, though, that try to make creating HTML documents easier and more friendly. Netscape Composer is one of those programs.

Creating basic HTML pages is fairly easy because Netscape Composer features an Editor interface that's a lot like popular word processors. Text manipulation such as adding bold, italics, and changing font faces is easy to accomplish. You can also create HTML lists and add horizontal rules and <BR> tags.

The heart of your Web site—hyperlinks and images—are easy enough in Netscape Composer as well. Gold doesn't have great support for image maps (and has no client-side support), but the basics are easy. Plus, once you've created an HTML document in Netscape Gold, you can always open it in a text editor for further enhancements.

Next in Chapter 24, we'll take a similar look at Microsoft's entry in the free development tools market: FrontPage Express.

Review Questions

1. Is it possible to change HTML styles in Composer before typing the text for a particular style?

2. To what other sort of computer application is Composer similar?

3. In what type of file does Composer save your HTML? Can you edit this with other programs?

4. What menu command allows you to change from an unordered to an ordered list type?

5. What does Composer call HTML definition lists?

6. Is there a menu command for
?

7. Why should you be careful when using the Browse button to create hypertext links?

8. How is the Browse button for images different from the Browse button for hyperlinks?

9. Can you type the Title of your document directly in the document window?

Review Exercises

1. Use Composer's definition lists and hyperlinks to create a page of book reviews. Clicking the book's name shows the user a graphic of the book. For instance, an entry might be the following:

   ```
   HTML By Example
   The best book ever written for learning HTML the right way.
   ```

2. Based on the preceding example, add another definition (DD) line that includes a link to order the book, the author's name, copyright information, and price. For instance:

   ```
   HTML By Example
   The best book ever written for learning HTML the right way.
   Ann Navarro, Todd Stauffer Copyright 1999, $34.99. Order this book.
   ```

3. Create a button bar interface using Composer. (No image map is necessary; just create a series of clickable images.)

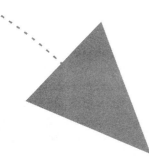

Using Microsoft FrontPage Express

FrontPage Express is Microsoft's entry in the freely available WYSIWYG HTML editing market. Most users will obtain it through the initial installation of Windows 95/98, though it's also available with Internet Explorer 5.

Though it shares a name with the commercial version of FrontPage, FrontPage Express is light on the site management features and other extended capabilities that the full version of FrontPage provides.

This chapter teaches you the following:

- How to do basic markup in FrontPage Express
- How to add links, images, and heads with FrontPage Express
- How to easily create forms with FrontPage Express

Basic Markup in FrontPage Express

FrontPage Express has many of the menu items, icons, and other user interface features that you'll be familiar with if you've ever used other Microsoft products, such as Word. Additional toolbars and menu items have been added to support the unique needs of an HTML authoring tool (see Figure 24.1).

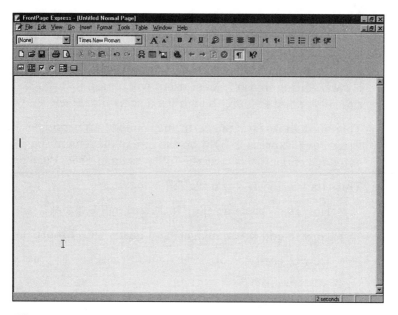

Figure 24.1: *The Microsoft FrontPage Express interface.*

Much like Netscape Composer (and any WYSIWYG tool, for that matter), basic markup in FrontPage Express is accomplished with typing and a few mouse clicks.

For example, I can type in the following paragraph:

```
Today is Wednesday. It's a nice day here in Southwest Florida, which really
isn't a surprise, since it's usually quite nice here this time of year. It is
especially nice when compared to some of the more northern climates as they
begin to see frost and snow!
```

I can then modify it as I would in a word processor by highlighting portions of the text and clicking toolbar icons to make changes (see Figure 24.2).

HTML Lists

Creating a list in FrontPage Express is pretty easy, too. There are even several different ways to do this, so you can pick the one that's easiest for you.

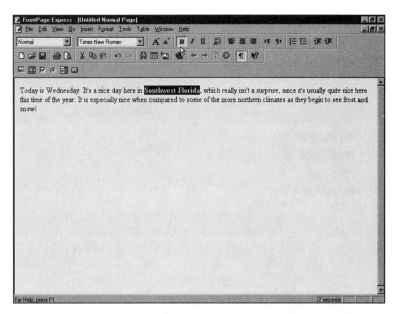

Figure 24.2: *Adding boldface to text is a simple one-click operation.*

For an ordered or unordered list, one method is to enter the text for your list, pressing Enter after each. For example:

Downloadable Support Files

Frequently Asked Questions

Send Us a Note

Toll-Free Numbers

Select the entire list with the mouse. With all the text highlighted, you can select the appropriate list button in the button bar or select the list type in the drop-down style menu. For instance, if you click the Bulleted List (UL) button in the button bar, you'll get something similar to Figure 24.3.

Definition Lists

Creating some HTML features within FrontPage Express isn't as intuitive as others may be. One example of this is the definition list. Ordered and unordered lists are easy; there's a toolbar icon specifically for them. No icons, or even menu options, are available for a definition list. The secret is to look in the drop-down list box just to the left of the font selection box.

Begin by selecting Defined Term from the drop-down list to the left of the font drop-down list. Then type the term. As soon as you hit Enter, notice that the drop-down list has changed from Defined Term to Definition (see Figure 24.4). That lets you just keep typing, in order to add the definition.

Hit Enter again, and the drop-down list changes back to a new Defined Term.

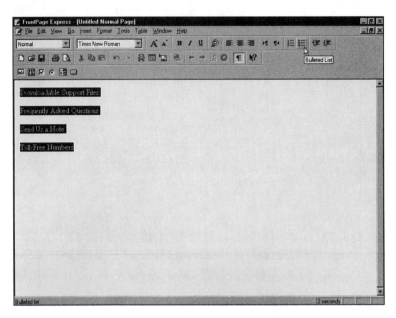

Figure 24.3: *Changing regular text to a bulleted list.*

Figure 24.4: *After typing the defined term, FrontPage Express automatically advances to the Definition.*

Continue with the process until you're finished with each term and definition. Then simply either press Enter twice after the last definition or use another menu option to move on to the next feature that you want to include.

Saving Your HTML Document

FrontPage Express retains the familiar File, Save As interface common to most Windows programs, though a bit of a curve ball comes first. When you first select File, Save As, you are presented with a Save As dialog that assumes you'll be publishing directly to a Web site (see Figure 24.5). You're asked for a page title and a URL location. To bypass this and save as a file on your hard drive, choose the As File button and save as you normally would.

Figure 24.5: *Click As File to save on your hard drive.*

EXAMPLE

Simple Markup with FrontPage Express

In this example, you'll create a simple page in FrontPage Express and use what you've learned so far to create a new HTML document. To begin, choose File, New. You may want to save this file to give it a name. Then, just type Listing 24.1 (or something similar) into the document.

Listing 24.1: fpe-test.htm A Sample Page for FrontPage Express

Foo Inc. Customer Service Pages

To help you get the most out of our products, or just help if you're having a problem, we've created the following Web pages with downloading files, tips, tricks, fixes and answers to your questions. Just click any link to get to that page.

Downloadable Support Files Fixes, drivers, free stuff, utility programs, documents and even a game or two written by our engineering and tech support staffs. If you can't find it here, BigCorp hasn't written it. (Or you'll have to buy it from us!)

Frequently Asked Questions Listing of questions that our tech support reps hear all the time. They're willing to answer them again, but that just means they get frustrated and take more breaks.

Send Us a Note Send email directly to the most prolific answer guy on our support staff.

Toll-Free Numbers Phone numbers for tech support, customer service, and, for good measure, we've even thrown in our toll-free, 24 hour sales numbers. Good of us, eh?

Now, the trick is to turn this into a more interesting page. You can start with the heading by selecting it and changing it to a Heading 1 style using the pull-down style menu.

In the descriptive text (first paragraph), there's nothing particularly special you need to do. You can always add bold and italic text where it seems appropriate by highlighting the text and clicking the buttons in the icon bar.

TIP

The Insert, Horizontal Line menu command can be used to insert an <HR> line in your document.

The next section is intended to be a definition list, even though the text isn't separated well. (FrontPage Express doesn't support the use of the Tab key.) To get there from here, start by highlighting the phrase Downloadable Support Files and choosing Defined Term from the pull-down style menu. Press Enter, highlight the remaining text that goes with that phrase, and select Definition from the same menu (see Figure 24.6).

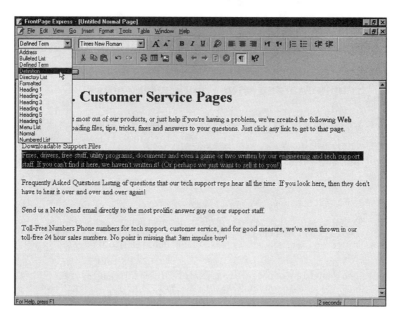

Figure 24.6: *Changing plain text into a definition list.*

Continue in this fashion with the remaining three items and text. Save the file as an HTML document, along with the appropriate file extension. You're set. Now open the file in the Web browser of your choice to see the results. It should look something like Figure 24.7.

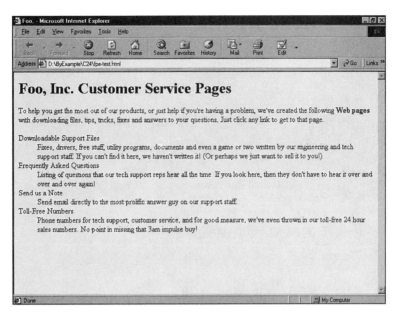

Figure 24.7: *The test file viewed in Internet Explorer.*

Links, Images, and Head Elements

FrontPage Express also gives you the ability to add the trappings of good Web pages, including hypertext links, images, and <HEAD> information. For the most part, you can do just about anything possible in HTML 4 through the menus, and it's all fairly straightforward. If it's not in one of the menus, you do have the choice of using the View, HTML option to enter your code directly.

Hypertext Links

To insert a hypertext link, highlight that text and click the Hyperlink button, or choose Insert, Hyperlink. The Create Hyperlink dialog box opens. This dialog allows you to choose a local file or URL as the document (or multimedia file) that this link references (see Figure 24.8) or even stage a new file to be created to fill that link. Click OK when finished, and your hypertext link will appear in the document..

Inserting an Image

Inserting an image in a FrontPage Express HTML document is similar to inserting a hypertext link. Start by placing your cursor in the document where you'd like the image to appear. Next, click the Picture button or choose Insert, Picture. Unfortunately, FrontPage Express doesn't prompt you to add details such as the ALT attribute text. To get to that dialog (see

Figure 24.9), you need to right-click within the image and select Image
Properties, or use the keyboard shortcut Alt+Enter.

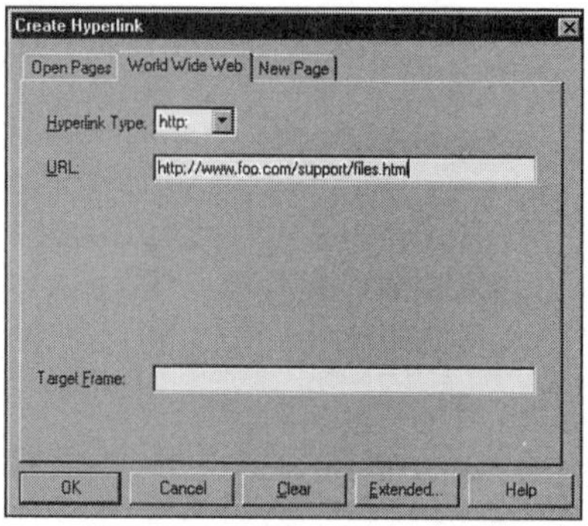

Figure 24.8: *Creating hypertext links.*

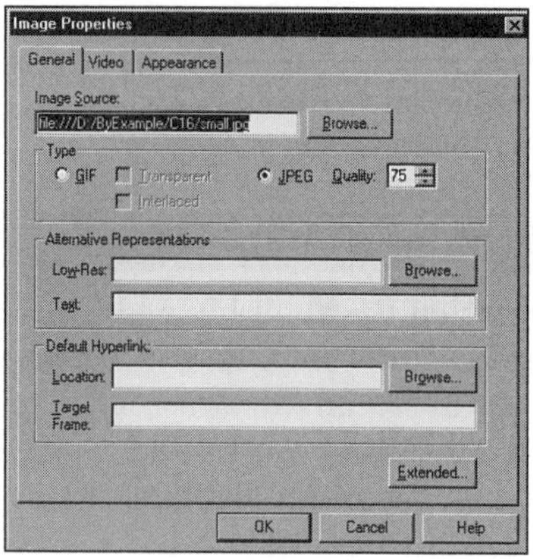

Figure 24.9: *Adding a picture with advanced settings.*

Additional features such as borders, spacing, alignment, and sizing can be
set from the Appearance tab within the same dialog.

Editing <HEAD> Elements, Colors, and Other Page Properties

FrontPage Express allows you to modify a host of information generally
found in the <HEAD> element and other global page properties. To begin,
choose File, Page Properties to bring up the Page Properties dialog box (see
Figure 24.10).

In this dialog box, enter the Title for your Web document. Click OK if that's
all you need to add. If you'd like to set color choices or add custom Meta
tags, you can do that from the Background and Custom tabs within the
dialog. When you're finished, click OK.

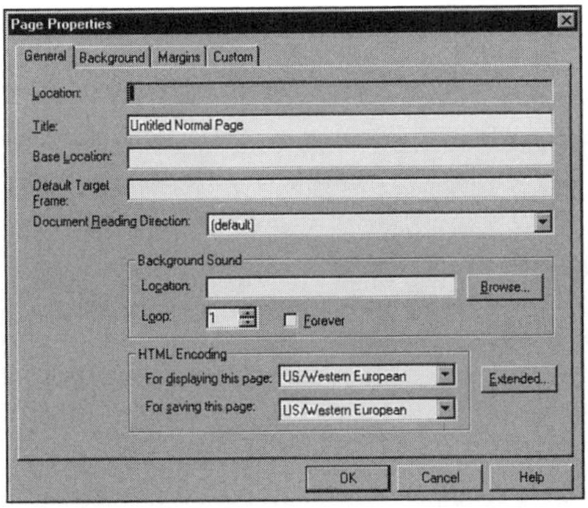

Figure shows a Page Properties dialog box.

Figure 24.10: *Several dozen options are available in the comprehensive Page Properties dialog box.*

Finishing the Page

In this example, you'll take the page you created in the first example and add links, images, and a title. If you use the same document (complete with markup) that you used in the original example, that's great. If not, re-enter the text from Listing 24.1 and save it as fpe-test2.html.

Start by adding an image to this page just before the heading. Place the cursor, and select the Picture button or choose Insert, Picture. The Picture dialog box should appear with the Picture tab open. In this dialog box, choose a graphic file. When you click OK, the picture will appear in your document. (You may want to press Enter after the graphic to place the heading text on the next line.) Don't forget to edit the image properties to include an ALT attribute.

Now create the hypertext links for the definition terms. Highlight each term with the mouse (for example, Downloadable Support Files) and click the Hyperlink button or choose Insert, Hyperlink. Enter the URL you want to use as a link (either relative or absolute).

Next, give your document a title. Select File, Page Properties to do so.

Finally, just for fun, change the text color from black to maroon, using the Background tab in the Page Properties dialog.

Click OK, and you're done. Save the file, then load it in your Web browser. It should look something like Figure 24.11.

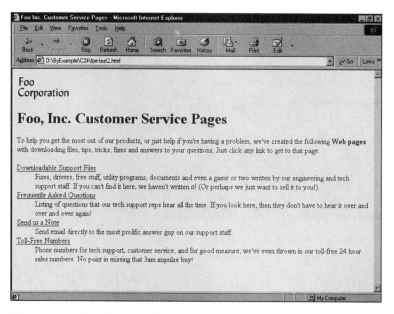

Figure 24.11: *The updated test page.*

Designing Forms

One of the strengths of FrontPage Express is the easy creation of HTML forms. You can work directly with the form elements or even use a Form Page Wizard that analyzes the type of information you want to collect and designs a form suited for that data.

Access the Form Page Wizard by choosing File, New. Choose Form Page Wizard from the Template or Wizard selections to get started (see Figure 24.12).

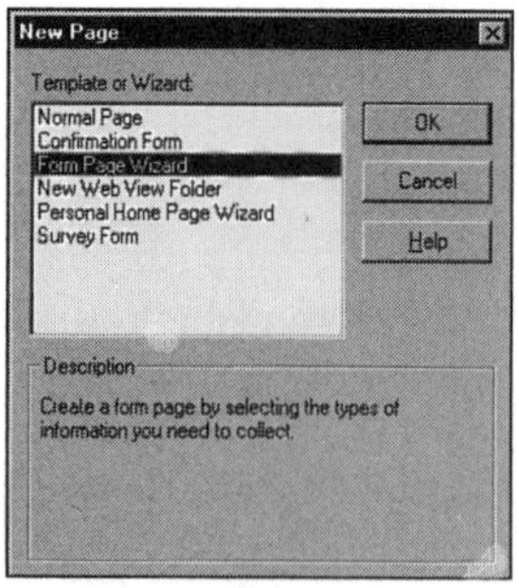

Figure 24.12: *Select the Form Page Wizard from the New Page dialog.*

The first bits of data to enter include the URL of the page you're creating and the page title. Continuing in the next pane of the wizard, you'll define each of the questions you want to use to collect data. Figure 24.13 illustrates the process of adding a question to collect the user's email address.

Figure 24.13: *Editing a form question.*

Additional data for the Form Page Wizard is collected in the next pane, after which you're returned to add more questions or finish your form.

The rough outline of the form is then generated on your page (see Figure 24.14). You can then edit the form title, edit supporting text, add or remove horizontal rules, and so on.

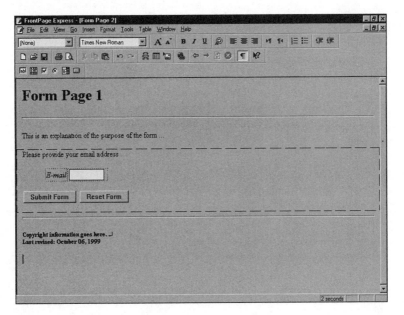

Figure 24.14: *The Form Page Wizard output.*

What's Next?

FrontPage Express is included in Windows 98 and newer bundles of Internet Explorer in order to provide a free and easy way for the average user to create HTML files and publish them on the Web.

Basic HTML is about as simple as creating a regular Word document—just type text and apply styles. Generally speaking, everything can be done a couple of different ways. You can click the Bold button, for example, or you can choose Format, Font from the menu.

Creating lists is also fairly simple in FrontPage Express, although creating definition lists can be a little tricky. Hypertext links, images, and head elements are all added via menu items and dialog boxes.

A strength of FrontPage Express is its handling of forms. Wizards help even the novice create complex forms, yet the direct access to form elements lets more experienced users do their own design work.

Up next, Chapter 25 is our final chapter, where you'll take the skills you've learned throughout the rest of the book and apply them in developing two different Web sites.

Review Questions

1. Where can you obtain FrontPage Express?
2. Is it possible to select an HTML style first, and then type your text?
3. In what type of file does FrontPage Express save your HTML? Can you edit this with other programs?
4. True or False: There's only one way to create a heading.
5. What command allows you to change from an unordered to an ordered list type?
6. What is the major difference between definition list creation and that of ordered or unordered lists?
7. What menu do you select to change the background color of your page?
8. Do you have to use the Form Page Wizard to insert a form in your document?
9. Can you edit the output of the Form Page Wizard after it's finished?

Review Exercises

1. Use definition lists and hyperlinks to create a page of book reviews. Clicking the book's name shows the user a graphic of the book. For instance, an entry might be the following:

   ```
   HTML By Example    The best book ever written for learning HTML the right
   way.
   ```

2. Based on this example, add another definition (DD) line that includes a link to order the book, the author's name, copyright info, and price. For instance:

   ```
   HTML By Example    The best book ever written for learning HTML the right
   way.

   Ann Navarro, Copyright 1999, $34.99. Order this book.
   ```

3. Create a basic form using the FrontPage Express Form Page Wizard. Ask for address information, and include a free-form question where the user can express an opinion.

HTML Examples

HTML Examples

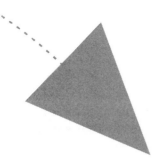

HTML Examples

It's time to see if you can apply just about everything you've learned to the world of the Web. This is also a wonderful opportunity to find a page that works well for the type of site you're trying to build. If you find a close match, you can get a head start on your own site by copying the example from the supporting Web site and altering it to fit your needs.

This chapter provides you with examples of the following:

- A basic HTML 4 Web page

- Several pages combined into a personal Web site

- The process of creating a larger, commercial Web site

NOTE

This is one chapter where the supporting files that can be found on the Web site can really help you out. If I've created a page that you think will work well for your site, just grab the HTML off the Web, change it to suit your needs, and toss it up on the World Wide Web. Hopefully, I've already done most of the work for you!

Back to Basics: Basic HTML 4 Pages

The beauty of designing HTML 4–compliant sites is that you never really have to worry about whether your users are happy, satisfied, and fully informed. Everyone, regardless of their browser, can see your entire site. If they're visiting with a modern browser, they'll most likely see your site just as you intended. Visitors with older browsers or assistive devices will still enjoy your site because HTML 4 "degrades gracefully" when presented on less-than-fully-capable browsers.

One of the most important rules to remember in HTML design is that your information is more important than the presentation. If using nothing but HTML 4 text, lists, and graphics helps you update your pages quicker and keep things interesting, you're doing better than the advanced Java programmer with nothing to say.

Let's see some examples of a "personal" Web site, perhaps useful for a home-based business or even just for fun. My examples are based on myself, for a purely fun and personal site that I might make if I had the time (and maybe this will serve as the basis for one!). We'll create four basic pages—an index page, a personal biography, a family page, and a page about recent travel. These days, sometimes you tell people your life story with little more than a URL.

EXAMPLE

The Personal Index Page

Because we're not talking about any major leaps of thought in HTML, I'll concentrate more on design issues with these personal pages. The keys to your index page will be an attractive presentation, while making it clear that things are dynamic on the page—you'll let people be immediately aware of the new or changed material. To create the index page, enter Listing 25.1 in your text editor.

Listing 25.1: index.html: The Personal Index Page

```
<!DOCTYPE HTML PUBLIC "-//W3C//DTD HTML 4.0 Transitional//EN">

<HTML>

<HEAD>

<TITLE>Ann Navarro's Home on the Web</TITLE>

</HEAD>

<BODY>

<IMG SRC="annlogo.gif" ALT="Ann's Place" WIDTH=337 HEIGHT=70>

<P ALIGN="center">

<A HREF="index.html">Index</A> ¦ <A HREF="about.html">About Ann</A> ¦

<A HREF="family.html">Our Family</A> ¦ <A HREF="travel.html">My Travels</A>
```

```
</P>
<H1>Welcome to My Place on the Web!</H1>
<P>I'm <A HREF="about.html">Ann Navarro</A>, and you've reached my little place
on the Web. If you were looking to find me here, thanks for the thought. If
you're here by accident, well, maybe there's something interesting. Stay a
while.</P>
<P><IMG SRC="new.gif" WIDTH=50 HEIGHT=20 ALT="New!">
<P>I just returned from Munich, Germany, where I attended a meeting of the <A
HREF="http://www.w3.org/MarkUp/Activity.html">W3C HTML Working Group</A>.</P>
<P><A HREF="byexample.html">The new book is done!</A> - My latest book, HTML By
Example, 2nd Edition, is done and soon to be on store shelves.</P>
<P><A HREF="summer99.html">Family Vacation Photos</A>! Some snapshots from our
trip to Orlando in July.</P>
<HR>
<H3>Stuff that I do that you may or may not find interesting...</H3>
<UL>
<LI>Computer book author - <A HREF="books/">The full list</A> of books I've
written or contributed to.
<LI>Director, Online Education for the <A HREF="http://www.hwg.org">HTML Writers
Guild</A>.
<LI>Somebody's <A HREF="linda.html">step-mom</A>.
</UL>
<H3>Your Feedback on this Web Site...</H3>
<P><A HREF="feedback.html">Feedback</A> Lots of folks have written in to tell me
what they like about this site. The feedback has been incredible, and I couldn't
be happier. Keep it coming! If you've got something to say, please
<A HREF="mailto:me@webgeek.com">send email</A>.</P>
<HR>
<P>Copyright 1999, Ann Navarro. All Rights Reserved.
</BODY>
</HTML>
```

Boring? I hope not. Let's call it "clean." This page uses a couple of different ways to get around on the site, including a text menu at the top of the page and links to relevant material throughout. It also features site news right up front and some invitations to wander the site. Simple graphics and logical formatting let users get a feel for the site quickly, so they know they're not missing anything (see Figure 25.1).

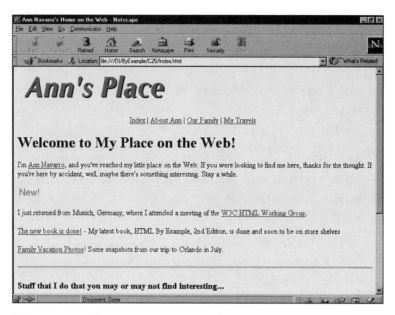

Figure 25.1: *An inviting, clean index page for a personal site.*

EXAMPLE

The Personal Biography

The next step is to create a biography page (see Listing 25.2 and Figure 25.2). Personal bios should probably be the most laid-back part of the site. Because I'm not using this site for business, I can feel free to talk about hobbies, personal likes and dislikes, my family, and so on. Although we all have freedom of expression on the Web, keep in mind that links and search engines can let your pages show up in some interesting ways. If you have some quirky hobbies, be prepared for business associates and others to come across your page at some time. (In other words, don't post it if you don't want your grandmother to see it!)

Listing 25.2: about.html: The Personal Bio Page

```
<!DOCTYPE HTML PUBLIC "-//W3C//DTD HTML 4.0 Transitional//EN">
<HTML>
<HEAD>
<TITLE>About Ann</TITLE>
</HEAD>
<BODY>
<IMG SRC="annlogo.gif" ALT="Ann's Place" WIDTH=337 HEIGHT=70>
<P ALIGN="center">
<A HREF="index.html">Index</A> ¦ About Ann ¦
```

```
<A HREF="family.html">Our Family</A> ¦ <A HREF="travel.html">My Travels</A>
</P>
<H1>A Little About Me</H1>
<P>Well, to start, I'm 33 years old, and I live in
<A HREF="http://www.charlotte-florida.com/community/">Port Charlotte,
Florida</A>. I moved here just over a year ago, coming from Carmel Valley,
California.
<P>My husband <A HREF="http://www.basicguru.com/navarro/">Dave</A> and I met
online back in 1995, through a forum on <A HREF="http://www.compuserve.com">
CompuServe</A>. We were married just over a year later, on August 17, 1996.
<P>I have one step-daughter, Linda, who's a rising soccer star. She hopes one
day to play on the US Women's Soccer team, and perhaps go to the Olympics. Linda
lives with her mom just outside of Nashville, Tennessee.
<P>We have one cat, <A HREF="http://www.webgeek.com/photos/sleepy.jpg">
Dizzy</A>, who spends most of her time sleeping, or demanding to be let outside.
<P>Dave and I are both dedicated geeks; we love tearing apart our computers and
upgrading them. So much so, that the covers seem to be permanently off of them!
When I'm not at the computer (which is rare!), I enjoy cooking, gardening, and
reading science fiction novels.
<P>I hope to add to these pages soon, as I convert some of my favorite recipes
to HTML, and draw some diagrams for my spring garden plans.
<HR>
<P>Copyright 1999, Ann Navarro. All Rights Reserved.
</BODY>
</HTML>
```

Also notice the consistency from page to page, like the text menu and logo at the top of the page. Most visitors like consistency in styling—they know that they're still on the same site, and they can quickly figure out how to get around if all the tools are in the same place. It makes you more memorable and reminds people that all this great information is part of your site. You don't have to be dull on your pages or even as simple as this example is, but I do suggest that you have a guiding design.

Incorporating Images: Full-Size and Thumbnail

EXAMPLE

Perhaps these next pages could be a little more graphically appealing, but I'm not a graphic artist, nor are most people. The aim of this page is to provide a photo of each member of the family and a distinct section of text that talks about them individually (see Listing 25.3). By changing the alignment of the images in relation to the text and by carefully placing headings and full line breaks, you can see that there are three distinct pieces of information (see Figure 25.3).

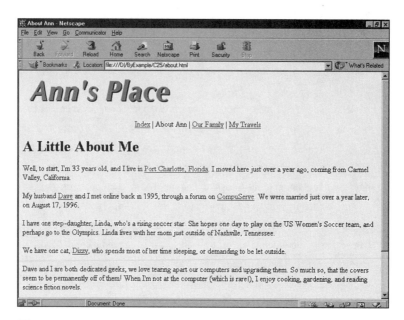

Figure 25.2: *The About Ann page.*

Listing 25.3: family.html: Associating Images with Distinct Blocks of Text

```
<!DOCTYPE HTML PUBLIC "-//W3C//DTD HTML 4.0 Transitional//EN">
<HTML>
<HEAD>
<TITLE>My Family</TITLE>
</HEAD>
<BODY>
<IMG SRC="annlogo.gif" ALT="Ann's Place" WIDTH=337 HEIGHT=70>
<P ALIGN="center">
<A HREF="index.html">Index</A> ¦ <A HREF="about.html">About Ann</A> ¦
Our Family ¦ <A HREF="travel.html">My Travels</A>
</P>
<H1>My Family</H1>
<H3>Linda</H3>
<P><IMG SRC="soccer.jpg" ALIGN=RIGHT ALT="Linda at the goal" WIDTH=150
```

HEIGHT=211>Linda is my step-daughter. She's 14, going on 24 (aren't they all?). She's a talented soccer player. She made first string goalkeeper on her high school's Junior Varsity team as a freshman this year. Her coach would have played her on the Varsity team, but he felt the remaining JV team needed her experience and expertise. Next year, she'll compete for starting goalkeeper on the Varsity squad.</P>

<P>Like most teens, she's into popular music, clothes. She recently left a string of broken hearts in SW Florida after she returned home from her summer visit with us.</P>

<P>She's most impatiently waiting for her 16th birthday, so she can get her driver's license.</P>

<BR CLEAR=ALL>

<IMG SRC="dave.jpg" ALT="Dave at the computer" ALIGN=LEFT WIDTH=308 HEIGHT=226>

<H3>Dave</H3><P> Dave is my husband, and my best friend. We're both very into computers and science fiction novels. He loves woodworking (has an autographed picture of Norm!), raquetball, and the Dallas Cowboys.</P>

<P>He thinks he's lord of the manor, though I just let him believe it!

<BR CLEAR=ALL>

<H3>Dizzy</H3>

<P><IMG SRC="dizzy.jpg" ALT="dizzy, snoozing" ALIGN=RIGHT WIDTH=300 HEIGHT=225> Dizzy was born in the Pacific Grove, CA, city maintenance yard. The animal control officer placed her with an elderly woman in town when she was just 4 weeks old. The woman's landlord didn't like the idea of pets, so the animal control officer called the 911 center where I worked to see if any of us would give the kitten a good home. I decided to take her in, and she's been a house cat ever since. <P>

<P>Dizzy also thinks she's queen of the castle, and that her "humans" are here to do her bidding. We play along most of the time!</P>

<BR CLEAR=ALL>

<HR>

<P>Copyright 1999, Ann Navarro. All Rights Reserved.

</BODY>

</HTML>

Finally, we have the travel page. This page makes use of thumbnail images, set in a table for easy organization (see Listing 25.4).

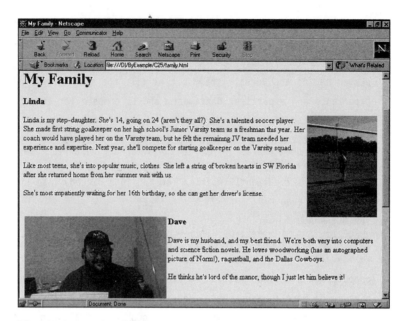

Figure 25.3: *Ann's family page.*

Listing 25.4: travel.html: Thumbnail Images Arranged in a Table

```
<!DOCTYPE HTML PUBLIC "-//W3C//DTD HTML 4.0 Transitional//EN">
<HTML>
<HEAD>
<TITLE>My Travels</TITLE>
</HEAD>
<BODY>
<IMG SRC="annlogo.gif" ALT="Ann's Place" WIDTH=337 HEIGHT=70>
<P ALIGN="center">
<A HREF="index.html">Index</A> ¦ <A HREF="about.html">About Ann</A> ¦
<A HREF="family.html">Our Family</A> ¦ My Travels
</P>
<H1>My Travels</H1>
<P>I've been very lucky to have travel be a part of my work life. In the
past 18
months, I've been to many exciting places, including these international cities:
<P><UL>
<LI>Geneva, Switzerland
<LI>Monte Carlo, Monaco
<LI>Nice, France
<LI>Paris, France
```

```
<LI>Kyoto, Japan
<LI>Amsterdam, The Netherlands
<LI>Toronto, Canada
<LI>Munich, Germany
</UL>
<P>I've gathered a collection of photographs from my trips. Each thumbnail image
presented here is linked to a full-sized photo. I hope you enjoy them!
<P>
<TABLE BORDER=1>
<TR>
<TD ALIGN=CENTER><A HREF="waag.jpg"><IMG SRC="waag-t.jpg" ALT="The Waag -
Thumbnail" BORDER=0 HEIGHT=60 WIDTH=80></A><BR>
The Waag - Amsterdam</TD>
<TD ALIGN=CENTER><A HREF="munich.jpg"><IMG SRC="munich-t.jpg" ALT="Chapel -
Thumbnail" BORDER=0 HEIGHT=60 WIDTH=80></A><BR>Chapel - Munich</TD>
<TD ALIGN=CENTER><A HREF="toronto.jpg"><IMG SRC="toronto-t.jpg" ALT="Royal
Museum - Thumbnail" BORDER=0 HEIGHT=60 WIDTH=80></A><BR>Royal Museum - Toronto
</TD>
</TR>
</TABLE>
<HR>
<P>Copyright 1999, Ann Navarro. All Rights Reserved.
</BODY>
</HTML>
```

Again, there's good continuity and clean design (see Figure 25.4). Can't ask for much more than that.

I think you can see where I'm going with this. The strongest point is this: You can do a lot on a site using HTML 4, and using only valid HTML ensures that your documents are available to the widest possible audience. Keep your site newsworthy, interesting, consistent, and personal, and you'll succeed with your small site.

CraftScape.com

In this section, you'll start by walking through the creation of a large Web site in an effort to apply most of the tags, extensions, programming, and theory you've learned throughout this book. I'll try to point out the major issues on each page as we go along.

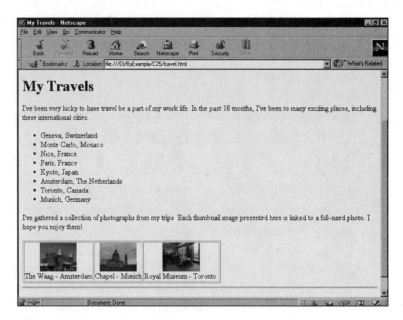

Figure 25.4: Ann's travels.

The Index Page

The first page many visitors will see will be the index for this site. You'll use client-side image map technology to link users to the various parts of CraftScape's Web presence, along with providing sufficient alternative navigation for users who can't read image maps and style sheets to set the site's basic appearance (see Listing 25.5).

Listing 25.5: index.html: The Index Page for CraftScape.com

```
<!DOCTYPE HTML PUBLIC "-//W3C//DTD HTML 4.0 Transitional//EN">

<HTML>

<HEAD>

<TITLE>

CraftScape.com</TITLE>

<STYLE>

<!--

H2 {color:navy}

-->

</STYLE>

</HEAD>

<BODY>

<MAP NAME="navmap">
```

```
<AREA HREF="patterns.html" SHAPE="POLY" COORDS="491,97,555,0,578,13,533,99,533,
99,491,97">
<AREA HREF="fabric.html" SHAPE="POLY" COORDS="441,93,494,8,520,26,480,99,444,99,
444,99,441,93">
<AREA HREF="notions.html" SHAPE="POLY" COORDS="393,96,452,0,475,15,423,99,423,
99,393,96">
<AREA HREF="crafts.html" SHAPE="POLY" COORDS="345,96,390,20,415,32,374,99,374,
99,345,96">
<AREA HREF="classes.html" SHAPE="POLY" COORDS="293,93,319,3,374,9,336,99,290,99,
291,99,291,99,293,93">
</MAP>
<img src="navbanner.gif" border=0 NAME="navmap" WIDTH="600" HEIGHT="100"
USEMAP="#navmap" ALIGN="RIGHT" ALT="Craftscape.com Navigation Map">
<BR CLEAR=ALL>
<H2><IMG SRC="sewing.jpg" WIDTH=200 HEIGHT=149 ALT="Busy Sewing" HSPACE=15
ALIGN=LEFT>Welcome!</H2>
<P>We hope you enjoy our Web site. Whether you're too busy to come down in
person,
or too far away, we're happy to have you here. Crafters from all across the
globe are welcome in our cyber-crafting community.
<BR CLEAR=ALL>
<H2><IMG SRC="fabric.jpg" WIDTH=200 HEIGHT=157 ALT="Choosing Fabric" ALIGN=RIGHT
HSPACE=15>February's Feature</H2><P>Check our Classes section for a new session
on
quilting, taught by our ever-present seamstress, Irma Gandalf. Winter is just
the right time to make something as cozy and comforting as a quilt!
<BR CLEAR=ALL>
<P ALIGN=CENTER> Index | <A HREF="classes.html">Classes</A> |
<A HREF="crafts.html">Crafts</A> | <A HREF="notions.html">Notions</A> |
<A HREF="fabric.html">Fabric</A> | <A HREF="patterns.html">Patterns</A></P>
<HR WIDTH="70%">
<P ALIGN="CENTER">CraftScape.com, 123 Main St, Anytown, FL 33555<BR>
Telephone - 941.555.1234, email - <A HREF="mailto:staff@craftscape.com">
staff@craftscape.com</A></P>
</BODY>
</HTML>
```

Notice that this page contains pointers to timely information such as sales and special events (the February features), as well as the regular links to the main subsections of the site (see Figure 25.5). Always provide contact information in the form of a street address, telephone number, and email address on this first page, or provide an obvious link to it.

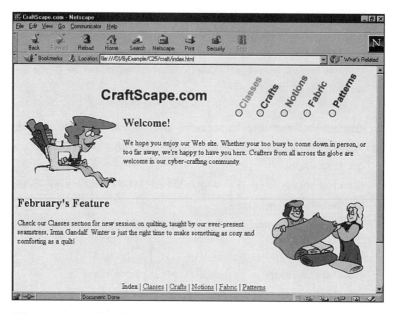

Figure 25.5: *The first look at CraftScape.com.*

TIP

Because the image map and text-based links will be on each page, it's easy to make a template for this site by clearing out the contents of the index.html file and resaving it as template.html or something similar.

CraftScape's Class Offerings in a Table

Sometimes your content just cries out for order. Even though CraftScape is offering only three courses this month, placing the information in a table provides a neat and concise view of what's happening (see Listing 25.6).

Listing 25.6: classes.html: Using Tables to Organize Data

```
<!DOCTYPE HTML PUBLIC "-//W3C//DTD HTML 4.0 Transitional//EN">

<HTML>

<HEAD>

<TITLE>

CraftScape.com</TITLE>

</HEAD>
```

```
<BODY>
<MAP NAME="navmap">
<AREA HREF="patterns.html" SHAPE="POLY" COORDS="491,97,555,0,578,13,533,99,533,
99,491,97">
<AREA HREF="fabric.html" SHAPE="POLY" COORDS="441,93,494,8,520,26,480,99,444,99,
444,99,441,93">
<AREA HREF="notions.html" SHAPE="POLY" COORDS="393,96,452,0,475,15,423,99,423,
99,393,96">
<AREA HREF="crafts.html" SHAPE="POLY" COORDS="345,96,390,20,415,32,374,99,374,
99,345,96">
<AREA HREF="classes.html" SHAPE="POLY" COORDS="293,93,319,3,374,9,336,99,290,99,
291,99,291,99,293,93">
</MAP>
<img src="navbanner.gif" border=0 NAME="navmap" WIDTH="600" HEIGHT="100"
USEMAP="#navmap" ALIGN="RIGHT" ALT="Craftscape.com Navigation Map">
<BR CLEAR=ALL>
<P>
<DIV ALIGN=CENTER>
<IMG SRC="classes.gif" ALT="February Classes" WIDTH=400 HEIGHT=100>
</DIV>
<P><IMG SRC="quilt.jpg" ALT="Irma's Quilt" WIDTH=200 HEIGHT=196 HSPACE=30
ALIGN=LEFT>
February is quilting month! Whether you're a beginner or a seasoned seamstress,
you'll find our selection of quilting classes to be both informative and
enjoyable. Bring your thimbles!
<P>
<TABLE BORDER=1>
<TR>
<TH>Class</TH>
<TH>Date and Time</TH>
</TR>
<TR>
<TD><A HREF="beginner.html">Beginning Quilting with Irma</A> - No experience
required!</TD>
<TD>Tuesdays and Thursdays, 9am to 11am</TD>
</TR>
<TR>
```

continues

Listing 25.6: continued

```
<TD><A HREF="traditional.html">Traditional Quilting Patterns</A> - How Great
Grandmother used to make them</TD>
<TD>Wednesdays, 1pm to 4pm</TD>
</TR>
<TR>
<TD><A HREF="bee.html">The Quilting Bee</A> - A fun, social time for everyone.
Work on a large group project and catch up on the week's news!</TD>
<TD>Mondays and Fridays, 10am to 12 noon</TD>
</TR>
</TABLE>
<P>All classes (except the Quilting Bee) have limited seating. Call today to
reserve your space, or <A HREF="signup.html">sign up online!</A>
<P ALIGN=CENTER> <A HREF="index.html">Index</A> ¦ Classes ¦
<A HREF="crafts.html">Crafts</A> ¦ <A HREF="notions.html">Notions</A> ¦
<A HREF="fabric.html">Fabric</A> ¦ <A HREF="patterns.html">Patterns</A></P>
</BODY>
</HTML>
```

All the data is presented in a very compact space, yet all the required information is present (see Figure 25.6).

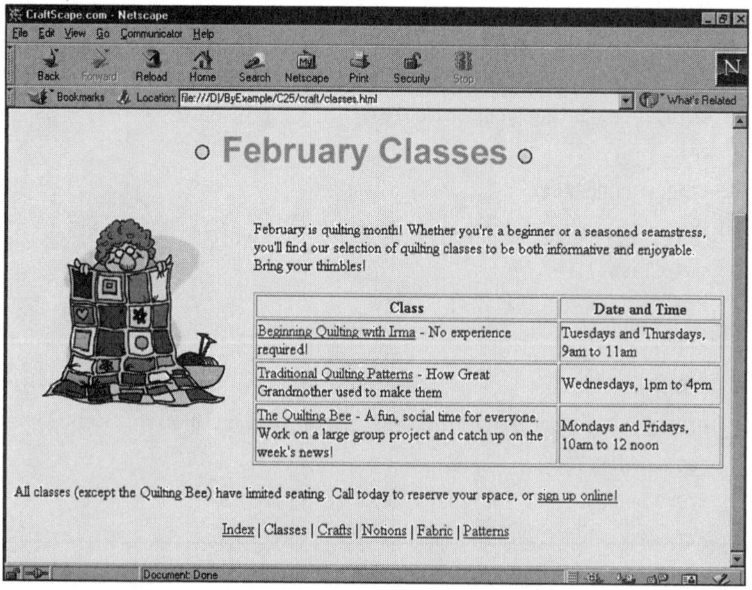

Figure 25.6: *Clear and to the point with tables.*

Collecting Data with Forms

Continuing with the client-oriented Web site, let's create a customer service form that allows customers to make a request (see Listing 25.7). CraftScape has one of the largest collections of notions (buttons, snaps, and so on) around, and their matching service is very popular. Your form will let customers request a search over the Web! Sound good?

Listing 25.7: search.html: Notion Search Page That Uses Tables and Forms to Collect Data

```
<!DOCTYPE HTML PUBLIC "-//W3C//DTD HTML 4.0 Transitional//EN">

<HTML>

<HEAD>

<TITLE>

CraftScape.com</TITLE>

</HEAD>

<BODY>

<IMG SRC="navbanner.gif" ALT="CraftScape.com Navigation Banner" WIDTH=600
HEIGHT=100 ALIGN=RIGHT>

<BR CLEAR=ALL>

<P>

<DIV ALIGN=CENTER>

<IMG SRC="search.gif" ALT="Notion Search" WIDTH=400 HEIGHT=100>

</DIV>

<P><IMG SRC="buttons.jpg" ALT="Buttons and Bobbins" WIDTH=200 HEIGHT=149
HSPACE=30 ALIGN=LEFT>

We're proud to have one of the largest collections of discontinued and
out-of-stock notions. Let us help you match that missing button, replace that
snap, or simply find a "retro" look for a new garment.

<BR CLEAR=ALL>

<P>

<FORM METHOD="POST" ACTION="http://www.craftscape.com/cgi-bin/search.cgi">

<DIV ALIGN=CENTER>

<TABLE BORDER=0>

<TR>

<TD>Name:</TD>

<TD><INPUT TYPE="text" NAME="name" SIZE="30"></TD>

</TR>

<TR>

<TD>Email Address:</TD>
```

continues

Listing 25.7: continued

```
<TD><INPUT TYPE="text" NAME="email" SIZE="30"></TD>
</TR>
<TR>
<TD>Telephone:</TD>
<TD><INPUT TYPE="text" NAME="phone" SIZE="12"></TD>
</TR>
<TR>
<TD>What type of notion are you looking for? </TD>
<TD><SELECT>
<OPTION>button
<OPTION>zipper
<OPTION>snap
<OPTION>hook and eye
<OPTION>trim
</SELECT>
</TD>
</TR>
<TR>
<TD>Manufacturer (if known):</TD>
<TD><INPUT TYPE="text" NAME="maker" SIZE="20"></TD>
</TR>
<TR>
<TD COLSPAN="2">Description (please be specific!)<BR>
<TEXTAREA COLS=60 ROWS=10></TEXTAREA>
</TD>
</TR>
<TR>
<TD COLSPAN="2">
<INPUT TYPE="submit" VALUE="Find my Notion!">
<INPUT TYPE="reset" VALUE="Start Over">
</TD>
</TR>
</TABLE>
</DIV>
</FORM>
<BODY>
</HTML>
```

The results of this code can be seen in Figure 25.7. The interface is straightforward, and a basic form-handling CGI script can send the data to CraftScape's employees.

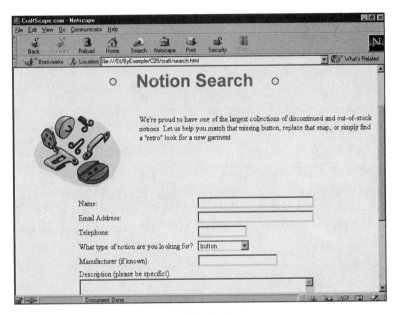

Figure 25.7: *Search form submissions.*

EXAMPLE

FTP and HTML

Perhaps it's not the most glamorous of possibilities with HTML, but many sites need to include a repository of files on their pages in order to better serve customers. In this example, you'll create the patterns page for CraftScape's site, giving users the opportunity to download sewing and needlework patterns that can be printed and used at home (see Listing 25.8).

Listing 25.8: patterns.html: Adding FTP to HTML Documents

```
<!DOCTYPE HTML PUBLIC "-//W3C//DTD HTML 4.0 Transitional//EN">

<HTML>

<HEAD>

<TITLE>

CraftScape.com</TITLE>

</HEAD>

<BODY>
```

continues

Listing 25.8: continued

```
<MAP NAME="navmap">
<AREA HREF="patterns.html" SHAPE="POLY" COORDS="491,97,555,0,578,13,533,99,533,
99,491,97">
<AREA HREF="fabric.html" SHAPE="POLY" COORDS="441,93,494,8,520,26,480,99,444,99,
444,99,441,93">
<AREA HREF="notions.html" SHAPE="POLY" COORDS="393,96,452,0,475,15,423,99,423,
99,393,96">
<AREA HREF="crafts.html" SHAPE="POLY" COORDS="345,96,390,20,415,32,374,99,374,
99,345,96">
<AREA HREF="classes.html" SHAPE="POLY" COORDS="293,93,319,3,374,9,336,99,290,99,
291,99,291,99,293,93">
</MAP>
<img src="navbanner.gif" border=0 NAME="navmap" WIDTH="600" HEIGHT="100"
USEMAP="#navmap" ALIGN="RIGHT" ALT="Craftscape.com Navigation Map">
<BR CLEAR=ALL>
<P>
<DIV ALIGN=CENTER>
<IMG SRC="patterns.gif" ALT="Downloadable Patterns" WIDTH=400 HEIGHT=100>
</DIV>
<P>
Thanks to the many highly creative crafters we have in the CraftScape community,
we're able to provide this library of downloadable patterns for your enjoyment.
Arranged by craft category, you'll find embroidery and needlepoint grids,
childrens clothes, stuffed toys, Christmas projects, and more.
<H2>Needlepoint</H2>
<DL>
<DT><A HREF="home.zip">Home Sweet Home Sampler</A>
<DD>A stitchery classic.
<DT><A HREF="baby.zip">Bundle of Joy</A>
<DD>Celebrate the new arrival in the family with this commemorative sampler.
<DT><A HREF="wedding.zip">Our Wedding Day</A>
<DD>A new bride's first project.
</DL>
<H2>Holiday Crafts</H2>
<DL>
```

```
<DT><A HREF="house.zip">Gingerbread House</A>
<DD>A holiday classic. Let your imagination run wild!
<DT><A HREF="wreath.zip">Wreath Collection</A>
<DD>Six festive wreath ideas.
<DT><A HREF="angels.zip">Angel Ornaments</A>
<DD>Sweet, pillowy angels to hang on your tree.
</DL>
<P>All files are stored in "Zip" format. Use Winzip or your favorite unzipping
software to extract and use the files inside.
<P ALIGN=CENTER> <A HREF="index.html">Index</A> ¦
<A HREF="classes.html">Classes</A> ¦ <A HREF="crafts.html">Crafts</A> ¦
<A HREF="notions.html">Notions</A> ¦ <A HREF="fabric.html">Fabric</A> ¦
Patterns</P>
</BODY>
</HTML>
```

It's pretty straightforward. You can use an FTP-style URL to access files for downloading across the Internet to your users (see Figure 25.8). Notice that each selection was described using a definition list.

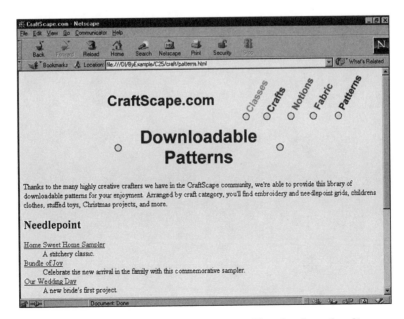

Figure 25.8: *The patterns page offers files for downloading.*

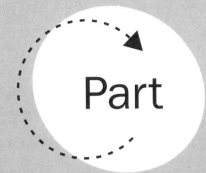

Part

Appendix

Answers to Review Questions

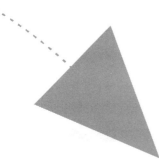

Answers to Review Questions

Chapter 1

1. No. It's a text markup language.

2. True.

3. SGML (Standard Generalized Mark-up Language).

4. False. WordPerfect documents are binary (that is, non-ASCII) computer files that can't be edited without a special word processing application.

5. Yes. The World Wide Web Consortium has several dozen Working Groups, one of which is the HTML Working Group.

6. No. The W3C also produces the XML family of specifications, CSS, P3P, and many others.

Chapter 2

1. Web protocols allow Web server computers to send many different types of data and information.

2. Hypertext is a system of documentation in which certain words in a document are linked to other documents. The Microsoft Windows help system is an example of hypertext.

3. False. Hypermedia links are hypertext links to multimedia files.

4. A site is a collection of Web documents and files. A page is a single Web document.

5. Helper applications are used to display or play some non-HTML files and documents, such as multimedia files.

6. File extensions help browsers determine the file types of multimedia files, as well as which helper applications or plug-ins are needed to display them.

7. Usenet and FTP.

8. Your email address.

Chapter 3

1. The original graphical browser was NCSA Mosaic. Which is the most popular is debatable, but it would probably be either Netscape Navigator or Microsoft Internet Explorer.

2. Lynx is a text-only browser.

3. A server address.

4. `mailto:` is followed by a simple email address instead of a server/path combination.

5. The forward slash (`/`).

6. Yes (assuming that the path and filename are correct).

7. True. All text and graphics on Web pages must be downloaded to the user's computer.

8. Binary
ASCII
Binary
Binary

Chapter 4

1. Yes. Customer service and technical support.

2. Multimedia makes the Web a unique marketing medium in which customers can interactively experience products and services.

3. The All-Rite travel site could be updated more frequently with special offers than could their brochures, with more appeal than direct mailings.

4. It can sit dormant and unchanged for weeks or months.

5. A Web page or site that acts as a front end for data processing.

6. The next logical medium for publication.

Chapter 5

1. False.

2. Web server software and a high-speed Internet connection.

3. Kbps stands for thousands of bits per second. Mbps stands for millions of bits per second.

4. Call your local phone company.

5. Throughput is the average amount of information per user multiplied by the number of users. ISPs charge for throughput to discourage one site from monopolizing the ISP's Internet connections.

6. Eight characters with a three-character extension (8.3).

7. The hybrid system uses separate directories for items that appear once (such as documents and files specific to a particular Web page), while commonly-accessed files are kept in their own directories (such as logos).

8. A graphics file—most likely a photo of a person. This graphic might be linked to the About the Company page on a Web site.

9. Put. Uploading means sending the file.

Chapter 6

1. No. You can use a simple text editor or word processing program.

2. HTML files are saved in the ASCII text file format. The extension should be .html or .htm.

3. `<!DOCTYPE>`, `<HTML>`, `<HEAD>`, and `<BODY>`.

4. `<TITLE>`.

5. Save it with a new filename and HTML extension.

6. Container tags have two parts, the opening and closing tags, and they act on a specific block of text. Empty tags have only one part and perform a function on their own.

7. `<HR>` (also `<BR>`).

8. The opening and closing tags aren't identical except for a forward slash (`/`).

9. True.

10. `<P>` is a container that defines a section of text; `<BR>` is an empty tag that forces a line return.

Chapter 7

1. Explicit is also known as physical styles; implicit is also known as logical styles.

2. Implicit tags let the browser choose the formatting; explicit tags let the designer choose.

3. Because it gives the browser no choice in how to render the affected text.

4. <I> will not work in a text browser. <EM> will.

5. <CODE>.

6. For internal documentation when your HTML document explains computer-related issues.

7. Yes.

8. The <P> paragraph tag (for its traditional presentation with blank lines before and after the content).

9. Yes.

Chapter 8

1. The list type container tag (<OL> and so on) and the list item empty tag (<LI>).

2. A bullet point (and a return).

3. Yes. Numbered, lettered, and Roman numeral lists are available.

4. By using the attribute TYPE="square" on the <UL> element.

5. Yes.

6. It can accept two different list item tags, <DT> and <DD>.

7. No.

8. B.

9. An unordered list (<UL>) nested within an ordered list (<OL>).

Chapter 9

1. The file size of the graphic.

2. True.

3. GIF and JPG. Yes, but many browsers require helper applications to view other graphics formats.

4. When compressed, the graphic file loses image quality.

5. Create the graphic. Download public-domain graphics. Use scanned photographs. Use graphics created by a digital camera.

6. Around 20 kilobytes.

7. Small images that are linked to the larger full-sized copy of the image.

8. An attribute in which the value is the image's URL.

9. It displays text in browsers that can't view the image file.

10. False.

11. It's the default value.

Chapter 10

1. An attribute.

2. No.

3. A fragment link. It will access another fragment of the same document.

4. Yes.

5. The <BASE> tag establishes the absolute base for relative URLs in your document. It appears between the <HEAD> tags.

6. False. It requires an absolute URL.

7. No. mailto: does not require a double slash (//).

8. <REL> and <REV> (also <HREF>).

9. No.

Chapter 11

1. False.

2. Yes, to emphasize the text used for the hypertext link.

3. <U> (underline).

4. No.

5. Yes. It accesses the section parttwo in the local document chapter1.html.

6. This is an anchor for a clickable graphic thumbnail. It is legal.

7. Yes, but it might not display automatically in the browser window or helper application.

Chapter 12

1. Pixels.

2. CELLPADDING is the distance between the cell walls and the cell's contents. CELLSPACING is the distance between neighboring cell walls.

3. False. The default (when no value is assigned) is a one-pixel border.

4. At the top of the table.

5. Yes.

6. This creates one cell with three lines of text. (Each name appears below the previous name within the cell.)

7. ALIGN.

8. If that particular cell needs special alignment (such as dollar amounts).

Chapter 13

1. GET and POST. POST is used more often.

2. The URL to a form-processing script or a mailto: URL.

3. <TEXTAREA> is used for free-form entry. The user enters data with the keyboard.

4. The default text for the text area (if any).

5. An attribute.

6. Checkboxes work independently of one another; radio buttons allow one selection among a number of choices.

7. Use the attribute CHECKED.

8. With a Submit button (TYPE="SUBMIT"). When the user clicks this button, the data is sent.

9. A pull-down menu.

10. It displays as a scrolling menu.

Chapter 14

1. <P> is designed as a container, not a line-return tag. <P> also adds varying levels of space in different browsers.

2. Yes. Yes.

3. A series of form elements that logically belong together (such as name and address).

4. Extra spacing. Multiple <BR> tags don't render consistently in different browsers.

5. Don't use the <BR> tag between them.

6. It doesn't allow the user to enter more than the defined number of characters. It's error checking for elements such as phone numbers or ZIP codes that should always have a certain number of characters.

7. It allows you to align elements without resorting to a monospaced font presentation, as with <PRE>. You don't lose anything.

8. The <OL> list is used to number form elements.

9. The POST method is more powerful because it allows for more data to be transferred. The GET method is a bit easier to use.

   Most scripts can use a standard print command to "standard out" for HTML output. The Web browser acts like a terminal console.

Chapter 15

1. It actually replaces the <BODY> tag.

2. False.

3. The page has two columns. One column is 25 percent of the screen and uninterrupted, while the second column is 75 percent of the screen and divided into two equal rows.

4. auto.

5. Netscape (and compatible browsers) are designed to ignore text between <NOFRAMES> tags. Browsers that don't recognize frame tags will ignore everything but the markup.

6. Don't start the name with an underscore (_).

7. <FORM> and <BASE>.

8. It forces all links on that page to target a particular frame window without requiring you to enter a TARGET attribute for every anchor.

9. False. Reserved targets are special commands that can't be performed any other way.

Chapter 16

1. LEFT, RIGHT, and CENTER.

2. True.

3. Inline.

4. Because that's the method prescribed by the HTML 4.0 Recommendation.

5. Unfortunately, not all browsers understand <OBJECT>, but many do understand <EMBED>.

6. It's used to display information to browsers that can't process <EMBED>, yet it doesn't rely on support for another marginally supported element (<OBJECT>).

7. Text and inline markup.

8. No. There are tools that can determine the hex codes for you.

9. A single image is repeated left-to-right and top-to-bottom.

Chapter 17

1. USEMAP. <MAP>.

2. Rectangle (RECT), circle (CIRCLE), and polygon (POLYGON).

3. The client-side map specification includes support for ALT hypertext links for text-only browsers. The browsers must be updated to recognize this standard so that the ALT text is rendered.

4. You can, but you should use caution when doing so.

5. The centers x-y coordinates and the radius.

Chapter 18

1. "text/css".

2. False. They can be placed in an external style sheet, in the <STYLE> container, or inline within an element.

3. Cascading.

4. font-style.

5. Pixels, percentages, and inches.

6. Its value is a URL.

7. False.

Chapter 19

1. False.

2. The <DOCTYPE>.

3. Yes. As long as the validator can locate the DTD, it can use any type.

4. An SGML-based validator checks the structural integrity of your HTML file.

5. False.

6. In the element immediately preceding the error.

7. When your page passes validation without errors.

8. A validator that checks stylistic issues.

9. No. They may instead be alerting you to instances of "bad form."

10. URI, cut and paste, or file upload.

Chapter 20

1. <APPLET>.

2. Yes.

3. The <PARAM> tag sends any parameters required by the Java program to the applet when it's started.

4. LANGUAGE.

5. A method.

6. It comes from the function call in the body of the document.

7. The end of the comment tag should have // in front of it to keep from confusing some browsers, as in the following:

   ```
   // -->
   ```

8. An event handler allows JavaScript to react to an event. An event can be defined as any action by the user.

9. False. The value could be named nearly anything.

10. `this.form.city.value` (also `document.form.city.value`).

11. It's the opposite of focus.

12. `stringname.length`.

Chapter 21

1. `player2.at_bats = 25`.

2. A method.

3. The name assigned to the object by the keyword `new`.

4. False.

5. The second is an assignment. Assignments always evaluate to true.

6. The script simply moves on to the next statement.

7. 1.

8. 6.

9. You can use the plus sign (+) to concatenate strings.

10. `stringname.link`.

Chapter 22

1. True.

2. Yes.

3. Acrobat.

4. They are generally downloaded and handed over to a helper application.

5. Microsoft Word for Windows 2.0 or above.

6. RTF files maintain a minimal level of formatting (such as font sizes and alignment), while ASCII maintains no formatting beyond basic characters, spaces, and returns.

Chapter 23

1. Yes.

2. A word processor.

3. ASCII. Yes.

4. Format, List, Numbered.

5. Description.

6. Yes (Insert, New Line Break).

7. The URL created may reference your hard drive instead of a valid URL.

8. The image is actually copied to the new directory location.

9. No.

Chapter 24

1. It ships with Windows and is a part of the Internet Explorer 5.0 download.

2. Yes.

3. An ASCII text file. Yes, you could use any text editor or word processor.

4. False.

5. Format, Bullets and Numbering.

6. You can't simply highlight the text and use a menu command to create a definition list. You must work with each individual term and definition.

7. Format, Background.

8. No.

9. Yes.

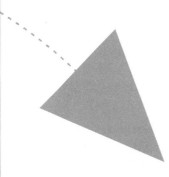

Index

R

RADIO attribute, <FORM> tags, 217

reading hypertext, 23

receiving data, CGI-BIN scripts, 247

relative links, 162

relative URLs, 166

requirements, sites, 71

RESET attribute, <FORM> tag, 218

resizing graphics (thumbnails), 149

returning values (JavaScript functions), 339-341

returns tags, 93

Rich Text Format (RTF), 383

rounding dollars, Math.round method code example, 370-372

rows, tables, 200-202

RTF (Rich Text Format), 383

S

sample Web page (completed), 97

samples

adding FTP to HTML documents, 437-439

adding HR tags to forms, 234

complete forms, 219-220

creating about pages, 432-434

creating customer service page, 435-437

creating event calendars, 203-204

creating frames, 257-258, 264

creating graphical menu bars, 186

creating index pages, 430-432

creating links, 178-179

creating product details table, 205

creating search pages, 435-437

creating tables, 198

creating Web sites (CraftScape.com), 429-439

customer feedback form, 237-239

customer service forms, 245

directory structures, 168

form appearance, 235

form text areas, 213

forms, 210

FrontPage Express Web page, 409

graphics in Web pages, 272

graphics listings, 184

HTML pages, 421-422

importing images, 426-427

list HTML, 126

nesting lists, 131

Netscape Composer documents, 393

Netscape Composer editing, 401

order forms, 223

personal biography page, 424-425

personal index page, 422-423

setting font style sheets, 303

Travel Agent Web site, 62-63

multimedia, 62

travel page, 427-429

Save As command (File menu), 147

Save As dialog box, 147

saving

documents, FrontPage Express, 409

graphics, 141

PhotoCD, 144

scanning photographs, 144

<SCRIPT> tags, 331-332

function declaration (JavaScript), 334

scripts

CGI-BIN, 246

output, 248

Perl, 248

scrolling in Web pages, 23

SCROLLING attribute, <FRAME> tag, 259-260

scrolling menus, 221

search pages, creating, 435-437

searching, Web, 60

section links, 162

secure sockets layer. *See* **SSL**